Clothing

Fashion • Fabrics • Construction

Second Edition

Jeanette Weber

Glencoe Publishing Company

Special Fashion, Clothing, and Textile Consultants
Irma Fischler
Sharon McKenzie
Rae Communale Pantalone
Ramona Rowan
Anne Marie Soto

Review Consultants
Nadine Hackler,
    Professor, Extension Clothing Specialist,
    University of Florida
Anne MacCleave-Frazier,
    Clothing and Textiles Specialist,
    The Pennsylvania State University
Sharon McKenzie,
    Curriculum Resource Teacher,
    Consumer and Family Studies,
    San Diego City Schools
Eloise Murray,
    Professor in Charge,
    Home Economics Education,
    The Pennsylvania State University
Darlene Kness
    Assistant Professor, Home Economics
    Central State University
    Edmond, Oklahoma

Thanks is given to Butterick Pattern Services for permission to reproduce pattern material on pages 376, 377, 379 of the *Effective Sewing Book.*

Send all inquiries to:
Glencoe Publishing Company
15319 Chatsworth Street
P.O. Box 9509
Mission Hills, California 91345-9509

Printed in the United States of America

ISBN 0-02-640161-4

1 2 3 4 5 6 7 8 9 10   93 92 91 90 89

Second Edition Cover and Interior Design
David Corona Design, Dubuque, Iowa

New and Revised Illustrations
Liz Purcell

Illustrators
Norman Nicholson
Phyllis Rockne
Gretchen Schields
Sally Shimizu
Ed Taber

Handbook Illustrators
Barbara Barnett
Phyllis Rockne
Sally Shimizu
Diana Thewlis

Cover and Unit Opening Photos (pp. 10, 68, 112, 160, 216, 286)
Bob Coyle

Photographers
After Six Formalwear, 122; Lee Bergthold, 169; Bettman Newsphotos, 100; Burlington Industries, 196, 200, 291; Deb Shop, 234, 351; E.I. Dupont de Nemours & Co., 281; David Frazier, 18; Cindy J. Ford, 166; Tony Freeman, 15, 294; Ann Garvin, 7, 13, 21, 28, 35, 36, 46, 64, 69, 92, 107, 109, 110, 113, 126, 130, 137, 161, 198, 216, 256, 263; Richard Hutchings, 38, 345; Susan Johns, 136; Stephen McBrady, 12, 75, 81, 157, 261, 320; Robert McElwee, 19; Fred Miller, 166; NASA, 185; North Wind Picture Archives, 82, 306; National Starch & Chemical Corp., 126; Alan Oddie, 20, 56, 70, 74, 104, 117, 121, 125, 154, 205, 207, 218, 231, 236, 240, 301, 307, 312, 324, 440; Tom Pantages, 162, 235, 319; Brent Phelps, 6, 11, 25, 113, 133, 143, 161, 170, 172, 217, 228, 244, 270, 273, 287, 349, 365; Smithsonian Institution, 104; Rick Sullivan, 62, 266; Suzanne's Discount Fashion Outlets, 13; Bob Taylor, 23, 163; Texas Highways, 79, 108; Duane R. Zehr, 3, 4, 5, 6, 11, 16, 40, 41, 50, 52, 57, 61, 69, 106, 113, 126, 161, 165, 166, 217, 220, 225, 230, 234, 243, 254, 274, 287, 288, 315, 329, 331, 339, 340, 351, 412, 417, 422, 466, 480.

Special thanks to P.A. Bergner (Pekin, Illinois) for providing props and special backgrounds for many of the photos.

Contents

Unit *Fabrics and Their Care*   160

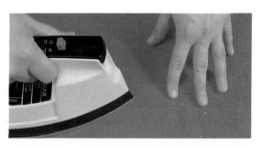

Effective Sewing Handbook

1

Clothes and You

1 | *Why Do People Wear Clothes?*

Pretend that you are at a large party, and you do not know anyone else who is there. How are you going to decide whom to talk to? You may glance around the party looking for people whom you would like to meet. You are looking for clues from people who will make you feel more comfortable and at ease.

But how do you decide all this before you walk up to someone and introduce yourself? Or how does someone decide to come up and talk to you?

The clothing that people are wearing offers some clues about themselves. Each person has chosen some type of outfit to wear to the party. Why did they choose what they did? Usually, the reasons are very complex, although the clothing decision may be made very quickly. Clothing is used to cover the body, to make you feel more attractive, and to communicate with others.

After reading this chapter, you will be able to:

- list the reasons why people wear clothes,
- explain how clothing identifies a person,
- describe how groups influence clothing choices,
- give examples of peer pressure.

The Reasons for Clothes

People wear clothes for many different reasons. Some of these reasons are physical. You wear clothes for comfort and protection. Others are for psychological and social reasons. Clothes give you self-confidence and express your personality. Clothes also help you identify with other people.

All people have basic human needs. Meeting these needs provides satisfaction and enjoyment in life. Clothing helps to meet some of these needs. Knowing something about the role of clothing helps you to understand yourself and others better. Clothing is a complex but fascinating part of everyone's life.

PROTECTION

In our world, we humans need to protect ourselves from our environment. We do not have a natural protective covering like most animals. The feathers and fur of animals protect them and keep them comfortable. Our skin is uncovered and exposed. We can be easily affected by the elements—rain, snow, wind, cold, and heat. We can be harmed or injured on the job or while participating in sports. In some cases, we need to protect others with our clothing.

Climate and Weather

If you lived in an environment that was completely controlled for human comfort, your clothing needs would be very simple. You would not need to consider the climate or changes in the weather. Large indoor shopping malls, hotel complexes, and many schools come close to such environments.

Even on balmy days or while inside climate-controlled buildings, clothing adds to your comfort. It absorbs perspiration, prevents sudden chills, and acts as a buffer between your body and accidental burns, scratches, and rough surfaces.

But it is outdoors under extreme weather conditions that clothing plays its most important physical role. The right garments can insulate your body against extremely hot or extremely cold temperatures.

All over the world, people have traditionally used clothing for comfort and protection in this way. People who live in severely cold climates, such as the Eskimos, keep warm by wearing pants and parkas with fur linings. The fur traps the warm air from their bodies and creates a life-saving insulating layer of warmth.

Desert nomads keep the harmful hot sun from dehydrating their bodies by covering up with long flowing robes and headdresses. Their clothing actually keeps them cooler than they would be without it.

Hats over the ears and thick mufflers prevent body heat from escaping on winter days.

Needs and Wants

In our vocabulary, the word *need* many times becomes identical with the word *want.* We often say that we *need* something new: "I need a new pair of blue shoes." Since we may already have several pairs of shoes in our closet, what we really mean is, "I *want* a new pair of blue shoes."

Shoes are needed to protect one's feet. There is no relationship between the color of the shoe and the protection provided.

Abraham Maslow, a psychologist, studied human needs and came to the conclusion that everyone has the same basic needs. He divided these needs into five categories. Then he organized these categories into a *hierarchy,* which means arranging them according to their level of importance:

1. *Survival.* Everyone needs food, water, clothing, and shelter in order to survive.
2. *Safety and Security.* People need to feel free from physical harm, and secure that their needs will be met.
3. *Belonging.* Everyone needs to belong to a family and other groups, and to love and be loved.
4. *Self-Esteem.* People need a feeling of self-respect and worthiness.
5. *Fulfillment.* People need to use their special talents, be creative, and reach personal goals through their own efforts.

As people's first needs are met, they can become concerned with the next level of needs. For example, once survival needs are met, people will begin to worry about safety and security. Once those needs are met, they will be concerned with their need for belonging. In a highly developed society, many members have the time and means to satisfy and develop all five categories of needs.

Can you think of examples of how shoes and clothes might be used to satisfy each level of basic needs? How do you define *needs* and *wants*?

These are extremes in weather conditions in which people have adapted their style of dress to their climate. In other areas, where the weather is more moderate or where it changes with the seasons, people dress with the weather in mind, too. Warm weather clothes include loose styles and light colors. Cold weather wear includes additional layers and bulkier fabrics than warm weather wear.

Safety

Clothing also serves to protect your skin from harm or injury. Some sports and occupations require protective clothing for safety reasons. Football players wear helmets and protective padding to help prevent injury during rough play. Soccer and hockey players wear shin guards to protect their legs from hard hits by

Heavy boots and thick water-repellent clothing protect the firefighter. How many protective items are on the bike rider?

the ball or puck. Amateur boxers wear protective headgear to reduce the blow from punches.

All of these protective aids were developed so that people could enjoy a sport and reduce the risk of injury.

Some people's work requires them to be in dangerous or hazardous conditions. Clothing can offer protection. Some items are even labeled with the term "safety" to identify them from regular day-to-day clothes and accessories.

Construction and mill workers wear safety shoes and boots with steel reinforced toes. Many workers must wear hard hats, too. Firefighters wear asbestos clothing in hazardous situations. Police officers wear bulletproof vests. Road workers wear fluorescent orange vests so that drivers can see them easily and prevent accidents.

Clothing can protect you in recreational situations, too. When at the beach, you may wear a shirt or jacket to prevent overexposure and a bad sunburn. While hiking through the woods, you may wear long pants and a long-sleeve shirt to avoid insect bites and scratches from the bushes. While sailing, you may wear a life vest as a precaution.

Sanitation

Special clothing and accessories are often worn for sanitation reasons. People who work in factories that produce food and medical products wear sanitary clothing, face masks, and hair coverings. This precaution prevents contamination of the products by germs.

In operating rooms, doctors and nurses wear special disposable sanitary uniforms, gloves, and face masks. Fast-food workers wear hats or hair nets to prevent their hair from falling into your food. These are examples of how other people protect you by wearing special clothing. Can you think of any other examples?

Clothing that is acceptable for the pool would be considered immodest for other places.

MODESTY

Modesty refers to *what people feel is the proper way for clothing to cover the body.* Different groups of people may have different standards of modesty. People follow these standards in order to fit in and be accepted by the group. Usually you can recognize what is considered modest or immodest because most people in the group dress in the acceptable manner.

Standards of modesty may vary from one situation or activity to another. For example, no one would think twice about a young man playing volleyball on the beach without his shirt. But it would be unacceptable for him to appear shirtless for his math class at school. Clothes that a woman might wear to a fancy party would probably be unacceptable at work the next day.

Sometimes standards of modesty are only minor variations of dress. For example, buttoning a shirt up to the neck would be more acceptable in some groups than leaving two or more buttons open.

Standards of modesty may differ from one culture to another. For example, some women of the Muslim religion are required to wear a long veil that completely covers them when they are in public. Only their eyes can show through a small opening. This is a very old tradition. In other parts of the world, it may not be considered immodest to wear very little clothing.

Modesty standards can also change over a period of time. Around the turn of the century, American women wore long skirts. And a woman always followed a man when walking up stairs. Why? It was unacceptable for him to see her ankles!

IDENTIFICATION

Clothing can also identify people as members of a group. Certain types of clothing, colors, and accessories have become representative of certain groups, activities, and occupations. Or by simply dressing alike, people can show that they belong to the same group.

Uniforms

A uniform is one of the easiest ways to identify group members. Uniforms can provide instant recognition or create a special image for the group.

Members of the police force, fire department, and military wear uniforms so that they can be recognized quickly and easily for public safety. Athletic teams wear different colors to identify their team and to tell them apart from their opponents. Different sports have different styles of uniforms. For example, rugby players wear car or type of equipment is a status symbol.

Designer clothing offers a sense of status for many people. Wearing an original garment made by a famous designer shows that the wearer can afford expensive clothes.

DECORATION

People decorate themselves to enhance their appearance. They wear clothes, jewelry, and cosmetics in hopes of improving their looks and attracting favorable attention. **Adornment,** or *decoration,* also helps people to express their uniqueness and creativity.

Throughout the world, different people have adorned their bodies in a variety of ways. (See the box feature SELF-ADORNMENT.) Some of these methods are still used today.

Clothing and accessories can be used to improve appearance in different ways. You can select the styles, colors, and fabrics that will best compliment your own characteristics. You will learn more about clothing selection in Chapters 10 and 21.

Clothing can also be decorated to make it special and unique. You can adorn your clothes with many types of needlework, painting, and trims. In Chapter 9, you will learn all about these different methods of creative arts.

Groups and Clothes

Groups are a part of everyone's life. You are an automatic member of one or more groups. You may choose to belong to many other groups. Within each group, you have a **role**, which is *a particular function or purpose of a group member.* The different groups and roles may have different clothing requirements. How do groups influence your choice of clothes?

A special celebration calls for special clothes to mark the event.

TYPES OF GROUPS

A **group** is *a number of people who share something in common.* It may be an interest, such as playing chess or acting in the school play. It may be a common characteristic, such as a similar age.

You automatically belong to your family group, school group, and community group. You may choose to join a club, team, band, group of friends, and many more.

Some of these groups have rules about clothing. You may be required to wear a uniform for school, sports, or a job. These uniforms give the members a sense of identification and belonging. When you wear the group's uniform, your actions reflect on the entire group. Thus, the uniform gives members a sense of responsibility to the group.

Other groups may have clothing requirements that are unwritten, but understood by the members. For example, you may wear a certain type of clothing, such as a special jacket, to a group meeting. Or you may wear the school colors to the basketball game to show enthusiasm and spirit for the group.

ROLES WITHIN GROUPS

Roles are divided into two categories—those that are given and those that are acquired. *Given roles* are those that occur automatically. These include your sex, age, and family status. You belong to a male or female group. You are a member of the group of people who are your own age. Within your family, you are a son or daughter and a grandchild. You may also be a sister or brother.

Acquired roles are those that you take on a part-time or day-to-day basis. You may be a sales clerk, a date, a club president, a ticket taker, a babysitter, a halfback on the team, or a wearer of braces.

In some groups, your role may be as a group member just like everyone else. Or you may have a special role. You may be the leader of the group, captain of the team, or treasurer of the club.

CLOTHING EXPECTATIONS

Many people have certain **clothing expectations**, or *thoughts about how people in different roles should dress*. For example, males do not wear skirts in our society. Teenagers may be expected to wear clothes that are not "too old." Your parents may have very definite ideas of how you should dress for different occasions. Sometimes conflicts occur when a teenager's choice of clothes, hair style, or makeup differs from the expectations of others.

Within your acquired roles, there also may be certain clothing expectations. Your employer, neighbor, customer, date, or club members may have certain expectations about how you should dress when you are with them.

For example, your employer expects a well-groomed appearance each time that you arrive at work. If you have a leadership position within a group, you may be expected to set an example for other members as to how to dress.

In Chapter 2, you will learn more about making clothing choices for different occasions.

Uniforms help to identify the group, focus on the action, and add excitement.

Many teenagers dress in similar ways in order to feel a part of their peer group.

Peer Groups and Peer Pressure

A **peer group** is made up of *members who have equal standing within the group.* Most people feel a strong need to fit in with other members of their peer group. Some will even adjust their habits and clothes to conform to the standards of the group. **Conformity** means *expressing yourself as being similar to others.*

APPEARANCE

Appearance may be regulated within the peer group by written or unwritten rules. Certain styles of clothes, brands, and colors may be approved or disapproved by the group.

Usually there is an "in" way of dressing. Certain accessories may be important to the group. The "right" shoes, boots, belts, hats, totes, or backpacks may be clearly identified.

Sometimes, members of the group are expected, and even pressured, to dress in the approved way. This *pressure by the peer group to conform* is called **peer pressure**. Clothing that does not conform to the group's standards and expectations may be criticized. The person may be talked about, laughed at, or teased.

Sometimes, peer pressure can be gentle and used to help members develop a sense of belonging and togetherness. Peer pressure can also be strong and cruel, forcing people to either conform or be excluded from the group.

To resist peer pressure, you need to have a clear understanding of your own values and identity. In Chapter 3, you will learn how you can balance your need for both conformity and individuality.

Chapter 1 Review

Summary

People wear clothes for many different reasons. Clothes provide protection, modesty, identification, status, and decoration. Uniforms, certain styles and colors, and special insignias can identify people as to occupation, groups, and roles. Groups can influence your choice of clothes. Some groups have special clothing requirements or expectations about how people should dress. Peer groups can apply peer pressure to make members conform to the group's standards and expectations of clothing.

Questions

1. List the reasons why people wear clothes.
2. In what different ways does clothing provide protection?
3. How do standards of modesty differ from one situation or activity to another?
4. Describe how uniforms can provide identification and status.
5. What are "status symbols"? Why are they popular?
6. What are the reasons why people adorn their bodies in a variety of ways?
7. How can groups influence clothing choices?
8. What is the difference between a given role and an acquired role? Give an example of each and what clothing expectations might be associated with that role.
9. Explain the positive and negative influences of peer pressure.

Activities

1. Look through current magazines and newspapers for illustrations of people wearing different types of clothing. For what reasons were the clothes being worn: protection, modesty, identification, status, or decoration? What information can you learn about each person from his or her clothing?

2. List all the different groups to which you belong. Identify any special clothing requirements or expectations for each group. How do you know what these clothing requirements or expectations are?

3. Discuss some of the ways that students exert peer pressure—either positive or negative—on clothing choices at your school. What is the "in" way of dressing by different groups?

You Be the Expert

Your school club is considering the purchase of special insignias to be worn by all club members on their jackets. What do you think are the advantages and disadvantages of such a proposal?

2 | *Clothing Choices*

TERMS TO LEARN

appropriate
consideration
goal
imitate
impulse
personality
resources
values

Each morning you are faced with a decision. What will you wear today? On some days, the decision will seem easy, and you will reach into the closet for the perfect outfit. On other days, the decision may seem hard, and you will have to think about it. You may even try on several garments until you find the right outfit to wear.

Each time that you decide what to wear, you consciously or unconsciously go through a decision-making process. There are many influences on your clothing decisions. You may consider where you are going, what you plan to do, who you will be with, what the weather is like outside, and how you feel that day.

In this chapter, you will learn about making clothing choices. After reading this chapter, you will be able to:

- identify the influences on your clothing choices,
- discuss appropriate dress for certain occasions,
- give examples of a variety of clothing decisions,
- describe the decision-making process.

Deciding What to Wear

To what occasions do you think the boy can wear the clothing he is selecting?

When you get dressed each day, you undoubtedly think about your plans. What activities are on your schedule for the day? Do you have school, practice for a sport, a part-time job, or a special occasion to attend?

Sometimes you have a wide choice of clothes that you could wear. At other times, the choice may be limited or made for you. For example, some schools have uniforms or a special clothing code, which lists what types of clothes may or may not be worn. Perhaps an employer requires that you wear a uniform or a certain style and color of clothing, such as black or navy pants with a white shirt.

When your choices are limited or made for you, your decision is easier. You have less to choose from.

However, when your choices are unlimited, how do you decide what clothes to wear? Would you dress differently for these three occasions: watching television with your brother, going to a party with friends, or being interviewed for a job by someone whom you have never met?

Probably there are many factors that influence your clothing choices for these occasions. Sometimes you may be uncertain as to which choice would be best. In making more difficult clothing choices, you have to decide what is important to you.

Your clothing choices depend on many things. Some of these include:

1. what you plan to do,
2. whom will be with you,
3. your mood,
4. your personality,
5. your values.

WHAT YOU PLAN TO DO

On Saturday morning, you may put on your old sweatshirt and comfortable blue jeans. You are planning to clean up your room and then work on a special hobby project. If you have a part-time job in a local store, you may put on a nice sweater and pair of slacks. Or you may be going swimming with several friends, so you put on your bathing suit under your clothes. The activities that you plan to do have determined what types of clothes to wear. You have chosen clothes that are **appropriate**, or *suitable,* for your activities.

Dressing for the Occasion

You can learn what type of clothing is appropriate for different occasions from your own experience and by observing what others wear. You probably have a variety of clothes that you wear to school that are similar to clothes worn by other students. You may wear these same clothes to other activities, such as a party, a football game, or a part-time job. Some special occasions may need a dressier outfit than what you wear to school.

You will learn more about dressing appropriately for special occasions in this chapter.

Fashion Focus

Dressing for Comfort

The smartest approach to dressing is to make yourself comfortable, not only in different activities but in all types of weather, too. If you understand how to promote body warmth and ventilation, you can enjoy yourself under most conditions.

Promote Body Warmth

- Wear several layers of lighter-weight clothing to trap air for added insulation.
- Choose darker colors to absorb heat.
- Wear natural fibers next to your skin to absorb moisture.
- Cover your head with a hat, hood, or scarf to prevent heat loss.
- Wear mittens instead of gloves to trap heat between the fingers; the thicker the mittens or gloves, the better.
- Choose close-fitting collars, cuffs, and waistbands to trap body heat.
- Wear socks or stockings; increase warmth with thicker fabrics, texture, longer lengths, or double layers.
- Choose closed shoes with thicker soles; fleece linings in boots add warmth.

- Remove layers and loosen clothing, as needed, to avoid overheating and sweating, which can cause excessive heat loss.

Keep Cool

- Wear white and light colors to reflect the sun's rays.
- Choose loose-fitting styles to allow air to circulate; open collars and roll-up sleeves.
- Wear fewer layers and avoid lined garments.
- Cover less body area by wearing short sleeve or sleeveless styles and shorts.
- Loosen or remove scarves, ties, and belts that trap body heat.
- Choose lightweight open-weave or open-knit fabrics to increase ventilation; avoid fabrics that cling to the body.
- Wear natural fibers that absorb perspiration and allow it to evaporate.
- Choose open shoes or sandals.
- Wear a hat in the sun.
- Select rainwear that is water-repellent, not waterproof.

If you are going hiking, shopping, or visiting a museum, you will need to wear comfortable shoes because you will be doing a lot of walking. If you are planning to participate in sports or exercise, you will be most comfortable in clothing that allows you to stretch and move easily. Dressing for the occasion is mainly a matter of common sense.

Dressing for the Weather

You should dress so that you can forget about being hot, cold, or wet. If you are going to be outdoors in cold weather, you need to dress to keep warm. Wearing several layers of clothes, plus a hat and gloves, is best. If it is snowing, boots will keep your feet warm and dry.

On rainy days, be sure to wear some type of rain gear. A slicker, boots, and an umbrella will keep you dry and protect your other clothes. Remember that leather shoes can be ruined by getting soaked too often.

WHOM YOU WILL BE WITH

Whom you plan to be with is another important influence on your clothing choice. With your family or best friend, you probably do not worry about what to wear. You feel very comfortable with them. Your know that you can relax around your home in your most casual clothes, such as a baggy shirt, patched jeans, and old worn sneakers. But would you feel comfortable if other people saw you dressed this way?

With school friends, you may want to wear similar types of clothing for certain activities. In some groups, teens will often telephone other members of the group to find out what they plan to wear to school, a party, or a special event. Then they can all dress in the same way.

On other occasions, you may be with people whom you do not know. You might be interviewing for a job, going on a "blind date," or attending a large celebration. On these occasions, you may take extra time to select an outfit that you feel is appropriate for the occasion. You may want to look your best and not have to worry about what you are wearing. In Chapter 3, you will learn more about how people judge others by their clothing.

YOUR MOOD

Your mood may affect your clothing choices for the day. If you are happy and cheerful, you may reach for bright, bold colors that reflect the way that you feel. If you are feeling down, you

We wear casual clothes around people whom we know and like. The informality of the clothes helps to create a relaxed atmosphere.

Which one of your outfits do you always enjoy wearing? Do you know why it is your favorite?

may unconsciously select a darker color. Or you may choose a favorite article of clothing that gives you a sense of comfort and security.

Everyone's mood affects personal clothing choices to some extent. As a teenager, your moods may change rapidly as you are growing and changing. Many times you may not be aware of these changes.

Think about your own wardrobe. Do you have an outfit that you always feel good in when you wear it? Does another outfit always feel comfortable? Almost everyone has favorites in his or her wardrobe. These are the clothes that you turn to and always enjoy wearing.

Sometimes clothes can help change your mood, too. On a day when you are feeling down, wearing a bright color or favorite outfit may lift your spirits a bit.

PERSONALITY

Your **personality** is *the combination of all your unique qualities.* You express your personality through your attitudes and behavior. Your personality also directly affects your clothing choices.

Are you outgoing and talkative, or quiet and

These young men value comfortable clothes that are practical and durable.

If you value *wealth*, then the symbols of wealth may be important to you. You will probably select clothing and other material goods that look expensive.

Practical people are concerned with comfort and durability. They want clothes that feel good and wear well over a long period of time. They may or may not concern themselves with current styles.

For others, *appearance* may be most important. They may sacrifice comfort and practicality to wear the latest up-to-the-minute fashions.

What is your own philosophy of clothing? Which of your values matters the most when you choose clothes? By answering these questions, you will learn more about your own clothing philosophy.

shy? Are you self-confident or unsure of yourself? Do you like to stand out in a group or blend in? Do you like to be a trend setter and unique in your clothing selection? Or do you prefer a middle-of-the-road approach?

The answers to these questions tell you about your personality. In turn, your personality influences the style of clothing that you prefer. In Chapter 3, you will learn how to express your personality through the clothes that you wear.

YOUR VALUES

Values also influence your clothing choices. Your **values** are *your ideas about what is important or good.* Your values may be shared by your family, your friends, and your community. Some of your values may differ from others, such as those held by your peer group.

Have you ever stopped to think how much clothes really mean to you? What values do you take into account when you make clothing choices? The way that you regard *wealth, practicality,* and *appearance* are examples of values.

Dressing for Special Occasions

Custom and tradition have established guidelines and rules as to what type of clothing is appropriate for certain occasions. These rules may be written or unwritten.

IN RESTAURANTS

Some restaurants require a jacket and tie for men and noncasual clothing for women. These requirements help to create a more formal atmosphere within the restaurant.

Almost all restaurants require you to wear shoes because of local health laws. In swimming and resort areas, you may see signs that say Shoes and Shirts Are Required. If you do not follow these rules, the restaurant has the right to refuse to serve you.

Wearing simple, understated clothes in moderate colors helps to create a businesslike setting in any office.

AT WORK AND AT PARTIES

Most offices have certain standards of dress. In many offices, a business suit is the standard outfit for both men and women. Employees who do not conform to the standard of their fellow workers may not be accepted by the group.

Clothing that may be appropriate at a picnic or a dance is unacceptable for the office. The rule for business is to wear nothing extreme – not too tight, too short, too low, too thin, too bold, or too bright.

When going to a party, men usually wear a suit and tie, and women wear dressier clothes. A formal dance may request "black tie." This means a tuxedo for men and formal dresses or gowns for women. When at parties and formal events, bright colors and high-fashion styles are very acceptable.

If you are uncertain as to what to wear to a special occasion, you can ask friends who have been to a similar event. Or you can talk to your parents or teachers as to what is acceptable.

For a special party, you can call the host or hostess or ask other guests what they plan to wear. Many people talk with others before they make their own clothing choice.

Conflicts over Clothing

Sometimes what you want to wear does not conform to what is appropriate to wear. This may create a conflict with your parents or other authority figures.

BE CONSIDERATE

When conflicts occur, it is important to have **consideration**, or *thoughtfulness,* for others. Perhaps it is a special occasion with your parents or other adults. By dressing appropriately, you are showing respect for their feelings and beliefs. At a party or dance, it is important to consider the feelings of your date and friends, too. Appropriate clothing can help to make an event special for all guests.

CLOTHING MISTAKES

You will probably feel more self-confident when you are dressed appropriately. In the "right" clothes, you will feel more relaxed and comfortable, especially if the situation is new for you.

Sometimes you may make a wrong clothing choice. When you arrive at an event, you may discover that you are not dressed appropriately. If this happens, try to forget about it. Concentrate on talking with other people. Get involved in the activity of the event. If you forget about what you are wearing, you will probably enjoy yourself much more. Everyone makes clothing mistakes once in a while.

Decision-Making

Each and every day you are faced with choices. *Choosing,* or making a decision about something, is the process of making up your mind. The process may be simple or complex.

You make many simple and complex decisions that relate to your clothing needs. Unconsciously picking a belt to wear with your jeans is a simple decision. Deciding what combination of clothing to wear, what to buy or sew, and what to discard are just a few of the more complex decisions.

As a child, your parent or another adult made your clothing decisions for you. You have been given the opportunity to make some choices. Perhaps you selected which outfit to wear on a certain day, or maybe you even participated in the buying process. But the adult had the final decision in the situation.

As you grow older and assume more responsibility and control over your wardrobe, you will want to develop successful decision-making

skills. Along the way, you will probably make a few mistakes or unconsciously slide into some decision-making pitfalls.

What makes you think this young man likes blue? What would you do to liven up his outfit?

SOME DECISION-MAKING PITFALLS

We make haphazard decisions mainly through habit, through imitation, through impulse, and through "coin-tossing."

Habit

Sometimes we purchase the same styles, fabrics, and colors of clothes just because we have always worn them. It is a clothing habit.

After a while, it is best to stop and evaluate what you buy to see if the decisions that you have been making are still the best ones. Your alternatives may have changed over time. The selection of clothing may have improved. There may be new fabrics and colors from which to choose. As you grow and your body changes, a new style may look better on you now than an old, familiar one.

Imitation

You may feel a strong desire to dress exactly like one of your friends or someone that you admire. Wearing what other teens at school wear provides you with a sense of identity, belonging, and security. It may make you feel accepted and part of a group. This strong desire may cause you to make clothing purchases that **imitate**, or *copy*, others.

You should consider yourself first when you make a clothing decision. How will the item really look on you? What looks good on your best friend may look dreadful on you. When buying clothes, good decision-making takes all the factors into consideration, measures them, and follows the path that leads to the best result.

Impulse

Buying clothes on **impulse** is *buying suddenly, without any thought or planning.* Impulse buying is emotional because you only react to the attraction of the items on display.

Can you think of a time when you have purchased an item of clothing on impulse? Has something in a store ever caught your eye, and you bought it without thinking?

Impulse purchases are often poor choices. The items may not be needed or may not match anything else in your wardrobe. And, often, money is wasted on items that are seldom

worn. When buying clothes, try to control your emotions so that you can make decisions that are best for you.

Coin-Tossing

Sometimes choosing which clothes to buy seems so hard that you cannot make a decision. Have you ever had to choose between two shirts, only to get more confused as you weighed the pros and cons of each? Some people solve such decision-making problems by tossing a coin in the air—heads for the blue shirt, tails for the beige one.

This is a haphazard way to make a choice since it is based on chance and not fact. If you are having trouble making a decision, walk away from it for a time. Later, it will be easier to see the facts more clearly, weigh the pros and cons, and make the right clothing choice.

THE DECISION-MAKING PROCESS

Making the best clothing choices for yourself on a regular basis requires good decision-making habits. Up to now, you may have learned whether your decisions were good ones only through the trial-and-error method. After you made a clothing choice, you could evaluate your selection and see why it did or did not work.

The blue plaid shirt that you bought is one of your favorites. It matches two pairs of slacks. It is a great fit, and the color looks good on you. The brown checked shirt that you bought at the same time just hangs in your closet. It does not match anything else in your wardrobe. It fits all right, but the color is wrong for you. The blue plaid shirt was a successful choice. The brown checked was a poor choice.

Evaluating, or analyzing, your success is a good habit, but the trial-and-error method is not very efficient. You will probably make several poor choices along with the good ones. If you follow a logical decision-making process, you will get better and more consistent results.

Each time that you go through the decision-making process, it will become easier for you. Good decision-making involves five steps:

1. Set a goal.
2. Identify all the alternatives.
3. Evaluate each alternative.
4. Select the best alternative.
5. Evaluate the result.

Set a Goal

A **goal** is *something that you want to accomplish or hope to obtain.* Your clothing goals may be to look your best at all times. Another clothing goal might be to round out your wardrobe by adding a blazer that coordinates with several other outfits.

Identify All the Alternatives

How do you reach your goal? Usually there are several ways. Think about the many choices that you can make that would help you reach your goal. You could buy a new blazer now or wait until one goes on sale. Perhaps you could make a blazer. Does an older brother or sister have a blazer that is no longer worn? Perhaps it could be passed on to you. What other alternatives do you have?

Evaluate Each Alternative

Consider the facts about each alternative that you have. What are the pros and cons of each one? Which one will help you reach your goal in the best way? You will have to consider your choices based upon your own **resources**—*your*

money, time, and skill. These facts play a big part in the decision-making process.

How much money can you spend for a blazer? Do you have the skill or the time to sew? Do you need a blazer now or can you wait until you find one on sale? How do you feel about wearing a secondhand jacket? It is important to evaluate all of your choices before you make your decision.

Select the Best Alternative

Based upon your evaluation of each alternative, which choice will help you reach your goal in the best way? When you have selected the best route to take, follow through on your decision. The sooner you act on your decision, the sooner you will reach your goal.

For instance, you decide to sew the blazer. In this way, you save money and can choose the exact type and color of fabric that you want.

Evaluate the Result

Once you have made your decision and followed through on it, take the time to evaluate it. Why did you make the decision that you did? Did the pros of one alternative outweigh the pros of another? Was there an important fact, once identified, that helped you to make your decision? In the long run, did you make the right choice? Did your selection fulfill your original goal?

When you evaluated your decision to sew the blazer, you were satisfied. Even though it took two weeks to make, it came out beautifully and is very special looking.

Evaluating the result of each decision that you make will help you to identify what is important in the future. Each time that you go through the decision-making process, you will improve your decision-making skills and be better prepared to make other decisions.

Chapter 2 Review

Summary

Your clothing choices depend on many things, such as what you plan to do, whom you will be with, your mood, your personality, and your values. Appropriate clothing for special occasions has been established by custom and tradition. When clothing conflicts occur, it is important to have consideration for others.

Every day you have to make many decisions. Some decisions are based on habit, imitation, impulse, or tossing a coin. But good decision-making habits can be developed. The decision-making process involves five steps: Set a goal, identify all the alternatives, evaluate each alternative, select the best alternative, and evaluate the result.

Questions

1. List and describe five factors that influence your clothing choices. What might limit your choice?

2. How does your mood affect your clothing choices?

3. How can values influence clothing decisions?

4. Describe the style of clothing that would be acceptable for a business office, a restaurant, and a formal dance.

5. How can you find out what type of clothes to wear for a special occasion?

6. What are four ways that people may make decisions about clothes? What are the advantages and disadvantages of each?

7. List the five steps of the decision-making process.

8. Why is it important to evaluate the results of each clothing decision?

Activities

1. Describe an outfit that always makes you feel good when you wear it. Why might this be?

2. Identify several different occasions that people attend, from picnics to formal dances. Using magazines and catalogues, cut out pictures of different types of clothing. Group the pictures according to which type of clothing would be appropriate for each type of occasion.

3. Select a personal goal that is related to clothing or your appearance. Go through the five steps of decision-making process and explain why you selected the alternative that you did. How could you evaluate the results of such a decision?

You Be the Expert

You are a member of the prom committee. After a discussion on whether or not to require tuxedos for the dance, the chairperson asks for a decision. How would you vote?

3 | *Expressing the Real You*

TERMS TO LEARN

impression
individuality
nonverbal messages
self-image
stereotype
verbal messages

Are you a people watcher? Do you ever sit in a shopping mall or other public place and watch the people pass by? Do you play a guessing game about them based on the way they look? Is the tall, young man in the football jacket an athlete? Is the couple in expensive-looking clothes really wealthy? Could the group in the outlandish clothes be members of a rock band?

When you play this game, you are forming impressions about people, using only their clothing, body features, and expressions as clues. Of these three factors, the clothing that a person wears has the strongest influence on the image that he or she projects.

After reading this chapter, you will be able to:

- discuss how first impressions influence others,
- describe how your self-image affects your clothing choices,
- identify and give examples of individuality and conformity in clothing,
- explain how clothes can express the real you.

First Impressions

When you leave your fingerprints on a glass or mark a piece of paper with a rubber stamp, you have left impressions on the glass and the paper. An **impression** is *an image that is transferred from one place to another.*

Just as you can create impressions with fingerprints or rubber stamps, you can create impressions about yourself, too. When you interact with other people, you are subconsciously making an impression. When you walk into a room, enter a conversation, or answer a question, you are creating an impression.

When others meet you for the first time, they develop a *first impression* about you in their minds. First impressions are often the basis of other people's opinions about you.

FORMING FIRST IMPRESSIONS

First impressions are formed in a very short time, usually less than a minute or two. Others quickly get their impression of you from the clues that you send out. Your clothes, body features, expressions, voice, and behavior are some of these clues. Have you ever made assumptions about someone based on one or more of these clues?

Sometimes people base first impressions on their own past experiences. You may form an opinion about someone because of a person that you already know. Both people may share a clue or signal. The clue could be the way that they speak, the style of their clothes, or the way that they wear their hair.

If you meet a new student who is wearing the same shirt as your best friend, you may make a positive association. You may have a favorable impression because the student reminds you of your best friend.

Clothes, features, expressions, voice, and behavior all help us to form a favorable or unfavorable impression. What is your first impression of this young man?

No matter who you are, you are often judged by first impressions. A teacher meeting a class, the politician on a platform, the entertainer on screen or stage, a speaker in a school assembly, clerks in stores, and receptionists in offices are all making impressions.

Verbal and Nonverbal Messages

How can people form an impression of you in only 30 seconds? They quickly observe the way that you look and the way that you act. Your appearance and behavior provide verbal and nonverbal messages about yourself.

VERBAL MESSAGES

Your **verbal messages** include *the tone of your voice and your choice of words.* It is both what you say and how you say it. What verbal clues do you send out? Try hearing yourself as others do. What kind of emotion does the tone of your voice express to others? Anger, joy, and sadness are just a few of the emotions that can be heard when you speak.

Your words can communicate many things about yourself. You can express your ideas and feelings clearly, or mask them behind other phrases. You can show politeness or rudeness with your words and tone of voice. How did you sound when you said "Good morning" to someone today? What impression would your teacher or employer have of you if you answered a question with a loud, slurred "Yeah?" or a clear "Yes, Mr. Martin?"

When you communicate with others, you send both verbal and nonverbal messages about yourself.

NONVERBAL MESSAGES

Your **nonverbal messages** include *your appearance and your behavior.* These are clues that people see—your clothes, grooming, body language, and manners.

- *Your Clothes.* What you wear may be the most obvious message that people first notice about you. The style, color, fit, and neatness of your clothes will influence opinions about you. Because clothes can send out strong messages to others, it is important to understand their impact. Later in this chapter, you will learn how to send the messages that you want about yourself.

- *Your Grooming.* Grooming refers to your general appearance and your clothes. Is your appearance clean or dirty, neat or sloppy? Clean, shiny hair gives a more favorable impression than dirty, dull hair. You will read more about grooming in Chapter 4.

- *Your Body Language.* This message includes your facial expressions, posture, movements, and behavior. Recent research shows that people form many opinions about others from their body language. (See the special box feature BODY LANGUAGE.)

- *Your Manners.* The way you act or behave with others shows much about you. Being polite gives one impression, while being rude implies another. Manners usually have a strong influence on whether someone forms a favorable or unfavorable impression about you.

ACCURACY OF IMPRESSIONS

First impressions can affect your judgment about others, just as your own appearance and behavior can affect how others think about you.

Body Language

What is body language? It is your body's nonverbal communication—your eyes, facial expression, posture, position of your arms and legs, and even the distance that you stand or sit from others.

What can we learn from a person's body language? Many feelings and attitudes are expressed, consciously or unconsciously, through body language. The science of *kinesics* explores the meaning of messages expressed through body movement.

- *Eye Contact.* Looking directly at another person shows interest, warmth, and self-confidence. Averting your eyes shows disinterest, shyness, or nervousness.

- *Facial Expression.* Your face has many muscles that control the expressions in your face. A raised eyebrow shows surprise, a frown shows disappointment. A smile is happy and friendly, a downturned mouth is sad. Much of what goes on in your mind finds expression in your face.

- *Posture.* An erect, comfortable posture shows self-assurance and a positive attitude. Sloping shoulders and slumping posture give a negative appearance.

- *Position of Arms and Legs.* Open and relaxed positions of your arms and hands demonstrate receptiveness and friendliness. Closed and clenched positions show anger, discomfort, and nervousness. Legs planted squarely or comfortably relaxed show that you are secure in the situation. Tapping fingers or foot probably means that you are bored or impatient with what's going on around you.

- *Distance.* How far you sit or stand from another person can indicate your feelings.

Everyone has a "personal space" around them. Coming too close to an individual and invading that space may make the person feel uncomfortable. Close friends may stand only 6″ to 8″ (15–20 cm) apart. Other people stand farther apart, and may slowly move closer together to show friendliness.

However, first impressions can be wrong. In all fairness, you must stop and evaluate your impression before you make a judgment about another person.

What impression would you make about someone who was wearing a soiled sweatshirt, baggy pants, and dirty shoes? Perhaps the person had a smudged face and messed-up hair. Was the person really sloppy and unkempt? Or had he just finished washing a car? Or perhaps he had just returned from a five-mile run? Until you know the facts, you should reserve your final judgment.

STEREOTYPES

Forming an opinion about a person because of a past association can be inaccurate, too. A **stereotype** is *an opinion based on ideas that you already have, whether they are accurate or not.*

People are often stereotyped by the way that they look and by the type of clothes that they wear. A crazy hair style may say that you are a rebel. Horn-rimmed glasses may imply that you are a serious student. A sports letter sweater says that you excel at sports. These are a few examples of stereotyping through appearance. Can you think of any more examples?

LEARNING ABOUT YOUR OWN IMPRESSION

As you mature, you begin to wonder how you look and relate to others. When you meet someone for the first time, what impression do you make? How do your family and friends see you in different situations?

To learn what image you project to others, you have to observe their reactions. Also, watch and listen to yourself. Then ask a relative or best friend about your behavior.

Your Self-Image

Have you looked at a recent photograph of yourself and said, "That doesn't look like me," or "I look great in that photo!" Or have you heard your voice on a cassette recording and asked, "Do I really sound like that?"

How do you see yourself? You are a unique combination of physical, mental, and emotional characteristics. You have your outward appearance, plus your inner qualities. You have special talents, interests, attitudes, and emotions. And you have certain shortcomings, too. *How you perceive all of your characteristics* is called your **self-image**.

Think about your self-image. What combination of characteristics makes you unique? You may look a lot like your sister or brother, but your talents and interests are not the same. Even identical twins have unique characteristics of their own. Make a list of your special qualities. Does your list give an accurate description of you?

All people have different qualities that make them look and feel unique.

What kind of self-image do you have? Is it positive, negative, or somewhere in between?

A HEALTHY SELF-IMAGE

Some people have a good self-image. They see themselves in a positive way. Others have a poor self-image. They see themselves in a negative way. These self-images can be accurate or inaccurate.

Sometimes people do not see themselves realistically, or the way that others do. For example, a teen may feel that her red hair is unattractive because no one else that she knows has hair the same color. Realistically, her red hair compliments her complexion beautifully, and her friends see her as a very pretty girl.

What kind of self-image do you have? Is it positive, negative, or somewhere in between? A positive self-image helps to make an individual actually look better. A person who shines from the inside out will project a positive feeling and make others feel good just to be with him or her. A person with a positive self-image does not need to be handsome or beautiful to look attractive.

YOUR PHYSICAL CHARACTERISTICS

Your physical characteristics make up your outward appearance. The shape of your body and face, your height and bone structure, and the coloring of your hair, eyes, and complexion are all physical characteristics of your body.

You inherit your physical characteristics from your parents. Physical characteristics are passed from generation to generation through genes that are every one of your body cells. Your genes include all the information that your body needs about you.

Almost all people have some features that they like, and some that they wish they could change. You can control some of your physical characteristics. You might firm up your muscle tone through sports, or trim your waistline with exercise. Or you may alter a feature through cosmetic surgery. But you cannot make yourself taller or shorter, or change the width of your shoulders.

However, you can select clothes that will emphasize or camouflage certain physical characteristics. In Chapters 11 and 12, you will learn how to use color and line to your advantage.

YOUR MENTAL CHARACTERISTICS

Your mental characteristics reflect your intellectual self. This self gives you the ability to think, know, understand, and remember things. Your intellectual self has talents and abilities just like your physical self. These talents can be developed by studying, practicing, and exploring through reading and experimentation.

One of your classmates may have a natural talent for working with computers. Her mind relates well to the logic on which computers are based. Another student may have a more creative mind. He may excel in less structured areas, such as the arts, fashion design, or clothing construction.

The real you is a combination of your physical, mental, and emotional characteristics.

YOUR EMOTIONAL CHARACTERISTICS

Your emotional characteristics are the ways that you express your feelings about everything in your environment. Feelings create emotions, such as love, hate, anger, joy, and sorrow. Emotions can make you laugh or cry, scream or withdraw, be happy or sad, feel enthusiastic or bored.

Your emotional self influences your intellectual self and vice versa. For example, your intellectual self gives you the ability to study for an exam, but your emotional self tells you that you "hate" doing it. Or your emotional self gets angry at your brother because he teases you.

But your intellectual self tells you to like him because he is another human being and a member of your family.

Growing up and maturing means being able to balance your intellectual and emotional sides. Young children may scream and cry when they are unhappy. They have not developed the ability to use their thinking self to analyze the situation. Adults are expected to behave more maturely than a child. They are expected not to scream and cry when something minor goes wrong.

As you grow older, it will be easier for you to control your emotions. And your emotional self will grow, too. You may feel new emotions, such as falling in love.

Expressing Your Personality

In Chapter 2, you learned how your personality can influence your clothing choices. Now you will discover how you can select clothes that will help to express your personality.

Have you ever been shopping with friends and heard them say, "Try this on! It looks just like you!"? What is the meaning behind this remark? Your friends are trying to say that they know something about you and your personality. They have some definite ideas about the kind of clothes that they think you prefer.

And what is your reaction? Do you agree with their selection of clothes for you? Or are you amazed that they picked out something that you do not like at all?

Everyone is a highly complex blend of many different personality traits. Your personality is the combination of your physical, mental, and emotional characteristics. You are an individual with definite interests, tastes, and preferences.

CLOTHES HELP

You can express your personality through the clothes that you wear. You can communicate what type of person you are—whether you are outgoing or reserved, a leader or follower, conservative or daring, confident or unsure, plus much more.

Sometimes people adopt extreme styles of clothing to create a false image of themselves.

What we wear shows aspects of our personality, our interests, and our values.

They may dress too old, too young, too extreme, or bizarre. Others may put too much emphasis on appearance. They spend so much time, effort, and money to look "just right" that other interests and activities are neglected.

At the other extreme are people who show no interest in their appearance and clothes. They may always look sloppy or wear the same clothes everywhere. Either too much or too little concern with clothes may limit your life.

Clothes cannot change your personality. But they can create favorable impressions that may lead to a new opportunity or experience.

Individuality Versus Conformity

As you seek your own identity as a person, you begin to get a clearer picture of yourself. Your self-image begins to emerge and you have a deep need to feel secure about that image. To feel good about yourself, you need the approval of others.

Most teenagers seek the approval of classmates and identify closely with a group. As your confidence grows, there is also an awareness of the need to be an individual—not just a carbon copy of others in the crowd. This dual drive contributes to a conflict: the strong desire to be part of a group, and a growing urge to be recognized as an individual in your own right.

CONFLICTS

This desire results in conflicts about what to wear. You may want to belong to the group and dress like the rest. At the same time, you may feel that you want your clothes to represent you, not everybody else. You want to express your own **individuality**, which is *the characteristics that make you unique or distinctive from others.*

If you have a conflict between individuality and conformity, perhaps you can find a middle ground in which you are comfortable. For example, if everyone in your group is wearing a certain style or brand of jeans, you may want to wear them, too. This will help you to feel a part of the group. However, you can express your individuality by wearing a unique shirt or sweater that you like with your jeans.

Even when wearing the same type of clothing that others in the group wear, you can express your individuality through your choice of colors, specific styles, or accessories. You may even start your own trend within your group. Others may like what you are wearing and want to dress the same way, too.

The Real You

It is hoped the clothes that you wear reflect the real you. If the image that you project does not reflect your real self, then others will get a cloudy picture of you. You will send mixed messages that are confusing to others and to yourself.

Perhaps you are not sure of your identity and how to present yourself to others. This is a time to look inward and evaluate who you are and who you want to be. You can experiment with your clothes and try new styles, colors, and fabrics. You will learn more about yourself—how you look, how you want to look, and how others see you. You will discover what you like and what is comfortable for you.

Summary

First impressions are formed in only a few seconds. They are based on a person's appearance and behavior and may not always be accurate. You can communicate many things about yourself through your verbal and non-verbal messages.

Your own self-image affects your clothing choices. Your combination of physical, mental, and emotional characteristics makes you unique. You can express your personality and your individuality through the clothes that you wear. Hopefully, your clothes express the real you to others.

Questions

1. Identify five clues that people use when making first impressions about others.

2. What is the difference between a verbal message and a nonverbal message?

3. How do stereotypes influence your first impression of others? Why may this be a negative clue?

4. Define self-image. How does a positive self-image affect your appearance?

5. What characteristics can you change or improve? What characteristics can you not change?

6. What three general characteristics make up your personality? How can clothes express your personality?

7. What is the difference between individuality and conformity? Give an example of how you can express both in the way that you dress.

8. Why should your clothes reflect the real you?

Activities

1. With another classmate, demonstrate two identical situations of two people meeting for the first time. In one, use negative body language and poor manners. In the other, use positive body language and good manners. Discuss how impressions differ.

2. On a piece of paper write how you see yourself. Describe your voice, body language, manners, grooming, and clothes. Then ask a close friend or relative to write how they see you. Compare the lists.

3. Read an article about "dressing for success." Do you agree or disagree with the advice in the article. Why?

You Be the Expert

Your brother is going to interview for a job in a clothing store. He is wearing a T-shirt and jeans. Your mother insists that he change into a shirt and slacks. He appeals to you to back his choice of clothes. What would you say?

4 Healthy Good Looks

TERMS TO LEARN

acne
anorexia nervosa
bulimia
calorie
dental hygiene
dermatologist
nutrients
nutrition
plaque
tartar

Healthy good looks. What does that phrase mean to you? Looking good involves much more than selecting the right type of clothes to wear. Looking good means developing a plan for your own physical well-being. It means finding the right combination of good nutrition, exercise, rest, and good grooming to make you look your best.

Looking good takes effort and a positive attitude about yourself. You are responsible for what and how much you eat, when and how much you exercise, and how much sleep your body gets. You are also responsible for your own cleanliness and personal grooming.

Your body is the only one that you will ever have. It cannot be replaced. Take good care of it so it will last a lifetime.

After reading this chapter, you will be able to:

- explain how nutrition, exercise, rest, and grooming contribute to your appearance,
- list the guidelines to follow when making good food choices,
- describe the benefits of regular exercise,
- apply the principles of good grooming.

Your Total Look

Your total look is the combination of your state of health and grooming, plus your clothes. Imagine the identical outfit on two different people. One has dirty hair, a dull complexion, and tired posture. The other has shiny hair, clean skin, and erect posture. The appearance of each person is totally different. Looking good is much more than just your choice of clothes.

A HEALTH CHECKLIST

- *Good Nutrition.* Eating healthful food is the cornerstone of all that you do for yourself. Your body needs good fuel to keep it running smoothly and properly. Nutrition affects your hair, skin, teeth, nails, weight, and level of energy.
- *Exercise.* Exercising helps your body stay in shape. A regular program of exercise, at least three or four times a week, can firm your body and reduce tension. Regular exercise can help you lose or maintain weight.
- *Sleep.* Sleep is important to looking and feeling good. While you are sleeping, your body performs housekeeping functions, such as cleaning your muscles to get them ready for the next day.
- *Grooming.* Caring for your body to make it look neat, clean, and attractive is also important. Your skin, hair, nails, and mouth all need daily attention for you to look your best.
- *A Positive Attitude.* Start off each day with a positive attitude. Feeling good about yourself is the first step to looking good. When your attitude is positive, others will notice that there is something special about you. Each morning, think about all the positive things that could happen to you that day.

Nutrition . . . Food for Fitness

Nutrition is the simple act of *nourishing or feeding yourself.* Plants and animals have little choice of what to eat. Plants get their nutrition from soil, water, and fertilizer. Animals eat whatever is available in their environment. People, on the other hand, have a tremendous variety of foods from which to choose.

As small children, your parents provided your food. They made your nutritional choices. You developed your eating habits from them.

As your environment broadened outside the family unit, you began to form eating habits of your own. Now you make many of your own choices, such as deciding what to buy in the school cafeteria or in a restaurant, or what to prepare for a meal or snack at home.

YOUR EATING HABITS

Have you ever evaluated the foods that you eat each day? Do they contain all the nutrients needed to keep you healthy and strong? **Nutrients** are *the substances needed by your body.* They include proteins, carbohydrates, fats, vitamins, minerals, and water.

Good eating habits include selecting foods from the basic food groups: (1) fruits and vegetables, (2) milk and milk products, (3) breads and cereals, and (4) meat, fish, poultry, eggs, and legumes. Within these groups, it is best to select foods that give you the most nutrition for the calories that you consume.

A **calorie** is *a unit of energy.* It is used to measure the amount of energy produced by a gram of food. For example, every gram of protein has four calories, and every gram of fat has

The Daily Food Guide

Fruit-Vegetable Group
Servings per day: 4
One serving can be:
- 1 medium fruit
- 1 cup (250 mL) fruit juice
- ½ cup (125 mL) cooked vegetables
- tossed salad

Milk-Milk Products Group
Servings per day: 4 or more for teenagers
One serving can be:
- 1 cup (250 mL) milk or yogurt
- 2 slices of American or Swiss cheese
- 1½ cups (375 mL) cottage cheese

Meat-Poultry-Fish-Eggs-Legumes Group
Servings per day: 2
One serving can be:
- 2 to 3 oz (60 to 85 g) lean meat, poultry, or fish
- 2 medium eggs
- 2 T (60 mL) peanut butter
- 1 cup (250 mL) cooked legumes

Bread-Cereal Group
Servings per day: 4
One serving can be:
- 1 slice bread, roll, biscuit, muffin, or bagel
- 1 cup (250 mL) ready-to-eat cereal
- ½ to ¾ cup (125 to 175 mL) cooked rice, pasta, cereal, or grits
- 2 tortillas

nine calories. Calories are also used to measure the energy used by your body. You might burn up 150 calories while swimming for 20 minutes.

Nutritionally Dense Foods

Foods that are low in calories and high in nutrients are called *nutritionally dense foods*. Some examples are broccoli, low-fat milk, broiled chicken, and cantaloupe. However, all high calorie foods are not bad.

A piece of pizza, although high in calories, is also high in nutritional value. Pizza includes carbohydrates from the breadlike crust, vitamin C from the tomato sauce, and protein from the cheese. On the other hand, a piece of cake is high in calories and low in nutritional value.

Spend your calories wisely. Be wary of foods that have "empty" calories with no nutritional value. These foods are usually high in

Healthy snacks are easy to prepare. You can make them from leftovers, vegetables, or fruit.

processed sugars, fats, and salt. To make wise choices, follow the dietary guidelines chart.

SNACKS

Good eating habits can include snacks, too. There may be a few times during the day when you will want to snack. Some people divide up their daily food intake to include their snacks. For example, instead of eating three large meals a day, they have three moderate meals and two small snacks.

Choosing Snacks

When choosing snacks, keep the basic dietary guidelines in mind. Avoid those that are high in sugars, salts, and fats. Did you know that one can of soda may contain 12 teaspoons of sugar?

Learn to look at the ingredients listed on the package. By law, ingredients must be listed in the order of the amounts in the product. So if sugar or sweetener is listed first or second, then it is one of the major ingredients.

Aim for foods that are closest to their natural state. For example, a fresh, crisp apple is better

for you than a slice of apple pie. Since both include apples, what is the difference? The fresh apple has lots of fiber and fewer calories. Its nutrients have not been lost through cooking, and its sugar content is natural. Apple pie has processed sugar added, and the crust is high in fat.

Healthy snacks do not necessarily have to be low in calories or uninteresting. Peanut butter on whole-grain crackers, a fresh-fruit salad, low-fat yogurt sprinkled with granola, raw vegetable sticks and slices, and whole grain muffins are all tasty and healthy snacks. Popcorn is a very good choice, especially when it is unbuttered and unsalted.

Make a milk shake with fresh fruits, stuff celery with cheese, or nibble on a nut and dried fruit mix. And don't forget fresh fruits. An orange, banana, or slice of melon is both refreshing and nutritious.

YOUR WEIGHT

Your ideal weight is based upon your height and body frame size according to your age. Most of us can control our weight with the proper eating and exercise programs. Be cautious of fad diets and eating too few calories as a method of losing weight. You need to eat enough to keep your energy level up throughout the day. The best way to lose weight is through a combination of healthy dieting and exercise.

If you are overweight, look for ways to cut back without really dieting. Cut down on high calorie snacks. Increase the amount of exercise that you get. Doing these two things will help you to balance your weight.

If you are underweight, you can be more generous at both snack and mealtime.

You can maintain your weight by balancing the calories that you eat with those that you burn. Reaching your ideal weight and maintaining it will help you feel and look better. And your clothes will probably fit better, too.

EATING DISORDERS

Two serious eating disorders are associated with food. **Anorexia nervosa** is *a severe loss of appetite over a long period of time resulting in extreme loss of weight.* **Bulimia** is *an abnormal craving for large amounts of food, followed by vomiting or the use of laxatives.*

Both of these disorders develop due to psychological reasons associated with a person's self-image. They are physically harmful to the body and need medical care.

As a young person, you are still growing. It is important to develop good eating habits so that your body has the right nutrients to promote a healthy growth pattern. Throughout your life, it is important to maintain good eating habits for a healthier you.

Exercise

Do you know people who seem to be in good health, yet complain of being tired all the time? They seem to lack the endurance to get through the school day without moping around. Chances are that if you look at their lifestyle, they sit a lot—during classes, on the school bus, watching television, and talking on the telephone. They do very little walking or other forms of exercise. Too much sitting makes your body slow, sluggish, and tired.

All types of exercise, from aerobics to bike riding, can take away the tiredness blues. Exercise builds strength, stamina, and self-confidence. You will look better because you will feel better.

Exercise improves your appearance because it makes your body function more efficiently. Your skin, hair, and nails will be healthier and look healthier. Your posture will be improved, another appearance plus. Good posture contributes to the smooth running of your body's functions. Digestion occurs more naturally if you sit and stand straight instead of slouching down on your internal organs.

Exercise helps your mind to relax and to reduce tension. People who exercise sleep better. Exercising on the day before a big exam will help you to be more alert during the exam.

ARE YOU IN SHAPE?

What does being in shape mean? Does it mean that you can do 15 pushups, 20 situps, and 25 jumping jacks without breathing hard or groaning with pain?

Being in shape means different things to different people. It does not mean that you have to be your school's top athlete. It does mean achieving the level of fitness as close to your maximum potential as you can.

Keeping your body fit depends upon many factors. Some you can control and some you cannot. Factors that you cannot control include your age, height, inherited traits, and possible birth defects and injuries. Each of us has limitations that we must work with or around. Yet, each of us can achieve a level of physical fitness that will help us to feel and look better.

The Benefits of Exercise

Now that you know what it means to be in shape, these charts can help you to choose the activities with the most shaping-up and calorie-burning benefits. The best exercise program is one that combines different types of activities and benefits.

Type of Activity	Number of Calories Burned in 30 Minutes	
	Females	Males
Resting	36	42
Bicycling	102	126
Walking	126	156
Tennis	174	213
Swimming	204	249
Basketball	219	270
Running	306	375

Exercise is the key to alertness and staying in shape. Perform some kind every day.

Activity	Benefit from Activity
Pushups, situps, pullups, weights, progressive resistant equipment	Increase muscular strength
Stretching exercises, yoga, gymnastics, soccer, karate, basketball, surfing, skiing	Improve flexibility
Aerobic dancing, running, jogging, walking, jumping rope, racquet sports, bicycling, swimming, basketball, cross-country skiing	Improve cardiovascular fitness

Adequate sleep makes you feel refreshed and more energetic. Too little sleep can affect your appearance and your mood.

ACTIVITIES AND EXERCISE

What exercise activities do you do? Do you ever walk instead of ride? Do you take the stairs instead of the elevator? How about biking to your friend's home or just biking for fun? What about organized exercise? List several activities from your daily routine that you can do to shape up or maintain your fitness level.

You can get regular exercise by playing sports, by dancing, or by doing gymnastics. You might consider participating on a team or working out with friends. Regular strenuous exercise through sports such as tennis, racquetball, volleyball, softball, basketball, soccer, swimming, cross country skiing, and running is a great way to contribute to your physical fitness. Or you may prefer to exercise on your own.

Find the type of exercise that is going to benefit you the most. Exercise can be *aerobic,* which benefits your heart and lungs. It can be body slimming, body shaping, or body building. (See the box feature on EXERCISE.)

Discuss exercise possibilities with a teacher,

coach, or someone who may know about exercise programs. Find one or more that you really like to do. If it is going to be a part of your weekly lifestyle plan, you have to enjoy doing it, or you will not exercise regularly.

Sleep

Sleep is the natural activity of letting your body rest and restore itself. Young people generally require 8 to 10 hours of sleep nightly to wake up feeling refreshed and ready to start a new day.

While you are sleeping, your body is rebuilding cells and tissues. When deprived of sleep, your muscles and joints may ache. The area around your eyes may become puffy and dark. You may be cranky and irritable. These symptoms are the result of not giving your body the time it needs to refresh itself through sleep.

Good Grooming

Good nutrition, exercise, and rest will help keep your body in good shape. Good grooming gives the finishing touch to an attractive appearance.

Step in front of a full-length mirror and take a look at yourself. Check your skin, hair, nails, and teeth. Is your skin clean and healthy-looking? Does your hair shine from being washed and brushed regularly? Are your nails trimmed neatly, with no chips or tears?

Does each area pass inspection? If not, zero in on those that need your help.

YOUR SKIN

Your skin is a valuable body organ. Without your skin for protection, you would die. It even has the power to repair itself without scarring when slightly damaged by minor cuts and burns.

The condition of your skin depends on many factors. You inherit the type of skin that you have. It may lean toward dryness, oiliness, acne, allergies, or well-balanced skin. Your skin is also influenced by your habits—eating, exercising, rest, bathing—and even nervousness.

Your environment greatly affects the quality of your skin. You may have to work hard to counter the effects of the elements of sun, cold, and wind. Also air conditioning, heating, and air pollution affect your skin. As the seasons change, you may notice your skin changing, too. Winter dryness may prompt you to use a moisturizer, which did not seem necessary during the hot summer months.

Daily Care

Bathing daily keeps your skin fresh and healthy. Your skin accumulates dirt, oil, bacteria, and dead skin cells, all of which need to be washed away regularly. To keep your skin clean, take a bath or shower daily. Wash your face both morning and night and in between if your face needs it. Use warm water and a mild soap, and rinse well. Soap residue can irritate your skin.

Perspiration is a natural function of your skin. The parts of your body with more sweat glands, such as your armpits, perspire more than others. Since perspiration can cause body odor, many people use a deodorant or antiperspirant after bathing.

A *deodorant* does not prevent you from perspiring, but covers up or destroys body odor. An *antiperspirant* stops both perspiration and odor from forming.

Acne

A tendency toward **acne**—*facial and body pimples*—is common during the teenage years. It is often blamed on heredity, hormonal changes, lack of cleanliness, certain foods, and stress. You cannot control heredity and hormonal changes, but you can control what you eat, and the amount of exercise and rest that you get.

There is no real proof that some foods are the cause of acne, although certain foods can cause allergic reactions that show up as skin rashes and blotches. Foods commonly blamed for aggravating skin problems are nuts, chocolate, hard cheeses, shellfish, fried foods, caffeinated sodas, and junk food in general. Drinking lots of water, not sodas, coffee or tea, is good for promoting healthy skin.

Exercise not only helps to relieve stress, a common acne villain, but also promotes the natural cleansing of the skin through perspiration. When perspiration mixes with the oils in the skin glands, it thins the oils so that they pass through the pores more easily and get to the surface. There they can be safely washed away

Cosmetics—Be a Smart Shopper

Cosmetics are anything that you use on your body to cleanse or change its appearance. These include products for your hair, skin, nails, and mouth—from shampoo and toothpaste to lipstick and perfume.

Expensive products do not always mean better results. With some products, you actually pay more for the fancy packaging and extensive advertising than for the product inside. With the ever-increasing number of products on the market, how can you be a smart shopper? Here are some hints:

- *Read all labels.* The Food and Drug Administration requires that all ingredients be listed on the label. If you have any allergies, you can avoid products that contain certain ingredients. If you have sensitive skin, look for *hypoallergenic products,* products that do not use common allergy-producing ingredients.

- *Take advantage of samples.* Try out tester products in the store. Buy promotional packages in small sizes to see which product is right for you.

- *Consider generic products.* A *generic product* is one which has no brand name. It may be just as good as the brand name products and much less expensive. For example, petroleum jelly is a very good moisturizer and a great lip gloss, which sells at a fraction of the price of many brand name products.

- *Compare products.* Compare size, quantity, and ingredients before making your final decision. To compare the price per ounce, divide the price by the number of ounces.

- *Get as much information as you can.* Pick up any leaflets and ask questions of trained sales representatives. Attend in-store demonstrations. Some companies have a toll-free 800 number to answer consumer questions about their products.

with soap and water before bacteria has time to grow. If the oil clogs your pores, it creates the perfect environment for blackheads, whiteheads, and pimples to grow. Keeping your face clean may not totally prevent acne, but it can help to reduce the effects. Do not squeeze pimples and blackheads because doing so could cause scarring. Severe cases of acne are treated by a **dermatologist**, *a skin specialist.*

Sun Protection

Spending time in the sun can be healthy. Sunshine not only makes you feel good, but it also provides you with natural vitamin D. And, like exercise, the warmth from the sun causes your skin to perspire and naturally cleanse pores.

But beware. Too much sun can damage your skin. You can get serious burns or develop skin cancer from overexposure to harmful ultraviolet rays. Your skin will toughen when exposed to the sun, even if you tan easily. It loses elasticity and wrinkles begin to form. Young people rarely worry about wrinkles, but the more you abuse your skin, the sooner the wrinkles will come.

Dermatologists recommend using a sunscreen or sunblocking lotion or cream to prevent skin damage. *Sunscreens* allow your skin to tan but protect against burning. *Sunblocks* prevent both tanning and burning.

Sunscreens and sunblocks are available in different degrees of strength. Read the product descriptions carefully to obtain the strength that you need to protect your skin type.

HAIR

Thick or thin, curly or straight, dry or oily, long or short, your hair should compliment your face and body shape. What cut will look best on you? What one is right for the type of hair that you have, and is easiest for the lifestyle that you

lead? Ask a hairdresser or barber for advice. They are trained to answer your questions and give you a cut that not only looks good on you but is easy to care for, too.

Have your hair trimmed regularly, even if you are letting the length grow longer. Trimming removes any split ends and keeps your hair more manageable.

Daily Care

Hair should be brushed daily, not only to keep it neatly styled, but also to make it shiny and free of dust and dirt. Wash your hair as often as it needs it. There is no right or wrong time limit to washings. For some people, daily washing is necessary; for others, every few days is fine. Always wash after swimming to remove chemicals that may damage your hair.

Choose a shampoo that cleans your hair without being harsh. Even oily hair can be cleaned

Good grooming adds to your appearance. Wash your hair when it is dirty or too oily.

properly with a mild shampoo. Purchase trial sizes of shampoos and use them for a few washings to see if your hair reacts favorably. Cream rinses make hair easier to comb through when wet. They also help to calm frizzy hair.

For common *dandruff,* or flaking of the scalp, special over-the-counter shampoos can help. For serious dandruff or scalp irritations, consult a dermatologist.

Hair Styling Equipment

Many people like to own two combs, one with wider teeth for combing wet hair and one with average teeth for everyday use. Hair is weaker when wet than dry. Using a wide comb helps to prevent damaging delicate, wet hair. The teeth of the combs should be smooth and without any burrs.

Blow dryers are available in many sizes, weights, shapes, and wattages. Use caution with the high-temperature setting since it may damage your hair with continued use.

Curling irons, styling wands and brushes, and heated rollers are available for curling hair. As with all electrical products, be safety conscious. Never use them near water, such as in the bathtub. Electrical shocks can be deadly.

HANDS AND FEET

To keep your hands looking neat and smooth, they need daily care. Apply a moisturizing lotion after washing your hands to keep them from getting chapped and dry. The *cuticle* of your nail, the little ridge of skin that grows at the base of your nail, dries out very easily. When this happens, it can split and be uncomfortable. To prevent this, wash your hands. Next, gently push the cuticle back toward your fingers with a towel. Then moisturize your hands and the nail area to help them from drying out.

Manicures are not only for females. Males should also follow a daily routine of cleaning their hands and nails and a weekly routine of trimming them. A nail brush can be used to help remove dirt from under the nails. Regular trimming and filing of any rough edges will help prevent nails from chipping and splitting.

Your feet also deserve attention. Toenails should always be trimmed straight across. Rough skin and callouses can be smoothed with lotion or by rubbing with a special stone, called pumice.

YOUR TEETH

Your smile says "Hello," "I like you," and "I like me." A smile is a good feeling coming from the inside to the outside. It also reveals the type of dental hygiene that you practice. **Dental hygiene** is *the care of your teeth and gums.* Regular brushing and flossing, along with a visit to the dentist every 6 to 12 months for a cleaning and a checkup, are necessary. You have only one chance with your permanent teeth, and regular care has a direct relationship to how long they last.

Brush your teeth each morning and night, and after eating, if possible. Floss daily. If you do not know how to floss, ask your dentist or dental hygienist for a lesson.

Daily flossing removes **plaque**, a thin layer of *mucus on your teeth that contains harmful bacteria.* An accumulation of plaque brings tooth decay and gum disease. When *plaque builds up and becomes hard,* it becomes **tartar**, which is even more harmful to your teeth and gums. Tartar can be removed by a dentist, but it is best to practice preventive dental hygiene and keep it from forming.

Make good grooming a part of your healthy lifestyle plan. Habits formed now will stay with you all through your life. You will feel better and look better all the time.

Summary

Looking good involves much more than selecting the right type of clothes to wear. Good nutrition, exercise, rest, and good grooming all contribute to your appearance. The Dietary Guidelines and The Daily Food Guide can help you make good food choices. Various forms of exercise can make your body look and feel better. Sleep can benefit your body in many ways. Good grooming involves the proper care of your skin, hair, hands, feet, and teeth. Each day you should take a bath or shower, brush your hair, clean your hands and nails, and brush and floss your teeth.

Questions

1. What are the five components of healthy good looks?

2. Why is good nutrition so important? How does it affect your body?

3. List the four basic food groups and the recommended daily servings for each group.

4. Describe nutritionally dense foods. Why are they good food choices?

5. List the dietary guidelines. Keeping the guidelines in mind, what snacks would be good choices? What would be poor choices?

6. How can you maintain your weight?

7. What are five benefits of regular exercise?

8. What is the purpose of sleep? What are the physical symptoms of a person who has not gotten enough sleep?

9. What good grooming steps should you do each day?

10. What cautions are associated with skin care?

Activities

1. List all the foods that you ate during one day. Indicate which foods were eaten as snacks. Evaluate the foods as to servings per food groups and the dietary guidelines. What changes could be made to obtain better nutrition?

2. Choose one of the dietary guidelines. Read an article related to the topic chosen. Use that information to evaluate why the dietary recommendation was made.

3. Regular exercise should be a part of everyone's life. Brainstorm with your classmates a list of sports and activities that are considered lifetime exercises to be done alone or with one or two other persons.

You Be the Expert

You are working in a local drug store. A customer asks your advice about various suntan lotions. What recommendations could you give the customer?

5 | Clothes and the Family

Do you remember the story of Cinderella and how her fairy godmother rescued her from having nothing to wear for the ball? Cinderella had no money to spend on a new gown, so the fairy godmother gave her a gown more beautiful than anything her family owned. Cinderella suddenly did not have to worry about how much the gown cost, if her family could afford it, or whether or not it was suitable for other occasions.

Fairy godmothers exist only in fairytales. In the real world, we all have to consider how being a part of a family can affect our clothing needs, wants, purchases, and responsibilities. After reading this chapter, you will be able to:

- understand how various factors, such as occupation, location, activities and interests, and family structure, affect the clothing needs of a family,
- recognize how family values, goals, and responsibilities influence clothing decisions,
- identify ways that a family can manage and stretch its clothing budget,
- take steps to develop your own clothing spending plan.

Clothing Needs for the Family

Every family has certain clothing needs. These are based on several different factors, such as the occupation of family members, location, activities and interests, and family structure. Thus, the lifestyle of the family and the family members affects clothing decisions.

OCCUPATION

Every family member has an occupation. It may be working outside the house, working in the home, or going to school.

A person who wears a uniform, or a person who works at home, will probably not need as great a variety of clothes as a person who works in an office or in a retail store.

A person who works outdoors will have very different clothing needs than a person who works inside. Well-constructed, wash-and-wear shirts in dark colors and rugged fabrics are more suitable for a construction worker than a banker. The construction worker might need only one dressy outfit, but several pairs of heavy-duty shirts and pants. On the other hand, the banker would need several business suits.

A person who is self-employed may need different types of clothes for different occasions. He or she may wear casual clothes when working at home or at a shop, and a business suit when going out to meet a client.

CHANGING NEEDS

A family member who changes jobs or receives a promotion may find that his or her clothing needs change. In some companies, there are different standards of dress for different types of jobs.

A parent who is at home caring for young children needs casual clothes that can be cleaned easily. If that parent takes on a part-time or full-time job, he or she may need different or additional clothes.

STUDENTS

As a student, your clothing needs are influenced by what is considered acceptable attire at your school. At many schools, students have flexibility as to what they can wear. Jeans, T-shirts, trousers, skirts, and sweaters are all worn.

Other schools have dress codes that prohibit the wearing of certain articles of clothing, such as shorts or sweatsuits, to class. Some schools require that their students wear uniforms.

If you have a part-time job, you may need different clothes than those that are appropriate for school. Some places, such as fast food restaurants, provide special uniforms. Others may require that you wear a jacket or suit.

This family wears everyday functional clothes, suitable for around-the-house activities.

LOCATION

Where your family lives also influences clothing needs. People who live and work in colder climates will have different needs than those who live and work in warmer climates. People in northern areas need almost two complete wardrobes—one for winter and one for summer. On the other hand, people who live in the Sun Belt need only warm weather clothes, plus a few jackets and sweaters for cooler days.

The type of community in which the family lives can also affect its clothing needs. Many people who live in cities need dressier clothes than people who live in the suburbs or in rural communities. The style of clothing worn in urban offices, restaurants, theaters, and at special events may be dressier than in smaller communities. Smaller towns usually have more casual styles of dress.

People who live in houses usually are involved in certain activities that apartment dwellers do not need to do. Some of these activities include gardening, raking leaves, and shoveling snow.

ACTIVITIES AND INTERESTS

Clothing needs are also influenced by how a family spends its time. What are the interests and hobbies of the family members? How do they spend their leisure time? A family that often goes camping would spend part of its clothing budget on clothes that are appropriate for the outdoors. A family that spends much of its time at cultural activities, such as concerts and plays, would have very different clothing needs. A family that prefers to stay at home, reading and watching television, would have other clothing priorities.

Some activities have special clothing requirements. For example, if a person in your family takes dancing lessons, then a leotard and special shoes or slippers might be needed. Skiers need parkas, boots, hats, and gloves. Family members who jog in the evening or early morning need reflective vests, in addition to their other jogging clothes.

FAMILY STRUCTURE

Family structure refers to *the number, ages, and relationships of the family members*. The more members in the family, the more demands that are placed on the resources of the family.

A working couple with no children and a single person with no family obligations have only themselves to consider when planning their clothing needs. Perhaps their clothing needs only focus on their job and social activities.

Children

If a family has children, then the needs of the children must be balanced with the needs of the adults.

- *Young Children.* A young couple with small children will need baby clothes, diapers, shoes, equipment, and toys. Children grow very quickly and outgrow clothing before it is worn out. Perhaps the parents will choose to put more priority on the clothing needs of the children at this stage in life than on their own needs. You will learn more about choosing clothing for children in Chapter 22.

- *Middle School Children.* Older children may be involved in a variety of activities that require special clothes. These may be sports, Scouts, 4-H, or special hobbies.

- *Teenage Children.* A family with teenage children will have different clothing needs. Clothing for teenagers is usually more expensive than children's clothes. Many teenagers are developing their own tastes and want to be involved in the selection and purchase of their clothes. This may cause conflict between parents and teenagers over the styles of clothing worn and the amount of clothing purchased.

However, teenagers can contribute their own resources of money or skill to help meet their personal clothing needs.

Retired People

Older couples who have retired will probably find that their clothing needs have changed. Since they now have more leisure time, their clothes will probably reflect this change in lifestyle. Casual clothing may replace business clothing.

A family that includes an elderly member or a disabled member will have special clothing needs, too. Certain styles of clothes may make it easier for the person to dress and undress or to feel more comfortable in their clothes. You will learn more about the special clothing needs of the elderly and disabled in Chapter 22.

Even though these two family members are wearing sleepwear, how might their individual ages and needs affect their clothing choices?

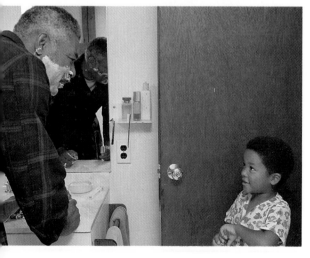

FAMILY VALUES

Some families place a special value on gifts that are handmade, rather than purchased. A scarf that is hand-knit by one of the family's members is a more valued birthday gift than one that is bought in the store, even if the store-bought one would be more expensive.

Some families value easy care in their clothing. They choose fabrics that are washable and require little or no ironing. They are willing to pay a little more money to get these features. Other families may value designer labels.

Many families have certain traditions or customs associated with clothing that they value. Perhaps every family member gets dressed up for special celebrations. Or they may wear certain articles of clothing that relate to their family heritage.

FAMILY GOALS

Both family and individual goals influence **priorities**, or *preferences,* relating to clothing. Most families have limited resources and must decide how and where to spend their money. If the family is planning to go to the beach, then swimming suits and shorts become the priority for the family members. However, if the family wants to attend a special wedding, then the need for appropriate clothing for the ceremony takes priority over casual clothes.

At times, families may decide that certain goals, such as buying a car, is very important. Then it may be necessary for all family members to limit their clothing purchases.

Personal goals also affect clothing decisions. If your goal after high school is to become a computer programmer, your clothing choices will be different than if you plan to be a diving instructor. If certain family members decide to work outside the home, then their changing wardrobe needs may take priority over other family members' needs.

Family Clothing Responsibilities

Clothing responsibilities include both the selection and care of clothes for family members. Someone must shop for clothes, wash, iron, or go to the dry cleaners. Someone must repair or alter clothing or perhaps sew new garments. Are these responsibilities given to one person, or are they shared? Or is each family member responsible for his or her own clothing? How these responsibilities are distributed affects clothing decisions.

DIVIDING RESPONSIBILITIES

The more often that laundry is done, the fewer clothes each family member needs. A family that can only do the wash once a week or that lives in an apartment house several blocks from the laundry will probably need more clothes. A family that owns a washing machine and has one or more members who can do the laundry frequently will need fewer clothes.

Suppose one member of the family has always done the laundry. If that member takes on additional responsibilities outside the home, such as a mother going back to work, one of two things will probably happen. Either the laundry will be done less often, or other family members will have to take on the responsibility of doing it.

Sometimes, one member of the family sews for the other members, or several members sew for themselves. This can increase the wardrobes of family members, provide better fit, and even save the family money during the year.

CONFLICTS OVER RESPONSIBILITIES

Sometimes family conflicts occur over the division of responsibilities within a family. Perhaps you want to wear a special outfit to a party tonight. Just as you are about to get dressed, you discover that the laundry had not been done today. You cannot wear the outfit, and you are very angry and disappointed. Whom do you blame? Do you yell at other family members? Or is it perhaps your own fault?

When purchasing clothes for family members or as special gifts, you assume the responsibility for meeting the needs and wants of others. How well you succeed at your task can result in either praise or conflict with others.

Family conflicts can be resolved by better communication between family members. Also, it may be important to clearly state the exact responsibilities for each family member so that there is no misunderstanding about each person's tasks.

A Family Clothing Budget

A **budget** is *a spending plan or schedule.* Its purpose is to adjust expenses to income during a certain period of time, such as monthly or yearly. A family budget must cover many things. Clothing is only one of these items. Other items include food, housing, transportation, recreation, medical expenses, and personal expenses for each member of the family.

A budget can be written or unwritten. However, to have it work effectively, a family must make certain decisions regarding expenses, resources, priorities, and management.

Lifestyle

Flammability Facts

Every year, many people are burned when their clothing accidentally catches on fire. The Flammability Fabrics Act sets standards for the flammability of fabrics. **Flammable** fabrics are *those that are easily set on fire or which burn quickly.* The standards cover children's sleepwear and apparel, as well as fabrics sold by-the-yard for children's clothing. Carpets, rugs, mattresses, and mattress pads are also covered. The Act requires that:

- all children's sleepwear must be labeled with information on flame resistance,
- permanent care labels must carry a warning if flame retardancy will be reduced or destroyed by laundering,
- products not meeting flammability standards must be labeled as such.

What can you do to protect yourself and your family?

- Buy flame-retardant clothing for children.
- Follow care label instructions for washing and ironing flame retardant fabrics.
- Don't wear full sleeves when cooking or lighting candles.
- Keep matches out of reach of children.
- Don't smoke in bed.

- Don't let children play near a hot stove, appliance, fireplace, or outdoor barbecue.
- Regularly clean the lint filter in a dryer to prevent a fire.
- Install smoke alarms.
- Keep fire extinguishers handy.
- Teach family members what to do in case their clothing catches on fire—*drop immediately to the ground and roll to smother the flames.* Wrap victim in a heavy blanket or coat to help extinguish the fire.

EXPENSES

Many of the items in a family budget are **fixed expenses**, which means that *they must be paid on a regular basis and always cost the same amount of money over a period of time.* Some examples of fixed expenses are most rent or mortgage payments, car payments, and insurance payments.

The *money that is left over after fixed expenses are paid* is called **disposable income**. Disposable income is used to pay for items such as food, clothing, entertainment, education, sports equipment, and other personal expenses.

Food and clothing are basic needs. Therefore, a portion of a family's disposable income must always be set aside for these two items. What percentage of money your family spends for clothing will be influenced by the family's lifestyle, stage of life, values and goals, and responsibilities.

Clothing expenses include not only the cost of different outfits for each family member, but also the cost of underwear, socks, accessories, and shoes. The cleaning and repair of clothes and shoes must also be included.

RESOURCES

There are many resources that a family can use to make its clothing dollars stretch. Money is only one of these resources. Other resources are time and personal skills. These skills can be used to save both money and shopping time.

Sewing Skills

Family members may sew for themselves or for other members. This can greatly reduce the percentage of the family budget that must be spent on clothing. Some families have others sew for them. They find that using a tailor or dressmaker is the best way to obtain alterations or even a special outfit, such as a prom dress.

Even if family members are not interested in learning how to make a complete garment, everyone can learn to do simple repairs and fitting adjustments, such as restitching a seam or shortening a hem.

Consumer Skills

Good consumer skills are also a family resource. Knowing how to shop wisely can help to save family members both time and money. Good shopping skills can be developed. In Unit 5, you will learn how to gather information from advertisements and labels. You will learn how to choose where and when to shop. Department stores, specialty shops, discount stores, outlets, mail order, variety stores, thrift shops, fairs, and garage sales are all sources of clothing. You will learn the advantages and disadvantages of different payment methods. The overuse of credit is a major problem for many families.

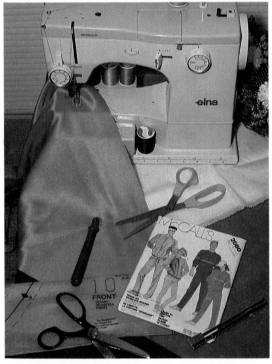

Hand and machine sewing saves you money, gives satisfaction, and insures a perfect fit.

Shopping

Shopping skills also include evaluating your selection before you finalize the purchase. Unit 5 will also present guidelines for evaluating the fit and quality of clothing. Certain compromises can then be made according to your needs and resources. Good shopping skills are also needed when shopping for a sewing project or when shopping for others.

Lifestyle

America Spends

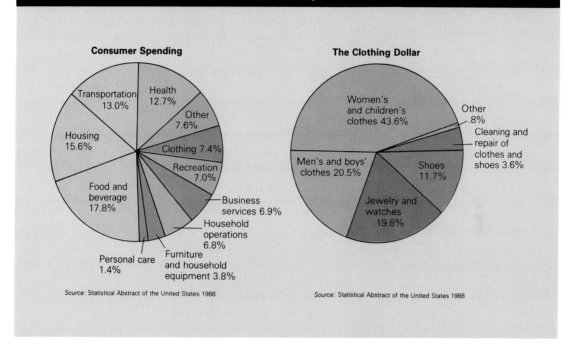

Consumer Spending

- Transportation 13.0%
- Health 12.7%
- Other 7.6%
- Housing 15.6%
- Clothing 7.4%
- Recreation 7.0%
- Food and beverage 17.8%
- Business services 6.9%
- Household operations 6.8%
- Personal care 1.4%
- Furniture and household equipment 3.8%

Source: Statistical Abstract of the United States 1988

The Clothing Dollar

- Women's and children's clothes 43.6%
- Other .8%
- Cleaning and repair of clothes and shoes 3.6%
- Men's and boys' clothes 20.5%
- Shoes 11.7%
- Jewelry and watches 19.8%

Source: Statistical Abstract of the United States 1988

Sharing

Another resource for a family is the use of a garment by different family members. Clothing can be handed down from one family member to another. Sharing and trading among family members are other ways of increasing each member's wardrobe. Clothing can also be recycled into new garments. Many ideas for redesigning and recycling are given in Chapter 13.

PRIORITIES

In order to follow a clothing budget, the family needs to decide on its priorities. How important to the family is clothing? Do all the family members share this same opinion about the importance of clothing? Which is more important to the family—time or money?

Many families find that both their time and money are limited, so they need to carefully balance both. If time is more important than money, the family may purchase more clothes that need to be drycleaned than home laundered. To save shopping time, clothing might be purchased through mail-order catalogues or in stores that have a large selection and a generous return policy.

If money is more important than time, family members may delay clothing purchases until the items go on sale, or shop in discount and outlet stores. Clothes that can be washed at home may be a better choice than clothes that must be sent to the dry cleaners.

MANAGEMENT

For a family to use a clothing budget successfully, the members need to make several management decisions:

- Who will manage the budget?
- How will the budget be organized? Will it be a monthly budget, a seasonal budget, or a yearly budget?
- How will the various family members account for what they spend?

In some families, the parents make all the decisions concerning how the money is spent for clothing. Family members must get approval before spending any money on clothes.

In other families, each member has his or her own clothing budget. As long as that person stays within the money limit set by the family, he or she can purchase whatever clothing is preferred.

In some families, the children receive an allowance to pay for part of their wardrobe needs, such as accessories, grooming aids, and minor clothing purchases. Major clothing items, such as new boots, come out of the family budget.

In other families, children use their own income to purchase all their clothes.

Only your own family can decide which method of management works best for its family members. There is no right or wrong method. However, it is important that all family members clearly understand their own responsibilities and budget limitations. Also, developing a personal clothing spending plan can help you to stay within your budget.

Family budgets must meet both ordinary and special expenses. Some money must also be put away for emergencies and savings.

Developing a Clothing Spending Plan

A spending plan will help you to spend your money wisely so that you can obtain your desired goals. In order to develop your plan, you and your family will need to agree on some guidelines. Who pays for what? Are you responsible for earning some, none, or all of the money that you spend on clothes? Does someone else in the family have to approve your clothing purchases? Who has the responsibility for taking care of your clothes? Are laundry and clothing repair tasks shared, or are you responsible for your own wardrobe?

Once these guidelines are set, there are four steps to establishing a good spending plan:

1. Determine your income.
2. Keep a record of your spending.
3. Plan your expenses.
4. Manage and evaluate your plan.

DETERMINE YOUR INCOME

Before you can plan your spending, you must know how much money will be available. Most planning periods cover one year. If you receive your paycheck or allowance monthly, estimate your income for each of the 12 months. If you receive your paycheck or allowance weekly, estimate your income for each of the 52 weeks.

Your income might **fluctuate**, or *go up or down*. Perhaps you work part-time for a company only when that company needs you. Perhaps you do alterations, or perhaps you babysit for different families. Some weeks you earn a great deal of money and other weeks you do not earn very much. Maybe you receive money as gifts for your birthday or holidays.

You may have to make two estimates of your yearly income. Figure out both the smallest and the largest amount of money that you will make. That way you will know how much you definitely have to spend on the essentials and how much you might have to spend on the extras.

KEEP A RECORD

The next step is to keep a careful record of how you are currently spending your money. Every day for a one- or two-month period, you should keep a record of everything that you buy. Write down the date, what you bought, where you bought it, and the cost of each item or service. At the end of this time, you can determine the average amount that you have spent.

PLAN YOUR EXPENSES

Now *analyze your spending record.* Group your expenses into as many different categories as you feel will be useful. You will probably have a category for:

- food, which would include snacks,
- entertainment, which would include movies, records, and sports events,
- clothing,
- personal items such as cosmetics,
- accessories.

Depending on your particular needs, interests, and hobbies, you might also include categories for items such as sports equipment, medical expenses, music lessons, or savings. Some of these items may be fixed expenses, which cannot be adjusted.

Next, determine the average amount that you spend for each of these categories per week, per month, and per year. Check to see that these all add up to an amount that is equal to, or less than, your estimated income.

It's never too early to plan for your clothing and other personal needs.

Evaluate where your money is going. Are you really spending it on the things that are the most necessary and important to you? Teenage boys tend to spend most of their money on transportation, food, and entertainment. Teenage girls tend to spend most of their money on food, clothes, cosmetics, and personal items. Decide which categories you will keep in your plan. The smart money manager always has a category for savings. Then he or she always has some money set aside for unexpected expenses.

Write down the names of each of the categories that you are keeping in your plan. Then list how much money you expect to spend in each of these categories. This is your spending plan:

- Do you need to increase the amount of money in one category and decrease it in another?

- What resources are available to you and your family that will help you do that?

Remember that if your income changes or your needs change, you will have to revise your plan.

MANAGE AND EVALUATE YOUR PLAN

A spending plan will not be helpful unless you stick to it. It requires self-control. You must be aware of how much you are spending each day, and stay within the limits that you have set.

Impulse buying is the Number One enemy of a spending plan. Some people are easily tempted by in-store displays. Other people do not feel a shopping trip is worthwhile unless they buy something. If you are one of these people, stay out of the stores until you know exactly what you are looking for. In Chapter 19, you will learn how to gather information before you go into the stores. This will help you cut down on impulse buying.

Evaluate your plan regularly to be sure that it is meeting your goals. If it is not, then you should adjust your plan to better meet your new needs or priorities.

A METHOD FOR LIFE

The good money management techniques that you learn and practice now will help you throughout your life. Both rich people and poor people go into debt. Many people, regardless of their income, feel that they do not have enough money to meet their needs and wants. This feeling often results from the fact that they do not know how to manage the money that they already have.

If you understand the importance of a budget and know how to develop a spending plan, you have a head start on planning for a secure financial future.

Chapter 5 Review

Summary

The selection, purchase, construction, and care of clothing involve family decisions. Clothing needs are based on the occupation of family members, location, activities, interests, and family structure. Family values and goals also affect clothing decisions. Responsibilities for the selection and care of clothes can be given to one person or shared. Families can stretch their clothing dollars by setting up a clothing budget and setting priorities. They can use other resources, such as sewing and consumer skills. Your own clothing spending plan can help you spend your money more wisely.

Questions

1. List four influences on the clothing needs of family members.

2. Why might changing jobs or moving result in different clothing needs?

3. How do family activities and interests influence clothing requirements?

4. Describe the possible clothing needs of three different families with different family structures.

5. How do family values and goals influence clothing decisions?

6. Identify the clothing responsibilities that occur in a family. How can conflicts be resolved?

7. What is the difference between fixed expenses and disposable income? Give examples of each in a family budget.

8. What different resources can a family use to stretch its clothing budget?

9. List the four steps in establishing a good spending plan. Why should a plan be evaluated regularly?

Activities

1. Discuss with family members the various influences on your family's clothing needs. What priorities are most important in your family's lifestyle?

2. List all the responsibilities that your family has for the clothing needs of family members. Identify the person or persons who handle each responsibility. What other ways could the responsibilities be divided up?

3. Develop a clothing spending plan for yourself: determine your income, keep a record of your spending for one month, and then analyze your expenses and develop a realistic plan. Be sure to evaluate your plan regularly.

You Be the Expert

Your parents say that the family spends to much money for clothes. So the family is going to sit down together and develop a clothing budget. What recommendations could you make about how to best manage the budget?

2 Clothes and Their Message

6 Clothing and Cultures

Suppose you are the director of your school play. The play has a large cast of characters. In order for the play to be successful, the audience must understand a great many facts about these characters in a very short time. How can you accomplish this? One way to do it is to use different costumes. The costumes you select for each member of the cast can give the audience clues about the character's background, occupation, wealth, and social status.

This chapter explores the many things that clothing can tell you about people and their culture. After reading this chapter, you will be able to:

- explain how clothes reflect the way that people think and live in a society,
- give examples of what clothes can tell you about a person's occupation, nationality, and cultural heritage,
- understand how technology and economics affect the kind of clothes that are available,
- discuss the influences that other cultures have on the clothes we wear today.

Clothing, Society, and Culture

The style of clothing that people wear – the fabrics, the designs, and the colors – can tell you many things about the way that people think and live. Clothing is a clue to a person's occupation, lifestyle, wealth, customs, status, values, and beliefs.

A **society** is *a group of individuals who live together in a particular area.* A **culture** is *the collection of ideas, skills, values, and institutions of a society at a particular time in history.* The American Indians are a society of people who have lived in North America since ancient times. Indian culture includes their special styles of art, architecture, dress, language, religion, and forms of government.

DEVELOPING SOCIETIES

The clothes that people wear in any society tell us something about the times in which they live. In a developing society, clothes tend to be strictly functional and very simple. The daily task of providing food, shelter, and clothing does not leave much time to decorate and embellish clothes for everyday wear.

As a society becomes more developed, a greater variety of styles and fabrics are available. The way that clothes look can become even more important than the protection that they provide. In some societies, clothing is considered a form of art.

Initially, the type of clothes that a society wears is determined by the climate and the natural materials that are available. The prehistoric peoples who lived in northern Europe, where the climate was dry and cold and the warm weather lasted only two or three months a year, developed a style of clothing made mostly from animal skins. The ancient Egyptians lived in a much warmer climate where plants, such as the flax plant, grew abundantly along the Nile River. Flax was woven into linen and styled into simple garments suitable to the hot climate of Egypt.

Clothing ideas are frequently shared among cultures. As early societies came in contact with one another, they began to exchange ideas and information that influenced their clothing. Sailors and merchants who established trade with other countries brought back fabrics, yarns, and trimmings. Soldiers who went away to war abroad saw how others lived and dressed. Missionaries who went to other lands taught the native people about the European style of clothing.

CLOTHES IN OTHER CULTURES

Every culture throughout history has had something special and unique about its clothing. The ancient Greeks wore gracefully draped garments that reflected the same qualities of beauty, harmony, and simplicity that were valued in art and architecture. French fashion in the 18th century, with its richly embellished fabrics, yards of ribbons and laces, and elaborate wigs, reflected the complicated manners and life at the court of Versailles.

In the early American colonies, many goods, such as clothing and furniture, were not easily available. If the colonists needed new clothes, they had to spin and weave their own fabrics, as well as sew the garments themselves. As a result, their clothes were plain and practical.

Many cultures developed a unique style of dress or national costume. Most of these items of clothing had very practical beginnings.

Ancient Celts in the Highlands of Scotland began to weave clan blankets with special plaid patterns to identify each clan. In the 16th cen-

Native Dress

Indian

Ancient Greek

17th-century
New Englander

17th-century
Frenchman

African

tury, they started wrapping these clan blankets around the body to form a short, belted-on, all-purpose garment called a *kilt*. The extra fabric was pulled up over the shoulder from the back and pinned in place.

In Middle Eastern countries, where the desert is very hot during the day and very cold at night, the *turban* became a common item of clothing. It absorbed sweat during the day and insulated the head at night.

In some parts of the world, such as Africa, China, and India, people still wear distinctive native costumes as part of their everyday dress. The African tribal robe, Chinese coat, and Indian *sari* have changed little over the centuries.

In other parts of the world, native costumes are usually worn only for festive occasions, such as holidays, parades, weddings, and dances. Why do you think this has occurred in different cultures?

Influences from the Past

Many of the clothes that you and your classmates wear every day are based on styles that were developed in Western Europe. Until the 14th century, European clothes were loose-fitting and draped. People from different cultures wore similar clothes. Around 1350, people started wearing more fitted styles of clothes. From then on, regional differences in dress began to develop in Western Europe. Many of these differences reflected the culture within the various countries.

For example, in countries such as Italy, Spain, and France, the Renaissance movement encouraged elegant styles, extravagant fabrics, and a great amount of decoration on clothing. The Reformation movement in Germany, Switzerland, Holland, and England encouraged dark colors, simple styles, and little decoration.

Throughout history, countries with wealth and power have influenced the fashions of other countries. When Spain and Portugal were exploring the New World, their fashions influenced styles throughout Europe. In the 17th century, France under the rule of Louis XIV became the most powerful country in Europe. French court dress became the fashionable dress. Since that time, France has been considered a leader in fashion.

In Africa and Asia, societies were not strongly influenced by Western Europe. As a result, clothing styles in these countries reflect their own unique cultures. What countries influence clothing styles today?

Many yards of various fabrics went into making the dresses of these fashion-conscious ladies.

CLOTHES TODAY

The clothes that we wear reflect a blend of many different cultures and our own highly industrialized society. Take a look around you to see what your classmates and teachers are wearing. Most of their clothes were probably **mass-produced** in a factory. This means that *many garments were made at the same time.* Those factories are located in many different cities or countries. Today you cannot always tell where a garment was made by looking at its style.

Almost all of today's clothes are made by machine. Few clothes have intricate detailing and handwork. Hems are usually machine-made. Even buttons can be sewn on by machine. As a result, garments can be made faster and cheaper than ever before.

While many of our styles today are similar, they come in a variety of colors, designs, and fabrics.

Clothes as Symbols

Societies have many symbols. A **symbol** is *something visible that represents something else.* A symbol can represent something that you cannot see, like an idea, a philosophy, or a custom. Clothing is one of these symbols.

HERITAGE

Some styles of clothing are identified with a particular area or country. A sombrero reminds us of Mexico, a kimono reminds us of Japan, a fur parka reminds us of Alaska. These national costumes are part of a person's heritage. **Heritage** is *the body of culture and tradition that has been handed down from one's ancestors.* The term **ethnic** is used to *identify a particular race or nationality.*

Although many different cultures developed garments that were similar in shape, each one personalized its clothes by adding unique forms of ornamentation. Traditional Hungarian clothes are decorated with leather. Colorful embroidery designs accent Scandinavian clothing. Hawaiian dress features various colored feathers, arranged in special patterns, and sewn to the cloth.

Some fabric designs are identified with a particular culture. Distinctive plaid fabrics remind us of Scotland. Batik fabric, with its unique designs, is associated with Indonesia. Guatemalans wear ponchos made from a certain type of woven striped fabric.

Styles of dress can vary within a country. In the United States, you can sometimes tell what region people are from by the way they dress. A Texan often wears cowboy boots with his business suit. People from warm climates, such as Florida and Hawaii, usually wear brighter colors than do people from Minnesota. People

In some societies, clothes are an indication of a person's social or economic class. In China, the farmers and villagers still wear dark cotton trousers and plain jackets, while many city residents wear clothes that have a Western influence.

In democratic societies such as ours, everyone tends to dress in similar styles. In fact, people all over the world tend to dress in somewhat similar styles today. The Western business suit is becoming the accepted standard of dress in most major cities. The Russian businessman and the American businessman wear the same type of suit.

As our society has become more relaxed and informal, our clothes have, too. At one time, a proper gentleman or lady never went anywhere without a hat and gloves. Years ago, in order to be dressed properly for all social occasions, a true gentleman was supposed to have 16 different outfits. He would not think of wearing the jacket from one outfit with the trousers from another. Today, we often wear one jacket or sweater with many different outfits for many different occasions. Sportswear once meant special clothes worn only for sports activities. Today it means the easy-care, simple-styled separates that are worn every day.

Almost every country in the world has one or more distinctive costumes. What country or countries do these costumes represent?

from large cities tend to wear more formal clothes than people from small towns. Can you think of some reasons for these regional differences in clothes?

In many societies, it is traditional for males and females to dress quite differently. Until recently, men always wore trousers and women always wore skirts in our Western society. Pants are now accepted clothing for everyone. Many styles look the same for both sexes.

In the 1970s, the unisex look was very popular. Men and women wore the same styles in the same fabrics and colors. It was fashionable for women to wear pantsuits, styled like men's suits, and neckties.

In many other cultures, skirts and robes are worn by men. Arab men wear long, flowing robes to protect them from the heat of the desert. In Malaysia, both men and women wear the *sarong,* a wrapped and draped skirt.

OCCUPATION AND STATUS

The clothes that people wear can tell something about their occupation and *status,* or rank in a society.

In the Past

Over the centuries, types and quality of clothes have been a way of distinguishing the nobility from the common person.

The colors used for clothing were another way to tell the status of the wearer. At one time, the only way to get purple dye was to extract it from the glands of a mollusk that was found on the coast of Asia Minor. Because this dye was rare and difficult to obtain, it was very expensive. Wearing purple garments became the sign of a very wealthy person. Soon, only royalty was allowed to wear purple.

Fashion Focus

Styles for Males and Females

In some cultures, males and females dress very differently. In other cultures, their clothing is very similar. Clothing styles associated with either sex evolve out of customs, traditions, religion, work, and leisure activities.

There are places in the world where pants have been appropriate attire for both males and females for many years. Eskimo and Lap men and women wear pants as protection against the subzero temperatures. In the rural areas of many societies, both males and females wear pants as they labor in the fields. But pants do not always have to be practical. Some Turkish women wear very full pants in elegant fabrics. Spanish bullfighters and Balinese dancers wear elaborately decorated pants.

In other parts of the world, males wear skirts or long robes just as females do. In Africa and the South Pacific Islands, males wear wrapped skirts or sarongs. Arabian males wear long, flowing robes. Chinese and Japanese men have worn silk robes, or kimonos, for centuries. Scotsmen still wear kilts for special occasions.

During the 13th century in Europe, when a wealthy middle class developed, it became difficult to identify people who were rich, but common, from those who were rich and noble. Special laws, called **sumptuary laws**, were made *to regulate what each class could wear.*

Some of these laws limited peasant clothes to certain colors and certain fabrics. At one time, peasants who looked like they were trying to imitate the clothing tastes of the upper class could be fined, imprisoned, or executed.

In late 13th-century France, there was a law that specified the number of dresses and the value of the materials worn by every class of society. Knights and their ladies were limited to three new robes per year!

In the Present

Today, we live in a much more democratic society where people are usually free to dress as they wish. However, we still have certain standards of dress that are influenced by our occupation and status. The business suit is out of place on a construction site. Blue jeans are out of place in many offices.

Uniforms are also symbols of occupation and status. Think about the policeman's uniform, the nurse's cap, and the priest's collar.

VALUES AND BELIEFS

Clothes can reflect the values and beliefs of a culture or a special group. They can be used to identify a person as a member of a religious group or to express a society's attitude toward a value.

Clothes and Charms

Much primitive dress reflects people's early belief in magic. When a hunter wrapped himself in the skin of a lion, he believed that he was transferring the skill and the strength of that lion to his own body.

A necklace of shark's teeth was believed to have an effect on the wearer that was similar to reciting a special prayer or casting a spell. It provided the wearer with all the qualities a fisherman needed to be successful. Masks and elaborate headdresses were used to ward off evil spirits.

Folktales are full of stories about things that give the wearer special powers, such as magic rings or cloaks that make the wearer invisible. Although we may laugh at these stories and think of them as ancient fairy tales, we sometimes act quite differently.

Some people carry special symbols, such as a rabbit's foot, to bring them good luck at an event where success is especially important.

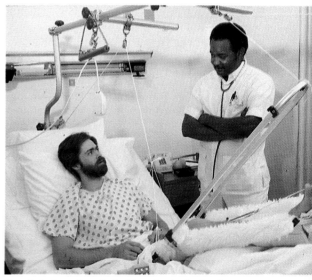

Special, functional clothing for both the doctor and patient are necessary in hospital care.

Clothes and Religion

Clothing and jewelry can indicate membership in a particular religious group. People wear crosses, stars, or other religious symbols as pins or necklaces.

Special clothes are also associated with certain religious ceremonies. These include christening gowns for baptisms, veils for weddings and first communion ceremonies, and prayer shawls and robes.

Clothes and Modesty

Standards for *modesty,* or what a society feels is the proper way for clothing to cover the body, can be very different. Nearly two centuries ago, women in Napoleon's time who wore very low-cut dresses in the front would never expose their shoulders.

Women in Victorian times might expose their shoulders, but would never expose their ankles. Even Victorian pianos had their "legs" covered with heavy, fringed shawls.

SOCIAL CUSTOMS

Social customs deal with traditions and etiquette. **Traditions** are those *customs used to emphasize various ceremonies or ways of doing things throughout a long period.* **Etiquette** deals with *acts that show consideration for events and people.*

Traditions

Every society develops its own set of rules for clothes that are appropriate for certain occasions. In our culture, the bride traditionally wears white. In China, she wears red. In our culture, a person in mourning wears black. In other cultures, a person in mourning wears white.

In Western society, men are expected to wear a tuxedo for formal occasions. In the Philippines, men wear a long-sleeved off-white embroidered shirt, called a *barong tagalog,* for formal events.

Although we may think of sportswear as casual clothing, sometimes it is very traditional. For example, white is the traditional color for tennis outfits. While other colors may be worn, most players in major tennis tournaments wear white.

Etiquette

In our democratic society, people are free to dress as they wish. However, custom has dictated that certain styles of dress are more appropriate to some occasions than to others. If you follow these guidelines, you will be more comfortable even if the occasion is new to you.

Wearing a gown and a tuxedo to a prom makes it a special event. Wearing dark colors to a funeral shows respect for the family's loss. Wearing your good clothes to someone's house for dinner shows that you are pleased by the invitation.

Effects of Technology and Economics

The style and quality of clothing that people wear can tell you a great deal about the technological and economic development of their culture. As a society becomes more advanced, a greater variety of clothing becomes available. Why do you think that this happens?

TECHNOLOGICAL DEVELOPMENT

Technology refers to *the way a culture uses its scientific knowledge to produce things.* Early people lived in a very simple economy. Their clothing was limited to the skins of animals they could hunt for on their own.

Then man discovered that he did not need to hunt for food and clothing. He settled down in one place and raised certain plants and animals that provided him with raw materials to make fabrics. For many centuries, the only fabrics available were those made from natural fibers, such as cotton, flax, wool, and silk.

Today, new types of fibers have been developed that look and feel like natural fibers. Unless you read the label, it is hard to tell what types of fibers are used in today's fabrics. New dyes and printing techniques have been developed that imitate or improve upon ancient hand techniques. In Unit 4, you will learn more about fabrics.

The Industrial Revolution of the 1700s and 1800s changed the way that goods were made. With the invention of power-drawn equipment and the development of factories, manufacturing was no longer done at home or in workshops. There was a great increase in the amount of fabrics and the number of finished garments that could be produced.

Computers are the newest development in technology. They can be programmed to tell a machine how to weave a fabric. They can analyze a color sample and tell you how to dye a particular fabric so that it matches your sample. Computers can even keep track of a store's inventory and forecast future sales. In Chapter 28, you will learn how computers affect the textile, apparel, and retailing industries.

ECONOMIC DEVELOPMENT

Economics refers to *the way that a society produces, distributes, and spends its wealth.* When people learned that they could *barter,* or trade their goods and skills for someone else's goods and talents, they were no longer limited to what was available in their own back yards. Soon trade developed between societies. As a result, ideas and technology were exchanged, along with goods.

For instance, during the 11th to the 13th century, the Crusades opened up trade routes between Western Europe and the Middle East and the Orient. Those who could pay the price could have garments made from the finest silks, damasks, and thin cottons. At first, only the fabrics were imported. Later, the technology was imported so that the fabrics could be made in Europe.

Trade also helps to balance out any excess of some supplies and scarcity of others between societies. For example, people might trade leather for cotton, or tools, or even food. Today, clothes made in many countries are sold all over the world. Your jeans may have been made in the United States, your shirt may have been made in Hong Kong, and your shoes may have been made in Spain.

Mass communication has made it possible for people to share ideas quickly. It no longer takes months for the newest styles to travel across the oceans.

The United States has often been described as a "melting pot." The way we dress today is the result of the influence of the many different people who settled here. Our basic style of dress is inherited from Europe, but many other cultures have contributed special items and details.

For example, the mandarin collar comes from China, and the caftan comes from Africa. Many styles of adornment were contributed by the Native Americans. The turquoise and silver jewelry of the Navajo tribes is highly prized.

Each of us has a heritage that is a unique combination of the cultures in which our parents and grandparents were born, the customs that our family has developed, and our own individuality.

This eldest daughter of a Swedish family enjoys wearing this traditional outfit to celebrate Lucia Day.

Chapter **6** *Review*

Summary

Clothes reflect the way that people think and live in a society. Many cultures developed a unique style of dress or national costume. Clothing ideas were frequently shared between cultures. Today, our clothes reflect a blend of many different cultures and our own highly industrialized society. Clothing can be a symbol of heritage, occupation, status, values, beliefs, and social customs. The style and quality of clothing can tell you about the technological and economic development of a culture or society.

Questions

1. How do a society and a culture differ from, yet interrelate to, each other?

2. How do weather and climate influence the type of clothing that a society develops? What other influences affect clothing styles?

3. Why do many people throughout the world dress in a similar style of clothing today?

4. Why is clothing a symbol of a society?

5. List eight styles of clothing that are identified with a particular country or area.

6. How can clothing reflect values and beliefs? Give examples.

7. Explain how traditions and etiquette influence clothing decisions in our society. Give examples.

8. How has technology and economics influenced the development of fabrics and fashions?

9. How do clothing styles in the United States reflect our "melting pot" heritage?

Activities

1. Look through magazines and books for illustrations of people in native costumes. Identify the particular country or region that each costume is associated with. Describe why each costume is unique.

2. Describe a special clothing item or outfit that you, a member of your family, or someone that you observed wore to participate in a religious ceremony. What was the significance of the clothing worn? What was unique about its style or color?

3. Research a style of clothing that was developed by the ancestors of your ethnic background. Identify its function and importance to that culture. How is it currently being worn?

You Be the Expert

You have volunteered to be the costume coordinator for the annual school play. When meeting with your committee members, what factors should the committee take into consideration as you plan the costumes?

7 | The History of Clothes

TERMS TO LEARN

agrarian society
factory
flax
fleece
Industrial Revolution
ready-to-wear
shuttle
wage

Have you ever thought about how clothes were made before the sewing machine was invented? What types of garments did people wear? How did they fasten these garments together? What types of fabrics did they use? Clothing has changed considerably from the animal skins worn by early man to the wide variety of choices available throughout the world today.

After reading this chapter, you will be able to:

- explain how people learned to grow, spin, weave, and make clothes from natural fibers,
- show how styles developed from simple, draped garments to complicated, tailored ones,
- evaluate how the Industrial Revolution affected the quality, quantity, and type of clothes available to everyone.

The First Clothes

Thousands of years ago, people learned to make clothing from the natural resources around them. In many climates, clothing was essential for protection from the cold weather or the blazing sun. Animal skins and hair, plants, grasses, and tree bark were some of the materials used for clothing.

LEARNING TO SEW LEATHER

Early cave drawings show animal skins being used as body coverings by people in Northern Europe. Untreated animal skins are very stiff and uncomfortable to wear. So primitive people discovered different ways to make the skins soft.

Some people beat the skins with stones, while other people chewed the skins to make them soft. Others beat the skins, then wet them, and rubbed them with oil. Much later, skins were *tanned,* or treated with tannic acid which is a substance that comes from a tree. With this method the skins stayed soft for a long time.

To hold the skins together, holes were punched in the leather. Then *sinews,* or string-like tendons from animals, were laced through the holes. With this crude form of sewing, several skins of small animals could be stitched together to form a garment.

LEARNING TO MAKE FABRIC

People in warmer climates, such as Africa and the South Pacific, needed protection from sun and rain. They learned to make garments from the trees and plants around them. Some

plants, such as the grasses, could be picked and used right away. Grasses were laced together to form the first woven fabric. It was probably

This frontier gentleman wears a coat and pants made out of animal skins.

Technology

Early Sewing Tools

Without the proper tools, we would not be able to sew the wide assortment of clothing that we have today. The development of these tools began with early people's need to cover themselves. As equipment improved, accomplishments grew, and the clothing industry evolved. Look at some of the early tools and their impact on sewing today.

The *eyed needle* allowed thread to be pulled through a fabric in one step. Before, a hole had to be punched in the fabric or skin. Then hairs or sinew were laced through the holes. With the eyed needle, thinner threads could be used and more delicate sewing could be done.

The *sewing plate* was a flat tool made of bone. It was used to push the needle through the hide or fabric, just as we use a thimble today. When the seam was finished, the thread was held across the plate and cut with a flint, which left a scratch on the edge of the plate.

The invention of the *sewing machine* is credited to Elias Howe, who patented the first practical lock-stitch machine. His machine had a needle with an eye near the point to hold the thread. The needle was fastened to a pivoting arm that forced the needle into the cloth. A shuttle held a small bobbin of thread underneath the fabric. The shuttle carried the under thread through the loop of the upper thread to form a lock stitch.

This is the same type of stitching that is done by today's home sewing machines. Early machines were operated by foot treadles. The Singer Sewing Machine Company added the first electric motor to sewing machines in 1889.

For over 50 years, patterns had no printing on them. In 1921, McCalls introduced the first printed pattern, which helped to simplify home sewing.

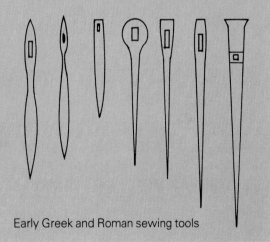

Early Greek and Roman sewing tools

used for mats and baskets rather than for clothing. Parts of plants, such as the bark of the trees, had to be soaked and treated until soft enough to be used as cloth.

People in colder climates began to cut up the animal skins for a better fit. As they did this, they found that the wet, matted clumps of animal hair formed a crude version of felt.

The Discovery of Natural Fibers

After thousands of years of wandering, people learned that *they could live in one place with other humans and grow what they needed.* This is known as an **agrarian society**. People learned how to raise certain animals for the meat and the skins. They learned to grow certain plants for food. People no longer had to spend all their time hunting and farming.

People learned how to spin bits of plants, reeds, horse hair, and bark into one continuous strand, or *yarn.* Then they discovered how to take these long pieces of yarn and weave them into fabric, just like they wove the grasses. People began to look around for other fibers they could use to make yarn. The cotton, wool, silk, and flax that they found are still the most common natural fibers today. Other fibers, such as alpaca from llamas and angora from rabbits, were discovered, but, even today, these fibers are too scarce and expensive to be widely used.

EARLY DEVELOPMENT

Although we know very little about how the process of weaving developed, ancient Egyptian wall paintings illustrate weaving techniques from as early as 5000 B.C. Other civilizations in the Middle East, Pakistan, and central Europe probably learned how to weave fibers into fabrics as early as 2500 B.C. The Chinese learned to weave sometime between 2500 B.C. and 1200 B.C. Here in America, the Pueblo Indians, along with other tribes from what is now the Southwestern part of the United States, developed the art of weaving cotton around A.D. 700.

Egyptian linen became famous all over the ancient world.

Flax

Flax, which is *a tall, slender plant used to make linen*, grew plentifully along the Nile River. It was discovered by the Egyptians, who learned to spin and weave the flax into linen fabric. This early linen was light, cool, and easy to launder. These characteristics made it particularly suitable to the Egyptian people. They needed work clothes that were cool and comfortable in the hot climate. Pieces of linen more than nine thousand years old have been found in Egyptian tombs. The fabric is as fine as any that is made today and may be seen in many museums.

Wool

Wool is the **fleece**, or *hair, of sheep*. Some wool also comes from lambs, goats, and camels.

Many cultures developed the art of spinning and weaving wool. Five thousand years ago, the Sumerians, who lived in the valley of the Tigris and Euphrates rivers, not only learned how to make fine wool but were also great traders. They exported wool to many other parts of the world.

In 150 B.C., the Romans introduced sheep into Spain and then crossbred them with sheep from Asia Minor. This new type of sheep was the ancestor of today's most important sheep, the *merino*. For centuries, the wealth of the Spanish Empire was based on these sheep. Spain's highest order of nobility was called the Order of the Golden Fleece. At one time, anyone caught smuggling merino sheep out of Spain could be put to death and his property seized by the Crown.

Gradually, however, these sheep were spread throughout the world by the Spanish royal family. Whenever one of them married someone from another royal family, merino sheep were always part of the *dowry,* or property given by the bride's family to the groom.

Cotton

Cotton comes from the cotton plant. We do not know very much about its beginnings. Probably it was first made into cloth by the people who lived in the areas known today as northern India and Pakistan. Sir John Mandeville, an English explorer who visited India in 1350, described the cotton balls as tiny lambs growing on a tree.

In the fourth century B.C., Alexander the Great's armies introduced cotton to North Africa. The Nile Valley in Egypt became a center for raising the "wool plant." Egyptian cotton soon surpassed Indian cotton in quality.

When the Spanish conquistadors arrived in the New World, they found cotton fabric being produced in Peru, Mexico, and southeast North America.

For thousands of years silk fabric was one of the most popular exports of China.

Silk

Silk is the fiber made by the silkworm as it builds its cocoon. The silkworm eats the leaves of the mulberry tree. There are ancient Sanskrit writings that claim that silk was produced in India as early as 4000 B.C. There are also written records from China, dating as far back as 2640 B.C., that talk about growing mulberry trees and mention the rare and valuable silk robes that were worn at that time.

The secret of making silk was carefully guarded by the Chinese for centuries. Although the punishment for revealing the secret was death by torture, people tried to steal it.

Eventually, in the East, this knowledge was smuggled to Japan via Korea. In the West, it was smuggled into the eastern Roman Empire by monks, who hid the little silkworms in their bamboo canes.

Because silk has a beautiful luster and can be dyed in many rich colors, it is still considered a luxury fabric today.

Changes in Clothing Styles

Early people were much too busy fighting and staying alive to worry about fashion. But once they learned how to live in one place by raising animals and growing their own crops, they had time to develop other skills and interests. As spinning and weaving skills developed, people learned how to shape fabric into a variety of garments.

Because ancient people left visual records, we do not need to guess at what these garments looked like. Drawings of these garments have been found on the walls of caves. Drawings, mummy cases, and actual fabrics have been discovered in the tombs of the Egyptian pharaohs. Surviving sculpture of the Greeks and Romans shows clothing styles of their times. Paintings, religious statues, and illustrated manuscripts show us how people in the Middle Ages dressed.

DRAPED, OR WRAPPED, GARMENTS

The very first draped garment was the animal skin that the cave dwellers wrapped around their shoulders. Later, people took a square or rectangle of fabric and draped, hung, or wrapped it around their body.

There are examples of draped garments in many cultures. The early Greeks wore a garment called a *himation,* which was an oblong piece of fabric nearly five yards or meters long. It could be worn as a cloak, or with one end draped over one shoulder and the other end draped over the opposite arm. They also wore a *chiton,* which was a tunic made from two rectangles of fabric joined at the shoulders.

The Romans wore a *toga,* a crescent-shaped piece of fabric with one straight end. It measured 4½ to 5½ yards or meters long and was wrapped and draped around the body.

Women in India wear a *sari,* which is a piece of silk or cotton fabric 45″ (1.1 m) wide and 80″

The Greeks and Romans wore simple garments that were easy to wash and to store.

Draped Clothing

Himation

Greek woman

Toga

Roman man

(2 m) long. One end is tucked into the waist-band of a petticoat. Then the fabric is pleated and wrapped around the body, and the other end goes over the head or the shoulder.

Draping was the quickest and easiest way to make a garment. It often took a long time to weave a beautiful piece of fabric. People did not want to cut it up. Since there were no modern washing machines or irons, it was easier to clean a rectangle of fabric. It could be washed and carefully smoothed out. When it dried, it was neatly pressed.

FITTED, OR SEAMED, GARMENTS

When early people learned how to punch holes in the animal skins and lace them together, they made the first fitted garment. A group of people known as Minoans lived on the Mediterranean island of Crete before the time of the ancient Greeks. The women wore some of the first recorded examples of fitted garments. They wore full skirts and very tight fitting jackets with elbow-length sleeves.

Gloves, developed by some of the early cultures that lived in cold climates, are another example of a fitted garment. Trousers were worn by northern invaders who swept into ancient Greece and Italy on horseback.

Today we wear many fitted garments. Slacks, blue jeans, T-shirts, and most suits are all fitted garments.

COMBINATION GARMENTS

Combination garments are garments that have been draped, then cut and sewn so that they hang loosely on the body. Examples of combination garments are the Arabian *kibr*, a hooded robe with sleeves; the Japanese *kimono;* the Hawaiian *muumuu;* and the *caftan* from many cultures.

The Development of Manufacturing

Until the 18th century, everything that had to do with making clothes was done by hand. Fabric was handwoven and all clothes were sewn by hand. Clothes took many hours of labor to construct. Garments were highly valued and expensive.

Wealthy people owned many garments. It was easy to tell how rich people were by the style and fabric of their clothes, and by the number of garments that they owned. Then, around 1760, James Watt, a Scottish inventor, developed the steam engine and everything changed.

THE INDUSTRIAL REVOLUTION

Watt's invention began what is now known as the **Industrial Revolution**. The term describes *the changes in society that resulted from the invention of power tools and machinery and the growth of factories.* Before this time, fabric was woven on a loom by hand. Many people worked long hours to weave a limited amount of fabric.

Now, a few people operated machines that could make many, many yards of fabric. Fabric was produced by faster and easier methods. This meant that there was more fabric that could be used to make more clothes for a larger amount of people.

After the sewing machine was invented in the 19th century, clothes could be made faster and cheaper. It became much harder to tell the difference between upper- , middle- , and lower-class people by looking only at their clothes. It was possible for almost everyone, rich or poor, to own more clothes.

The Industrial Revolution had an impact on the styles of clothing that people wore. Before the Industrial Revolution, an English gentleman's clothes were as elaborate as an English lady's clothes. Both wore light colors and delicate fabrics.

However, because the machinery in the new factories created a lot of dark and dirty smoke, middle-class businessmen began to wear darker colors and practical fabrics.

Inventions

The Industrial Revolution began in England in the early 18th century. Along with the development of the steam engine, new mechanical processes were invented for use in weaving, spinning, and knitting.

The first was the *flying shuttle,* invented by John Kay, an Englishman, in 1733. A **shuttle** is *an instrument that is used to weave the crosswise threads in and out, back and forth, on a loom.* Until the 18th century, the shuttle was moved by hand.

The flying shuttle came with two boxes, one on either side of the loom. When the weaver pulled a stick, the shuttle was released from one box and "flew" across the loom to the other box. Fabrics could now be woven faster, and they could also be made wider.

The next invention, the *spinning jenny,* was developed in 1767 by James Hargreaves, an Englishman who named it in honor of his wife. Until the Industrial Revolution, yarn was spun by hand on a rod or stick called a *spindle.* The spinning jenny had eight spindles so that eight yarns could be spun at the same time.

In 1769, another Englishman, Sir Richard Arkwright, invented the *water frame,* a machine powered by water rather than by animals.

In 1779, it was followed by the *spinning mule.* This machine could produce as much yarn as 200 hand spinners. At the time it was invented, it was the largest machine in the world. Samuel Crompton, the Englishman who developed it, combined many of the ideas utilized in the spinning jenny and the water frame.

The textile industry began to grow in the United States, too. Cotton was already the major crop in the Southern states when Eli Whitney invented the cotton gin in 1793. This machine separated the cotton fibers from the seeds. As a result, much more cotton fabric could be produced.

THE DEVELOPMENT OF FACTORIES

Factories were developed because all of these wonderful new machines needed to be put somewhere. A **factory** is *a place that houses many machines and many workers.* The first factories were developed in Europe. They were dark, noisy, dirty, unpleasant, and overcrowded places to work. The factory worker was paid a **wage**, a certain *amount of money per hour or per day of work.* Factory owners became very rich, but factory workers stayed very poor.

American Factories

The plans for all these new machines and factories were carefully guarded secrets. A man named Samuel Slater was responsible for introducing factories to the United States. In 1789, he sailed from England to the United States. Soon after he arrived here, he built a cotton mill in Rhode Island from the plans that he had memorized in England.

Many different textile factories were established in New England. In 1825, the first men's clothing factory was established in the United States. Its specialty was making sailors' suits. In 1842, the first loom especially designed for weaving silk was set up in a factory in Paterson, New Jersey. Paterson was the silk center of the world until the early 1930s.

THE DEVELOPMENT OF THE GARMENT INDUSTRY

While some people were inventing faster ways to make more fabric, others were inventing faster ways to make more garments. Before the Industrial Revolution, men's clothes were made by tailors. Women's clothes were made by dressmakers or by the women themselves. Each person's measurements were taken by using strips of paper cut to size and then marked as "waist," "shoulder," "neck," and so on. There were no standard measurements or sizes.

The Tape Measure

Then someone got the bright idea of marking these strips into certain segments, or measurements, and the tape measure was invented. Now there was a universal way to record everyone's measurements. Soon people noticed that a person's chest, waist, and hips were in proportion to each other and that some combinations of measurements occurred more often than others. Using the most common combination of measurements, the concept of *sizes* was developed.

The Sewing Machine

The sewing machine came next. It was the combined result of the ideas and work of many inventors. In 1790, the first patent was given to Thomas Saint, an Englishman, for a machine that sewed on leather.

In 1832, Walter Hunt developed a machine in his shop in New York City that incorporated two new ideas. These were the eye-pointed needle and a locking stitch.

Many other people contributed to the development of the sewing machine. In 1845, Elias Howe, an apprentice watchmaker from Boston, made a sewing machine that had a curved eye-pointed needle and an underthread

The change from hand to machine sewing meant that more people were needed to fill the demand for mass-produced goods.

shuttle. This machine could sew 250 stitches per minute. That was five times as fast as the fastest hand sewer. In 1846, Isaac M. Singer, an American, produced a machine that had a straight needle and could sew continuously.

By the 1860s, large quantities of ready-made clothes were available. Although the quality was not good, the clothes were inexpensive.

The Paper Pattern

The paper pattern was an American invention. Very wealthy gentlemen had their shirts made by a *chemisier,* or shirtmaker. Everyone else's shirts were made at home.

A Massachusetts tailor named Ebenezer Butterick developed a paper pattern that his wife used to make his shirts. Friends and neighbors soon began to buy the patterns. By 1865, the Buttericks had moved to New York and were selling paper patterns by mail to customers from all over the world.

In 1870, James McCall, a tailor and an author of a system for drafting patterns, began to manufacture dress patterns in New York City. Although other people tried, and failed, to start pattern companies, for many years these two companies were the only ones that survived.

MARKETING AND SELLING CLOTHES

Once people developed ways to make clothes faster and cheaper, they looked for ways to sell them more efficiently. With more people working in factories, a new middle class arose that was made up mostly of laborers. Merchants realized that these people had some money to spend on clothes.

There were also pioneers, miners, and sailors who needed simple, durable clothing and could not wait for a tailor to make up a garment. Catalogue or mail-order selling became a popular way to reach all these people.

The Stores

Dry goods stores were common when everyone's clothes were made by tailors, dressmakers, or at home. At first, these stores sold fabric, thread, and ribbons, but then some stores began to sell the mass-produced clothing that was made in the factories.

These stores expanded and carried so much merchandise that shirts were sold in one area, trousers in another, and so on. By 1850, the *department store* was born. A large store in Boston was the first one to use special marketing techniques like "sales" and "specials." The method spread quickly.

Men's and Women's Fashions

Because men's clothing was easy to sew and did not change style very often, the market for **ready-to-wear**, or *mass-produced garments,* for men grew very quickly.

In the 1850s, women who could afford to do so were still wearing clothes made by dressmakers from expensive fabrics. Because women's fashions changed frequently and were difficult to sew, the first ready-to-wear items were simple capes and shawls. Later, garments that would not go out of fashion quickly, such as robes, underwear, and petticoats, began to be manufactured.

In the 1890s, girls who worked in factories and offices began to wear a style called the Gibson Girl look. It was named after illustrations drawn by Charles Dana Gibson, an American artist. These simple skirts and white linen blouses, called *shirtwaists,* were easy to manufacture in proportioned sizes. After that, many more styles of clothing were manufactured for women. By 1900, New York City had about 475 shirtwaist factories that employed over 18,000 workers. You will learn more about the clothing industry in Unit Six of this book.

Chapter 7 Review

Summary

People first used animal skins for clothing. Later they learned how to spin yarns and weave them into fabric. The natural fibers—flax, wool, cotton, and silk—were discovered thousands of years ago. Clothing styles changed over the centuries from draped or wrapped garments to fitted or seamed garments. In the 18th century, the Industrial Revolution changed the fabric and clothing industries. Many different inventions contributed to the growth of these industries. As a result, fabrics and garments could be made faster and cheaper.

Questions

1. How did primitive people use natural materials for clothing?

2. Briefly describe the evolution of the four natural fibers used for clothing: flax, wool, cotton, and silk. Where were they originally used?

3. Give examples of the three basic styles of clothing.

4. How did the Industrial Revolution affect clothing?

5. How did each of the following inventions increase the production of fabric: flying shuttle, spinning jenny, spinning mule, and cotton gin?

6. What contributions did the following people make toward the development of the garment industry: Samuel Slater, Elias Howe, Isaac Singer, Ebenezer Butterick, and James McCall?

7. How did the marketing and selling of clothes change over the years?

8. Define ready-to-wear.

Activities

1. Choose one of the natural fibers. Research the methods used today for producing the fiber for the textile industry.

2. With another classmate, design a draped or wrapped garment using a square or rectangular piece of fabric. Demonstrate and model your design.

3. On a world map, locate the various countries and areas discussed in this chapter as being places where fibers or clothing styles originated. Indicate the locations on the map with markers. Trace how various fibers and their use spread to other countries.

You Be the Expert

In your history class, a student asks what type of clothing was worn in ancient civilizations, such as Egypt and China. The teacher asks if anyone knows the answer to this question. You raise your hand. How will you describe the fabrics and clothing styles of the ancient civilizations?

8 *Clothes and Fashion*

TERMS TO LEARN

classic
fad
fashion
haute couture
old-fashioned
status symbol
style
trend

What is fashion all about? Why does the shirt that you couldn't wait to own last year suddenly look "old" to you this year? Why do the clothes in pictures of your mother as a teenager look very old-fashioned, while the clothes in pictures of your grandmother may seem more attractive to you? Why do some fashions seems to last longer than others?

After reading this chapter, you will be able to:

- determine the difference between fashion and style, between a fad and a classic,
- explain why fashions change,
- describe how new fashions start and what influences them,
- talk about why fashion is exciting and enjoyable.

What Is Fashion?

Fashion is *anything that is currently "in."* Fashion usually means clothes, but there are fashions in hair styles, in home decorating, and in the foods that we eat. Several years ago, very few people ate yogurt. Now yogurt is very popular and fashionable.

Many years ago, fashion changed very slowly. Changes in technology occurred gradually and communication between groups of people took a long time. People often wore the same style of clothing for their whole life.

Sometimes a particular style of clothing continued for more than a lifetime. An outfit that was worn for special occasions was often handed down from generation to generation. The nobility might be able to afford new styles of clothing, but the lower classes could not.

Today, fashion changes very quickly. New technology creates new fashion. New forms of communication, such as radio, television, and the computer, can tell us this afternoon what people in London were wearing this morning.

FASHION TERMS

Advertisements and articles about fashion contain terms such as "fad," "classic," and "status symbol." If you understand what these terms mean, it will help you to become a wiser and more informed consumer. You will be able to select clothes that meet your own needs and wants. You will be able to better evaluate clothing styles as to how long they might stay in fashion.

A Fad

A **fad** is *a fashion that is very popular for a short time.* Then suddenly it seems as if nobody

This young man's jacket is a classic: a simple dark blue coat with gold buttons.

is wearing it. A fad can be a color, such as mauve or chartreuse. It can be an accessory, such as Earth shoes or rhinestone jewelry. Fads can also be an item of clothing. Short mini-skirts and paratrooper pants with many pockets are examples of a fad. Fads can even be a certain look, such as "punk-rock" or "safari."

Fads usually involve less expensive items of clothing or accessories. For example, wearing colored shoelaces in your sneakers is a fad. "Pop-it" plastic necklaces were a fad in the 1950s. Fluorescent socks, camouflage pants, and leg warmers were fads in the early 1980s.

Many fads are popular only with teenagers. Fads help the teenager express two important needs. The first need is to belong to a group. Many teenagers want to be a part of a group that is special and different from the rest of the world. The other need is for individuality. Teenagers may adapt fads in unique ways to express their own individuality within a group. What fads are currently popular in your school?

Past Fashion Fads

1940s

1960s

1980s

Style

Style refers to *the shape of a particular item of clothing that makes it easy to recognize.* Straight, A-line, and circular are all styles of skirts. Set-in, kimono and raglan are all styles of sleeves. Certain styles of garments are more fashionable at one time than another.

Classic

A **classic** is *a traditional style that can stay in fashion for a very long time.* The blazer jacket is a classic. Blue jeans are a classic. A tailored shirt and a cardigan sweater are classics.

A Status Symbol

A **status symbol** is *an item of clothing that gives the wearer a special feeling of importance or wealth.* Fashion designers are celebrities today. They put their names, initials, or symbols on the clothes they design to show that the clothes are special. People who wear those clothes are trying to communicate that they are special, too. Some status symbols, such as a mink coat, are so expensive that very few people can afford them.

Old-Fashioned

Old-fashioned is a term that describes *any style that we have grown tired of looking at.* With today's instant communication, our brain receives a great deal of new information every day. Nothing seems new for very long. A garment can look old-fashioned to us in a very short time. However, the fashion pendulum swings back and forth so that some styles do return. Some examples of this are buttondown

Fashion shows can start fashion trends and make a current "look" seem old-fashioned.

What criteria do people use to decide when clothing is old-fashioned or no longer in style? There are no specific rules or guidelines to follow. Instead, people's attitudes are influenced by designers, manufacturers, magazines, television, friends, family, and even their local community. You will read more about the influence of fashion advertising in Chapter 19. How do you decide when something is old-fashioned?

FASHION CYCLES AND TRENDS

Every fashion has a life cycle. A fashion is born when someone begins to wear it. The person who wears it could be a model in a magazine, a celebrity, or a small group of people with similar tastes. **Haute couture**, or *high fashion*, refers to a style or trend when it is first introduced and becoming popular. A fashion matures when many people start to wear it. It is old-fashioned, or "out," when people do not want to wear it anymore.

When the fashion cycle happens quickly, it is a fad. When *the fashion cycle happens quite slowly*, it is a **trend**. In the 1950s, the most popular style of dress had a fitted bodice, a belted waistline, and a full skirt. By the middle 1960s, a loose-fitting, unbelted dress was the most popular style. In the early 1980s, fitted dresses and suits were popular again. By 1985, large, loose-fitting jackets, shirts, and dresses were in fashion.

Men's neckties undergo a similar fashion cycle. In the 1940s, ties were very wide in order to balance the double-breasted suits with wide lapels that were fashionable. In the 1960s, when Ivy League suits were stylish, ties became very skinny. As suits with wider lapels again became popular in the mid-1970s, ties got wider, too. In the 1980s they narrowed to a medium width. These changes happened very gradually.

shirts, skinny ties, and V-neck sweaters.

Sometimes an old-fashioned look, such as the clothes of the 1940s and the 1950s, becomes an important look in fashion. Because some people want to wear the original clothes, not updated versions, attics and thrift shops turn into a popular source for such garments.

Sometimes bits and pieces of old clothes will be recycled into new styles. In the 1960s, there was a fad for long skirts made from discarded ties. Today antique laces are often used for parts of new blouses and dresses.

Fashion Focus

The Evolution of Modern Fashion

18th Century

The 1700s was a time of colonization in America, followed by the Revolutionary War. The textile industry was developing after the Industrial Revolution.

Fashions for both men and women were elaborate and elegant, with laces, ribbons, and colorful silks.

19th Century

The 1800s saw the Civil War, as well as expansion of the United States to the West Coast. Clothing styles changed rapidly, too. During the early 1800s, women wore lighter-weight, plainer gowns with high Empire waistlines. Men wore cutaway coats over long, tight-fitting pantaloons.

By the middle of the century, dresses were full-skirted and supported by crinolines and hoops. The knee-length frock coat replaced the tailcoat for men.

In the 1880s, full skirts gave way to back bustles. Shirtwaist blouses and suits for women were introduced. Men's fashions featured a shorter coat, the forerunner to today's business suit.

20th Century

In the 1920s, short, unfitted dresses were worn with long necklaces. The 1940s saw tailored styles with padded shoulders for both men and women.

Short miniskirts were in fashion during the 1960s. Styles in the 1980s were loose and full with broad, padded shoulders. Skirt lengths ranged from long to short.

1770s   1880s   1980s

Why Fashions Change

In the past, some fashion changes occurred because people wanted to imitate royalty. Other changes occurred because of the influence of historical events, such as a revolution or colonization. Today, people and events continue to change and influence fashion.

FASHION ORIGINATORS

For many hundreds of years, kings and queens and their courts set the style. They were the only groups who could afford to change their fashions. When people saw members of the royal court, they copied their style of clothing. However, fashion changes spread slowly.

Fashion Babies

In the late 1700s, *fashion babies* were used to spread fashion news. Fashion babies were small dolls about a foot high that were carefully dressed in the latest styles. Rose Bertin, Queen Marie Antoinette's dressmaker, made the first fashion babies in the 1770s. She dressed them in copies of the French queen's newest clothes and sent them from Paris to London.

Dressmakers in London could then see and copy the newest look. The babies then traveled to America. The dolls continued to be the most important form of fashion communication up until the Civil War. After the Civil War, fashion magazines replaced the fashion babies as a means of communicating the latest styles.

Designer Gowns

In the mid-19th century, an English gentleman named Charles Worth began to design

Fashion babies, or dolls, were masterpieces of design. They can be seen in museums today.

clothes for the French royal family. He was the first designer to make *designer gowns.* These gowns were worn in his salon by elegant, attractive women who were the first fashion models. Other designers imitated him. Thus the high fashion, or *haute couture,* industry was established in France.

Seasonal Showings

Meanwhile, new and efficient methods of producing ready-to-wear were being developed. Because high fashion could now be copied quickly and cheaply, the fashion cycle became much shorter. Designers began introducing new styles every season.

Although many of the well-known fashion designers are still based in Paris, other cities have become important design centers. London, Milan, Tokyo, New York, and Los Angeles are all important centers for garment industries. Today's American fashion designers create relaxed sportswear looks that are famous all over the world.

HISTORICAL EVENTS

Major historical events can influence fashion. After the French Revolution, France changed from a monarchy to a democracy. Clothes became more democratic, too. Everyone dressed in simpler styles.

Before World War I, women's clothes were designed more for appearance than for practicality. Dresses had long skirts with bustles or crinolines, high necklines, and very full sleeves. During the war, more women worked in shops, offices, and factories, so more practical fashions developed.

After World War I, women did not want to return to their former way of life or dress. Clothes became shorter and less fitted for both comfort and practicality.

During World War II, there was a shortage of fabric because so many textiles were being used for military uniforms and equipment. As a result, styles became slimmer, and shorter skirts became fashionable. Nylon stockings were almost impossible to get, so women had to wear cotton ones.

After World War II, styles changed radically. People were tired of the clothes that they had worn during the war and fabric was easily available again. Christian Dior, a French designer, introduced his "New Look" for women. These clothes featured very full skirts and longer lengths. Soon this style became very popular.

ECONOMICS

A society's economic system can affect how quickly fashion changes. In a highly industrialized, free enterprise system, such as in the United States or Western Europe, there is a great amount of competition among businesses. When you go shopping you can choose from many different styles of clothes in many different types of stores. Because so much variety is available, fashion changes very quickly.

In a society such as Russia or China, there is almost no competition. All manufacturers produce similar goods. There is little or no advertising. As a result, fashion changes very slowly because people do not have many choices.

SOCIAL TRENDS

Fashion can also reflect the trends and values of a society. In the Victorian society of the late 1800s, women were looked upon as fragile and delicate creatures. The style of clothing reflected and contributed to this belief.

Women's and Men's Styles

A lady's frame, or skeletal structure, was believed to be weak and delicate. The corset, an intricate cage of heavy canvas reinforced with whalebone or steel, was thought to be an absolutely essential undergarment. Victorians believed that it was needed to support the body, as well as provide a fashionable look. This corset was so restrictive that women did, indeed, develop health problems and become fragile.

In addition to the corset, the Victorian lady wore several layers of *undergarments,* which consisted of at least three petticoats, a hoop skirt, and a long dress that contained up to 20 yards of fabric. When she went out, she added a heavy woolen shawl and a large bonnet. All of this could weigh from 10 to 30 pounds. It is no wonder that the proper Victorian lady never went anywhere without her smelling salts.

The role of women in our society has changed dramatically since the 1800s. How is this reflected in clothing today? Do any extreme fashions still exist?

Styles for men have also changed over the years. In the 17th and 18th centuries, men wore silks, satins, ribbons, and lace. They wore fancy plumed hats over their long hair or large powdered wigs. Some of their garments were more elegant and decorative than women's styles. By the 19th century, men's clothes were plainer. They began wearing trousers instead of knee breeches, and coats were similar to styles today.

Then in the 1960s, many younger men started wearing colorful fabrics and jewelry. Soon men of all ages were wearing shirts in stripes, checks, and many colors with their business suits. Some men grew beards and moustaches and wore longer hair.

Styles for All

By the 1970s, fashions for both men and women were often similar. Blazers, trousers, jeans, trench coats, and tailored shirts were styled the same for everyone. Today, health and physical fitness are very important for both men and women. Exercise clothes, such as leotards and jogging suits, are fashionable to wear even if you are not exercising. Casual clothes and active sportswear are very popular for all ages.

THE DESIRE FOR CHANGE

Sometimes fashion changes because the events that created hardships pass, and people no longer wish to wear clothes that remind them of these events. Sometimes fashion changes because people simply get bored with one type of look.

Since the 1960s, fashion has changed rapidly. There are many theories as to why this is occurring. Probably there is no one single cause. Perhaps fashion is reflecting the many changes that are happening within our society. What do you think?

Simple, elegant styles were introduced for men in the early 19th century. Tight-laced corsets were a must for fashionable late 19th- and early 20th-century ladies.

The clothing designed for the Olympic team reflects current fashion and may make certain styles more popular in future years.

What Inspires Fashion?

There is a theory in fashion called the "trickle down" theory. It means that a new fashion starts at the top, with a fashion designer or an important personality, and then trickles down until it is accepted by everyone.

In recent years, however, fashion has begun to "trickle up." This means that a fashion is started by a group, sometimes teenagers. Blue jeans are a good example of a trickle-up fashion. When teenagers began to wear them, everyone thought blue jeans were just a fad. Now people of all ages wear them and fashion designers are manufacturing designer jeans.

What inspires fashion? There are many sources of inspiration and influence. They include designers, media events and personalities, cultural events, foreign influences, technology, and groups of people.

FASHION DESIGNERS

Fashion designers create the styles of clothes that we see in magazines, newspapers, catalogues, and stores. They decide the type of lines, colors, and fabric for each garment. Have you ever wondered what inspires a fashion designer? Have you ever wondered how many different fashion designers can come up with similar ideas at the same time? It is because they are influenced by the world that we live in.

Most designers attend art exhibits, study the history of costume, go to the movies, read the newspapers, and travel. They look at the way people around them dress. All of this provides new ideas for new designs.

MEDIA EVENTS AND PERSONALITIES

A popular movie, a television series, a musical group, a sports event, a newspaper headline, or a political event can all inspire fashions. When the Beatles became popular in the 1960s, young men changed their haircuts and began to wear collarless jackets. In the 1980s, Michael Jackson and Madonna created popular fads in clothing and accessories. The TV series, "Miami Vice," popularized loose, unlined jackets for men. The hairstyles of Princess Diana of England are copied around the world.

CULTURAL EVENTS

Cultural events, such as a stage play, an art exhibit or a costume exhibit, can inspire fashion trends. New York's Metropolitan Museum of Art regularly produces an historical costume exhibit. Often you can see the influence of the latest exhibit in the New York designers' collections. You can see it in the style of the clothes, the trim that is used, or in the fabrics and prints that are selected.

Cultural events in other major fashion cities, such as Paris, London, and Milan, have similar influences.

FOREIGN INFLUENCES

Other countries can have an influence on the fashions that we wear. This has been true throughout history.

In the late 1700s, some fashionable and well-traveled young men began to wear exaggerated versions of the pompadour-style hairdo that they saw in Italy. These elaborate, up-swept hair styles were called *macaronies*. Although you may not realize it, you are already familiar with this fashion. When Yankee Doodle "stuck a feather in his cap and called it macaroni," he was imitating these young men.

Foreign influences continue even today. After President Nixon's historic trip to China in 1972 to reestablish trade relations, oriental prints and silk fabrics became very fashionable.

TECHNOLOGY

Technology has a great influence on fashion. In the 1960s something happened that was called the "double-knit revolution." Fabric companies were able to manufacture a great variety of polyester double-knit fabrics. These fabrics were inexpensive to produce. Because they were also washable, they were very popular. However, these fabrics were more suitable to simple straight styles than soft, draped garments. As a result, clothing styles were very similar.

Because of new developments in fiber and fabric technology, a variety of styles are fashionable today. These recent developments have produced fabrics made from manufactured fibers that look and feel like fabrics from natural fibers. For example, polyester can now be knitted or woven so that it drapes like silk at less cost and easier care.

Other developments have produced fabrics with characteristics that are not possible with 100% natural fibers. One example is the stretch fabrics used for swimwear and exercise wear. Another example is Gore-Tex,® a fabric that is popular with runners, hikers, and skiers because rain and snow cannot penetrate it.

You will learn more about fiber and fabric technology in Unit 4.

GROUPS OF PEOPLE

People, in small and large groups, can influence fashions. With mass communication today, representatives of the fashion industry are able to monitor fashion trends in all parts of our society. They may report a unique style being worn by people in a certain region, or occupation, or age group. Popular rock groups and teenagers are major influences and have, in the 1980s, popularized painter's pants, lumber jackets, sweatshirts, and cowboy boots.

Summary

Many years ago, fashions changed slowly. Today, fashions change rapidly. Some common fashion terms include fad, style, classic, status symbol, and old-fashioned. Each fashion has its own life cycle which can be long or short. Throughout history, people, events, economics, and social trends have influenced and changed fashion. Today, fashions are inspired by fashion designers, media events, personalities, cultural events, foreign countries, technology, and groups of people.

Questions

1. Why are fads so popular with teenagers?
2. Describe the difference between a fashion, a fad, a style, and a classic.
3. Explain the life cycle of a particular fashion. Why do you think some styles keep coming back as a fashion? Give examples of such fashion cycles.
4. How were fashion babies used to communicate styles?
5. Describe how World War I and World War II influenced fashion.
6. How does competition in the economic system affect the amount of choices that consumers have?
7. How can fashion reflect the values and trends of a society? How have the changing roles of males and females influenced fashion changes?
8. What is the "trickle up" effect on fashion?
9. List at least five sources of fashion inspiration.

Activities

1. Choose a classic clothing style. Discover its origin and its reoccurrence in fashion throughout its history.

2. Identify an event in history, the entertainment industry, your home town, or your school that influenced a fashion change. Describe the fashion style that emerged.

3. Research three famous fashion designers. Identify their nationality and the major fashion influences of their designs. Choose from Christian Dior, Coco Chanel, Yves Saint Laurent, Valentino, Givenchy, Bill Blass, Mary Quant, Oscar de la Renta, Jean Muir, Calvin Klein, Ralph Lauren, Donna Karan, Patrick Kelly, and Christian Lacroix.

You Be the Expert

You are looking through an old photo album with your family. Your younger sister asks why some clothes look old-fashioned and others look almost like clothes that we wear today. What explanation can you give her?

9 Clothes and Creativity

You and your friends probably wear similar styles of clothes, but each of you wear them with your own individual flair. The T-shirt that everyone owns is a very simple styled garment. In its most basic shape, it is only a front, a back, and two sleeves. Think about how many T-shirts that you and your friends own and how different they all are. Some are printed, some are plain. Some may be trimmed with embroidery or appliqués. You can have a closet full of T-shirts with no two alike.

This chapter will explore some of the ways that people use to express their individuality in clothing. After reading this chapter you will be able to:

- explain man's basic need for creativity and self-expression,
- give examples of how different cultures have expressed this need,
- suggest ways that special handicrafts can add variety and originality to your clothes,
- discuss how clothes can express your personal creativity.

Creativity and Self-Expression

We use clothing to express our individuality. It is a basic human need to want to be part of the crowd, and, at the same time, to stand out as a separate person. Whether we are aware of it or not, all clothing sends out messages to the rest of the world. Even a person who wears the plainest, most unimaginative clothes is sending out a message. The message may be "I don't want to be noticed."

Throughout history, all people have expressed their creativity through clothing and accessories.

DEVELOPING A FEEL FOR ART AND BEAUTY

People can use clothing as a means to express their personal standards of art and beauty. We speak of a person who has *high standards* as a person of **good taste**.

How is good taste developed? How do we know the difference between bad taste and good taste? Some people are born with good taste. Other people acquire it because they are taught it as they grow up. Some people have to develop it on their own. You can do this by going to museums, visiting art galleries, and studying the world around you.

Carefully observe those objects and paintings that are generally accepted as beautiful and pleasing to the eye. If some of them are not pleasing to you, try to analyze the reasons why. Remember, the famous critics do not always agree!

WHAT INFLUENCES OUR STANDARDS?

Imagine an ancient Greek trying to agree with a 17th-century Frenchman on what is tasteful and beautiful. The Greek valued simplicity and balance, while the Frenchman admired elaborate decoration and intricate details. The **aesthetic**, or *artistic*, tastes of every society are influenced by its *traditions*, its *environment*, and its current *lifestyle*.

Traditions

Since the United States was first founded by people who mainly came from England, or were of English ancestry, English *traditions* concerning law and government were used to establish our own legal and governmental traditions.

Environment

The *environment* that we live in can also affect our standards. Many historians have said that the United States was largely built by using its tremendous natural resources in a very wasteful way. Nature was our plaything. Today, with dwindling resources, we must be careful of their use. We are now very conscious of using our natural resources well and sparingly.

Lifestyle

Our standards of beauty are also influenced by our *lifestyle.* We live in a very complicated world, where technology has discovered more ways to do more things by machine. Fewer and fewer jobs are being done by hand. At the same time, we are rediscovering the beauty of hand-made items. Hand-knit and hand-crocheted sweaters are highly admired. Some fashion designers now include them in their most expensive collections.

We are seeking antique items that our great-grandparents and their parents made and used. Old quilts and embroidered samplers have become very valuable.

Some people have a theory about this trend. They call it "high tech, high touch." It means that when much of our world is highly technological, people need to surround themselves with things that feel good to touch and that remind them of the past. Do you agree with this theory? Why? Why not?

CREATIVE OUTLETS

There are many ways that you can express creativity and good taste through the clothes that you wear. How you coordinate your clothes is one way. When you decide what belt, shoes, sweater, shirt, and slacks to wear, you are putting together a look that is uniquely you.

The style of clothing that you choose is another way. Some people like to dress in a very conservative manner. Other people like to wear whatever is the latest fashion. Some people prefer dark colors, while others like to dress in bright colors. Sewing is a creative outlet for many people. When you sew, you can choose the style, the fabric, and the color that you want. The result is a garment that is special and original.

Special Handicrafts

You can decorate your clothes with special sewing work, such as embroidery, quilting, appliqué, and patchwork. Machines today can also weave, embroider, print, and dye fabric. However, there is a special satisfaction in doing these things yourself. The result is a special beauty that cannot be duplicated by a machine. **Handicrafts** are *forms of art that are created by using your hands.*

THE YARN CRAFTS

Fabric is the basic material for most garments. Yarns can be put together in many different ways to form fabric. They can also be twisted or knotted together in special ways. The result can be lace, macramé, or braid, depending on the kind of knots and the thickness of the yarn.

Weaving

Weaving is the process of interlacing two sets of yarns to form fabric. One set of yarns, called

Weaving is done on a loom. The warp yarns are held between two beams. The filling yarns are inserted and then pushed back to make the fabric.

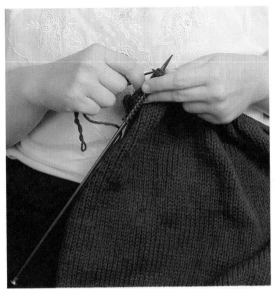

This woman is hand knitting a sweater. When you do this, you are able to choose the color and insure perfect fit.

the warp, is at right angles to another set, called the *filling*. You will learn more about weaving techniques in Chapter 16.

Today, almost all woven fabrics are made by machines. Hand weaving has become a valued craft. Because a weaver can reach only so far when sitting at a loom, handwoven fabric is narrower than machine-woven fabric.

Knitting

Knitting can also be done by hand or by machine. You will learn about machine-knitted fabrics in Chapter 16.

Knitting by hand requires knitting needles that are anywhere from 7″ to 14″ (18–35 cm) long. A single yarn is twisted and looped off of one needle and onto the other.

Using only two basic stitches, a knit stitch and a purl stitch, a skillful knitter can loop and twist the yarn to form many different patterns and textures. The knitter shapes the sections of a sweater or hat by increasing and decreasing the number of stitches on the needle.

Crochet

Crochet work looks similar to knitting, but it has a slightly lacier appearance. Crocheting is done with only one needle, called a *crochet hook*. The hook is used to pull the yarn through a loop, or a series of loops. Crochet work, just like knitting, uses only one yarn at a time. Some of the items that can be crocheted are blankets, hats, scarves, mittens, and sweaters.

Lacemaking

Lacemaking is the most complicated of the knotting and looping arts. Whether the lace is made by machine or by hand, the process is quite similar. Many yarns are wound onto bobbins and then the bobbins are twisted and crossed around needles to create the lace patterns.

Lace can be made as fabric to be used for large items, such as tablecloths. Also it can be made into very small shapes or narrow widths and used as trim.

Macramé

Macramé is the decorative art of tying knots. Sailors often spent idle hours on a sea voyage doing macramé using heavy rope that was available on the ship. Today, macramé knots are often combined with beads threaded onto the cord. Macramé is used for wall hangings, plant hangers, jewelry, handbags, and other craft items.

Braiding

Braiding is the process of overlapping and wrapping several strips of yarn, fabric, or leather around each other. Braiding can be used to make belts, headbands, straps, or watchbands. Wide strips of fabric can be braided and then sewn together to form braided rugs.

THE STITCHING CRAFTS

Sewing, embroidery, needlepoint, patchwork, quilting, appliqué, and beadwork all involve the use of a needle and thread. Using these techniques, fabric is joined or decorated either by machine or by hand.

Sewing

Sewing, the most basic of the stitching crafts, is the art of using stitches to join pieces of fabric together. Sewing is a skill that can provide you with many hours of pleasure. It can also help you save money.

Embroidery

Embroidery is an art that includes *many different types of decorative stitches used on fabric.* Embroidery can be done with silk or cotton thread for a delicate effect. It can also be done with heavy yarns for a bolder effect. There are many different kinds of embroidery.

Many people enjoy doing crafts such as macramé, needlepoint, counted cross-stitch, and braiding to produce things that are both decorative and useful.

Crewel embroidery is done with wool yarns. It is used on wall hangings, pillows, and chair seats. *Counted cross-stitch embroidery* is a series of small "x's" carefully combined to form a picture or a design. *Chicken scratch* is special form of cross-stitch embroidery done on gingham fabric. *Candlewicking* is a series of knot stitches done with coarse cotton thread. The name comes from colonial times when coarse thread was used to make candlewicks.

Needlepoint

Needlepoint is the technique of forming stitches on a special open-weave fabric called canvas. Embroidery thread or wool yarn is pulled in and out of the holes in the canvas to form a variety of stitches. Needlepoint is used to make pillows, cushions, chair coverings, rugs, and wall hangings.

Quilting

In America, pioneer women and girls created colorful patchwork quilts for their homes. The early designs were called "crazy quilts" because the top of the bed covering was made up of many different sizes, shapes, and colors of fabrics.

Later on, as fabric became more available, the fabric scraps were cut into simple shapes and joined together to create interesting squares, or blocks. These blocks were given names, such as Log Cabin, Turkey Trot, Lone Star, and Dresden Plate, that had special meaning to the settlers who created them. At quilting bees in small towns, women sewed the quilt layers together with tiny stitches. Then the quilt edges were bound with bias strips of fabric.

Today, many of the famous block patterns are used in modern quilt designs. Antique quilts have become collector's items and are very valuable.

Patchwork

Patchwork is the technique of cutting out small shapes of fabric and sewing them together to form larger shapes. Because fabric was scarce, early American settlers used patchwork as a way to utilize all the valuable scraps. These patchwork designs were fashioned into quilts that are famous throughout the world as a uniquely American craft.

Quilting

Quilting is the process of stitching together two layers of fabric with a soft material in between. The stitches can be sewn by hand or by machine in straight lines or in patterns. Hand-quilted items are the most valuable because the many tiny stitches require patience and skill. The air pockets that form between the stitches make quilted items especially warm.

Appliqué

Appliqué is the art of *sewing one or more pieces of fabric to the top of a larger piece of fabric.* The fabric pieces can be cut in different shapes to create a design. Either small hemming stitches or machine zigzag stitches can be used to stitch the appliqué in place.

A special type of appliqué is called *reverse appliqué.* The design is drawn on the base fabric and then cut out so that you have a window in the fabric. The base fabric is placed on top of another fabric, and the two layers are stitched together.

Beadwork

Beadwork is a craft that was perfected by the North American Plains Indians. Early beads were made from shells, seeds, animal bones, and teeth. Later on, traders introduced the Indians to beads manufactured in Europe. The beads are stitched to fabric to form intricate and colorful designs.

DYEING AND PRINTING

Dyes can be applied to an entire piece of fabric so that it is all one color. Or they can be applied with dyeing and printing techniques that give special effects.

Tie Dyeing

Tie dyeing is a very old method. The fabric is tightly tied in certain places, then dipped into the dye. The dye will not penetrate in the spots where the fabric is tied. The fabric can be re-tied and dipped in a different color of dye. In the 1970s and again in the late 1980s, tie-dyed T-shirts were popular among young people.

Batik Printing

Batik printing is created by first applying hot wax to the areas of the fabric that will not be dyed. The fabric is then dipped into a dye and left to dry. New wax can be applied to other areas before the fabric is dipped into another

Appliqués, beaded belts, and tie dying can give just the colorful accent that an outfit needs.

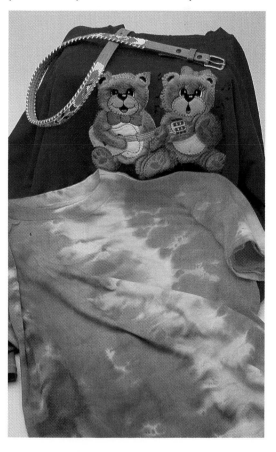

Silk screen printing can be used to print posters, t-shirts, bags, and many other items.

color. Batik fabric can have elaborate designs by applying different layers of wax and dye.

Block Printing

Block printing is a method that is similar to using a rubber stamp. A design is carved on a block. The first blocks were made from clay, but today they can also be made from wood, linoleum, or metal. The block is covered with dye and pressed on the fabric so that the design is transferred from the block to the fabric.

Silk Screen Printing

Silk screen printing gets its name from the fact that finely woven silk was originally used as the printing screen. Today other types of fabric can be used. The screen is attached to a frame and a sealer is applied. This sealer covers all the areas of the screen that should not be printed. The screen is placed over the fabric, and the dye is applied to the screen. The

dye seeps through the unsealed areas to create the design on the fabric. A separate screen is needed for each color of the design.

Painting

Painting on fabric is similar to painting on any other surface. The color can be applied with a brush, a pen, or a marker. Hand-painted silk is used for very expensive garments. Designs are also painted on T-shirts, sweatshirts, canvas bags, and umbrellas.

YOUR OWN CREATIVITY— YOUR OWN MESSAGE

When you add your own creative touch to your clothes, you will have a wardrobe that is uniquely yours. Sewing, decorating, and coordinating your garments will give you a feeling of pride and accomplishment. Clothing can be much more than protection. It can be exciting.

Summary

Everyone has a need for creativity and self-expression. Throughout history, people have expressed their ideas about beauty and taste in different ways. Special handicrafts can be used to create or decorate fabric and clothing. Yarns can be put together in different ways to form fabric or decorative items. Weaving, knitting, crochet, lacemaking, macramé, and braiding are yarn crafts. The stitching crafts, which use a needle and thread, including sewing, embroider, needlepoint, patchwork, quilting, appliqué, and beadwork. Fabric can also be decorated by different methods of dyeing and printing.

Questions

1. Why do different cultures have different standards of taste and beauty?

2. How can you express creativity through the clothes that you wear?

3. Explain the differences in making a garment by weaving, knitting, and crocheting. What types of garments can be made by each of these methods?

4. What is macramé? What items can be made by this technique?

5. In what ways is needlepoint similar to embroidery? How does it differ?

6. Both patchwork and appliqué techniques use small pieces of fabric. How are they different?

7. What handicrafts were popular with the early pioneers? Why did some of these crafts develop?

8. Describe the techniques of tie dyeing, batik printing, block printing, and silk screen printing.

9. Why are handicraft techniques so popular with many people today?

Activities

1. Interview someone who enjoys weaving, knitting, crocheting, or doing embroidery or needlepoint. Ask them to demonstrate the stitches used for making various projects. What satisfaction do they receive from creating these handmade items?

2. Visit a local yarn store. What is the price of a beginner's knitting or crocheting kit? How does the cost of making the item compare to buying a ready-to-wear item?

3. Visit a craft shop that features finished textile and yarn crafts that are sold. Make a list of the various craft techniques used to create the projects for sale.

You Be the Expert

You have a summer job at a yarn and crafts store. A customer asks you to recommend some simple fabric or yarn projects that she and her children could make on vacation. What crafts could you recommend?

3 *You and Your Wardrobe*

CHAPTER
10
**Developing a
Wardrobe Plan**

CHAPTER
12
Understanding Design

CHAPTER
13
**Redesigning and
Recycling**

CHAPTER
11
Understanding Color

10 | *Developing a Wardrobe Plan*

TERMS TO LEARN

economical
inventory
prioritize
versatile
wardrobe plan

Suppose you are going to drive across the country. You are starting your trip in Boston and want to end up in San Francisco. How are you going to know which roads to take? You could just point your car westward and hope that you eventually reach San Francisco.

However, it would be a lot easier if you got a map and planned your route before you left Boston. That way you could avoid wrong turns, drive on the better roads, and arrive at your destination in a shorter time.

Putting your wardrobe together with the aid of a wardrobe plan is just like driving with a road map. It is the fastest and most efficient way to get the best results. After reading this chapter, you will be able to:

- explain the benefits of a wardrobe plan,
- evaluate your present wardrobe to determine your clothing needs,
- expand your wardrobe by creating new clothing combinations,
- develop a personal wardrobe plan.

What Is a Wardrobe Plan?

A **wardrobe plan**, or *clothing review,* has several purposes. First, it will help you make better use of items that you already own. As you develop your plan, you may find new ways to combine the clothes that are already in your wardrobe.

Second, a wardrobe plan will help you decide what you need to add to your wardrobe. You will be able to determine whether a pair of black wool slacks or a pair of denim jeans is a more useful addition to your wardrobe at this time.

Third, it will serve as a guide for future additions. You will be able to determine which items are wearing out or beginning to look dated. This will give you a head start on knowing what you will need to add next season or next year.

A wardrobe plan is a guideline for the clothes and accessories that are appropriate for you and your lifestyle. You should review your plan each season. It should be flexible enough to change as your needs, wants, and lifestyle change in life.

Steps to Take

To investigate your wardrobe and its possibilities, follow these steps:

1. Take inventory of what clothes you have.
2. Make a wardrobe plan chart.
3. Sort your clothing into categories.

Planning your wardrobe wisely will save you time, money, and disappointment.

TAKE INVENTORY

If you were a store owner who needed to know exactly what merchandise was available in the store, you would take physical **inventory**. This means that *all the merchandise would be counted,* whether it was on racks, in bins, under the counter, on shelves, or part of a display. Then you could decide what should be added to the store's inventory.

You need to do the same thing with your wardrobe. It is best to take your clothing inventory at the beginning of each season or school year, instead of at the end, when you are tired of your clothes. You will be able to take a fresh look at what you own.

Set aside a day when you will have enough time to take everything out of your closet and drawers, and then put all the items back again.

MAKE A CHART

Before you begin to sort and count your clothes, create a wardrobe chart. Working with a chart will help you to make better use of what you already own. It will also help you to deter-

A Wardrobe Plan Chart

	School	Casual	Work	Dressy	Remain	Repair	Revise
Slacks							
Shirts							
Jackets							
Skirts							
Jackets							
Accessories							

mine if you have too many of one type of clothes and not enough of another. In addition, a chart will show you what you need, so that you can plan your clothing purchases.

Across the top of your chart, write down all of your different activities. Include school, sports, clubs, jobs, and social activities. Also write categories on the condition of the garments, for example, "Remain" (clothes OK)," Repair," or "Revise." On the left-hand side of the chart, list all the different types of items that are in your wardrobe. These may be pants, shirts or blouses, skirts, sweaters, jackets, dresses, coats, and accessories.

SORT CLOTHING INTO CATEGORIES

You need to sort all of your clothing into four different piles, or categories, before you record any of your clothes on your wardrobe chart. If you are like most people, your wardrobe will contain clothes that you wear frequently, plus clothes that you seldom or never wear. It is important to include these clothes in your inventory, too.

The four categories are:

1. clothes that will *remain* in your wardrobe,
2. clothes that need *repair* before you can wear them,
3. clothes that you need to *revise* because you seldom wear them,
4. clothes that you need to *retire* because you can no longer wear them.

Clothes That Remain

These are the clothes that you like and wear often. Organize them by type. For example, put all the pants together, and all the shirts or blouses together. Then you can see how many you have of each type and what colors they are.

Record each item on your wardrobe chart. Next, check off all the activities that each item is suitable for. Because many clothes can be worn for more than one type of activity, you may check off several activities for each item. For example, your jeans may be worn for school, parties, sports events, or just getting together with friends. Your dressy blouse or good shirt is suitable for dances and special occasions.

Ask yourself why you like and enjoy wearing the clothes in this category. Does it have something to do with the style, the fabric, the color, or the type of care that they require? Your answers will give you guidelines for making future purchases.

Clothes That Need Repair

These are the clothes that you could wear if only a button was sewn back on, the rip in the seam was mended, the hem was repaired, or the hole was patched.

As soon as possible, set aside time to repair these clothes. You might do it while watching television, listening to music, or talking on the phone. Chapter 18 shows you how to make simple repairs. Then you can add these clothes to your *repair* list on your chart.

Some repairs require extra time and creativity. Perhaps a garment has a stubborn stain that cannot be removed. Or the fabric ripped when it caught on a nail. These clothes may need some redesigning to make them wearable again. Move these items to your *revise* pile.

Sometimes a garment cannot be repaired without a major investment in time and money. If so, you will have to decide whether to repair it or move it to your *retire* pile.

Clothes to be Revised

These are the clothes that you seldom wear. Look carefully at the clothes in this group. Think about why you do not wear each particular garment.

Does the garment not go with other clothes in your wardrobe? Perhaps you could try a new color or fabric combination. Or you could try wearing it in a new way.

Later in this chapter, you will learn how to mix and match your wardrobe to create different outfits. In the future, you may need to limit

What should I do? Retain? Repair? Revise? Retire?

your purchases to a few basic colors so that you can be sure that everything will coordinate.

Does the garment not fit well? Is it uncomfortable to wear? If so, you might be able to make a simple alteration to improve its fit. Do you simply not like it anymore? Perhaps a change of style, quality, color, or trim could update it or give it a new look. In Chapter 12, many redesigning ideas will be discussed.

Sometimes a garment is simply a mistake. It may not fit in with your tastes, your wardrobe, or your lifestyle. In that case, the best thing to do is to make a mental note as to why it does not suit you. Then you can avoid making the same mistake again. Put it in your *retire* pile.

Clothes to be Retired

This category includes the clothes that you have outgrown or that have worn out. You may have added some that cannot be revised or redesigned, or some that are simply mistakes.

If the clothing is still wearable, pass it along to relatives, neighbors, or a charity. In Chapter 13, you will learn various ways that garments

This plaid shirt can be worn in many different ways to give an informal, casual appearance.

can be recycled to other people and for other uses. If the garment is no longer wearable, the fabric may still be in good condition. You can recycle it into projects or household uses.

You may have a garment that you cannot wear, but you cannot bear to give it away. It may have been a gift from someone special. In that case, wash or dry clean and store it out of the way. Keep the space in your closet or drawers for clothes that are an active part of your wardrobe.

Develop a Personal Wardrobe Plan

Now take a look at your wardrobe chart. You should have the most check marks under the columns for the activities that you participate in most often. If there are any "holes" in your chart, you need to rethink how you wear garments that you already own, or you could plan to buy or sew new garments.

USE EVERYTHING THAT YOU OWN

The easiest way to expand your wardrobe is to think of ways to use all of your clothes. It is also the most **economical**, or *inexpensive*, method because it does not cost you any money.

Try New Combinations

Perhaps you are in the habit of always wearing the same sweater with the same pair of pants. Now you have a chance to try out new combinations. Take a look at the coordinated outfits that you already own. Separate them into individual pieces, such as pants, skirts, shirts, sweaters, and jackets. Now see if the pieces from one outfit will mix and match with the pieces from another outfit.

Fashion Focus

Planning Your Wardrobe: Mix and Match

The mix-and-match wardrobe is the most economical way to get the greatest mileage out of your wardrobe dollars. It's also the best way to guarantee that most of your clothing will work together.

Start with a basic plan:

Male	*Female*
2 pr. slacks	1 pr. pants
1 pr. jeans	1 blazer
1 blazer	1 skirt
1 shirt	2 blouses
1 polo shirt	1 sweater
1 turtle neck	1 pr. shorts
	1 vest

How many different outfits can you put together from each of these wardrobes?

Experiment with new color mixes. Some seasons, unusual color combinations, such as turquoise and orange, or purple and red, are very fashionable. Perhaps you always wear your beige sweater with your tweed slacks. Try combining the slacks with another color, such as bright blue or red.

Experiment with new fabric combinations. The jacket from your corduroy suit can be worn with a variety of other fabrics. Some seasons, combining more than one print in an outfit is fashionable. Checks might be worn with stripes, and prints with plaids. However, the patterns and colors must be carefully combined to create an outfit that is pleasing to the eye. In other seasons, they may be out-of-fashion.

Try New Uses

Perhaps you can think of new ways to wear the clothes that you already own. You might be able to wear your favorite flannel shirt as both a shirt and a shirt-jacket. The turtleneck that you always wear with your blue jeans could be worn with your slacks and a sweater for a dressier look. The vest that you usually wear under a jacket might be worn over a dress or top. A sun dress might double as a jumper. A change of accessories might transform an outfit from casual to dressy.

Try belting a large, loose-fitting jacket to create a slimmer look. Substitute a tie or a scarf for a belt. Tuck pants into boots. Layer tops in a different order.

DECIDE WHAT YOU NEED

Once you have explored all the different ways to wear the clothes that you already own, it is time to take a look at what you need to add to your wardrobe.

Needs versus Wants

Wardrobe planning involves both needs and wants. In Chapter 1, you learned about needs. A "want" is a desire for something that gives you satisfaction.

Emotional needs often create wants. You may want a special item because wearing it will make you feel attractive, confident, slimmer, taller, or shorter. You may want it because it will help you to fit in with the crowd or stand out from everyone else.

The item may be a status symbol for you, making you feel important. Or it may create an image that you would like others to see.

Prioritize

You should **prioritize**, or *rank*, the clothes that you need. If you have outgrown or worn out a major item, such as a coat or a pair of boots, you will need to replace it. You may need certain clothes for a part-time job or new activities. Your wardrobe chart can help you identify the clothes that you need in your wardrobe.

Then you can consider the clothes that you would like to add to your wardrobe. Perhaps one new garment could enable you to coordinate several other outfits. For example, a new shirt could go with several skirts or pants, as well as your jacket. It could also be combined with two of your sweaters. Look for clothes that are **versatile**, or *able to be worn or combined in a variety of ways*.

Your wardrobe plan can also include some items that you want because they are fun, exciting, up-to-date, or will help you to express the real you. However, it is important that you spend your resources to first meet your needs. Then you can add the extra "wants," if you so desire. The best addition to your wardrobe is a garment that will help to satisfy *both* your needs and your wants.

This girl is purchasing a blouse. Other ways of adding items to your wardrobe are by sewing them, sharing or trading, or by renting.

EVALUATE YOUR ALTERNATIVES

Most people would love to be able to have all the clothes that they need and want. However, most of us have limited resources. We may not have enough money to buy everything we want.

There are many different ways to go about adding items to your wardrobe.

- You might purchase some of the things that you need.
- You might sew some new garments, or redesign older garments that you already own.
- You might share clothes with a relative or a friend.
- You might also explore trading clothes or renting them.

Buying

Buying offers you the advantage of trying on a finished garment to see if it is right for you.

You can evaluate the style, quality, and fit before you make your final decision. Buying can be a fast and easy alternative. However, it is the most expensive alternative in terms of money.

To help your money go farther, you can develop good shopping skills. These can also help you to save time when shopping. Unit 5 discusses shopping guidelines that will help you in your wardrobe planning.

Sewing

Sewing offers many advantages in following your wardrobe plan. It usually saves you money. Sometimes you can sew a garment for one-third the cost of buying it.

Sewing gives you the opportunity to express yourself. You can be creative and sew clothes in the color, size, and style that you want. You can make accessories to match. And you can customize your clothes to fit you perfectly.

There is a feeling of pride and accomplishment in wearing something special that you made yourself. In Chapter 23, you will learn more about sewing selections.

You can also use your sewing skills to redesign a garment that you seldom or no longer wear. However, sewing takes time and a certain amount of skill.

Sharing and Trading

These are two good ways to stretch your wardrobe. You might consider sharing or trading clothes with a family member or friend. Instead of investing in a new outfit for a special occasion, sharing is a good alternative. Trading clothes with another person gives both of your wardrobes a new addition at no cost to either of you. By sharing and trading, you can recycle clothes for new uses by others.

Renting

Renting clothing is an option that has traditionally been used for formal occasions. Caps and gowns are rented for graduation. Tuxedos can be rented for school dances, weddings, and other special events. In some large cities, there are shops that rent formal clothing for females as well as for males. Uniforms and costumes can also be rented.

KNOW YOURSELF

The more that you know about yourself, the easier it is to plan a wardrobe that you will enjoy wearing. In Unit 1, you learned how clothing choices are influenced by your lifestyle, personality, values, family, friends, and other groups.

Your personality and values are expressed through your preference for certain styles, colors, and fabrics. What you do and where you

Formal wear, especially for men, is usually rented from formal wear outlets.

live influence the variety of clothes that you need in your wardrobe. Special activities, interests, and occasions determine your need for special types of clothes.

Even the roles and responsibilities that you have within your family and other groups influence your wardrobe. And for some people, peer group pressure and advertising are a major influence.

Finally, your physical characteristics affect the way that you look in clothes. In the next chapters, you will learn how to use color and design to select the clothes that are the most flattering to you.

Every time that you consider adding a new item to your wardrobe, you should ask yourself the following questions:

- Do I really need it?
- Does it go with other items in my wardrobe?
- Can I wear it for more than one type of occasion?
- Can I change the look by changing the accessories?
- Are the color, style, and texture flattering to my personal coloring and body shape?

Your wardrobe plan is your road map for choosing the best clothing for *you.*

Body Shapes

Here is some information that will help you to pinpoint your body shape. Then in the next chapters, you will find out how to play up your best features.

- *Height.* Are you tall, short, or somewhere in-between? Have you reached your full height or are you still growing? How is your posture? Poor posture does not make you look shorter—but it does make your clothes look like they do not fit properly.

- *Frame.* Your body's frame is the skeletal structure of your bones. It may be small, medium, or large. The size of your frame influences how you appear to others. Two people of the same height and weight may look very different. A person with a larger bone structure will appear bigger than a person with a small frame.

- *Shape.* Bodies come in many different shapes. Some of the most common are the *triangle shape,* which has narrow shoulders and wide hips; the *inverted triangle,* which has wide shoulders and small hips; and the *rectangle,* which has shoulders, waistline, and hips that are approximately the same size. The *hourglass* shape has a small waist with chest and hips that are approximately equal in size.

- *Proportion.* Proportion represents the relationship of the parts of the body to one another and to the whole body.

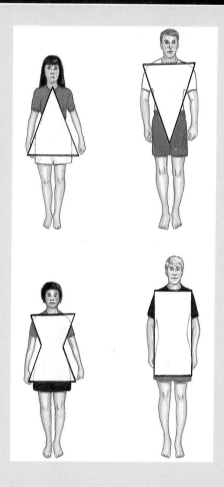

Some people have arms and legs that are long, while others have ones that are average in length. Two people who are the same height can have very different body proportions. One may have a long torso and short legs, while the other may have a short torso and long legs.

Chapter 10 *Review*

Summary

A wardrobe plan will help you make better use of items that you already own. It can also help you decide what you need to add to your wardrobe. The first step is to take an inventory of your wardrobe. Sort all your clothing into four categories—remain, repair, revise, and retire. Using the clothes you own in new combinations and new ways can help expand your wardrobe. You should prioritize, or rank, the clothes that you want to add to your wardrobe. Evaluate different alternatives, such as buying, sewing, sharing, trading, and renting.

Questions

1. What are three benefits of making a wardrobe plan?

2. Describe how to take an inventory of your wardrobe. What are the categories into which you should sort your clothes?

3. Why is it beneficial to repair clothing as soon as possible?

4. What should you do with clothes that you seldom or never wear?

5. How can mixing and matching extend your wardrobe? Give examples.

6. How should you prioritize your needs and wants when deciding to add to your wardrobe?

7. Why should you look for clothes that are versatile?

8. What are four alternative methods of expanding your wardrobe? What are the advantages and disadvantages of each?

9. List the questions you should ask yourself each time you consider adding a new item to your wardrobe.

Activities

1. Make your own wardrobe chart. Take an inventory of your clothes and mark the activities for which each is suited. What "holes" do you have in your wardrobe? Can any clothes in the *repair* or *revise* categories be used to meet those needs?

2. For one week, wear the clothes in your wardrobe in combinations that you have never tried before. How many new combinations can you create?

3. Some wardrobe experts recommend that no item be purchased unless it can coordinate with at least five other items in your wardrobe. Do you agree or disagree? Describe what impact that would have on your shopping habits.

You Be the Expert

While shopping with a friend, he decides to purchase a sweater that is very similar to one that he owns. You ask, "Do you really need it?" He replies, "I want it . . . isn't that the same?" How can you explain the difference between needs and wants?

11 Understanding Color

TERMS TO LEARN

color scheme
hue
intensity
intermediate color
optical illusions
primary colors
secondary color
spectrum
value

What would our world look like in shades of gray? Would it seem dull and depressing to you? Try to imagine sitting down to a meal with all gray food. Would you enjoy wearing clothes that were only black, white, and gray? You can visualize the change to a completely gray world when you compare the picture on a black and white television set to one on a color model. Color definitely makes a difference.

Although we may not notice it, color influences our lives in many different ways. Often the effects of color are very subtle, or hard to detect. After reading this chapter, you will be able to:

- explain how colors help to communicate, influence moods, suggest temperature, and create optical illusions,
- define the language of color,
- develop color schemes that work well together,
- choose colors that compliment your coloring and body shape.

The Message of Color

Colors convey many messages. They act as symbols and communicate feelings. They can affect our mood and influence our appearance.

Some colors suggest coolness while others appear hot. Some fade into the background while others stand out. Optical tricks cause us to see color that is not there. Certain color combinations can even appear to quiver.

COLOR AND SYMBOLS

A stoplight at a busy intersection sends messages without words. Red means stop, yellow means caution, and green means go. Without these symbols, traffic would quickly jam up.

Red is also used for fire engines. Pink and blue are associated with babies. White is worn for weddings, and black is worn for funerals.

Think of the colors associated with special holidays or celebrations—orange and black for Halloween, red and green for Christmas, and

These photos give off certain color messages. What do these colors convey to you?

red, white, and blue for the Fourth of July.

Colors are also associated with the flags of different countries and the uniforms of athletic teams. What are the colors of your favorite professional baseball or football team? What are your school colors?

Our language is rich in expressions about color. You can *see red* when you are angry, and *feel blue* when you are sad. *In the black* means that you are making a profit, while *in the red* means that you owe money. A *gray day* and *green with envy* are just a few common phrases that use colors. Can you think of any others?

COLOR AND MOOD

Reds, oranges, and yellows express excitement and stimulate action. They encourage us to be cheerful. Blues, greens, and violets have a subduing effect. They give a sense of calm and relaxation. These feelings and qualities are important when planning colors for a home or office, as well as for clothing.

You may reach for a red or yellow raincoat on a dreary day to help brighten your mood.

Fast-food restaurants are decorated with bright, cheerful colors, which invite you to order and eat more food. Shades of blues and greens are used in places where a feeling of restfulness is desired. Doctors' offices and hospitals are now decorated in these colors instead of sterile white. Even surgeons and other medical personnel in operating rooms wear soft green clothing.

Color can also imply levelheadedness and confidence. The typical business suit is deep blue, which indicates professionalism. If a red tie is added, what effect might it create?

You may have pleasant or unpleasant memories associated with color. Sometimes you may dislike a color, yet have no idea why. Perhaps the color does not suit your personality. Maybe you were wearing it when you had an accident or a bad experience. It is also possible that one of your parents dislikes the color, and you grew to dislike it, too.

On the other hand, you probably have one or more favorite colors. Do you know why? Do you receive compliments when you wear it? Does it make you feel happy and cheerful?

Think about colors and how you feel about them. If you could buy a whole new wardrobe, what colors would you choose? Would you choose the same colors for decorating your room?

COLOR AND TEMPERATURE

Colors suggest temperatures that are associated with nature. Red, orange, and yellow look like fire and sunlight. Blue is the color of deep waters, clear skies, and ice. Green represents grassy lawns and shade trees. Violet is seen in the shadows of a cool evening or the sparkle of snow.

Such associations make us seek cool, crisp colors on a hot day. Blues, blue-violets, and greens are considered cool colors. Warm colors make us feel more comfortable in colder weather. Reds, oranges, and yellows are considered warm colors.

Designers and display artists consider these qualities when choosing colors. There are usually more blues, blue-greens, and greens in spring and summer clothes. In fall and winter, colors turn more to red, orange, gold, and brown.

OPTICAL ILLUSIONS

Color can create visual images, not unlike the special effects that you see in films, but on a much simpler scale. Sometimes the *special effects make you think that your eyes are playing tricks on you.* These are called **optical illusions**.

Color Illusions

Try this for fun. Draw a bright green circle on a piece of white paper. Now stare at it intensely for 20 to 30 seconds. Then look away at a blank piece of white paper. What do you see? You should see a red circle, the complement of green.

Complementary colors are those that are opposite each other on the color wheel (see page 129). They create an after-image effect in this experiment. Try it again with two other complementary colors, such as blue and orange.

Movement Illusions

Colors also create optical illusions of movement. Warm colors tend to *advance,* or move toward you. Dark colors tend to *recede,* or move away from you.

Try this experiment with the two same size circles below—one bright yellow, and one bright blue. Glance at them quickly. Which seems larger? Even though you know they are the same size, the yellow one appears larger. Because it advances, the yellow circle gives the illusion of being larger.

Have you ever noticed that an umpire's black-and-white-striped shirt seems to hurt your eyes when you look at it? When two colors of equal brightness, such as black and white, or yellow and blue, are used together in a bold pattern, they seem to vibrate. The reason that your eyes seem to hurt is that they are having trouble focusing. Each of the equally bright and intense colors are fighting for your eyes' attention.

Illusions Working for You

By understanding these optical illusions, you can choose color combinations that work for you, instead of against you. After-images can affect your complexion. A bright blue sweater might make your skin look more yellow; a bright green might make it look more red.

Advancing and receding colors can emphasize or minimize your size. When you are in a crowd, notice which colors stand out. Finally, vivid color combinations might actually become tiring.

The Language of Color

Have you ever owned a box of crayons or paints that contained more names of colors than you could remember? As a child, it was fun to use all of them and fill up a page with a truly original color mix.

Learning about color offers a challenge. Remembering their names is not as important as learning how to combine them in creative, yet pleasing, color combinations. It is helpful to study the basics of color, its language, and its many variations. Then you will understand how to select the colors and color combinations that are best for you.

THE COLOR WHEEL

Colors are called hues. A **hue** is the name given to *a specific color,* such as pink or green. The three **primary colors** are *red, yellow, and blue.* All other colors are made from a combination of these three basic colors.

To understand the relationship of one color to another, it is helpful to use a color wheel. The primary colors, red, yellow, and blue, form the points of an equal-sided triangle on the color wheel.

When you combine equal amounts of two of the primary colors, you create a **secondary color**. Blue and yellow make green. Red and yellow make orange. Red and blue make violet, which is often called purple.

If you combine a primary color with a secondary color you create an *in-between,* or **intermediate color**. Blue combines with green to make blue-green. Red combines with orange to make red-orange. Using the color wheel, what other intermediate colors can you make?

Colors that are directly opposite each other on the color wheel are called *complementary*

colors. Red and green are complementary colors. What are the other complementary colors on the color wheel?

Color Wheel

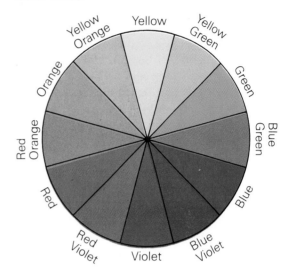

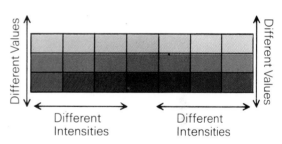

Find the primary, secondary, and intermediate colors on the color wheel.

COLOR VARIATIONS

On a color wheel, the colors are very bright and vivid. However, the majority of colors that you see around you are not bold or intense. Most colors are lighter, darker, or softer than the hues on the color wheel.

Value describes *the lightness or darkness of a color.* Every color has a wide range of value, from very light to very dark.

For example, red can go from a very pale pink to a dark burgundy. Value is created by adding white or black to the pure color. Colors combined with white are called *tints*. The light pastel colors of pink, mint green, and baby blue are tints. Colors that are darkened by the addition of black are called *shades*. Navy blue is a shade of blue, and brown is a shade of orange.

Intensity is the *brightness or dullness of a color*. Blue can be a strong vivid blue or a dull grayed blue. Both tints and shades can be bright or dull. For example, pink can be very soft and pale, or fluorescent bright.

The intensity of a color varies with the amount of color pigment in it. Bright colors are very color-intense. Colors referred to as jewel tones, such as emerald green and ruby red, are examples of high-intensity colors. Dulled colors are less intense and softer. They have been dulled by adding their complementary color or black. Khaki green and beige are two examples.

Neutral colors are those with an absence of true color pigment. They include white, black, and gray, which is the combination of white and black. Tints and shades of beige are often considered neutrals; they are not true neutrals because they have a yellow or green base.

Color Schemes

The *way that you use a color or combination of colors when planning an outfit or decorating a room* is called a **color scheme**. Some modern artists use a haphazard mix of colors very successfully. However, they have an understanding of color and the subtle differences between the many intensities and shades. This method does not usually work for the amateur. Instead, it is better to follow one of several time-tested color schemes as a guideline.

MONOCHROMATIC

Mono is the prefix meaning *one*. *Chromatic* refers to color. Thus a *monochromatic color scheme* uses the values and intensities of just one color.

In planning a monochromatic color scheme, you can choose values that have a lot of contrast or very little contrast between them. For example, you might wear a pale blue shirt with navy blue slacks. This will create strong contrast between the upper and lower halves of your body. Or you might choose a sweater that is only a shade lighter than the slacks. This combination has little contrast and creates a more continuous look.

Shades and Tints

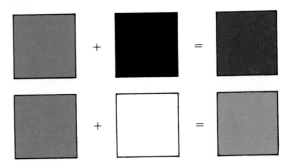

Tints *are colors combined with white.* Shades *are colors that are darkened by the addition of black.*

ANALOGOUS

An *analogous color scheme* is two or more colors that are next to each other on the color wheel. For example, yellow, yellow-orange, and orange are analogous colors, so is a blue-green shirt with blue shorts.

Basic Color Schemes

 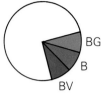 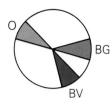 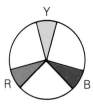

| Monochromatic | Analogous | Complementary | Split Complementary | Triad |

When using an analogous color scheme, the colors will blend better if they are close in value and intensity. Red and red-violet are more harmonious than pink and red-violet, even though pink is a tint of red. Pink and pink-lavender would mix well. Why?

COMPLEMENTARY

Each color on the color wheel has a complement that is located directly across from it. A *complementary color scheme* combines colors that are direct opposites, such as red and green, and orange and blue.

When complementary colors are used together in equal intensity, a very bold color scheme is created. The colors emphasize each other. Wearing an outfit of two bright complements will call attention to you, more than you might want.

A softer effect can be obtained by using different values and intensities. For example, instead of using red and green, try pairing up pink and forest green. Or choose a rust and navy plaid, instead of orange and blue.

Another method is to use one of the complementary colors as an accent. A yellow blouse with violet trim, or a red tie with a narrow green stripe are also complementary color schemes.

SPLIT COMPLEMENTARY

One color used with the two colors on either side of its direct complement make up a *split complementary color scheme*. This color scheme is more common and easier to wear than a complementary color scheme. The color combinations are less bold.

You will often find a split complementary scheme used in a plaid or print fabric. A blue and green plaid with an accent stripe of red-orange within the plaid is an example.

TRIAD

Three colors that are of equal distance from one another on the color wheel create a *triadic color scheme*. Orange, violet, and green is one example. The primary colors of red, blue, and yellow is another. A triadic color mix of bold, bright colors would be more difficult to wear than one of softer, duller colors.

ACCENTED NEUTRAL

Since neutrals have no color, they combine well with other hues. When a color is matched with white, black, or gray, it is considered an *accented neutral color scheme*. The accent color is used in smaller amounts to brighten up the neutral color.

What Is Color?

Light is the source of all color. When a ray of light passes through a glass prism, it forms *a band of colors* called a **spectrum.** The colors of the spectrum blend into each other: *red, orange, yellow, green, blue, and violet.* Each color has its own wavelength, or rate of energy. The longest wavelength produces red; the shortest, violet. When sunlight passes through raindrops, the light forms the colors of a rainbow.

We see objects as different colors because of the light that is reflected from the object. When light strikes a red apple, the red wavelength is reflected and all others are absorbed. When you look at a yellow banana, you see yellow because only the yellow wavelength is reflected. When light strikes something white, all wavelengths are reflected and none are absorbed. Thus, white is the absence of color. Black represents the combination of all colors since all wavelengths are absorbed.

Your eye can distinguish hundreds of colors. The retina, which is the light sensitive area of the eye, contains cells that receive all light stimuli and send these messages to the brain. Research has shown that many animals, including dogs and cats, do not see colors. They probably see objects as various shades of gray.

Color is also affected by different types of light. Have you ever noticed that some colors that you wear seem to change when you go from home to outdoors to school? A blue shirt that you bought in a store may

appear more green when you get home. This is the result of seeing colors under different kinds of lighting.

Natural sunlight reflects the true colors of an object. Incandescent light might add a touch of yellow, while fluorescent light adds blue. Some light bulbs are "soft pink" and add a subtle pink tone to colors.

Color blindness, or daltonism, is not being able to tell all colors apart. Some people can see a wide range of yellows and blues, but may confuse reds and greens. Others may confuse some reds and greens with some yellows. Only a very few people can see no color at all.

People can be easily tested for color blindness. In these tests, colored shapes lie buried in a jumble of dots. The examiner can determine a person's ability to see colors by the colored shapes that they identify. More than 4 out of every 100 males and 1 out of every 200 females are color-blind.

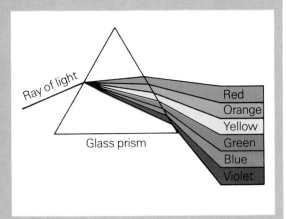

The accent color often serves as a center of interest in an outfit. The eye is drawn to it, making it more noticeable than the other parts of the outfit. A man wearing a gray suit might accent it with a yellow tie or a blue handkerchief.

You can find the best fabric colors to go with your personal coloring by the use of a mirror.

Choosing the Best Colors for You

How do you choose colors? Which of the many beautiful hues of the spectrum are for you? What about the warm reds, oranges, and yellows, or the cool blues, blue-violets, and greens? Some color experts say that everyone can wear every color, as long as it is the right value and intensity for you.

When selecting colors for your wardrobe, you should consider your personal coloring and your body shape. The right values and intensities will compliment your coloring and flatter your body shape.

YOUR PERSONAL COLORING

Your personal coloring is made up of the natural color of your skin, hair, and eyes. Your personal coloring may change. Your hair color may darken as you grow older, or you may change its color. Your skin may tan or darken in the summer. Whatever your personal color combination, it becomes the basis for choosing the colors of your clothing and accessories.

To find out which colors look best on you, you should compare actual colors. Look in a mirror and hold colors underneath your chin. The colors can be clothing, pieces of fabric, or even colored paper. Have a friend or relative help you with your evaluation.

When you look in the mirror, which do you see first, the color sample or your face? Your best colors are those that accent you. Your complexion should look healthy and glowing. If the color takes the attention away from your face, you may seem pale by comparison. Then it is not one of your best colors.

Do you look better in bright, clear colors or softer hues? Are cool colors or warm colors more flattering? For example, do you look better in clear red, blue-red, or orange-red? Is your best green an olive green, a blue-green, or a true green? Is pure white or ivory more attractive for you? Sometimes a particular color will seem to accent your eyes or hair and give them sparkle. Choose colors that create a positive, healthy look for you.

COLOR AND ILLUSIONS

Colors can create illusions about the way that you look. Remember the optical illusions described in the beginning of this chapter? They apply to your clothing selections, too.

You can use color to accent or play down certain areas of your body. You can create illusions of height and size. Color can be used to emphasize a special feature or the color of your eyes. Some people with blue-gray eyes appear to have very blue eyes when they wear a blue shirt. Learn to use color to your advantage.

Size

Colors can be used to make you look larger or smaller. If you look at two identical size cubes, one white and one black, the black one will look smaller. Why? White reflects light and makes objects look larger. Black absorbs light and makes objects look smaller.

The same is true for advancing and receding colors that you read about earlier in this chapter. Therefore, if you want to look larger, choose light colors, warm colors, and bright colors. If you want to look smaller, choose dark shades, cool colors, and dulled or soft colors. Compare two outfits in the same style, one in bright red and the other in a soft, burgundy shade. What illusions would be created by each color?

You can use these color guidelines to help emphasize or camouflage certain body areas. If you want to accent your broad shoulders, what colors should you choose for a shirt or a sweater? If you want to de-emphasize your hips, should you wear a pair of white or tan pants?

Height

Colors can also help you to look taller or shorter. Wearing one or more colors that are close in value and intensity will help to make you look taller. An unbroken block of color from the neckline to the hem gives a taller illusion.

Wearing sharply contrasting colors, either in hue or in value, will make you look shorter. A bright red shirt and bright blue pants will cut your height. The same is true when you wear a light colored top with a dark shade below. The broken blocks of color create a shorter illusion.

Emphasis

Color can be used as an accent or center of interest. Wearing a collar in a contrasting color moves the center of attention away from the body and toward the face. If you have a slim waistline, you might like to emphasize it by wearing a belt in a bright, contrasting color. On the other hand, if you want to hide your waistline, wear a narrow belt in the same color as your dress, skirt, or pants. Do not make it the center of attention.

YOUR WARDROBE

When choosing colors for your wardrobe, select ones that flatter your coloring and your body shape. Choose colors that you like and that make you feel good. These will be the colors that will bring you compliments on your appearance and wardrobe. Plus, it is fun to wear colors that make you feel special.

Chapter 11 Review

Summary

Colors convey many messages. They act as symbols, influence moods, suggest temperature, and create optical illusions. The three primary colors can be combined to create all other colors, or hues. Every color has many different values and intensities. Color schemes help you combine colors that work well together. Some common color schemes are: monochromatic, analogous, complementary, split complementary, triad, and accented neutral. When selecting colors for your wardrobe, you should consider your personal coloring and your body shape.

Questions

1. List eight examples of colors used as symbols.

2. What are warm colors and cool colors? What moods do they express?

3. What is meant by colors advancing or receding?

4. Name the primary colors. What combinations make the secondary colors? What combinations make the intermediate colors?

5. What is the relationship between values and tints? values and shades?

6. Why are some colors more intense than other colors?

7. Define each of the following color schemes and given an example of each: monochromatic, analogous, split complementary, and accented neutral.

8. When choosing colors for your wardrobe, what two factors should you consider?

9. How can you use colors and optical illusions to emphasize or minimize your body shape?

Activities

1. Using water-based paints, create a tint, a shade, a dulled intensity, a secondary color, and an intermediate color from a primary color.

2. Collect photographs or illustrations of various articles of clothing in different colors. Mix and match the pieces to create different color schemes. Describe the different effects created. Which color combinations do you think are most harmonious? Why?

3. With another classmate, evaluate your best colors. Use actual garments or swatches of fabric. Compare their effect on your coloring. What colors do each of you look best in? Demonstrate the different effects to the class.

You Be the Expert

Your friend has red hair and has heard that redheads should never wear any color of red. What advice can you give your friend about color selection?

12 Understanding Design

TERMS TO LEARN

balance

elements of design

emphasis

harmony

line

principles of design

proportion

rhythm

shape

silhouette

space

texture

Do you have a special outfit that always brings a compliment? Do you know why? Your special outfit probably includes the elements of design that work best for you.

This chapter introduces the elements and principles of design—what they are and how to use them in clothing selection. After reading this chapter, you will be able to:

- understand the language of design and the techniques used by designers,
- demonstrate how to use lines, shapes, and spaces to create fashion illusions,
- describe how fabric textures and patterns can affect your appearance,
- use the design elements and design principles to create the look you want.

The Language of Design

Designers, those who make images and objects that we see and use, have studied the universal language of design. If a designer studied in Europe or Japan, he or she learned the same language of design as someone who studied in the United States.

Artists, architects, interior designers, and fashion designers all learn this same language. Whether designing artworks, clothing, furniture, homes, offices, or even gymnasiums, designers use the same basic "building blocks" to put together their creation.

These building blocks are called the **elements of design**. They include *line, shape, space, texture, and color.* You learned about the importance of color in the preceding chapter. Now let us look at the other elements of design.

- A **line** is *a series of points connected together to form a narrow path.* You may have studied "lines" in a math class. Lines divide areas into shapes and spaces.

- **Shape** is *the outline, or silhouette, of an object.* Look at the objects around you—they all have an outer shape. What are the shapes of your classroom chalkboard, your living room sofa, and your pants or skirt?

- **Space** is *the area inside the shape, or outline, of an object.* It may be divided by lines. How many panels is the chalkboard divided into? How many cushions are on the sofa? How do the seams of your pants break up its space?

- **Texture** is *the surface characteristics, or feel, of an object.* The chalkboard feels hard and smooth. Your sofa may be soft and nubby. Touch the fabric of your clothing. Does it feel soft or crisp, smooth or fuzzy?

Line, shape, space, and texture are all clearly and dramatically shown in this model's outfit.

Designers learn how to combine the elements of design within an object to create a finished project. A good design is one that is pleasing to look at, time and time again.

UNDERSTANDING LINE

Line is the most basic element of design because it divides areas into shapes and spaces. Line can also give direction, or a feeling of movement, to a design. Individual lines can be straight or curved.

Straight Lines

Straight lines are divided into three types: vertical, horizontal, or diagonal.

- **Vertical lines** *go up and down* on a garment. They generally give you a taller, more slender look. They have a feeling of strength, dignity, and formality.

- **Horizontal lines** *go across* on a garment. They can give a shorter, wider look. They tend to create a feeling of stability and restfulness. However, the spacing and width of horizontal lines can affect the feeling they create.

- **Diagonal lines** *move at an angle* on a garment. They add movement and excitement to clothing. The effect of diagonal lines depends upon whether the lines slant in a more vertical or horizontal direction. Zigzag diagonal lines create the most excitement.

Straight lines can also suggest a certain style. Such lines have a crisp look and are usually used in classic or conservative designs. Most men's and women's business suits have crisp vertical and horizontal lines at the shoulders, sleeves, pockets, cuffs, and hems. Many businessmen select a tie with stripes or a straight-line pattern instead of one that has a round design.

Diagonal lines are dramatic and more trendy in nature. They are often seen in high-fashion clothes and sportswear.

Curved Lines

Curved lines can be *circular or gently waved*. They add softness and roundness to a garment.

Curved lines can move in a vertical, horizontal, or diagonal direction.

Curved lines create a softer, more casual image. A Western-style shirt with a curved seam across the chest and back has a more casual look than a tailored shirt.

LINE AND ILLUSION

Have you ever seen someone disappear in a magic act? Do you really believe that they turned into a puff of smoke? Of course not. It is just an optical illusion. An *illusion* is something that deceives or misleads us when we look at it.

Illusions can make things appear quite differently than they actually are. In fashion design, illusions cannot make people disappear, but they do create a bit of magic. You can use them to emphasize, minimize, or camouflage your body shape.

Creating Positive Illusions

In order to create positive illusions with lines, you must understand how they work. Look at the illusions shown here. These are created by the direction in which the eye moves when looking at the lines and the shapes created. A change in line direction can change the apparent length of a line. A change in the location of a line can change the apparent size of an area.

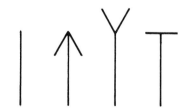

VERTICAL LINES

DIAGONAL LINES

HORIZONTAL LINES

CURVED LINES

How lines work together also determines the overall impression. The thickness of lines and the amount of space between lines affect the illusion. Very wide vertical stripes may give the impression of added width because the eye starts moving sideways across the lines. With horizontal stripes, the same is true. Horizontal lines spaced far apart make the eye move up and down instead of sideways.

Vertical lines give an illusion of thinness. Horizontal lines give one of bulk.

How can you use optical illusions in fashion? Our eyes naturally follow the dominant line in a garment. This line may be a center seam, a waistline, a curved neckline, or a bold stripe. Whatever it is, it will have the most influence on the total look of a garment or outfit.

Thus, you can use vertical lines to add height and lessen width. Horizontal lines at the shoulder, waist, or hemline can add width or help a tall person look shorter.

SHAPE AND SPACE

Look at a framed painting. What do you see? First, you see the outline of the picture as defined by the frame. Your eye records its shape: round, rectangular, or square. Then your eye looks inside the frame at the artwork. It moves around the space and focuses on the dominant areas. In fashion, the shape is the *frame,* and the space inside it is the *artwork.*

Fashion Shapes

Study the **silhouettes**, or *outer shapes,* of your classmates' clothing. If you cannot see the shapes quickly, try squinting at them. When you squint at an object, you can see its outline or shape more easily. How many different garment shapes can you identify? Is one shape more common than the others?

Are any classmates wearing skirts or pants that are straight and narrow, flaring and bell-shaped, or full and rounded? Can you tell where their actual waistlines are?

Most clothes are one of four basic shapes: *natural, tubular, bell,* or *full.*

• The *natural* shape is one that follows your body's proportion. Clothes of this shape are close to the body and emphasize your natural waistline. This shape is the most classic.

• The *tubular* shape is rectangular with vertical emphasis. The dominant lines go up and down. Usually the waistline is not defined. A T-shirt dress, straight leg pants, and a tailored business suit are examples of tubular shapes.

• The *bell* shape combines both vertical and horizontal lines in a silhouette and is flattering to most people. A-line skirts and dresses, flaired pants and jackets, and capes are all bell shapes.

• *Full* shapes have more horizontal and curved lines than do the other shapes. Gathered skirts and dresses, full sleeves, and pants with wide legs are examples of full shapes.

Four Basic Clothing Shapes

NATURAL

TUBULAR

BELL

FULL

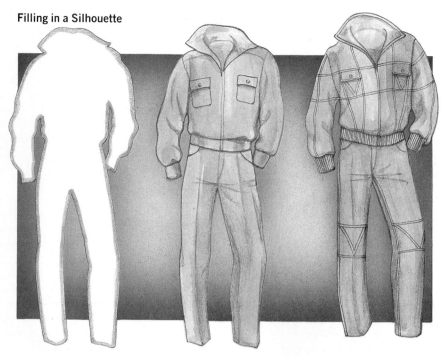

Filling in a Silhouette

SILHOUETTE   **STRUCTURAL LINES**   **DECORATIVE LINES**

Fashion trends influence which shapes are in style during a fashion season. Usually silhouettes change gradually from year to year, but occasionally a whole new shape is introduced by fashion designers. Styles may suddenly swing from full to tubular if a "new look" is promoted by designers, magazines, or stores.

Fashion Spaces

The area inside the shape of your garment is just as important as the silhouette. The lines created within this area by seams and trims divide your garment and you into inner spaces. These internal lines can be either structural or decorative.

• *Structural lines* are formed by sewing the different parts of a garment together. They include seams, darts, tucks, gathers, pleats, necklines, armholes, waistlines, and hems. Some seams may be purely design lines, such as a yoke or panel, but are still considered structural lines.

• *Decorative lines* are created by adding trims, such as braid, edgings, lace, and buttons, to a garment. See if you can identify the structural and decorative lines on the clothing you are wearing today.

Both structural and decorative lines can create strong illusions. The bolder the lines are, the more emphasis they will create. When choosing a garment to buy or sew, be sure to note where the structural and decorative lines fall on your body.

For example, pants or skirts with a fitted yoke will emphasize your hipline. Do you want emphasis here? Usually, the fewer the lines within a garment, the less attention they will attract. You can use lines, shapes, and spaces to create the illusions and effects that you want.

TEXTURE

Fabric selection plays an important role in the final look of a garment. Imagine a favorite shirt. How would it look if it was made of a heavy wool plaid, a crisp striped cotton, a soft nubby knit, or a shiny satin? Each result would be totally different!

All four fabrics differ in one important characteristic—texture. Just as color and line can create different illusions, texture can also make you look taller, shorter, larger, or smaller.

Fabric Texture

The texture of a fabric is determined by the type of fiber, yarn, construction, and finish of the fabric. The texture determines how the fabric feels, looks, and moves when it is worn. Fabric texture can be soft or crisp, smooth or nubby, and dull or shiny. Each texture has a different effect on the impression it creates.

- *Soft or clingy fabrics,* such as jersey and chiffon, hug the body and emphasize any figure irregularities. However, when draped into soft silhouettes, these fabrics can be very flattering to most figures.

- *Moderately crisp or stiff fabrics,* such as corduroy and denim, stand away from the body just enough to conceal figure faults.

- *Extra-crisp fabrics,* such as taffeta and vinyl, may create a stiff outer shell and make the body seem larger.

- *Smooth fabrics* with a dull finish do not seem to create illusions about size and shape. Some examples of smooth fabrics are flannel, broadcloth, gabardine, and wool jersey.

- *Nubby or bulky fabrics* add dimension and can make you appear larger. Fabrics such as wide-wale corduroy, mohair, and heavy tweeds look best on a slim to average figure of medium to tall height.

- *Dull fabrics* absorb light and tend to make a figure look smaller. Flannel, denim, and gingham all have dull surfaces.

- *Shiny fabrics* reflect light and give an impression of added size. Some shiny fabrics are satin, polished cotton, nylon, and vinyl. Sequined and metallic fabrics also have shiny surfaces.

Fabric texture can also help create different moods. Rough, bulky fabrics give a more casual appearance. Delicate and glittery fabrics look more formal. However, do not be afraid to mix textures within an outfit. Years ago, fashion had "rules" about mixing different types of fabrics. Today all types of combinations are possible—from velveteen and tweed, to denim and satin!

Name as many textures as you can see in the clothing worn by this young man.

Fashion Focus

Garment Terms

- **Bodice.** The portion of the garment above the waist
- **Dart.** Triangular-shaped folds of fabric stitched to control fullness and give shape to the garment
- **Facing.** An extra piece of fabric that covers raw edges at the neckline, armhole, and other garment openings
- **Fasteners.** Items used to hold a garment closed, such as buttons, snaps, hooks and eyes, and zippers
- **Gathers.** Soft, unstitched folds of fabric used to control fullness
- **Hem.** Fabric folded back at the bottom edge of a garment to finish off the edge
  - **Hem allowance.** The width of the fabric forming the hem
  - **Hem finish.** A technique used to prevent edge of the fabric from fraying
- **Interfacing.** An extra layer of fabric placed between the garment and the facing to add shape or body
- **Lapel.** Part of the garment that turns back below the collar
- **Lining.** An extra layer of fabric used to prevent stretching and to finish off the inside of the garment
- **Placket.** A garment opening finished with a strip of fabric or zipper
- **Pleat.** A wider fold of fabric pressed or stitched flat
- **Seam.** A row of stitching used to hold two pieces of fabric together
  - **Seam allowance.** The width of the fabric between the seam and the edge of the fabric
  - **Seam finish.** A technique used to prevent the edge from fraying
- **Trim.** Some form of decoration added to a garment, such as braid, lace, or rickrack
- **Tuck.** Narrow fold of fabric stitched flat
- **Waistline.** A horizontal seam attaching the upper and lower sections of a garment; it can be located above, at, or below the natural waistline
- **Yoke.** A fitted section at the shoulder or hips to which garment is attached

Fabric Patterns

Pattern designs on fabric are created by color, lines, shapes, and spaces. They come in an endless variety—stripes, plaids, geometrics, florals, scenics, borders, and many others. The designs can be large or small, even or uneven, light or dark, spaced or clustered, muted or bold. All will affect how a fabric will look on you.

Fabric patterns, just like fabric texture, can create illusions in design. Small prints in subdued colors usually decrease apparent size. Large, overall designs increase size. Widely spaced motifs will also make you seem larger. Prints with large curves give a feeling of added roundness and size.

Different Fabric Patterns

LARGE PRINT   SMALL PRINT

VIVID PRINT   SUBTLE PRINT

LARGE PLAID   SMALL PLAID

Which of these fabric patterns could be used for a large person or a small person?

When selecting striped or plaid fabrics, follow the basic theory of line and illusion. Identify the dominant stripe of the fabric. If you cannot identify it easily, try the squint test. As you squint at the fabric, note which stripe you see first. This will be the dominant one. Placement of this stripe is important. How will it divide up the space within your garment? Is it vertical, horizontal, or diagonal?

Where on the body do the stripes fall? For example, a bold horizontal stripe across the hipline or waistline will make either look larger. What happens when the stripes meet at the seams? Do they match horizontally or vertically? Do they *chevron*, or form angles, at the seams?

Select prints, stripes, and plaids that are in *scale*, or in proportional size, with your own body size. Small designs look best on the small to average person, but they look out of place and lost on a large figure. On the other hand, large designs are best worn by the average to tall person as these designs can overwhelm a small figure.

The Principles of Design

How can you successfully combine all the elements of design—line, shape, space, texture, and color—in clothes so they will look good on you? The **principles of design** are *artistic guidelines for using the various design elements within a garment.* These principles include *balance, proportion, emphasis, rhythm,* and *harmony.*

BALANCE

Balance is *how the internal spaces of a shape work together.* The area of a design may be broken up by structural lines, trims, fabric pattern, texture, or color. Balance can be symmetrical or asymmetrical.

- *Symmetrical balance* occurs when the space within a garment is divided into equal parts. A simple skirt with a center front seam and a simple shirt with a center front closing are examples of symmetrical balance. Both the left front and the right front of each garment are the same. Symmetrical balance usually has a more formal or tailored look.

- *Asymmetrical balance* occurs when the space within a garment is divided unequally. A skirt with a side front wrap is an example of asymmetrical balance. A shirt with a bold pocket design on only one side is another example. Although the space is divided unequally, it can be balanced by adding design details, color, or accessories to the other section. Asymmetrical balance has an informal or exciting look.

PROPORTION

Proportion is *the size relationship of each of the internal spaces within a garment to one another and to the total look.* The most pleasing

Which outfits show symmetrical and asymmetrical balance?

How do the different jacket lengths affect the proportion of this outfit?

proportions are those that are unequal. For example, a garment split exactly in half by a belt or horizontal seam is usually less attractive than one that is divided unevenly.

Clothing should also be in proportion or scale to your own size. If you are short or small-framed, stay away from large, overpowering details, such as wide lapels and collars, or huge pockets and bows. If you are tall or large-framed, avoid tiny details. If the parts do not relate well to one another or to yourself, they are said to be *out of proportion.*

The selection of accessories also involves an understanding of proportion. Ties, belts, jewelry, hats, handbags, shoes, and boots are available in a wide range of shapes and sizes. Be sure that the accessories you choose are in proportion to your outfit and to you.

EMPHASIS

Emphasis is *the focal point, or center of interest, of a garment.* In fashion design, emphasis should highlight your best features and draw attention away from your figure faults. Emphasis can be accomplished with line, design details, color, texture, trims, or accessories. For example, a colorful belt would emphasize a waistline. A contrasting collar would focus attention on your neckline. A bright tie or shiny buttons could be a center of interest.

Well-planned emphasis will lead the eye quickly to the center of interest. Poorly planned emphasis confuses the eye so that it does not know where to focus. What happens when wide, contrasting trim outlines the collar, cuffs, pockets, belt, and hemline of an outfit?

Wearing many busy, contrasting fabrics at one time tends to confuse the eyes. All that was needed here for emphasis was a tie for the boy and a bowed blouse for the girl.

RHYTHM

Rhythm is *the flow of the lines, shapes, space, and texture of a garment.* The flow should gently carry the eye from one area of the garment to another. Good rhythm is apparent when all the lines of an outfit work well together. For example, a curved pocket compliments the curve of a jacket hem. A pointed shirt collar repeats the point of a jacket lapel. Conflicting lines, such as curved seams and striped fabric, help to break the rhythm of an outfit.

Rhythm can also be achieved through repetition. Rows and rows of ruffles have rhythm. There is rhythm in a gradual change of size or color. Unmatched stripes and plaids can destroy the rhythm of an outfit. The breaks in the fabric pattern along the unmatched seamlines upset the natural rhythm of the fabric design. Jagged or jerky lines are seldom attractive.

HARMONY

Harmony is *the pleasing arrangement of all the parts of a garment.* Harmony is achieved when the design elements work well together. The colors, lines, shapes, spaces, and textures look like they belong together. However, the total result is not perfect unless the design is also harmonious with you—your size and shape, your coloring, and your personality.

Which figure presents a more harmonious appearance?

Design Equation			
Use These Design Elements	**According to These Principles**		**To Create**
line shape space + texture color	balance proportion emphasis = rhythm harmony		good design

PUTTING IT ALL TOGETHER

Each of us has body characteristics that we cannot change. They help to make each of us look unique. Some of us may have wide shoulders, narrow hips, or a bit more waistline than we would like. The key to improving your appearance is learning how to select clothing that brings your total look into balance. You can use your knowledge of the design elements and the design principles to enhance the way you look.

Planning a wardrobe that is complimentary to you will become easier as you become more aware of yourself. Study your size and shape, your coloring, and even your face and hair. Which fashion combinations are best for you? Once you know about them and use them, you will show yourself to best advantage.

Summary

The elements of design include line, shape, space, texture, and color. Vertical, horizontal, diagonal, and curved lines can create a feeling of movement, suggest a certain style, and create illusions. The four basic shapes of clothing are natural, tubular, bell, and full. The outer shape creates the silhouette of a garment. The inner space can be divided by structural or decorative lines. Texture can also create illusions and express a feeling or mood. The principles of design are guidelines for using the various design elements within a garment. The principles of design include balance, proportion, emphasis, rhythm, and harmony.

Questions

1. Name the five elements of design. Explain how each one contributes to the look of an outfit.

2. What are four types of lines used in design? What look or feeling does each one create?

3. Explain how illusions can be created by lines.

4. Describe the four basic shapes, or silhouettes, of clothing.

5. How can texture create different illusions? Give examples.

6. What guidelines should you follow when selecting fabric designs such as prints and stripes?

7. List the five principles of design. How do they differ from the elements of design? How do they all work together?

8. What are two guidelines for determining good proportions?

9. How could you create a focal point of a garment? Give examples.

Activities

1. Collect photographs of clothes that illustrate vertical, horizontal, diagonal, and curved lines. Use felt-tipped pens to highlight the dominant lines. Describe the effect of the line direction on each garment.

2. Collect fabric swatches with different textures and design patterns. Divide into two groups: fabrics that are best for taller or larger-framed people, and those for shorter or smaller-framed persons. Can any fabrics be worn by both groups?

3. Demonstrate the principles of proportion by having two or more students of different heights try on sweaters or jackets of different lengths. Discuss how the proportion of the different garments affect each student's appearance.

You Be the Expert

Your brother is shorter than many of his classmates. What styles of clothing could you recommend that would make him appear a little taller?

13 Redesigning and Recycling

TERMS TO LEARN

conservation
consignment store
recycling
redesigning

What do you do with clothes that you no longer wear? Redesigning and recycling are two methods that people use to maximize their clothing wardrobes. They help you to get the most from your clothes and your clothing dollar.

So the next time that you look at something that you no longer wear, think how you can put this item back into use by yourself or someone else.

After reading this chapter, you will be able to:

- update the fashion look of older clothes,
- improve the quality and fit of your clothes,
- use color in a variety of ways to change the look of an outfit,
- recycle clothes and fabrics for new uses.

Advantages of Redesigning

Redesigning is *taking an already existing garment and changing it to better meet your needs.* You can change the style, quality, fit, or color of a garment. Redesigning can be a simple adjustment of the hem length, or an update of the total look of the garment.

Redesigning is a very practical method of expanding your wardrobe. It helps you to get the most from what you already have. By making only minor changes, you may be able to achieve the current fashion look. Thus, you can get added wear out of many of your clothes.

Redesigning also offers you the opportunity to be creative. You can give your clothes a unique look that expresses your individuality. Redesigning can save you money. By using your time and skills, you can expand your wardrobe with very little cost.

Where to begin? After you have completed your wardrobe inventory, sort through the clothes that you seldom or never wear. This is the clothing category that was labeled *revise* in Chapter 10. Look at each garment and imagine how you might improve it.

- Was it a reject because of style, fit, or color?
- Does the workmanship need to be improved?
- Or does it need a creative touch to freshen it?

STYLE

Fashion changes from time to time. It may be from season to season or year to year. These trends influence the shape of clothes. This season, clothes may be full- or close-fitting, worn loose or belted. Pants and skirt lengths change from short to long to short again. Collars, cuffs,

It is possible to redesign even the most unfashionable garment. What would you do with this one?

and ties are sometimes wide and sometimes narrow. As fashion trends change, some of your clothes may look out-of-date.

Updating

Often you can redesign older clothes to give them an updated look. Hemlines can be shortened and sometimes lengthened. A very loose-fitting jacket can be taken in to look more fitted. A full-cut dress may be belted at the waist or hips for a more controlled look. Flared pants legs can be turned into straight legs. These simple techniques can give a newer look to older clothes.

Restyling

You can also change the entire style of a garment to keep it in your wardrobe. Long pants can be cut off to make cropped pants or shorts. A short-sleeved shirt can be made from a long-sleeved one. You can remove the sleeves of a jacket and turn it into a vest. You can shorten a coat to make a jacket.

Fashion Focus

Altering Ready-to-Wear

Have you ever received a gift that did not fit quite right and could not be returned? Did you ever find something on sale that was a fantastic buy but was too long for you? Or has someone ever offered you a secondhand garment that was in excellent condition but was a little too big? By knowing how to alter ready-to-wear, you can overcome these problems.

- *Adjusting the length.* Most hems can be shortened but not always lengthened. To shorten a hem, mark the new hem length. Remove the old stitching and fold up the fabric along the new hemline. It may be necessary to trim the hem allowance and to finish the new hem edge. Finally, sew the hem to the garment by hand or machine.

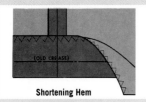

Shortening Hem

To lengthen a hem, press the old hemline carefully to remove the crease. If the new hem allowance is too narrow, stitch wide hem facing tape to the fabric edge to create a hem allowance. Sew hem in place.

- *Adjusting the width.* Small width adjustments should be made at the side seams. To make a garment smaller, try it on and have someone else pin the new seams. Transfer the markings to the inside of the garment. Carefully stitch the new seams, tapering smoothly to join the original stitching and press seams open. If seam allowances are too wide, trim and finish edges.

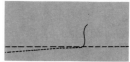

Making a Garment Larger

To make a garment larger, check the seam allowances to see if there is enough fabric for the new seams. Remove stitching before trying on the garment and having the seams pinned. Transfer markings, stitch, and press. If seam allowances are very narrow, machine zigzag both together.

For additional directions, see pages 154–155 and the Sewing Handbook.

Lengthening Hem

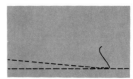

Making a Garment Smaller

Planning

Before you begin any redesign project, work out the steps and solutions. Before cutting off pant legs or sleeves, be sure that you leave enough fabric for a hem or cuff. Before you take out the sleeves of a jacket, plan how you will finish the armholes of the new vest.

If you want to make a more major design change, such as changing a neckline or the width of jacket lapels, refer to an alterations book in your public library.

QUALITY

Quality refers to the condition of the garment's appearance and construction. Sometimes quality can be improved by simple repairs or replacements. Restitching hems and seams, changing buttons, adding snaps or hooks and eyes, and mending small tears and holes usually take only a few minutes to do.

Seams and Hems

Restitching a seam or a hem is an easy way to improve quality. Sometimes the stitches break, creating openings in the seam or a sagging hemline. You can repair the stitches with machine or hand stitching.

Sometimes a hem in a new garment puckers or pulls. The stitches may be very obvious on the right side of the garment. To make it look better, remove the old stitches and restitch the hem. Be sure that your stitching does not show on the outside. See the Sewing Handbook for instructions.

Buttons and Fasteners

Changing buttons can upgrade a new garment or add life to an old one. Sometimes manufacturers use inexpensive buttons to help

Knowing how to hand and machine sew will help to make your redesign plans a success.

keep the cost of clothes down. Old buttons sometimes fade after many washings or cleanings. Replacing these buttons will improve the appearance of a garment.

Sometimes snaps or hooks and eyes on ready-to-wear clothes are not stitched securely. You can restitch these fasteners quickly by hand. You can also add a snap or hook and eye at a neckline, front closing, or waistband. This will help hold the fabric together more securely or smoothly. Refer to the Sewing Handbook for sewing methods.

Small Tears and Holes

Small tears and holes in fabric often can be mended invisibly with tiny stitches. A patch can also be applied underneath a hole by fusing or stitching. Or you can cover up a hole with a decorative appliqué or trim.

Worn or Stained Areas

Sometimes an area of a garment becomes worn or frayed, while the rest of the garment is in excellent condition.

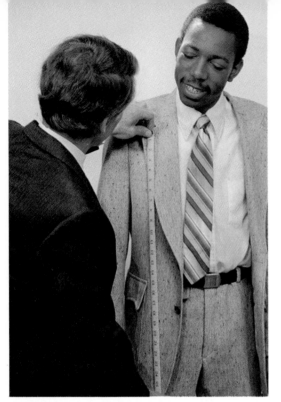

A good fit means that you will be comfortable in the garment and will wear it often.

Elbows of a sweater, jacket, or heavy shirt can be covered with oval patches that are top-stitched or fused to the area. Use contrasting fabric, such as leather, suede, corduroy, or flannel.

Apply a row of trim, fold-over braid, or bias binding to hide the worn edge of a sleeve or pants leg. Patches can be stitched or pressed to the inside or outside of a pants leg to reinforce the knee. Stubborn stains that cannot be removed can be hidden with trim or appliqués.

FIT

How a garment fits affects both your appearance and comfort. Are your black pants so long that they hang down over your shoes? If so, you may seldom wear them because you know that they do not look right. Or perhaps a waistband is so tight that your skirt or slacks are uncomfortable to wear. Moving the hook or button over just a little bit may give you the added comfort that you need.

A garment that you bought in September may be too short by February. Or you may receive a jacket handed down from an older brother or sister. It coordinates well with your wardrobe, but it is just a little too big for you. All of these fitting problems may result in clothes not being worn.

Most minor fitting problems can be corrected with some time and basic sewing skills. For more major problems, better sewing skills are usually needed. If you or someone in your family does not have this experience, it may be economical for you to pay a dressmaker or tailor to alter the garment for you.

Length

Most garments can be shortened easily. Hems of skirts, dresses, jackets and tops can be measured, refolded, and restitched. So can sleeves and pants that do not have cuffs. Cuffed garments require extra planning and construction steps.

When shortening a hemline, you may need to trim away some of the new hem allowance. Most hems should be no wider than 2″ to 3″ (5–6.6 cm) in width. A too-wide hem can add bulk and result in a hem that is uneven and too obvious. You will learn the specifics of hemming in the Sewing Handbook.

It may not be as easy to lengthen a garment as it is to shorten it. First, you must check the existing hem allowance. See if there is enough fabric to create the added length. If not, you may be able to add wide hem facing tape on the inside of the garment to complete the hem.

Second, you must be sure that the old hemline will not show.

For used garments, check the edge of the hemline for signs of soil, wear, and a permanent fold line. Even some new garments have a hemline crease that is impossible to remove.

One solution may be to cover the original hemline with trim or several rows of machine stitching. Too often, however, this method looks like it is a cover-up instead of being part of the garment design.

Width

Adjusting the width of a garment is often more complicated than adjusting its length. Most minor width adjustments can be made at the side seams of the garment. The amount to be adjusted is distributed equally between the two side seams.

For example, if you want to adjust the width of a skirt or pair of pants 1″ (2.5 cm), you will adjust each side seam a total of ½″ (1.3 cm). Since each side seam has two layers of fabric, you will sew the new seam only ¼″ (6 mm) from the original seam. This will give you an adjustment of ¼″ (6 mm) on the left front, the left back, the right front, and the right back for a total of 1″ (2.5 cm).

To take in a garment, or make it smaller, you will stitch the new seam within the garment itself. To let out a garment, or make it larger, you will stitch the new seam outside the original seam in the seam allowance. Therefore, it is extremely important to check the width of the seam allowances to be sure that there is enough fabric to stitch a new seam.

Some ready-to-wear garments have seams that are trimmed and finished to ¼″ (6 mm). With such a narrow seam allowance, you would not be able to make the garment wider.

When adjusting a garment's width, always pin the new seams and try on the garment before you stitch. Have someone else help you check the fit. You do not want to create any new problems while trying to solve the original one.

COLOR

Redesigning clothes through color can open up many alternatives for your wardrobe. You can quickly change the mood or look of an outfit by adding or subtracting color. By mixing and matching clothes and accessories, you can get an updated fashion look. You can add decorative touches to your garment to create a new feeling. Or you can change the color of the garment entirely.

Accessories

You can update an outfit by adding new accessories in the latest fashion colors. A new belt, scarf, tie, buttons, or jewelry can create a new look for an old outfit.

Check the fashion magazines and pattern catalogues to see what are the new trends in colors and accessories. This season, a bright red belt may make the right accent. For another season, natural-colored accessories, such as a tan rope belt, may be the important look.

Decorative Trims

Decorative trims can add a touch of color or create a new mood for a garment. Lace can add romantic feeling to clothes, while rickrack gives a more casual look. Braids and ribbons can be tailored or dressy. Piping used around the yoke of a shirt gives it a Western look. Embroidery and appliqués can create very colorful accents.

The use of trims gives you an opportunity to express your creativity while redesigning. But use color accents carefully. Aim for a well-coordinated, balanced look. One well-selected color of trim is usually better than a combination of several colors in a garment.

You must also consider the overall effect of the trim on the garment. Just covering up a spot may look awkward. You might want to add two rows of trim instead of one. Or you can repeat the trim at the hem of the sleeve, as well as at the bottom of the skirt. An appliqué on both patch pockets may look better than on one.

Experiment by pinning the trim in place before you attach it permanently. Most trims and appliqués can be stitched in place by hand or by machine. Embroidery takes longer to apply than ready-made trims, but it adds a special, personalized design. Refer to the Sewing Handbook for different applications of trims.

DYEING FABRIC

Another alternative for redesigning clothes is to change the color entirely by dyeing the fabric. Fabric dyes are available in liquid and powder forms. Read the instructions on the package carefully. Some fibers will dye better than others. When dyeing fabrics, it is important to follow the step-by-step directions exactly. Otherwise, the dye may not be permanent, and the color may fade when you wash the garment.

Special dyeing techniques can also be used on fabrics. Two of these are tie dyeing and batik, which are described in Chapter 9.

Advantages of Recycling

Recycling means *to reclaim items for another use.* You can recycle clothes by passing them along to others, or by making something new out of them. Recycling helps to prevent waste by extending the life of either the garment or the fabric. Something that you might no longer need could exactly meet the needs of someone else.

Many families and communities are involved in recycling glass, aluminum, and paper. This helps to conserve our resources, both now and in the future. **Conservation** is *the protection and preservation, or saving, of resources.*

Recycling clothing also helps to conserve resources. Fabrics are made from either natural or manufactured fibers. Recycling helps to conserve not only the sources of these fibers but also the energy used to manufacture the fibers and fabrics.

Recycling helps families to save money. You can pass a garment along to another family member at no cost. You can utilize old fabrics for new projects at no cost. You can sell clothing at garage sales or consignment stores.

A **consignment store** is *one that will pay you a percentage of the selling price after the store sells your clothes.* In turn, you can buy clothing at these locations for a lower price than you would pay for new clothing.

However, you need to check each item for quality and size. Used clothing is sold "as is" and cannot be returned. Or you can help other families save money by passing your clothing on to them or donating it to charities.

PASSING IT ON

Wearable clothing can be handed down to a younger brother, sister, cousin, or neighbor. Or you can pass it along to a friend.

Sometimes friends will have a clothing swap. Your best friend may have always admired the red sweater that you no longer wear. You might trade it for a shirt or lightweight jacket that your friend no longer likes. Now you each have added to your wardrobe without spending any money.

Your usable, but unwanted, clothing can be passed on to someone less fortunate. You can donate it to religious groups or other charitable organizations that give clothing to the needy.

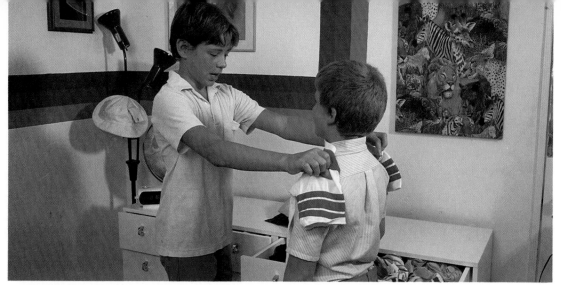

The most common form of passing on clothing is within a family. Younger brothers and sisters can wear older siblings outgrown garments.

They may help families that have lost their belongings in a fire or flood. Check in your area for organizations that accept used clothing.

You can also sell used clothing at tag sales, garage sales, bazaars, and flea markets, for a little money. Some secondhand stores or thrift shops may also pay you on consignment for your clothing. You will read more about these types of retail operations in Chapter 20.

OTHER USES

If clothing can no longer be passed along to others, you can recycle the fabric. Make an accessory item, clothing for children, or a patchwork project. Or save it for cleaning use.

Accessories

Be imaginative. What accessory could you make from an old pair of jeans? How about a sturdy tote bag made from one of the pants legs. An old sweatshirt could be turned into a vest or a pillow.

And do not forget other fabrics in your home.

A tablecloth that is badly stained could be transformed into a set of placemats. A colorful old towel can make a carry-all for the beach.

Children's Clothes

Used fabric can be employed for many children's clothes, from a corduroy jumper made from an old skirt, to a quilted robe made from a

Children love to dress up. Bits of fabric, old shirts, belts, and costume jewelry will be used.

larger robe. Shorts, pants, jackets, shirts, dresses, and sleepwear can all be made from fabric that is in good condition. And because it is old but in good shape, it will feel better to wear than new fabric.

Many children like the feel of such fabrics, because they are softer and more comfortable. It is the same for adults who choose to pay a premium price for prewashed designer blue jeans.

Old clothing can also be used for playing "dressup." Children love to have clothes that they can use for all types of creative play. A box of old clothes is an excellent source of inspiration for costume parties, Halloween, and class plays at school.

Patchwork Projects

Patchwork is a method of sewing together small fabric shapes to create a new, decorative piece of fabric. In Chapter 9, you read about patchwork quilts being used for centuries. Today, patchwork can be used for a variety of projects, in addition to quilts. You can make pillows, wallhangings, placemats, tote bags, and stuffed toys from patchwork.

Patchwork clothing, such as vests, jackets, belts, and aprons, can be created by using a variety of patchwork designs. You can get ideas from craft books or magazines for planning patchwork projects.

You can be very creative in your fabric choices, combining colors and prints that blend or contrast. However, do select fabrics that are firmly woven and compatible in care. Since the pieces of fabric will be stitched together, it is important that they wear and clean the same.

Household Use

What do you use to dust your furniture? Every family needs some household rags for

Patchwork quilting is fun. First, collect patches and then arrange them in color combinations.

cleaning. Small pieces of fabric can be used for dusting and wiping. Larger pieces of fabric can be used to cover the floor when painting, sanding, or staining. When clothing is too worn or damaged to be repaired or recycled, the fabric may be still good enough for additional use. The same is true for old towels, sheets, and other household fabrics.

Save fabrics that will be absorbent, such as 100% cotton or cotton blends. Be sure to remove all buttons, zippers, snaps, hooks and eyes, or other fasteners. These may scratch the surfaces that you clean. You may want to cut off any trims or bulky areas, such as pockets, to make the fabric easier to handle.

You can also use some items, such as stockings and panty hose, for stuffing toys and pillows. Buttons, fasteners, and trims can be saved for use on future projects.

Finally, fibers can be recycled for use in padding and in paper. Some organizations collect old clothing and fabrics for such recycling.

Redesigning and recycling are ways of using an item to its fullest potential. Not only can you use your creative skills, but you can help to save both personal and natural resources. And you can gain a great deal of satisfaction from helping others meet their clothing needs.

Chapter 13 Review

Summary

Redesigning and recycling can help you stretch your clothing budget and update your wardrobe at the same time. Redesigning can change the style, quality, fit, or color of a garment so that it will better meet your needs. Redesigning also offers the opportunity to be creative and express your individuality. Recycling can reclaim items for another use. You can recycle clothes by passing them along to others or by making something new out of them, such as accessories, children's clothes, patchwork projects, or household rags.

Questions

1. Define redesigning and recycling.
2. When redesigning a garment, what are four changes that you could make?
3. What are three benefits of redesigning clothes?
4. How can older clothes be updated for a newer, more fashionable look?
5. What specific steps can be taken to improve the quality of clothes that are redesigned?
6. What must be considered about the fabric before lengthening a hem or letting out a seam?
7. How can color be added to clothes without dyeing the fabric?
8. When adding decorative trim to a garment, how should the principles of balance be applied?
9. List three advantages of recycling clothes.
10. When clothes can no longer be worn by yourself or others, how can you recycle the fabric? Give examples.

Activities

1. Choose one item in your wardrobe to redesign for yourself or for another family member. Or you could recycle the fabric into a new clothing or household item. Explain what steps or techniques you would use. If possible, take *before* and *after* photographs to share with the class.

2. Write an article for your school newspaper, explaining the process and value of redesigning and recycling clothes.

3. Contact stores and organizations in your community that recycle clothing. What are their policies and methods of collecting and distributing the clothing?

You Be the Expert

You are working during the summer as a dressmaker. A customer brings in some clothes that look "out of date," but the fabrics are in excellent condition. What suggestions could you make for restyling jackets, skirts, and pants to make them more fashionable?

4 Fabrics and Their Care

14 | *The World of Fabrics*

What does a pair of socks have in common with a felt-tip pen? What does an artificial heart have in common with a T-shirt? Many socks are made of nylon; the felt-tip pen has a nylon point. The artificial heart has a lining made from finely woven polyester; the T-shirt is probably a cotton and polyester knit.

Fibers and fabrics are all around us. Sometimes their uses are very obvious. Everyone expects a shirt to be made from fabric. At other times, their uses are the result of several technologies working together. A knowledge of textile chemistry and a knowledge of medicine helped to create the artificial heart.

After reading this chapter, you will be able to:

- explain why a knowledge of fabric can help you to make wise consumer decisions,
- describe the different characteristics of fabrics,
- explain how fabric characteristics affect fabric performance,
- evaluate fabrics for use in clothing, home furnishings, and recreational items.

Fabrics Are Everywhere

According to the American Textile Manufacturers Institute, the average American uses 60 pounds of textiles each year. This is twice as much as a person living in Western Europe uses and 10 times as much as a person living in any other part of the world.

Not all of these textiles go into clothing. A large amount is used for home furnishings. Take a look around your home. You may see curtains or draperies, upholstery or slipcovers, carpets or rugs, bedspreads, sheets, blankets, towels, table linens, lamp shades, and closet accessories made of fabric.

Clothing and home furnishings still do not account for all the textiles that are used in the world. Other uses for textiles include the recreational, industrial, medical, and transportation areas.

Carbon-fiber reinforced plastics increase the strength, but decrease the weight, of tennis rackets, fishing rods, golf clubs, ski poles, and the hulls of some sailboats and canoes. Fibers are used for rope, cording, and fishing lines.

Buildings are designed and built by using huge "skins" made of fabrics. This type of structure is popular for restaurants, stadiums, theaters, parking garages, and other public gathering places. Disposable surgical products, such as gowns, surgical masks, and bandages, are made from nonwoven fabrics.

The next time that you are in a car, bus, train, or airplane, take a good look around you. You will discover that fibers and fabrics have many functional, decorative, and comfort uses. Consider polyester tires and seat belts, synthetic fillers for seat cushions, vinyl or woven seat covers, carpets, and more. Fabrics used in both

The first balloons were made of canvas sail. Now they are made of special lightweight fabric.

private and commercial transportation vehicles have been developed to take continuous hard wear.

Some fabrics are chosen for their strength. Others, such as airplane carpets, are chosen for their flame-resistant qualities. The space program uses fibers and fabrics in spacesuits, interiors of the spacecrafts, booster rockets, and even the heat shield of the space shuttle.

Fabric Knowledge Is Important

If you take the time to learn about fibers and fabrics, your knowledge will help to improve your consumer skills. You will have the confidence that you need to make wise fabric choices, whether you are buying your clothes or making them. Once you have made your selection, this knowledge will help you to take better care of your purchases. Your clothes will last longer, and you will be more satisfied with them.

As an experiment, take a close look at the garments that are hanging in your closet. Which items still look and feel good, even though you have worn them over and over again?

Take your favorites out of the closet, and look at the labels that are sewn into the back of the neck or along one of the major seams. Labels, by law, must identify the fiber content of the fabric and a recommended care procedure.

Note the fiber contents of your favorite clothing. How are they the same? How are they different? Which fiber or fiber blends have performed well for you?

MAKING YOU A BETTER SHOPPER

When you are aware of the similarities and differences between certain fibers and fabrics, you will be able to better evaluate the textiles that you are thinking about purchasing. You can also make better comparisons between similar items.

Should you buy the wool slacks or the cotton corduroys? Would the woven silk shirt or the polyester knit shirt be best? Do you prefer underwear that is 100% cotton, a cotton blend, or 100% nylon? What type of fabrics should you choose for decorating your new room?

Deciding Which to Buy

Suppose that you are shopping for a new sweatshirt. You have narrowed your choices down to two. Both sweatshirts are the right style and color. The label on one sweatshirt says "100% cotton." The label on the other sweatshirt says "100% acrylic." The cotton sweatshirt is a little more expensive than the acrylic one. Which are you going to buy?

Sometimes, the manufacturer will attach hangtags to the garment that will give you some clues about what to expect from the fabric. These hangtags might include information, such as "easy care" or "will not fade."

However, in order to make the best decision, you will need to know something about the differences between cotton and acrylic. You also need to know something about the type of fabric that is used in sweatshirts. This information will help you decide which sweatshirt is the best value for your money.

CARE OF CLOTHES AND OTHER FABRICS

Fiber and fabric knowledge will also help you to know what to expect when it comes to taking care of your purchases. Labels contain valuable information about a garment's fiber content and its method of care. When you are buying fabric by the yard, this same information is printed on the end of the fabric bolt. The Care Labeling Rule, issued by the Federal Trade Commission, regulates the information that must be listed on the care labels. In Chapter 18, you will learn more about care labels.

Technology

Space-Age Fabrics

Space-age fabrics are being used for active sportswear and outdoor clothing. These new fabrics can keep you warm and dry, even in very cold and wet weather. Runners, skiers, hikers, and climbers want garments that are lightweight, yet insulate well.

Polypropylene does not absorb moisture. Instead, warm moisture is pulled away from the skin to the surface of the fabric. There it can bead up and evaporate. You stay dry and warm, rather than becoming wet and losing body heat while exercising.

Polypropylene, an olefin fiber, is being used for all types of exercise and outdoor wear—from turtlenecks and underwear, to hats and gloves. With its excellent wicking ability, polypropylene is replacing cotton, wool, and silk as the next-to-the-skin layer for outdoor activities.

Gore-Tex® is another unique material. By stretching it as thin as possible during the manufacturing process, billions of tiny holes per square inch (6.45/square cm) are created. Garments made from this material can breathe through the micropores, yet are waterproof.

Because Gore-Tex® is far too thin to be made into clothing, it is lamiated between layers of sturdier fabrics. Unlike traditional rubberized raingear, Gore-Tex® is comfortable to wear. On the outside it sheds raindrops, but on the inside perspiration can pass freely through the material to the outside. And it's windproof, too.

Characteristics of fabrics used for clothing often differ from those used for upholstery, rugs, towels, and other household uses.

Fabric Characteristics and Performance

Fabrics have many different characteristics, or qualities. These characteristics affect a fabric's performance, the way that the fabric reacts when it is used. Our own expectations about fabrics depend on the type of garment or item. You would not expect the fabric in a prom dress to be as durable, as soil-resistant, or to last as long as the fabric on an upholstered couch. You would not expect a scarf to be as absorbent as a bath towel. And you would not expect your own raincoat to be as water-repellent as a fireman's coat.

What determines how a fabric performs? It is a combination of three factors:

1. how the fibers are used,
2. how the fibers are formed into fabrics,
3. how the finishes are applied to the fabric.

In Chapters 15, 16, and 17, you will learn about specific fibers, fabrics, and finishes.

FABRIC CHARACTERISTICS

Fabric characteristics are those traits that distinguish one fabric from another. These include the *type of fabric construction, texture, hand,* and *weight.*

Type of Fabric Construction

Some types of fabrics are easily identified by their construction. You can recognize terry cloth by its loops. Velvet has a *raised surface,* or **pile**, while ribbed corduroy has rows of pile. Satin has a shiny look produced by its special type of weave. Refer to Chapter 16 for various fabric descriptions.

Texture

Texture refers to how the surface of a fabric looks and feels. It can be smooth, rough, dull, shiny, nubby, fuzzy, or a combination. In Chapter 12, you learned how fabric texture can influence the illusion of size. Texture also can express a feeling or mood, such as "dressy" or "casual."

As a result, the texture of a fabric often dictates its end use. For example, a rough, dull texture would look out of place in a formal environment of smooth, silky fabrics.

Hand

How a fabric handles and feels is called the fabric's **hand**. It can be described as soft, firm, crisp, stiff, or *drapeable,* which is the ability to hang in loose folds. You can learn how a fabric handles or behaves by draping it over your hands.

Some fabrics, such as crepe and jersey, have a soft, drapeable hand. They are appropriate for garments with full silhouettes or design details, such as gathers, soft pleats, or ruffles.

Other fabrics, such as denim and corduroy, have a stiffer, firmer hand. They usually look best when they are made into more tailored clothes.

Some fabrics, such as gabardine and linen, have a crisp hand. They are appropriate for garments with straight silhouettes and design details, such as pressed pleats.

Some fabrics, such as taffeta and chintz, can be both soft and crisp.

Weight

Fabrics can range in weight from very light to very heavy. Weight is determined by the yarns and the type of fabric construction.

Chiffon and batiste are very lightweight fabrics, while canvas and coating fabrics are

Tens of thousands of fabrics are available today. You can make good fabric choices by knowing something about their characteristics.

heavyweight fabrics. Bulky fabrics, such as thick knits and some fake furs, are also considered heavyweight.

Weight is not always related to hand. A lightweight fabric can be very soft or very crisp. Although a woolen blanket is heavier than a cotton sheet, the sheet is crisper than the blanket.

Even the same type of fabric can vary in weight. For example, velvet can be lightweight enough to be gathered into a soft evening skirt. Velvet can also be heavy and thick for use in draperies and upholstery.

If you own a pair of cotton slacks and a cotton shirt, you will probably find that the fabric in the slacks is heavier than the fabric in the shirt. Why is this usually so?

FABRIC PERFORMANCE

Performance refers to how a fabric will react during the life of the garment or item. Does it wrinkle? Is it comfortable to wear? Does it breathe, letting air and moisture pass from the body? Does it resist or absorb stains? Will it shrink when laundered? Is it strong and durable? Does it need ironing? Sometimes a fabric's performance is a result of the fibers that are used. At other times, special finishes can be applied to the fabric to provide characteristics that are not natural to the fibers.

Fabric performance can be divided into three areas: *durability, comfort,* and *ease of care.*

Durability

Durability refers to all *those characteristics that affect how long you will be able to wear or to use a particular garment or item.* These include *strength, shape retention, resiliency, abrasion resistance,* and *colorfastness.*

- **Strength**. Is the fabric going to be strong enough for the way that you plan to use it? Different fibers have different **tensile strengths**, or *ability to withstand tension or pulling.* Strength is also related to the fabric construction. Tightly woven or knitted fabrics are usually stronger than loosely woven or knitted fabrics. For example, canvas is used as chair seats, while a sheer open-weave fabric is used for curtains.

- **Shape Retention**. Will the fabric retain its shape after wearing or cleaning? Or will it stretch so that you end up with baggy knees and elbows? Shape can also be lost when the fabric is washed or machine-dried. Some fibers shrink when exposed to water or heat.

- **Resiliency.** Is the fabric **resilient,** or *able to spring or bounce back into shape after crushing or wrinkling?* Will the wrinkles hang out of the garment, or must the fabric be pressed? The fibers in a wool carpet may flatten underneath a piece of heavy furniture. But they will spring back into shape when the carpet is steamed.

- **Abrasion Resistance.** Will the fabric resist abrasion? **Abrasion** is a *worn spot that can develop when the fabric rubs against something.* This can occur on the inside of a collar where it rubs the back of your neck, or at your side where you carry your books. Some fabrics can pill, or form tiny balls of fiber on the fabric.

- **Colorfastness.** Will the color fade when the fabric is washed? Will the colors *bleed,* or run, into other areas of the garment? **Colorfastness** means that *the color in the fabric will not change.* It will not fade from washing, from chlorine in a pool, or from exposure to sunlight. However, some fabrics are designed to fade or bleed. Some denim blue jeans are meant to lighten when washed. Madras, a woven plaid fabric, is meant to bleed so that the plaid becomes softer and less distinct.

The new fabrics used in tents today make them cool in daytime and warm and dry in evening.

Comfort

Comfort is another factor to consider when selecting fabric. A fabric can be the right weight and texture, durable and easy to care for, but uncomfortable to wear. It may be too hot, too cold, or too clammy. A fabric's *absorbency, wicking ability, breatheability,* and *stretchability* all affect how comfortable the fabric is on your body.

- **Absorbency.** This term refers to *how well the fabric takes in moisture.* Some fibers, such as cotton and wool, are very absorbent. Other fibers, such as polyester and nylon, are not. That is why you may feel very clammy when you wear 100% polyester fabric on a hot summer day. Your perspiration stays on the surface of your skin and is not absorbed by the fabric. That is also why you can dry yourself faster with a terry cloth towel made from 100% cotton than with one made from a cotton and polyester blend. However, special finishes can be applied to improve the absorbency of fabrics.

- **Wicking.** This term refers to a fabric's ability to draw moisture away from your body, so that the moisture can evaporate. The wicking ability of some fibers makes up for the fact that they are not very absorbent. Olefin, a fabric that you will be learning more about, has wicking properties.

What fabric performance features should you look for when shopping for exercise clothing?

- **Breatheability.** This characteristic is another important factor to consider when choosing comfortable fabrics. It refers to *the ability for air or moisture to pass through fabric.* Some fabrics have special finishes to prevent rain and moisture from penetrating the fabric. These finishes also prevent body moisture from evaporating through the fabric. That is why your feet and your body often sweat when you wear rubber boots and a rubber raincoat. Manufacturers sometimes compensate for this in waterproof clothes by adding small grommet holes under the arms to act as air vents. You will learn more about waterproof and water-resistant finishes in Chapter 17.

- **Stretchability.** This term describes *the fabric's ability to "give" and stretch with the body.* How much stretchability you will need in your clothes depends on your activities. You might want extra stretchability in your swimsuit, ski pants, and exercise wear.

Ease of Care

The type of care that a fabric requires determines how easy it is to care for a garment or other item. Washing, dry cleaning, ironing, brushing, and folding are all methods of fabric care.

Some fabrics require more routine care than others. When selecting fabrics, choose those that match your lifestyle. *Washability, soil* and *stain resistance,* and *wrinkle resistance* are some factors that influence fabric care.

- **Washability.** Can the fabric be washed or must it be dry cleaned? Over a long period of time, your dry cleaning bills may add up to more than the cost of the garment. Do you have the time and space to hand wash and dry different garments? Although it is easy to hand wash a sweater, will you set aside the time to do it? Will the fabric shrink more than one or two percent? If so, it might affect the fit of the garment.

Lifestyle

Accessories Make the Room

Here are 10 project ideas to make your room something special.

1. A *fitted coverlet* makes your bed in a breeze—just tie it on! Snug corners keep it looking neat at all times.

2. *Fabric-filled-in-shutters* add a nice touch of color to your room, while giving you lots of privacy. Panels can be changed whenever you want a new look.

3. A *coordinated window shade* can be made to match the coverlet or shutter panels. Kits for roll-up shades make it easy to do.

4. An *exercise mat* unrolls, and doubles as an extra sleeping pad for overnight guests.

5. A *pillow corner* is a great place to entertain friends or to relax by yourself—make them in assorted sizes, shapes, and fabrics.

6. A *duffle bag* will help you organize your gear for any sport.

7. *Pockets* make a handy wall organizer for school supplies, sewing tools, and accessories. Design it to suit your personal needs.

8. *Desk accessories* take on a special look when you cover them with fabric. Try a pencil cup, address book, book ends, picture frame, or even a wastebasket.

9. A *laundry stash* can coordinate with any of your other room accessories, while keeping your clothes out of sight.

10. A *wallhanging* is a great way to accent your room. Make a fabric collage with glue or appliqué, paint on fabric, tie dye a design, or stretch printed fabric on a frame.

- **Stain and Spot Resistance.** Is the fabric resistant to stains and spots? Some fibers absorb stains, but special finishes can help the fabric to repel the stain or to release it during cleaning. Carpets, upholstery, coats and jackets, and children's clothes often have special finishes.

- **Wrinkle Resistance.** Do you have to iron the fabric every time that it is washed? Do you have to press a garment before every wearing? Or will the wrinkles hang out after a short time? Fibers have different characteristics that affect wrinkling. For example, polyester is very wrinkle-resistant, but cotton and rayon wrinkle easily. Special finishes, such as durable press, can be applied to fabrics to improve their wrinkle resistance.

Function, expectations, personal taste, and compatibility all enter into fabric selection.

FABRIC GUIDELINES

Whether you are buying or making a bedspread, a swimsuit, a sweater, or a tent, you should ask yourself the same four questions.

1. *What is the function of this garment or item?*
   It should meet the purpose for which you want it. If you need a coat to wear in the rain, does the fabric have a water-repellent finish? If you need a coat for warmth, does it have insulating qualities?

2. *Will this fabric meet your expectations?*
   Examine it closely. Feel its texture and weight. Is it durable enough to withstand its expected use? Read the labels and hangtags for information about performance and care. Can the sweater be washed? Must the tablecloth be ironed? Is the jogging suit absorbent? Must the dark color be washed separately? Will the fabric shrink?

3. *Does this fabric reflect your personal taste?*
   Do you like the color, pattern, and texture of the fabric? Will it coordinate with other items in your wardrobe or in your decorating scheme?

4. *Is this fabric compatible with your personal values?*
   Sometimes, in order to make a final decision, you will need to decide which characteristics are more important to you. You may have to make trade-offs. For example, if you are looking for a dressy garment, you may have to sacrifice washability. If you are looking for a garment that is very comfortable, you may not find it in your favorite color.

Fabrics may even be more of a part of our world in the future. Fiber technology is developing new and advanced products in textile laboratories. Scientists and textile engineers are creating new uses for fibers and fabrics. The next three chapters introduce you to the inside world of fabrics, beginning with fibers — the basic ingredient of fabrics.

Summary

Knowledge of fabrics can help you be a better shopper. It can help you take better care of your clothes and other fabrics. Fabrics have many different characteristics. These include type of fabric construction, texture, hand, and weight. A fabric's performance is affected by the fibers used, the way the yarns are formed into fabric, and the finishes applied to the fabric. Performance can be judged by a fabric's durability, comfort, and ease of care. When evaluating fabrics, you should consider the item's function and your own expectations, tastes, and values.

Questions

1. What are four areas, other than clothing, in which fabrics are used?

2. How can knowledge about fibers and fabrics help to improve your consumer skills?

3. Explain the relationship between fabric characteristics and fabric performance.

4. Identify four general fabric characteristics that distinguish one fabric from another.

5. What is the difference between a fabric's hand and its weight? Give examples of each.

6. List at least four fabric characteristics that affect durability.

7. Why is comfort an important factor to consider when selecting fabrics?

8. Some fabrics require less care than others. Which characteristics would be most important for children's clothes? upholstery? business suits? casual shirts? table linens?

9. What four questions should you ask yourself when you are selecting any item made of fabric?

Activities

1. Separate your wardrobe into two categories: fabrics that you enjoy wearing, and those that you do not. Analyze whether there are any similarities in the characteristics of each group of fabrics.

2. Visit a sporting goods store to see the various types of fabrics used in clothing, equipment, and accessories. Read labels for fiber and care information. What similarities and differences do you find?

3. Bring a garment or fabric item to class that did not perform or last in the manner in which you had expected. Discuss the factors that might have led to this poor performance.

You Be the Expert

You are working part-time in a furniture store. When customers ask you about the performance of various upholstery fabrics, what guidelines could you give them about durability and ease of care?

15 | *Fibers*

Fray or unravel a scrap of any fabric until you find a single thread or yarn. Then untwist the thread or yarn so that you can pull out one hairlike unit. It will be so fine that you can scarcely see it. That is a **fiber.** Tiny as it is, a fiber is *the basic unit from which fabric is made.*

Not all fibers can be made into fabrics. A fiber must have certain characteristics, which are also called *properties,* that make it suitable for fabric. To make it easier to understand the various fibers and their properties, fibers are grouped according to their origin.

After reading this chapter, you will be able to:

- describe the fiber characteristics needed for use in fabrics,
- identify the different classifications of fibers,
- explain how manufactured fibers are made,
- list the various fibers and describe their characteristics.

Fibers for Fabrics

Take the fiber that you have pulled out and examine it closely. Is it long or short? Is it straight or crimped? Is it dull or shiny, smooth or coarse? Pull on it. Does it break easily? Does it spring back when stretched, or does it stay extended?

These are just a few of the many different fiber characteristics that you can identify. If you would look at the fiber under a microscope, you would see even more identifying features.

ESSENTIAL PROPERTIES

For use in fabrics, a fiber should have four essential properties:

1. It must be fairly *strong* or it is worthless.

2. The fiber must be *pliable,* or able to bend without breaking. Otherwise it cannot be twisted into a yarn and then woven or knitted into fabric.

3. The fiber must have some *elasticity,* or ability to stretch and return to shape. This characteristic influences the fabric's stretchability and resiliency.

4. Finally, the fiber must be *long* enough to be able to be spun into yarns.

In addition, each fiber will have its own individual characteristics that will influence appearance and performance. You learned about many of these characteristics in the previous chapter.

FIBER CLASSIFICATION

Fibers come from various sources, or origins. *Those that come from natural sources,* such as plants and animals, are called **natural fibers.**

Other fibers are the result of scientific experimentation and development. These "test tube" fibers are called **manufactured fibers.**

In many publications and advertisements, you will see manufactured fibers referred to as *man-made* fibers. Sometimes the term *synthetic* is used, although not all manufactured fibers are produced from chemicals.

Fibers are also classified by name. Each fiber has a **generic name,** which indicates *a general classification of fibers of similar composition.* Cotton, wool, nylon, rayon, and polyester are examples of generic names.

In addition, manufacturers of manufactured fibers have a **trade name** for each fiber that they produce. These names are *registered as trademarks and are protected by law.* No other company can legally use the same name for the same type of product.

For example, polyester is a generic name for a manufactured fiber. Its trade name may be Dacron®, a DuPont product; Kodel®, an Eastman product; or Fortrel®, a Celanese product.

The Textiles Fiber Products Identification Act requires that the generic name of fibers be listed on the label of all textile products. Trade names are optional. Manufacturers may include them on labels or hangtags.

Natural Fibers

Natural fibers come from plants and animals. They exist as part of the natural element, or source.

Cotton, flax, and ramie are plant fibers. They are made from **cellulose,** which is *a fibrous substance found in plants.* Cotton is a seed fiber. Flax and ramie are stem fibers. A less common plant fiber is jute.

Wool and silk are animal fibers and are made

of protein. Wool comes from sheep, and silk is spun by silkworms. Other animal fibers include the hair fibers, such as cashmere, mohair, camel, alpaca, vicuna, and angora.

Two other natural sources of fibers are asbestos and rubber.

COTTON

Cotton comes from the *boll,* or seed pod, of the cotton plant. After the seed pods are harvested, the cotton fiber is separated from the seeds and processed.

Under a microscope, a cotton fiber looks like a twisted ribbon. Some types of cotton plants produce seed bolls with fibers as long as 2″ (5 cm). These are known as *long staple fibers* and are used for fine quality cotton fabrics.

Cotton is strong, absorbent, comfortable to wear, and washable. It can be washed in high temperatures and with strong soaps or detergents. Cotton accepts dyes readily.

However, cotton wrinkles easily and can shrink. It also mildews easily and is flammable. Special finishes can be applied to cotton fabrics for wrinkle resistance, shrinkage control, mildrew resistance, and flame retardance. Cotton can also be **mercerized** to *give the fiber added strength and luster.*

Cotton is used for a wide variety of fabrics, for both clothing and home furnishings. It is often combined with other fibers.

FLAX AND LINEN

Flax is the name of the fiber that comes from the inside of the stem of the flax plant. When flax is made into fabric it is called linen. The flax fibers can be separated from each other by soaking the stems in chemically treated water. Under a microscope, a flax fiber looks like a bamboo pole.

Flax is stronger than cotton and is very absorbent. It is lint-free and dries more quickly

The cotton fiber is bursting out of the pods. Cotton is the most widely used natural fiber.

The stems of flax plants furnish long fibers that are made into various weights of linen fabric.

than cotton. It can be washed, bleached, and ironed at high temperatures without scorching.

Flax is not very resilient, and it wrinkles easily. It can shrink and be damaged by mildew.

Linen fabric is used for both clothing and home decorating items, such as towels and tableclothes. To reduce its natural tendency to wrinkle, linen is often given a wrinkle-resistant finish or blended with other fibers.

RAMIE AND JUTE

Ramie comes from the stems of China grass that is grown primarily in Southeast Asia. It has a natural silklike luster. When seen under a microscope, ramie is very similar to flax.

Ramie is one of the strongest fibers known. It is very resistant to insects and mildew. However it is stiff and brittle, with poor elasticity and resiliency. As a result, ramie is usually combined with other fibers, such as cotton or flax. It is used in sweaters, knitted tops, shirts, placemats, and upholstery.

Jute is the name of a plant that produces a coarse, rough fiber. It is used primarily for burlap fabric that can be used for gunny sacks, bags, and decorative fabrics. It wrinkles easily, breaks easily along folds, and produces lint. However, jute is inexpensive.

WOOL

Wool comes from the fleece of sheep. Wool from sheep that are less than eight months old is called lamb's wool. The quality of the wool depends on the breed of sheep and the climate in which the animal was raised. Sheep are sheared once or twice a year. The fleece must be washed and then *carded,* or combed.

Wool is a comfortable, durable, and versatile fiber. If you look at a wool fiber through a mi-

Wool is especially good to wear in cold weather. It keeps in body warmth and is very comfortable.

croscope, it is covered with scales. It also looks wavy and crimped. Wool fibers trap air, which in turn prevents the loss of body heat. This helps you to feel warm in cold weather. The overlapping scales help to shed raindrops. Yet wool absorbs moisture from the air or body and still feels dry.

Wool is resilient. The fiber is very springy or elastic and returns to its original shape and size after being stretched. That is why wrinkles and creases will hang or steam out easily. Wool is naturally flame-resistant, and a wool blanket can be used to smother a fire.

Wool has one property that is not shared by other fibers. When heat and moisture are applied to wool, the scales spread and soften slightly. This is called *felting.* If the fabric is rubbed or pressed hard, the scales interlock and the fabric mats and shrinks.

Thus, most wool fabrics should usually be dry cleaned or washed carefully by hand in cold water. Washable wool fabrics have been treated with a special finish to prevent felting, or blended with other fibers, such as nylon.

Wool also can be damaged by moths, carpet beetles, and other insects. Special finishes can

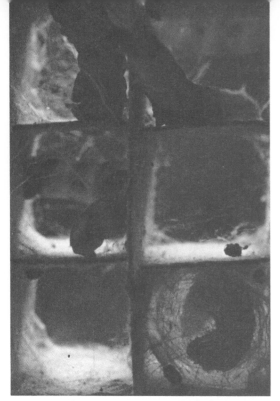

The silkworm larvae in their cubicles are at different stages of spinning their cocoons.

Under a microscope, silk looks like a glass rod with an irregular surface. This surface texture provides its superb **luster,** or *gloss and sheen.*

Silk feels very soft and smooth. It is strong, yet lightweight and comfortable to wear. Silk has elasticity and resists wrinkling. It can be dyed in brilliant colors and prints.

Silk is usually dry cleaned, but some silks can be washed, depending on their dye and finish. Strong soaps, bleaches, perspiration, abrasion, and high ironing temperatures can weaken or discolor silk fabrics.

Silk is used for a variety of fabrics for both clothing and home furnishings. It can range from sheer to heavy, textured fabrics.

SPECIALTY ANIMAL FIBERS

Specialty animal fibers include angora, alpaca, cashmere, camel's hair, mohair, and vicuna. They are usually expensive because they are not available in large quantities. Their characteristics are similar to those of sheep's wool. These specialty fibers may be used alone or with sheep's wool to produce softness or luster effects. Dry cleaning is usually recommended for these fibers.

be applied to wool for moth resistance.

Wool is used for clothing, blankets, carpets, and other household items. Wool fabrics tailor more beautifully than fabrics from other fibers because of wool's ability to be shaped with steam. Wool also wears well and resists abrasion or rubbing. It can also be blended.

SILK

Silk is formed when the silkworm larvae spin their cocoons. The fiber is one continuous filament that can be as long as one mile. The cocoons are harvested before the silkworm emerges. If the worm breaks through the wall of its cocoon, the single filament would be broken into many shorter fibers. The cocoons are placed in a bath, which dissolves the natural gum that holds the fibers together.

RUBBER

Natural rubber is made from a milky liquid, called *latex,* that comes from rubber trees. It is used to waterproof coats, hats, boots, gloves, and aprons. It also can provide elasticity for waistbands, and support garments. It is used as a backing for rugs and for recreational items.

Synthetic rubber is made from chemicals. Spandex, a manufactured fiber, has many more advantages for stretchability in fabrics than does rubber.

Manufactured Fibers

Manufactured fibers come from substances that are found in nature, such as wood pulp, petroleum, natural gas, and air. But unlike cotton, flax, wool, and silk, these substances are not fibers in their original state. Chemical engineers transform these substances into fibers that have specific characteristics.

Since the first manufactured fiber was produced in the United States in 1910, a total of 23 generic manufactured fibers have been developed. Not all of them are currently produced. But each generic fiber differs significantly in its chemical composition.

There are two basic types of manufactured fibers: *cellulosic and noncellulosic.*

Cellulosic fibers are produced primarily from wood pulp with a minimum of chemical steps. The three cellulosic fibers are *rayon, acetate,* and *triacetate.*

Noncellulosic fibers are made from molecules that come from petroleum, natural gas, air, and water. Nylon and polyester are noncellulosic.

Today, fiber research is focusing on modifying manufactured fibers and improving their performance, rather than creating new generic fibers. These variants are sometimes called second-and third-generation fibers.

Fibers can be engineered to produce fabrics that have specific qualities, such as colorfastness or flame resistance for specific end uses. Many of the manufactured fibers are designed to resemble the natural fibers, but with improved performance and care properties.

RAYON

The first of the many manufactured fibers now on the market was rayon. It is a cellulosic fiber that can be produced in many different variations for different end uses. Like cotton and linen, it is absorbent and comfortable to wear. It dyes well and can be printed with bright designs.

Rayon wrinkles easily and can shrink unless specially treated. It is also weak when wet and can be weakened by long exposure to light and high temperatures. However, special finishes can be applied to improve all of these performance qualities.

Rayon is used in a wide variety of clothing and household fabrics. It is often used for blouses, shirts, and linenlike fabrics. It can be washed or dry cleaned.

ACETATE

Acetate is also a cellulosic fiber. Thus, some of its characteristics are similar to those of rayon. It is absorbent and dries faster than rayon. It can be dyed and printed, but special dyes must be used.

Acetate has an attractive hand and appearance. It has a silky feel and drapes well. It is resilient, holds creases well, and is flame-resistant.

Acetate is heat sensitive, so it must be ironed at low temperatures. It also can be dissolved by acetone, which is contained in nail polishes and removers. It may cling to the body unless treated with an antistatic finish.

Many different types of fabrics are made from acetate. Some common ones are satin, taffeta, and silklike fabrics. Usually acetate fabrics are dry cleaned, but some may be washed, depending on care instructions.

TRIACETATE

Triacetate has many similar qualities as acetate. It has good abrasion resistance, wrinkle resistance, and is not as sensitive to heat as ace-

Spinneret

The little silkworm was the inspiration for the production of manufactured fibers. The silkworm gives off a liquid substance through its glands. The substance hardens as it emerges into the air, forming a strand of silk.

Chemists concluded that perhaps a thick syrupy substance could be forced through a metal plate with tiny holes and hardened

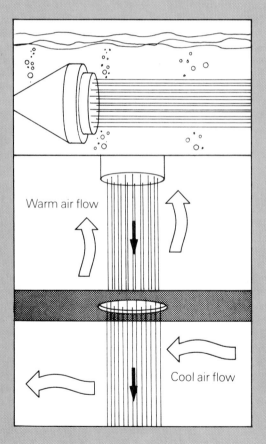

Warm air flow

Cool air flow

into a fiber. The metal plate, called a *spinneret,* is similar to a shower head. It may have from one to thousands of tiny holes.

Cellulosic fibers are made from wood pulp, which is dissolved into a liquid to go through the spinneret. Noncellulosic fibers are made from large molecules, called *polymers,* that are melted or dissolved. After the fibers emerge from the holes in the spinneret, they are hardened.

Three methods of forcing are used:

- *Dry spinning* forces the solution through the tiny holes into warm air where the solvent evaporates and the fiber solidifies.
- *Wet spinning* forces the solution through the tiny holes into another solution where it coagulates into a solid fiber.
- *Melt spinning* first melts the substance and then after being forced through the spinneret hardens it by cooling.

Fibers can be forced from the spinneret in different thicknesses according to the size of holes used. This can create very thin or very thick fibers. Fibers can be forced in different shapes, which gives different characteristics to the fibers.

Also, certain additives can be mixed into the solution before it is used. These can add color or special properties, such as flame resistancy or less transparency.

After being forced through the spinneret, the fibers are stretched to align their molecules and to increase their ultimate strength and elasticity.

tate. One of its unique characteristics is that white triacetate fabrics stay white better than most other fibers. Permanent pleats can be heat set. Triacetate is washable and is used in light to heavyweight fabrics.

NYLON

Nylon was introduced in 1939 as a "miracle fiber" because of its excellent strength, elasticity, and washability. It was the first noncellulosic fiber to be produced. It is lightweight and quick-drying. It is resilient and can be blended with many other fibers.

Because nylon does not absorb moisture well, it can feel uncomfortably warm in hot weather and cool in cold weather. It also collects static electricity, unless specially treated.

Although nylon is easy to wash, it may yellow or gray after a period of time. Some nylon fabrics absorb and hold oil stains. Because it is heat sensitive, it must be ironed at low temperatures.

Nylon is a very versatile fiber with many consumer and industrial uses. You will find nylon in lingerie, pantyhose, swimsuits, outerwear, carpets, tents, and car tires. It may be washed or dry cleaned.

POLYESTER

One of the most widely used manufactured fibers on the market is polyester. It is a strong, high performance fiber that is used alone or blended with many other fibers. It has excellent resilience and outstanding wrinkle resistance. It also washes easily and needs little or no pressing.

Polyester fabrics retain heat-set creases and pleats better than other fabrics. When combined with other fibers, polyester adds strength and wrinkle resistance.

One of the best characteristics of many manufactured fabrics is that they resist stains.

Polyester is not very absorbent. Thus, some 100% polyester fabrics feel hot and uncomfortable in warm weather. Recent developments have improved its moisture absorbency properties.

Some polyester and polyester-blend fabrics have a tendency to pill. Polyester also attracts and holds oil-based soil unless the fabric is pretreated with a soil releasing agent.

Polyester fibers are used in a wide range of textiles that can look like cotton, silk, or wool. Both woven and knitted fabrics in a variety of weights are used for clothing and home furnishings.

Polyester is also used for fillers in parkas, jackets, and comforters. One of its most common uses is blending with cotton for durable press garments, sheets, and other fabrics.

ACRYLIC

Acrylic is a soft, resilient fiber that has high bulking power. It resists wrinkling and offers warmth without added weight. It is often substituted for wool because it is nonallergenic, yet has similar characteristics. It is also washable. Because acrylic fibers have good resistance to sunlight, they are suitable for curtains, draperies, and upholstery.

Some acrylic fabrics will pill or collect static electricity. They may hold oil-based stains. They are heat sensitive and should not be dried or ironed at high temperatures.

Acrylic fibers are used in sweaters, woollike fabrics, carpets, blankets, and upholstery fabrics. They can be washed or dry cleaned.

MODACRYLIC

Modacrylic fibers share many of the characteristics of acrylic fibers. They are often used in pile fabrics, fake furs, children's sleepers, and even wigs.

OLEFIN

Olefin is heat sensitive and does not absorb moisture. It has good abrasion and spot resistance. Hard-to-remove stains, such as ink and grease, can be easily removed from olefin fibers.

Olefin is used in indoor-outdoor carpeting, upholstery, and placemats. Polypropylene, a type of olefin fiber is being used in a variety of outdoor garments and exercise wear. Because it does not absorb moisture and will wick perspiration away from the skin, it keeps the body warm and dry in even cold, damp weather.

ARAMID

Aramid fibers have exceptional strength and heat and flame resistance. Even at high temperatures, these fibers maintain their shape and form. They are also very resistant to abrasion.

Aramid fibers are used in protective clothing, such as firefighters' apparel, race-car drivers' suits, and light weight bullet-proof vests. Aramid is also found in radial tires, cables, aircraft furnishings, and other industrial products.

SPANDEX

Spandex is an elastic fiber with excellent stretchability and recovery. Even after repeated stretching, it still retains its elasticity. Because it is resistant to sunlight, perspiration, oil, and abrasion, this fiber has replaced rubber in most clothing uses.

Using high temperatures when washing or machine drying this fiber can cause it to discolor and lose some of its stretching power. It can also be damaged by chlorine in bleach and in swimming pools.

Spandex can be covered with other yarns or left uncovered. It is used in elastics, underwear, swimwear, and active sportswear.

GLASS

Fiberglass is a fiber produced from glass beads. It has outstanding heat-resistant and nonflammability properties. It is strong, yet can break because it is brittle. It is nonabsorbent and water-repellent.

Fiberglass is not suitable for clothing. However, it is used in draperies, insulation, and in some boat hulls and sports car bodies. The newest use of fiberglass fibers is for fiber optics for communication lines.

METALLIC

Metallic fibers can be added to fabrics, primarily for decoration. They can be made entirely of metal, or they can be combined with plastic. Metallic fibers are used in dressy fabrics, accessories, and industrial products.

Textile Fibers

Natural Fibers	Characteristics
Cotton	Extremely versatile; strong and durable; comfortable, absorbent; wrinkles and shrinks unless treated; will mildew; easily laundered; can be ironed at high temperature
Flax (Linen)	Strong, durable; comfortable, absorbent; does not lint; wrinkles and shrinks unless treated; will mildew; easily laundered; can be ironed at high temperature
Ramie	Silklike luster; very strong; resistant to insects and mildew; stiff and brittle with poor elasticity and resiliency; usually combined with other fibers; washable
Wool	Very versatile and durable; provides warmth; very resilient; absorbs moisture; can shrink and be damaged by insects; dry cleaned, sometimes washable
Silk	Natural luster; strong and smooth; absorbent; weakened by sunlight and perspiration; usually dry cleaned, sometimes washable

Manufactured Fibers (Trade Names)	Characteristics
Acetate (Celanese, Chromspun)	Silklike appearance; soft and drapeable; may wrinkle and fade; dries quickly; resistant to shrinking, moths, mildew; usually dry cleaned; heat sensitive; damaged by acetone
Acrylic (Acrilan, Creslan)	Soft, warm, and lightweight; wrinkle-resistant; resistant to moths and sunlight; may pill; may accumulate static electricity; dry cleaned or laundered; heat sensitive
Aramid (Nomex, Kevlar)	Exceptional strength; exceptional heat and flame resistance; very resistant to abrasion
Modacrylic (Verel)	Soft and resilient; retains shape; abrasion- and flame-resistant; quick-drying; resistant to moths, mildew, and sunlight; dry cleaned or laundered; very heat sensitive
Nylon (Antron, Cantrece, Celanese)	Very strong and resilient; lustrous; does not absorb moisture; dries quickly; easily laundered, but may yellow or gray; heat sensitive, press at low temperature
Olefin (Herculon)	Nonabsorbent, with wicking properties; strong and lightweight; quick-drying; resistant to abrasion, soil, mildew, perspiration, weather; washable; heat sensitive
Polyester (Dacron, Fortrel, Kodel, Trevia)	Excellent wrinkle resistance; strong and resistant to abrasion; blends well with other fibers; dries quickly; low absorbency; easily laundered, needs little or no pressing
Rayon (Arvil, Fabro)	Absorbs moisture; soft and comfortable; drapeable; may wrinkle or shrink unless treated; usually dry cleaned, sometimes washable
Spandex (Lycra)	Excellent elasticity and recovery; stronger and more durable than rubber; resistant to body oils; washable, but avoid chlorine bleach
Triacetate (Arnel)	Can be permanently pleated; wrinkle- and shrink-resistant; crisp finish; easily laundered; not as heat sensitive as acetate

Summary

A fiber is the basic unit from which fabric is made. For use in fabrics, a fiber should be strong, pliable, have some elasticity, and be long enough to be spun into yarns. Fibers are identified by a generic name and sometimes by a trade name. Fibers are classified according to their origin. Natural fibers come from plants and animals. They include cotton, flax, ramie, wool, silk, and others. Manufactured fibers are the result of scientific experimentation and development. They include rayon, acetate, nylon, polyester, acrylic, olefin, spandex, and others. Each of the natural and manufactured fibers has specific characteristics that can affect a fabric's appearance and performance.

Questions

1. Identify four properties that a fiber must have to be used in fabrics.

2. In what two ways can fibers be classified? Give examples of each.

3. What is the difference between a generic name and a trade name for a fiber?

4. List four natural fibers. What are the strengths and weaknesses, as well as the advantages and disadvantages, of each fiber?

5. Why are cotton fabrics and wool fabrics comfortable to wear?

6. What is sometimes done to natural fibers to improve their performance and care?

7. Explain how chemical engineers develop and change manufactured fibers.

8. What characteristics do nylon and polyester fibers have in common?

9. Identify two advantages of each of the following manufactured fibers: acrylic, polyester, rayon, aramid, and spandex.

Activities

1. Examine a variety of fibers and yarns under a microscope to identify their characteristics.

2. Compare a natural fiber to a manufactured fiber. Use two fabrics, one made from each fiber. Test each fabric for characteristics such as wrinkle resistance, stretchability, stain resistance, and absorbency. Wash a sample of both fabrics and compare results with an unwashed sample.

3. Research the latest developments in fiber technology. Create a display that shows the use of new generation fibers in home furnishings, medicaine, sports, or industry.

You Be the Expert

You have a summer job working in a clothing store. Customers often complain about feeling hot and sticky in certain fabrics. What fibers would you recommend that customers look for when purchasing summer clothes?

16 | *Fabrics*

TERMS TO LEARN

blends
fabric
filling yarns
knitting
nonwoven fabrics
selvage
warp yarns
weaving
yarns

All **fabrics** or *cloth of any kind,* begin with fibers. However-
er, the fibers must be held together in some manner to create
fabrics. For most fabrics, the next step in fabric construction
is to spin the fibers into yarns.

Try this experiment. From a small ball of cotton, loosen
several fibers. Carefully pull the fibers from the ball, twisting
them with your fingers as you pull. Notice how much stronger
the twisted yarn is, when compared with the strength of the
loose fibers.

All woven and knitted fabrics are made from yarns, which
are then interlaced or looped together. After reading this
chapter, you will be able to:

- explain how yarns are formed,
- describe the characteristics of woven fabrics made by different weaving techniques,
- identify the characteristics of knitted fabrics,
- understand characteristics of fabrics made by other methods.

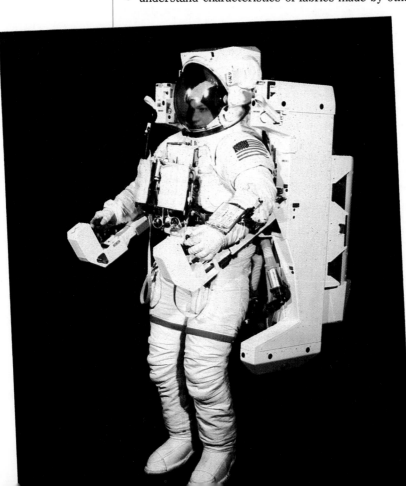

Yarn Variations

Most fabrics are made from **yarns** that have been *created from fibers twisted together or laid side by side.* The fibers that make up the yarns may be natural, manufactured, or a combination of both. Much of the beauty, texture, performance, and variety of fabrics is due to the difference in the yarns.

LENGTH OF FIBERS

Fibers are classified according to their length. They can be either staples or filaments.

1. *Staple fibers* are short fibers that are measured in inches or centimeters. All natural fibers, except silk, are staples. Manufactured fibers can be cut into shorter lengths to make staple fibers.
2. *Filament fibers* are long continuous fibers that are measured in yards or meters. Silk and manufactured fibers are filaments.

Yarns made from staple fibers are rougher and fuzzier than those made from filament fibers. Thus, fabrics made of staple fibers are not as smooth as those made from filaments. Manufactured fibers can be cut into staple lengths to help give fabrics the appearance of cotton, linen, or wool.

TYPES OF YARNS

The simplest yarn is a *monofilament.* It has only one strand of filament. A silk fiber in its natural state is a monofilament. Nylon sewing thread and fishing line are monofilament yarns. A simple yarn can also be made by twisting two strands of fibers together to form a *single yarn.* An example of this is sewing thread.

All other yarns are made by twisting two or more single yarns together to form a *ply yarn.* Two or more ply yarns twisted together are called a *cable yarn.* A *novelty yarn* is made from two or more single yarns that are not alike. They may have loops or different thicknesses. Novelty yarns can create a wide variety of interesting textures.

Plies and Twists

Look at several different yarns. Those used for knitting or embroidery are good examples.

Simple yarns have been in use for thousands of years. Textured yarns and novelty yarns have been recently invented. Textile researchers continue to add to the kinds of textured and novelty yarns available.

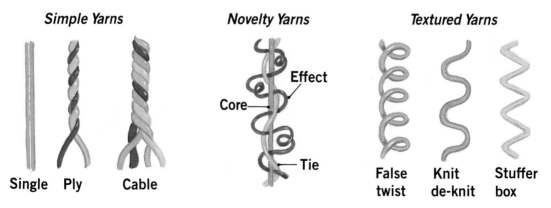

Simple Yarns   **Novelty Yarns**   **Textured Yarns**

Single   Ply   Cable   Effect, Core, Tie   False twist   Knit de-knit   Stuffer box

How many plies do they have? How tightly are they twisted? How does the number of plies and amount of twist affect the appearance and feel of the yarn?

The purpose of twisting is to bind the fibers together and hold in the loose ends of the fiber. The amount of twist affects both the yarn's appearance and behavior.

- *High twist yarns* are firm, strong, dull in texture, and relatively fine in size.
- *Low twist yarns* are softer, weaker, and more lustrous than tightly twisted yarns.
- *Loosely twisted yarns* may fuzz or pill on the surface. They usually pick up soil more readily.
- *Tightly twisted yarns,* such as crepe, may shrink.

Cotton and polyester are blended to form a fabric that is very suitable for T-shirts.

BULK YARNS

Special machines can give manufactured filament yarns different textures and stretch properties. *Bulk yarns* are permanently set into ripples, waves, zigzags, or various twists. This is done to give the yarns more softness and texture. It increases the stretch and recovery of the yarns. It can increase wrinkle resistance and improve wash and wear properties.

By increasing the space between the filaments, the fabric has more breatheability and is more comfortable to wear. It also helps to prevent static buildup. By adding bulk to manufactured yarns, some of the disadvantages of the fiber's original characteristics are overcome. For the change to be permanent, the yarns are heat set.

BLENDING

Different fibers can be combined into one yarn. These yarns are called **blends** because they are engineered to obtain the best qualities of each fiber. Natural fibers can be combined, such as wool and silk. Manufactured fibers can be combined, such as nylon and acetate. Or a natural fiber and a manufactured fiber can be combined, such as cotton and polyester.

Fibers are usually blended to improve fabric performance. A very common blend is polyester and cotton. The cotton offers comfort, softness, and absorbency. The polyester adds strength, wrinkle resistance, shrink resistance, mildew resistance, and quick drying.

A polyester and cotton fabric is easy to wash and needs little or no ironing. The fabric should have at least 15 percent of a fiber in order to benefit from its characteristics.

Fibers can also be blended just for appearance. An angora fiber may be added to wool to give more texture and softness to a sweater. Silk may be included for shine or luster. Can you think of any other blends that could be created for appearance?

Plain

Twill

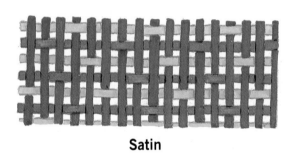

Satin

Fabric Construction

The two most common methods of fabric construction are weaving and knitting. **Weaving** is done by *interlacing two sets of yarns at right angles to each other.* **Knitting** is *a method of looping yarns together.* A few fabrics are made by other methods.

WOVEN FABRICS

Fabric can be woven by hand on small looms. The textile industry uses high speed, high performance computerized looms that can produce many yards or meters of fabric in one hour. The shuttle has been replaced with a stream of water or an air jet to carry the yarn across the width of the fabric at high speeds.

The Process of Weaving

Weaving is done by interlacing lengthwise and crosswise yarns. The *yarns that run the length of the fabric* are called **warp yarns**. These yarns are usually the stronger of the yarns used and are positioned on the loom first.

The *crosswise yarns* are known as **filling yarns**. They are woven or interlaced into the warp yarns, following a specific pattern.

Along each edge of woven fabric, there is a **selvage** or *self-edge.* It is formed by the filling yarn when it turns to go back in the other direction. The selvage is usually a little stiffer and firmer. It will not ravel.

Fabric is woven in different widths, depending on the yarns, the end use of the fabric, and the type of loom used. The newer looms can weave fabrics that are 60″ or more (1.5 m) wide. Some air and water jet looms are capable of weaving two widths of fabric, each 72″ (1.8 m) wide, at one time. Because these looms operate at incredibly fast speeds, the warp yarns must be very strong and durable.

There are many, many variations of woven fabrics that are used for clothing and home furnishings. They range from very lightweight, open-mesh fabrics to heavy, firm, tightly woven upholstery fabrics. If you examine a woven fabric closely, you can see how it is woven. The weave differs in how the lengthwise and crosswise yarns are interlaced together.

BASIC WEAVES

The three basic weaves are the *plain weave, twill weave,* and *satin weave.* Almost all other fabrics are some type of variation of these three basic weaves. Two other types of weaves are the *pile weave,* which uses three sets of yarns, and the *leno weave,* which twists the yarns in a unique way.

Plain Weave

The plain weave is the simplest of all weaves. The filling yarns pass over and under each warp yarn. The yarns alternate in each row to form an even, balanced weave. Plain weave fabrics have no right or wrong sides unless they are printed or finished differently. The yarns can be tightly or loosely woven.

Some examples of plain weaves are muslin, voile, broadcloth, percale, taffeta, and crepe. Plain weave fabrics are used for shirtings, handkerchiefs, and sheets.

A *ribbed weave* is a variation of the plain weave. The rib is created by using filling yarns that are thicker than the warp yarns. Poplin and faille are ribbed fabrics.

A *basket weave* is another plain weave variation. Two or more yarns are grouped side by side in each direction and woven as one. Hopsacking is a basket weave.

Twill Weave

A twill weave is recognized by parallel diagonal ridges on the fabric surface. In a twill weave, filling yarns pass over and under one or more warp yarns. Each successive row shifts to the right or left to give the diagonal line.

Twill weaves are firmer, heavier, and more durable than plain weaves. Denim, chino, and gabardine are examples of twill weaves. Twill weaves are often used for strong, sturdy work clothes.

Satin Weave

A satin weave has yarns that float on the surface to give it a luster or shine. Either the warp or filling yarns pass over four to eight yarns at a time. The long floats appear on the right side of the fabric. The satin weave creates a smooth surface with lots of sheen. However, satin weaves can snag easily. Satin fabrics are used for blouses, evening wear, and bed linens.

Pile Weave

A pile weave uses three sets of yarns. The extra yarns are brought to the fabric surface as loops during the weaving process. The back of the fabric can be a plain, twill, or satin weave.

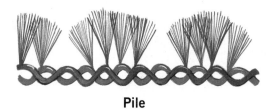

Pile

The loops can be left uncut for terry cloth. Or the loops can be cut to form velvet, velveteen, velour, or corduroy. In most corduroy, the pile yarn is woven in a striped effect to create the rows. *The width of the pile* can range from narrow pinwale to wide wale corduroy. The surface loops of velvet and velveteen can be sculptured when cut to form a decorative surface texture.

Leno Weave

In a leno weave, the warp yarns cross and twist between the filling yarns. This produces open or sheer fabrics with good stability because the filling yarns cannot shift.

A sheer, gauzy fabric used for curtains and evening wear is called *marquisette.* Leno weaves are also used for bulkier yarns to make open weave curtains and draperies.

Figure Weaves

Various patterns or designs can be woven in fabric by changing the way that the yarns are interlaced. Small geometric designs are woven by means of a dobby attachment on the loom. Bird's-eye and honeycomb are two examples of a *dobby weave.*

Large, elaborate designs can be produced by the *Jacquard weave.* Special looms are used to produce the intricate designs and combinations of weaves. Some examples are brocades and damasks, which are used for table lines.

KNIT FABRICS

Fabric can be knitted by hand, using various sizes of knitting needles. In the textile industry, knitting machines can duplicate any hand knitting stitches or patterns. Some knitting machines produce knitted fabric, either flat or tubular. Other machines knit the item directly, such as socks and pantyhose.

A knit fabric has a lengthwise and crosswise direction, the same as a woven fabric. In a knit, the lengthwise rows of stitches are called *wales.* The crosswise stitches are called *courses.* A knit usually has a greater degree of stretch ability in either the lengthwise or crosswise direction.

Leno weave

Wale

Course

Knit fabrics are very versatile. They can be made in a variety of fibers, weights, and types of construction. Knits are easy to care for and comfortable to wear. They do not wrinkle easily.

Because of their stretchability, knits move with the body. As a result, they are less stable than woven fabrics. Knits provide good insulation for warmth, but they do not resist wind due to their open construction.

BASIC KNITS

There are two basic types of knits—*weft knits* and *warp knits.* They differ in the number of yarns used and in the method of construction.

Weft Knits

Weft, or *filling, knits* are made with only one yarn. When you hand knit, you are making a weft knit. Weft knits can be made on either a flat knitting machine or a circular machine, which produces tubular fabric. Most weft knits have two-way stretch in both the lengthwise and crosswise directions. Because of their single yarn construction, most weft knits can run.

- A *plain knit* is the most common type of weft knit. It is sometimes called *jersey.* The front and the back have a different appearance. The right side of the fabric is the one with the vertical wales, which looks like the "knit" stitch in hand knitting. Hosiery, T-shirts, sports shirts, dresses, and sweaters can be plain knits.

- A *purl knit* looks the same on both sides. It looks like the wrong side of a jersey. Purl knits stretch in both the lengthwise and crosswise directions. They are used for sweaters.

- A *rib knit* has vertical ribs or columns of stitches that alternate on the front and the back. Rib knits are often used as neck, wrist, and bottom bands on sweaters and jackets.

Weft and Warp Knit

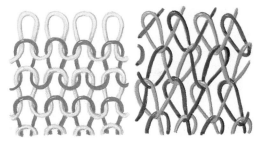

Weft Knit   **Warp Knit**

- A *double knit* is a variation of the rib knit that uses two yarns and two sets of needles. The loops are drawn through from both directions. A double knit is heavier, firmer, and sturdier than other knits. It will not run or ravel. Double knits can be used for a variety of garments.

Warp Knits

Warp knits are made with several yarns. The flat fabric is constructed by looping the multiple warp yarns so that they interlock. Thus, each loop is made up of two yarns. The fabric is usually run-resistant.

The two kinds of warp knit fabric are *tricot* and *raschel.*

- *Tricot knits* have very fine vertical wales on the right side and crosswise courses on the back. They are used for lingerie, underwear, shirts, and dresses.

- *Raschel knits* may have an extra yarn stitched in to produce a textured or patterned design. Open and lacey knits can be created.

NONWOVEN FABRICS

Nonwoven fabrics are made by *interlocking the fibers with heat and moisture or with an adhesive substance.* Felt has long been made by applying heat, moisture and pressure to wool fibers. It depends on the natural ability of wool fibers to shrink and lock together to form a mat. Felt is used primarily for hats, craft projects, and industrial uses.

Manufactured fibers can be joined or fused together using an adhesive or bonding agent. These types of nonwoven fabrics are used for sew-in and fusible interfacings, disposable surgical gowns, and disposable diapers.

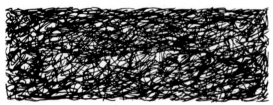
Nonwoven

Nonwoven fabrics do not ravel or fray. They are flexible and have good shape retention. However, they may have weak areas and may tear easy. They also do not have good abrasion resistance. Most nonwoven fabrics are inexpensive to produce.

OTHER FABRIC CONSTRUCTIONS

There are many other types of fabric constructions. The basic ones are also the most popular ones.

Laces and Nets

Laces and nets are made by twisting or looping threads or yarns together. Special machines can make very intricate lace designs for use in garments and home furnishings.

Bonded and Laminated Fabrics

Fabrics can be *bonded,* or permanently joined, to another fabric, vinyl, clear films, or rubberized coatings. This can be done to give more body to the fabric, or to create a special surface. Simulated leather has vinyl bonded to a woven or knitted base. Rubberized coatings can be added to fabrics, such as raingear, for water repellency.

Many of these fabrics cannot be dry cleaned. Instead, they should be wiped off or washed gently. An outer fabric and a backing can be laminated to a layer of foam. This may be used to give additional warmth to outerwear.

Quilted Fabrics

Quilted fabrics consist of two layers of fabric with a batting between them. The three layers of fabric can be held together with machine stitching in a decorative pattern or in rows.

Pinsonic quilting is a method of holding the layers of fabric together without any stitching. Instead, the fabric is quilted by heat fusion. This method has no stitching threads that can break. However, holes can develop in the fabric at the point of the heat fusion.

Pinsonic quilting is used for bedspreads, mattress pads, and placemats. It may soon be used for garment fabrics as well.

Stretch Fabrics

Stretch fabrics are woven or knitted fabrics that have been constructed to stretch more than they normally would do. Stretch fabrics are made of yarns that have increased stretchability. These fabrics use bulk yarns or yarns that have been wrapped around an elastic core. Spandex, natural rubber, or synthetic rubber can be used also.

Stretch fabrics can be designed to stretch in the warp direction, the filling direction, or in both directions. Two-way stretch fabrics are especially desirable for swimsuits, exercise wear, and active sports wear.

Fashion Focus

Fabric Dictionary

- **Batiste.** A soft, sheer plain-weave fabric, usually cotton-blend, used for blouses, children's wear, and nightwear

- **Broadcloth.** A closely woven plain-weave fabric of cotton, wool, or silk; used for shirts, sportswear, suits, and coats

- **Brocade.** A Jacquard-woven fabric with an elaborate design that is raised slightly above the firmly woven background; used for evening dresses and upholstery

- **Burlap.** A coarse, rough-textured fabric made of jute; used for accessories and decorating projects

- **Calico.** A lightweight plain-weave fabric with a small printed pattern; used for sportswear

- **Canvas.** A strong, heavyweight plain-weave fabric of cotton or manufactured fibers; used for sportswear, accessories, and recreational items

- **Cashmere.** A very soft, expensive fabric knitted or woven from the soft, glossy hair of the Kashmir goat; used for sweaters, coats, and suits

- **Challis.** A lightweight plain-weave fabric with a slightly napped, soft finish often printed with small floral designs; used for blouses and dresses

- **Chiffon.** A soft, very sheer plain-weave fabric of silk or manufactured fibers; used for dressy clothes or scarves

- **Chino.** A sturdy, mediumweight twill-weave fabric of cotton on cotton blends; used for pants, sportswear, and uniforms

- **Chintz.** A plain-weave glazed cotton fabric used for clothing, curtains, and slipcovers

- **Corduroy.** A sturdy pile fabric of cotton or manufactured fibers, usually with rows of cut pile that vary from narrow to wide; used for sportswear suits, and upholstery

- **Crepe.** A fabric with a crinkled surface created by highly twisted yarns or a special finish; used for blouses, dresses, and lingerie

- **Denim.** A strong twill-weave fabric of cotton or cotton-blend with colored warp yarns and white filling yarns; used for sportswear and jeans

- **Dotted Swiss.** A crisp, sheer fabric with woven dots; used for dresses and curtains

- **Double Knit.** A sturdy knitted fabric of wool or polyester made with two sets of needles to produce a double thickness of fabric; used for sportswear, dresses, and suits

- **Duck.** A durable, plain-weave cotton fabric used for sportswear and upholstery

- **Faille.** A ribbed fabric used for dresses and draperies

- **Fake Fur.** A pile fabric, usually made of modacrylic fibers, that simulates animal fur; used for coats, jackets, hats, upholstery, and stuffed toys

- **Felt.** A nonwoven fabric created by matting short wool or other fibers with moisture, heat, and pressure; used for hats and crafts

- **Flannel.** A soft, napped fabric of cotton, wool, or rayon used for shirts, dresses, skirts, slacks suits, nightwear, and sheets

- **Gabardine.** A strong medium- to heavy-weight twill fabric of wool, cotton, or manufactured fibers; used for sportswear, suits, and coats

- **Gingham.** A light- to mediumweight plain-weave cotton fabric made from dyed yarns to create plaids, checks, and stripes; used for shirts, dresses, and curtains

- **Jersey.** A smooth, drapeable, lightweight knit of cotton, wool, silk, or manufactured fibers; used for dresses, shirts, sports-wear, and underwear

Fashion Focus

Fabric Dictionary (continued)

- **Lace.** A decorative, open-work fabric used for fancy blouses, dresses, trim, curtains, and tablecloths
- **Madras.** A plain-weave cotton fabric in plaid, checks, or stripes with noncolorfast dyes so that the colors bleed for a faded look; used for sportswear
- **Malimo.** A fabric made from warp and filling yarns that are stitched, not woven, together; used for curtains
- **Muslin.** A firm plain-weave cotton fabric in a variety of weights and qualities; used for dresses, sheets, and draperies
- **Net.** An open-mesh fabric formed by twisting yarns together; used for evening dresses, veils, and curtains
- **Organdy** and **Organza.** A crisp, sheer plain-weave fabric; organdy is made from cotton, organza from silk or rayon; used for dressy clothes and curtains
- **Oxford Cloth.** A plain-weave medium-weight fabric with a colored warp and a white filling; used for shirts
- **Percale.** A firm, smooth plain-weave fabric of cotton or cotton and polyester blend that is similar to muslin but woven of finer yarns; used for shirts, dresses, and sheets
- **Piqué.** A mediumweight fabric in a dobby weave with small geometric designs, such as bird's eye and honeycomb; used for dresses and children's wear
- **Poplin.** A mediumweight finely ribbed fabric that is slightly heavier than broadcloth; used for sportswear and dresses
- **Sailcloth.** A very strong, durable cotton fabric; originally used for sails, now used for sportswear
- **Sateen** and **Satin.** A smooth, shiny fabric woven in a satin weave; sateen is made from cotton, satin from silk or acetate;

used for dresses, evening dresses, and draperies
- **Seersucker.** A plain-weave cotton or cotton-blend fabric with puckered stripes; used for summer suits and sportswear
- **Suede Cloth.** A woven or knitted fabric with a napped finish that looks like suede, which is a leather; used for coats, jackets, accessories, and upholstery
- **Taffeta.** A crisp plain-weave fabric that has a sheen and rustles when it moves, usually of manufactured fibers; used for dressy clothes and bows
- **Terry Cloth.** A very absorbent woven or knitted pile fabric that has uncut loops on one or both sides; used for towels, robes, and beachwear
- **Tulle.** A fine, lightweight machine-made net; used for bridal veils and formal gowns.
- **Tweed.** A sturdy, rough fabric made from wool or wool blends in a plain or twill weave with a nubby surface; used for jackets, suits, skirts, coats, and upholstery
- **Velour.** A soft woven or knitted fabric with a thick pile surface; wool velour is used for coats, cotton or nylon velour is used for sportswear and casual wear
- **Velvet** and **Velveteen.** A lustrous fabric with a short cut pile; velvet is made of silk or manufactured fibers, velveteen of cotton; used for jackets, dressy clothes, robes, draperies, and upholstery
- **Vinyl.** A woven or knitted fabric coated with vinyl to look like leather or rubberized fabric; used for coats, rainwear, and upholstery
- **Voile.** A soft, very sheer plain-weave fabric similar to organdy and batiste; used for blouses, dresses, and curtains

Summary

Most fabrics are made from yarns that are created from fibers twisted together or laid side by side. Yarns made from staple fibers are rougher and fuzzier than those made from filament fibers. Bulk yarns have been heat set for added softness, texture, and stretchability. Different fibers can also be combined into one yarn to create blends. Most fabrics are constructed by weaving or knitting. Types of weaves include: plain, twill, satin, pile, leno, and figure weaves. The two basic types of knits are weft knits and warp knits. Other fabric constructions include nonwoven fabrics; laces and nets; and bonded, laminated, quilted, and stretch fabrics.

Questions

1. Explain the difference between staple fibers and filament fibers. What effect do they have on the finished fabric?

2. Identify a single yarn, a ply yarn, a cable yarn, and a novelty yarn.

3. What advantages do bulk yarns give fabrics?

4. What are blends and why are they created? Give examples of at least two blends and their advantages.

5. Why must the warp yarns be strong when weaving fabric?

6. Describe each of the three basic weaves. Give examples of common fabrics that are woven by each method.

7. How is a pile weave created?

8. What is the difference between a weft knit and a warp knit?

9. Name several products that are made from nonwoven fabrics.

Activities

1. Recreate the three basic weaves using thin strips of paper to represent the yarns.

2. Collect a variety of fabric swatches. Identify each according to type of weave or knit and name of fabric. Mount the swatches in a notebook and write a description of each fabric and its characteristics.

3. Compare a woven and a knit fabric made of the same fiber content. Stretch each fabric in different directions. In which direction was the greatest amount of stretch? Did the fabric recover its shape after being stretched?

You Be the Expert

You are a copywriter for a mail-order catalogue. When describing different fabrics, what characteristics or benefits might you include in the copy? What information could you use to be sure your advertising statements are accurate?

17 Finishes

TERMS TO LEARN

dyes
finishes
gray goods
printing
waterproof
water-repellent

When *fabric first comes from the loom,* it is called **gray goods.** It looks nothing like the finished fabric that you will see as a shirt, jacket, or towel. Many of the fabrics have no color—they are gray or off-white. The warp yarns may have been stiffened to withstand the strain during weaving. The fabric may be limp, or fuzzy, or dull, or very shiny. How then are fabrics transformed into beautiful, colorful, comfortable, and serviceable materials that you want to buy and wear?

The answer is **finishes,** which are any *special treatments that are applied to fabrics.* After reading this chapter, you will be able to:

- understand the dyeing process,
- describe the various printing techniques,
- explain how a fabric's texture can be changed,
- identify the finishes that can improve a fabric's performance.

Finishing Processes

Finishes can be applied to fabrics to improve their appearance, their texture, and their performance. Every fiber and type of fabric has certain desirable and undesirable characteristics. Finishes can be added that reduce the undesirable characteristics or improve the desirable ones.

Some finishes are added to create a specific design, such as a stripe or a print. Other finishes offer a softer, firmer, or smoother hand. Many finishes are used to add a specific property or quality to the fabric, such as wrinkle resistance or improved absorbency.

Fabric finishes may be permanent or temporary. *Permanent finishes* last throughout the life of the fabric. *Temporary finishes* may last through only one or two cleanings.

But, before any gray goods are finished, they must be cleaned to remove any oils, resins, gums, or soil that would prevent the finish from penetrating the fabric.

Color and Design Finishes

Manufacturers can alter the appearance of gray goods by dyeing or printing the fabric. As far back as prehistoric times, people have decorated their clothing with color.

Dyes are *compounds that penetrate and color fibers.* They can be used to color the entire fabric, or to create special designs on the fabric. In Chapter 14, you learned about colorfastness and how it relates to fabrics.

HOW FAST IS COLORFAST?

A color is said to be "fast" when it does not fade. The fastness of a color depends on three factors:

- the type of dye,
- the chemical structure of the fiber,
- the method of application.

Most dyes are not colorfast to everything. Some may be more affected by washing, dry cleaning, sunlight, or perspiration. Some may *crock,* or rub off onto your skin or other clothing.

Manufacturers select dyes that are most suitable to the fiber content and the intended use of the fabric. Colorfastness to washing is important for children's clothes and sportswear. Fastness to sunlight is more important for draperies, upholstery, and carpets. Swimwear needs to be colorfast to sunlight, washing, and chlorine. Fabric used for a coat lining should be colorfast to crocking, perspiration, and dry cleaning.

It is important to read the label or hangtag for information about colorfastness. You cannot tell how fast a color will be by looking at the fabric. Also, follow directions for the recommended method of care.

DYEING TEXTILES

For centuries, natural dyes were obtained from plants, insects, shellfish, and minerals. The first synthetic dye was discovered by accident in 1856. Then a whole new industry developed for textiles.

Textile colorists are constantly seeking better dyes for different fibers and blends. Today, they are assisted by computers in the development of exact formulas for dyeing different fibers a certain color. This means that our dyeing range is almost limitless.

Dyes

There are two types of dyes—natural and synthetic. *Natural dyes* are made from bark, roots, leaves, berries, flowers, insects, and animals. These materials are boiled, squeezed, soaked, or pounded to obtain the liquid color. Then the fabric is soaked in the dye.

Some of the earliest natural dyes included red maddar dye, made by the Egyptians from plant roots, and Indigo blue, made in India from a plant. Saffron yellow was extracted from a fall-flowering crocus by the Greeks and Romans.

Cochineal was a red dye made by the Aztecs from insects, and Tyrian purple was made by the Phoenicians from snails. Orange-red henna came from a shrub in North Africa and the Middle East. Some of the dyes were very scarce and very expensive.

With the introduction of *synthetic dye* in 1856, a new industry developed. It was found that coal tar could be used to produce the whole spectrum of colors. Synthetic dyes had greater colorfastness and were much less expensive. Today, synthetic dyes have almost entirely replaced natural dyes for commercial dyeing.

Methods of Dyeing

There are five different methods of dyeing:

- **Stock Dyeing.** Fibers are dyed before being spun into yarns. It permits the spinning of tweed and multicolored yarns.
- **Solution Dyeing.** Dye is added to the chemical solution before it is forced through spinnerets. The color becomes a permanent part of the manufactured fiber.
- **Yarn Dyeing.** Yarns are dyed before they are woven or knitted into fabric. This method is used for plaids, checks, and stripes.
- **Piece Dyeing.** Fabric is dyed after being woven or knitted. Manufacturers can store undyed fabric and then dye it a specific color, according to their orders.
- **Product Dyeing.** The fabric is cut and sewn into the finished product. Then the entire garment or item is dyed, according to orders.

Piece dyeing is taking place in this textile plant. The woven fabric is being dyed to a customer's specifications.

PRINTING TEXTILES

Fabrics can be printed in a variety of ways. **Printing** involves *transferring color to the surface of a fabric.* Some printing methods are very old techniques that are still used by crafts people today. However, the textile industry uses high-speed electronic machines for textile printing. Some specialty fabrics, such as scarves and evening gowns, may be printed by hand.

METHODS OF PRINTING

• **Roller Printing**. The roller printing press contains circular rollers, or printing plates, one for each color of the desired design. Each roller is chemically etched with its colored part of the pattern, leaving high and low areas on the rollers. The raised sections of the roller pick up the desired color. The fabric is printed as it passes through the press and makes contact with the raised sections of each roller. The

different areas of color will coincide to form the completed design.

Two variations of roller printing include discharge printing and resist printing.

In *discharge printing,* some of the dye is bleached or chemically removed to create a white design on a colored fabric.

In *resist printing,* the fabric is printed using a dye-resistant chemical. Then the fabric is dyed. The printed area resists the dye and remains uncolored.

• **Screen Printing**. A fabric or metal mesh screen is stretched on a frame. The design is traced onto the screen. Then all the areas not included in the design to be printed are blocked out with a special coating. The color is then pressed through the screen onto the fabric, using a squeegee or roller. A separate screen is used for each color of the design. Large designs, such as those often used in home furnishings fabrics, can be printed using this method.

Rotary screen printing combines the advantages of roller printing and screen printing. The

Technology

Designing by Computer

The traditional method of designing a new fabric is a very time-consuming process. The design must be slowly and carefully worked out on graph paper. Then someone has to make a handwoven sample on a small loom. If the designer wants to change the colors, the type of thread, or the pattern of the weave, it means many more hours of work.

With a CAD (Computer Aided Design) system, it takes only a few minutes to develop designs that once took hours. Using a special pen, called a stylus, a fabric designer can sketch a design on a special pad, called a tablet. After viewing the design on the computer's display screen, the designer can easily erase any sections and re-sketch the design.

Next, the designer tells the computer what yarns are going to be used. The picture on the display screen automatically shows how different yarns will affect the texture of the design. Using the computer's special color system, the designer can experiment with different color combinations. Some very advanced CAD systems can duplicate up to 16 million colors.

Finally, the computer takes the design that appears on the color monitor, or display screen, and prints it on paper. Once the final design is approved, the computer in the designer's workroom can send a message to the computer at the fabric mill. In only a few hours, the designer's idea can become actual fabric.

rotary screens, made from metal foil, are less costly than the printing plates. It is a faster method than flat screen printing.

- **Transfer Printing**. This is a popular method for transferring designs, insignias, and words onto fabric. The design is printed in reverse with heat sensitive dyes on paper. When the paper pattern is placed face down on the fabric and heat is applied, the design is transferred to the fabric.

Other printing methods include block printing, batik, and tie dying, all of which are discussed in Chapter 9.

Texture Finishes

Most fabrics have some type of finish applied to improve surface texture and hand. These finishes may also help to improve the comfort or performance of the fabric.

What types of texture finishes could you add to various textiles in this photo?

TYPES OF TEXTURE FINISHES

- **Calendering**. Fabric passes between two heated rollers that smooth the fabric and improve the luster.

- **Glazing**. A resin is applied during calendering to produce a high polish or glaze on the surface of the fabric. Chintz is a glazed fabric.

- **Napping**. Rotating wire brushes are used to raise the short fiber ends of staple yarns to create a soft, fuzzy surface. Flannel is a napped fabric.

- **Lustering**. Fabric is treated with heat and pressure to add luster.

- **Beetling**. Cotton or linen fabrics are flattened to fill out the weave and add luster.

- **Delustering**. Fibers or fabrics are treated with chemicals to reduce their gloss.

- **Embossing**. Fabrics are given a raised design on their surface by being calendered with rollers engraved with the design.

- **Ciré**. A super glossy finish is obtained by applying wax or some other substance before calendering. Ciré nylon is sometimes used for lightweight jackets.

- **Moiré**. A watered or wavy pattern is obtained by calendering two layers of fabric slightly off-grain. Moiré fabric is used for evening wear.

- **Sizing**. Starches or resins are added to the fabric for extra body. Sizing is usually only a temporary finish.

Performance Finishes

Many different types of finishes can be applied to fabrics to increase their performance. Some finishes improve durability, and others make the fabrics more comfortable to wear. Several finishes are designed to make the fabrics easier to care for because they control wrinkling. Other finishes are used to protect the fabric from bacteria, mildew, insects, and perspiration.

Labels and hangtags on textile items use different terms to describe finishes:

- *Proof* means that the finish provides complete protection from the influence.
- *Resistant* and *repellent* means that the finish offers partial protection.

Durable press garments are very popular, especially for sportswear and children's wear.

TYPES OF COMMON PERFORMANCE FINISHES

Here is a list of some of the more common performance finishes that you will find listed on labels and hangtags.

- **Crease Resistant and Wrinkle-Resistant Finishes**. These help fabrics to resist wrinkling and to recover more rapidly from wrinkling caused by normal wear. Wrinkles tend to flatten or disappear when the garment is hung up.

- **Durable Press and Wash and Wear Finishes**. The fabric can be washed and dried by machine and will need little or no ironing. The fabric will resist wrinkling during wear, and the garment will maintain its shape, pleats, and creases.

   In many advertisements and articles, you will see the term "permanent press" used. Fabric experts prefer the term "durable press," which means that the fabric or garment will perform as expected, with proper care. However, if care instructions are not followed, some wrinkling may occur. The word "permanent" implies that wrinkling can never occur.

- **Shrinkage-Controlled Finishes**. Shrinkage should only be minimum, even after repeated launderings. It does not guarantee that no shrinkage will occur. The term "Sanforized" is an assurance that the fabric will not shrink more than one percent in washing. Washable wool fabrics have been treated so they will not felt or shrink when laundered as directed on the label. If a fabric is "preshrunk," then some shrinkage process has already occurred.

- **Stain- and Spot-Resistant Finishes**. These help fabrics to repel water- and oil-based stains. These finishes are often used on table linens and upholstery fabrics, in addition to clothing.

- **Soil-Release Finishes**. These make it easier to remove soil and oily stains from durable press fabrics and manufactured fibers during laundering.

- **Antistatic Finishes**. These help prevent fabrics from clinging.

- **Absorbent Finishes**. These make the fabric absorb moisture more easily and thus become more comfortable to wear.

- **Water-Repellent and Waterproof Finishes**. These are designed to help keep the fabric and the wearer dry. **Water-repellent fabrics** have been treated to *resist water, but eventually they will become wet.* The fabric remains porous. The finish may need to be renewed when the garment is dry cleaned.

   Waterproof fabrics have been coated or treated so that *no water will penetrate.* The fabric has been made nonporous and thus may be uncomfortable to wear. New *microporous waterproof finishes* have recently been developed that allow body moisture to escape while not allowing water to penetrate.

- **Flame-Retardant Finishes**. These help to reduce flaming and burning in fabrics that have been exposed to a flame or high heat. These finishes are used on children's sleepwear and other clothing. Special care may be needed to maintain the finish.

- **Antibacterial Finishes**. These check the growth of bacteria and perspiration odors.

- **Mildew-Resistant Finishes**. These resist the growth of mildew and other molds.

- **Moth-Resistant Finishes**. These repel moths and other fiber-eating insects.

PROPER CARE

Many of the fabric finishes can be diminished or destroyed by improper care of the fabric. Be sure to read the care labels carefully and follow the manufacturer's recommendations. In the next chapter, you will learn more about caring for your clothes and fabrics.

Textile technology is continuing to develop new finishes that will enhance and improve fibers and fabrics. Look for them on the market.

Performance finishes can protect clothes against everything from flames to moths to the carelessness of people.

Summary

A wide variety of finishes can be applied to fabrics to improve their appearance, texture, and performance. Some finishes are permanent; others only temporary. To add color, fabrics can be dyed or printed using various methods. The surface texture of a fabric can be made smooth or fuzzy, dull or shiny, or given a special design. Performance finishes can be applied to improve durability, comfort, or ease of care. Some finishes can be diminished or destroyed by improper fabric care.

Questions

1. Identify the three benefits that a fabric finish can provide.

2. What is the difference between a permanent finish and a temporary finish?

3. What type of colorfastness would be most important for draperies? children's clothes? coat linings? swimwear?

4. What are the five different methods of dyeing fabrics?

5. How can designs be applied to fabrics?

6. List 5 of the 10 finishes that can be applied to improve texture.

7. What types of finishes can be added to improve the care of fabrics?

8. What is the difference between waterproof and water-repellent? What new type of waterproof finish has been developed?

9. What types of resistant finishes can be added to fabrics?

10. Why is it important to read care labels and follow recommendations when caring for clothes and fabrics?

Activities

1. Gather hangtags or advertisements that list various types of finishes. Make a chart that identifies the trade names, such as Sanforized, of different types of finishes.

2. Test the water repellency of different types of raingear, including umbrellas. Use an eyedroper or small measuring spoon to place droplets of water on the different fabrics. Record how long it takes for the water to be absorbed, if ever.

3. Print your own designs on fabric, using screen printing or block printing. For block printing, you can carve designs out of wood or firm vegetables, such as potatoes, carrots, or turnips.

You Be the Expert

You are working in a children's clothing store. A parent begins asking questions about which play clothes would be easy to care for? What guidelines could you suggest that the parent follow to better evaluate the different fabrics?

18 | *Fabric and Clothing Care*

TERMS TO LEARN

detergent
dry cleaning
laundering
soap
solvent

Have you ever had your favorite white shirt turn pink in the wash? Or discovered that your new sweater was now two sizes smaller when you took it out of the dryer?

Have you been ready to leave for a party only to find that your outfit was stained or ripped? All of these problems resulted from improper care of fabrics and clothing.

If you are like most people, you would rather buy, sew, and wear clothes than think about caring for them. You may enjoy using fabric placemats, towels, and sheets but seldom think of how long they will last.

But proper care of your fabrics and clothing will save you both time and money in the long run. After reading this chapter, you will be able to:

- explain how to care for clothing and fabrics on a routine basis,
- understand care-labeling information,
- choose the best method for cleaning a garment or fabric item,
- describe how to store clothing.

Organization

Are you responsible for your own clothes? Do you wash, dry, press, mend, fold, and put them away? Or do you share in the clothing care for all family members? Who is responsible for household fabrics such as sheets, towels, and table linens?

However the tasks are divided, it is important that family members understand their own responsibility. Sometimes family members rotate tasks. Perhaps you are responsible for washing the clothes one week. The next week you might be responsible for folding the family laundry and putting items away.

GETTING ORGANIZED

Organization means setting aside specific time to do different tasks, such as hand washing a sweater or mending a hem.

It helps to have some type of routine schedule and deadline for your clothing care. Schedules are just guidelines and should be flexible. Deadlines are not.

Organization also means having the right laundry products and equipment available for you to use. Suddenly discovering that you have run out of detergent makes washing your clothes a more complicated task than it should be.

Routine Care

Why should you learn about clothing and fabric care? First, it will help you save money.

When a garment is ruined through improper care, it costs you money to replace it.

By learning how to remove spots and stains, you can save cleaning bills. And by learning how to take care of fabrics, you are able to extend their length of service to you.

Every time that you wear a garment, it should become a part of your daily routine for clothing care. It only takes a few seconds to check it over before you put it away.

CHECK FOR SPOTS, STAINS, AND SOIL

Does the garment need to be laundered or dry cleaned? Light-colored fabrics show soil and stains clearly, so you can evaluate them easily. However, dark-colored clothes also need to be cleaned regularly. If you allow fabrics to get too dirty, they will be more difficult to clean.

Garments that need to be laundered should be set aside in a particular location that you or your family uses for dirty clothes. Then they will not be overlooked when laundry time comes.

Check the garment for any signs of stains. It is best to remove any spots or stains as soon as they happen or shortly afterward. The longer a stain remains on a fabric, the harder it will be to remove.

Some stains need to be pretreated before they are laundered. (Refer to the STAIN REMOVAL CHART.) Some difficult-to-remove stains may be successfully treated by a professional dry cleaner. This is especially true for fabrics that cannot be washed.

Stains and spots should also be treated as soon as possible on seat covers, upholstery fabrics, and table linens. A good method to keep spots and stains under control is to quickly examine your clothes each evening when you undress. Put any stained garments aside for cleaning.

CHECK FOR REPAIRS

Has a button popped off? Has the hem come loose? Has a small rip appeared in a seam? No matter how careful you are with clothes, small repairs are often needed. Plan to repair the garment as soon as possible. Otherwise, the rip may become longer, or the entire hem will fall down. If you do not set it aside, you may forget about the needed repair until you want to wear the garment again. And then you may not have the time to do it.

Many repairs can be done in only a few minutes with hand sewing. Restitching a loose button, snap, or hook and eye takes only a few stitches. It is easier to reanchor a loose fastener than to wait until it comes off completely.

Sometimes a garment can no longer be worn because the zipper is broken or the elastic is loose. For a broken zipper, carefully remove the old one and pin a new zipper in place. Stitch, following the original stitching lines.

Worn-out elastic can be replaced by inserting new elastic into the casing. Refer to the Sewing Handbook for specific instructions for different sewing techniques.

AIR OR BRUSH IT

Some garments may not need to be washed or dry cleaned, but they do need to be freshened before wearing again. Hang a woven garment, such as a jacket or dress, where the air can circulate around it. This will help to remove any odors that the fabric has picked up from either the air or your skin. Knitted garments, such as a sweater, can be draped over a chair.

If the garment has picked up any dust, lint, or animal hair, it can be gently brushed to remove the substance. Use a special clothing brush, lint brush, or a specially designed roller with an adhesive surface.

Lightly brushing clothes keeps them free of lint and refreshes the fabric nap.

Hang or Fold

Get into the habit of putting your clothes away in a closet, drawer, or shelf. This will help to prevent wrinkling and save you from pressing clothes before you want to wear them again. Also you will be able to locate them easier and faster when you know exactly where they have been placed. Resist the temptation to toss your shirt on your bed or on the floor.

Most woven garments should be hung on hangers. For jackets and any clothes that might be marked or creased by the narrow metal hangers, use plastic or wooden hangers that are a little wider. These will better support the shoulder area of the garment.

Weekly Care

At least once a week, you should set aside some time for specific clothing tasks. These might include hand washing a garment, mending, or pressing. Clothes may need to be laundered or taken to the dry cleaners. A quick glance at your wardrobe will help you keep everything in tip-top shape.

Stain Removal Chart

- Always remove a stain before laundering a garment or item because hot water and heat can "set" a stain, making it very difficult to remove.
- For stubborn stains, try a presoak or prewash spray.
- When using a chemical stain remover, always pretest it on a nonvisible part of the garment or item.
- For nonwashable fabrics, identify the stain for the dry cleaner.

Blood	Soak in cold water as soon as possible for 30 minutes or longer. Rub detergent to stain and launder. If yellow stain remains, soak with bleach and relaunder.
Chewing Gum, Candle Wax	Harden gum or wax by placing them in freezer or rubbing with an ice cube. Scrape off as much as possible with a dull knife or fingernail. For wax, place stained area between paper towels and press with warm iron. If stain remains, sponge fabric with cleaning fluid. Launder.
Chocolate	Scrape off chocolate. Soak in cool or lukewarm water. Apply detergent to area and launder. If any stain remains, bleach and relaunder.
Cosmetics	Rub detergent into area and launder. If stain is stubborn, sponge fabric with cleaning fluid.
Grass, Foliage	Rub detergent into area and launder, using hottest water as possible for fabric. If stain remains, bleach and relaunder.
Grease, Oil	Scrape off as much as possible or blot with paper toweling. Rub detergent into area and launder. For grimy grease, place stain between paper toweling and press with warm iron. If necessary, sponge fabric with cleaning fluid and launder, using plenty of detergent.
Ink, Ball-Point Pen	Spray lightly with hair spray or sponge with rubbing alcohol. Leave on for a few minutes and blot off as much as possible. Repeat, if necessry. Rub in detergent and launder.
Nail Polish	Sponge with nail polish remover (do not use acetone on acetate fabric) or cleaning fluid. Launder.
Paint, Varnish	Treat immediately. For latex paint, saturate fabric with warm water and launder. For oil-base paint, saturate fabric with paint solvent, such as turpentine, and rinse with cool water. Launder.
Perspiration	Soak in warm water with presoak product, or sponge with ammonia. For old stain, sponge with white vinegar and rinse. Rub detergent into stain and wash in the hottest water possible for fabric.
Soft Drinks	Sponge or soak in cool water, and launder.

This care label gives information on hand and machine washing and drying, as well as dry cleaning and ironing.

Care-Labeling Terms

Remember these points when reading a care instruction:

1. Only the *washing* or *dry cleaning process* listed in the instruction has been checked for safe use.

2. If no *temperature* is mentioned, it is safe to use any temperature or setting—hot, warm, or cold.

3. If no *ironing* instruction is given, it should not be necessary to iron the product.

4. If *bleach* is not mentioned, any type of bleach may be used when needed.

5. If *no warnings* are given, you do not need to make adjustments to the care processes listed in the instruction.

Care Labels

The Care Labeling Rule, first passed in 1972, requires that permanent care labels be placed in all textile clothing. The label must be permanently attached and remain readable for the life of the garment.

In 1984, a revision in the rule went into effect that made the information listed on the label more complete and uniform. The new care labels provide more detailed information.

For example, a label that recommends washing as a care procedure must also tell you the washing method, safe water temperature, and method and safe temperature for drying.

If ironing is needed, the temperature for ironing must be included. If chlorine bleach is not safe to use, then a warning must be added.

Manufacturers are encouraged to use common terms from a new glossary that is part of the revised rule. Some common directions, such as "Machine Wash, Warm," have been standardized. However, the manufacturer is now required to list only one method of safe care, even though other methods may be used safely. Also, the manufacturer does not have to warn you about any other method that may not be safe.

CARE LABEL INFORMATION

• **Washing**. A "machine wash and dry" label means that you can wash and dry the garment by any method at any temperature. Otherwise, the label will indicate the appropriate temperatures and wash cycle to use, and must specify air drying if needed.

• **Ironing**. If ironing is needed, even for a "touch-up," the label must say so. If it is not safe to use the hottest setting, then the label must indicate "warm iron" or "cool iron." A label that states "do not iron" means that even the coolest setting could be harmful to the fabric.

- **Bleaching**. You can assume that it is safe to bleach the fabric if the label does not warn against it. If only chlorine bleach is harmful, the label will state "use only nonchlorine bleach when needed." If all types of bleach are harmful, the label must warn "no bleach."

- **Dry Cleaning**. A garment may be dry-cleaned by any method, including a coin-operated machine, if the label says "dry clean only." Any specific warning concerning solvents or steaming must be given when necessary. In the past, if dry cleaning was harmful, the label had to state so. Now, you cannot assume that a washable garment or item can also be dry cleaned. Always check with your dry cleaner about a garment labeled "washable."

- **Yard Goods**. Care instructions will only be printed on the end of the fabric bolt, so you must make note of them when buying fabric.

Dry Cleaning

Dry cleaning is a *process that uses special liquids containing organic solvents to clean fabrics.* A **solvent** is a *substance used to dissolve another substance.* Clothing is placed into a machine that resembles an automatic washer. The solvent is released and agitated with the clothing to remove soil. Then the solvent is spun away, and the clothing is tumbled or air dried until all traces of the solvent are gone. Steam pressing restores creases and pleats.

Laundering Clothes

Washing fabric by hand or by machine with a soil removing product is called **laundering**. Different types of fabrics need to be laundered by different methods. Some things to consider before washing a garment are its type of fiber, fabric construction, finishes, color, and amount of soil. For best laundering results, follow the guidelines in this section.

SORT CLOTHES

You must first decide what clothes can be washed together. Refer to the care labels for recommended procedures. Then group the fabrics according to washing method — machine or hand, and recommended water temperature.

Next, separate the fabrics according to color. In order to prevent any bleeding of colors, wash all dark colors together. White fabrics should also be washed separately. Many white fabrics, especially those made from manufactured fibers, will pick up color even from colorfast fabrics. Over time, the white fabric may become dull and gray.

Finally, consider the type of fabrics being laundered. Delicate fabrics should be washed on a gentle machine cycle or hand washed. Durable press fabrics should be washed in warm or cool water with a cool rinse to prevent wrinkling.

Some fabrics create lint, such as terry cloth and corduroy. They should not be washed with fabrics that have a very smooth surface and might attract lint. It is a good idea to turn lint-producing fabrics inside out in order to reduce the lint pickup by other fabrics.

PRETREAT STAINS

Remove any stains before laundering fabrics. Heavy soil on collars and children's clothing should be pretreated. You can apply liquid detergent or make a paste of powdered detergent and water to apply to the area. Or you can use a product specially designed for pretreating fabrics. Follow the manufacturer's directions.

Fashion Focus

Simple Repairs

Stitch a Ripped Seam

Restitch seam by machine or hand, using a small backstitch. Overlap ends of stitching for added strength. If the seam is in an area that receives extra stress, such as the underarm or crotch seam, use a double row of stitching ⅛″ (3 mm) apart.

Fix a Snag

Knitted or loosely woven fabrics often get snags, or loops of fabric pulled out. Use a small crochet hook, snag fixer, or needle threader, and insert through the fabric directly under the snag. Grasp snag with hook and pull back to underside of fabric. To smooth out any puckers caused by the snag, gently stretch the fabric in the direction of the pulled thread.

Mend a Tear

A straight tear can be mended by stitching back and forth across the tear to hold the torn edges together. Begin and end stitches about ¼″ (6 mm) above and below the tear.

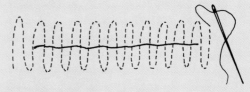

Patch a Hole.

A patch can be applied by hand stitching, machine stitching, or fusing.

Trim away any frayed threads from around hole. Cut out a patch of fabric, slightly larger than hole. Pin patch to inside of garment. On right side, turn under edges of hole and slipstitch to patch. On inside, fold in edges of patch and sew to garment. For added strength, topstitch around folded edge on outside of garment.

To fuse a patch, cut patch the exact size of hole. Place fabric wrong side up on ironing board. Insert patch in hole. Cover area with a piece of fusible web and then a piece of firmly woven fabric. Press from wrong side to fuse patch in place. Or you can purchase iron-on patches or mending tape. Press, following manufacturer's directions.

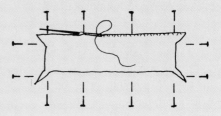

Sorting the wash takes time, but the clothes will clean more thoroughly if you do it.

SELECT WASHING METHOD

You can wash fabrics by hand or by machine. Many machines have two or more wash cycles. The cycles may be programmed for different agitation speeds, such as normal and gentle, and for different rinse temperatures.

For example, a durable press cycle would have a cool rinse. Different cycles also have different lengths. A delicate cycle would be shorter than a regular cycle. More heavily soiled fabrics need a longer washing period.

Be sure to check all garment pockets for any items. Close zippers and any hook and loop fasteners. Do not load too many fabrics into the machine. They must be able to move freely for good cleaning action. Overloading can cause wrinkling, especially of durable press fabrics. For best results, mix small items with large items. If you are not washing a full load, select a lower water level. If possible, refer to the machine's instruction book for additional recommendations.

SELECT WATER TEMPERATURE

Fabrics can be washed in water temperatures that range from very hot to cold. Follow the directions on the care label of the garments to select the proper water temperature. Hot water gets fabrics the cleanest and offers sanitizing benefits, too. It can usually be used for white fabrics that are not delicate and colorfast fabrics. Water that is too hot can shrink some fabrics.

Warm water is recommended for delicate fabrics and colors that are not colorfast. It is also used for durable press and wash and wear fabrics. Cold water does not have much cleaning power, but it can be used for lightly soiled fabrics.

SELECT LAUNDRY PRODUCTS

Soaps and detergents are cleansing agents designed to remove soil from fabrics. **Soaps** are *made by mixing an alkali with a fat* and work best in soft water. **Detergents** are *made from chemicals or petroleum* and work well in either hard or soft water.

Many other laundry products are also available on the market:

- **Prewash Spray.** This liquid helps remove stains.

- **Presoak.** This method helps break down protein-type stains, such as blood and meat juice.

- **Bleach.** This chemical mixture removes stains, whitens and brightens fabrics, and destroys bacteria. Chlorine bleaches are the most effective but cannot be used on all fabrics. Nonchlorine or oxygen bleaches are mild and can be used on both whites and colors.

- **Water Softener.** This substance softens hard water.

- **Fabric Softener**. This product makes fabric feel softer and reduces static electricity. Liquid fabric softeners are added to the final rinse. Special nonwoven sheets can be used in the dryer.
- **Starch**. This substance is used to stiffen fabric, such as cotton.

DRYING

Fabrics can be dried by machine, or they can be hung up or laid flat to dry. Always check the care label for drying instructions. Many automatic dryers have different temperature settings or specific cycle settings. Manufactured fibers should be dried at a lower temperature than cotton or linen. Heavier fabrics will take longer to dry than lightweight fabrics.

For best results, do not overload the dryer since this slows down drying time, increases wrinkling, and decreases fluffiness. Durable press fabrics should be removed before they are completely dry to prevent any wrinkling. Do not dry lint-producing fabrics with other types of fabrics. Be sure to clean the lint filter after each load.

IRONING AND PRESSING

Wrinkles can be removed from fabrics with heat, moisture, and slight pressure. Ironing and pressing are two methods of smoothing away fabric wrinkles. *Ironing* is done with a back and forward motion of the iron. It should always be done in the lengthwise or crosswise direction of the fabric to avoid stretching the fabric. *Pressing* is accomplished by raising and lowering the iron from one area to the next.

Different fibers and fabrics have different sensitivity to heat. Many manufactured fibers have low heat sensitivity and should be ironed at lower temperatures. Cottons and linens are not as heat sensitive and require higher temperatures to effectively remove wrinkles. Most irons have several temperature settings that are labeled with fabric types, such as "permanent press, wool, cotton, and linen."

Storing Your Clothing

Organize your storage space to keep your clothes neater and easier to find. Arrange the closet to use the space to your best advantage.

STEPS TO TAKE

Group similar clothing together. It will be easier to find your blue shirt if it is among the shirts, instead of hidden between other types of clothes. By hanging similar lengths together, there will be space underneath to place shelves or baskets to hold other items in the closet.

Closet Hints

- Multiple shirt, skirt, and pants hangers enable six garments to be hung on one hanger.
- Plastic or cardboard boxes can be used to store folded items and accessories on shelves.
- Shoe bags can be hung on a door to hold shoes.
- Or use shoe bag pockets to store rolled up belts, scarves, shoe polish supplies, hangtags, or the extra buttons and yarns that come attached to garments.
- Use cup hooks to hang belts, necklaces, and chains.
- If closet space is tight, purchase a second rod to hang clothes on to literally double your space.

Arranging Bureau Drawers

Arrange your drawers in similar fashion. Store the same type of items together, such as socks, underwear, and T-shirts. Use a tray on top of a chest or dresser to hold small items, such as a watch or jewelry.

And do not forget the space under your bed. Low boxes or metal chests can be used to store out-of-season or seldom-worn garments.

SEASONAL STORAGE

If you live in a seasonal climate, you may want to store off-season clothing in large garment bags, boxes, or chests.

Moths and Mildew

Always store clothes and accessories that are clean. Soiled fabrics attract moths and other insects that will eat holes in fabric. Laundering or dry cleaning will remove moth larvae or eggs. Moths are particularly fond of oil-based soils on wool clothing.

Do not store clothing or fabrics in damp places where they might be subject to mildew. If mildew grows on your clothing, it can stain or deteriorate the fabric and be difficult to remove. Do not store leather or fur items in plastic bags. They need to be stored where air can circulate. Instead, they can be draped with a piece of fabric.

Closet Hints

1. A tie rack on the door holds ties, belts, and scarves.

2. A fabric shoe bag stores not only shoes but also socks and underwear.

3. Luggage can be stored on hard-to-reach top shelves.

4. Decorative boxes keep out-of-season clothing protected.

5. A two-tiered hanging system helps to divide shirts, skirts, and jeans.

6. Sweaters and T-shirts fold easily into wire or plastic baskets.

7. Longer garments can hang in a narrow compartment with organized shelving both at top and bottom.

8. Small cubicles help to keep shoes separated.

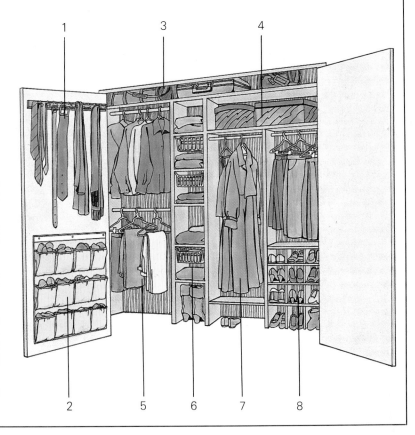

Summary

Taking good care of your clothes and fabrics can save you money, time, and energy. You should establish a daily and weekly routine for clothing care that includes laundering, mending, and proper storage. Permanent care labels list the recommended care method to use. Some fabrics must be dry cleaned with solvents. Laundry procedures depend upon the type of fiber, fabric construction, finishes, color, and amount of soil. You should follow guidelines for sorting clothes, removing stains, selecting washing methods and laundry products, drying, and ironing or pressing. By organizing your storage space, you can keep your clothes neater and easier to find.

Questions

1. Why should you learn about clothing and fabric care?
2. What routine clothing care should you do each time you wear a garment?
3. Why should stains be treated quickly?
4. What type of information might be included on a care label?
5. In the dry cleaning process, what is used to clean fabrics?
6. Why is it very important to sort clothes before laundering? How should the clothes be separated?
7. Describe the steps that should be followed when laundering.
8. What is the difference between soaps and detergents? Explain what bleach does to fabrics.
9. What guidelines should be followed when drying fabrics in an automatic dryer?
10. Why should clothes and fabrics always be clean when stored?

Activities

1. Choose a variety of laundry products and read the labels on each package. Which product provides the most useful consumer information? Explain the reasons for your choice.

2. Gather information from various care labels. List the type of fiber and recommended method of care for each item. Note any pattern of fiber/fabric care that is similar.

3. Soak a piece of red fabric that is not colorfast with samples of white or light-colored fabrics. Once the red color bleeds into the other fabrics, test whether additional washings or bleaching products can restore the original color of the other fabrics.

You Be the Expert

Your younger brother is doing his laundry for the first time. He starts to toss all of his clothes—T-shirts, blue jeans, sweaters, and underwear—into the automatic washing machine. What should you do?

5 Shopping

CHAPTER

19

Gathering Information

CHAPTER

21

Evaluating Your Selection

CHAPTER

23

Sewing Selections

CHAPTER

24

Consumer Rights, Protection, and Responsibilities

CHAPTER

20

Shopping—Where, When, How

CHAPTER

22

Shopping for Others

19 *Gathering Information*

TERMS TO LEARN

comparison shopping
impulse
logo
mandatory
media
recreational shopping
sales promotion
trademark
warranty

As you glance through a new magazine, many advertisements for a variety of products compete for your attention. The items have a new and exciting look. The colors and styles are fresh and appealing. Suddenly, almost everything you have been wearing seems to be "old." You dream of going out and buying a whole new wardrobe!

However, none of us can afford to replace all of our clothes every few months. Yet, we are constantly tempted by advertisements in magazines, newspapers, catalogues, and on television to buy.

After reading this chapter, you will be able to:

- develop a "plan of action" for your clothing purchases,
- understand how advertising techniques can affect your purchasing decisions,
- identify the information printed on labels and hangtags,
- discuss ways that comparison shopping can help you to gather information.

A Plan of Action

Putting together a shopping plan requires time and thought. However, it will save you time and money later when you need to sew or shop for new items.

STEPS TO THE PLAN

There are four steps to developing a good shopping plan.

1. *You need to gather information.*

   It will help you make an informed decision. Analyzing advertisements, understanding the information printed on labels and hangtags, and careful comparison shopping are all activities that will help you gather this information.

2. *Consider your alternatives and their consequences.*

   Should you buy a new garment, make a new garment, or remodel something you already own? Where will you purchase it? You have many choices of stores, such as a department store, a boutique or specialty store, a discount store, or a mail-order firm. In Chapter 20, you will learn about the advantages and disadvantages of shopping in different types of stores.

3. *Make your own decisions.*

   In Chapter 10, you learned how to develop a wardrobe plan. Once you have established your overall plan, you must decide exactly what you are going to buy or make. Should your new sweater be dressy or casual? Should it be a cardigan or a pullover? Should it be blue, like your old one, or would another color work better with your wardrobe? Remember that your wardrobe plan can change as your clothing needs change.

4. *Evaluate your selection.*

   Does it fit properly? Is it within your budget? Is it well made? Is the fabric a good quality? How much will it cost you to take care of this garment? Can you wash it or will it need to be dry cleaned frequently? In Chapter 21, you will learn what to look for when you are evaluating your selection.

It takes determination and organization to develop and follow both a wardrobe plan and a shopping plan. However, the results are worth it. You will have a better-looking wardrobe that satisfies your needs and wants without putting a strain on your time, budget, or sewing skills.

Gathering Information

Gathering information about what kind of clothing is available and what it is made of can be found through advertisements, through studying fashions themselves, through carefully reading labels and hangtags, and through comparison shopping.

ADVERTISING

The purpose of advertising is to sell us something. Advertisements can tempt us to buy something we really do not need or something that is too expensive for our budget. Advertising attempts to influence us to buy a product by appealing to many different emotions.

Some advertisements are designed to appeal to our dreams and fantasies. Others are designed to appeal to our desire to win the approval of others, our desire for the "very latest," our desire for adventure, or our desire for individuality.

Ads: Information or Image

Advertisements, whether they appear in magazines, catalogues, newspapers, on radio, or on television, can be sources of information and inspiration. There are two basic types of advertising. One type provides you with information. The other type promotes an image.

- **Information Ads.** Information ads tell you many details about the product. They will describe the style and the fabric. They will include the size range, price, fiber content, care, name and location of the store, and brand name.

By reading these ads carefully, you can compare information without having to go from store to store. However, some ads provide more complete information than others. Stating that the fabric is "50% cotton/50% polyester" is more informative than saying that the fabric is a "cotton blend." Newspapers and catalogues carry many information ads.

- **Image Ads.** Image ads are designed to appeal to your fantasies, make a fashion statement, or promote a designer's or a manufacturer's name. These ads are usually very visual. Most of the ad is devoted to illustrations or photographs.

Although image ads give little information about the actual product, they can provide ideas for styles, colors, and textures to add to your wardrobe. You can learn about new fashions and get ideas for new ways to wear clothes you already have. Most magazine and television advertisements are image ads.

Advertising Media

Advertising is designed to give us a message. **Media** is *the method that is used to communicate that message.* Radio and television are *electronic media.* Magazines and newspapers are examples of *print media.* Each of the different medias have certain requirements and limitations that affect the format of the advertisements.

- **Radio and Television.** Because most radio and television ads are only 30 seconds or 60 seconds long, they usually do not give you much information. The people who develop these ads concentrate on ways to make them short and splashy. Their aim is to capture your attention and make you remember the product or the company name. Both radio and television are used to advertise special sales.

- **Magazines.** Most magazine ads are used to create an image of a certain product or brand. They usually have a large photograph or illustration and contain some information about the product. Most magazine ads do not tell you how much the product costs or where you can buy it.

- **Newspapers.** Except for some special ads in large Sunday newspapers, most newspaper ads are black and white drawings. Photographs usually do not reproduce clearly. Some newspaper ads appeal to the same desires and fantasies as the magazine ads. However, they also include more information, such as where you can buy the product, what hours the store is open, what sizes are available, and how much the product costs.

- **Other Print Media.** Other print media include billboards and posters found along the highway or on the sides of a bus. You only see these ads for a very short time, so the message is brief and bold.

- **Promotional Articles.** A magazine or a newspaper will often have a promotional article or an editorial on subjects, such as the newest styles or how to plan your wardrobe. If you read these carefully, you will discover that many of the products mentioned in the article are also advertised in the paper or magazine.

Editors try to support the advertisers. There is nothing dishonest about this. Just remember that what you are reading may be a biased article. However, if you are an alert reader, you will get some new information or new ideas about the product.

- **Fashion Shows and Demonstrations.** Fashion shows give you the opportunity to see the product in person on a model. Remember that a garment may not look the same on you as it does on a professional model. These models are usually tall and slim, and they are wearing accessories carefully chosen to enhance the outfit.

Demonstrations show you how to use the product. Cosmetic demonstrations often give you the opportunity to try out the product on your own skin.

Fashion shows and demonstrations can be free or there may be a charge to attend. These are both very *subtle forms of advertising* that are sometimes called **sales promotions**.

THE INFLUENCE OF FASHION

Because fashion is an industry, its main purpose is to stay in business by selling more clothes. In order to do this, fashion must change constantly. Every season there are articles that talk about the "new looks."

What to Look For

As you learned in Chapter 8, fashion actually changes very slowly. A new style may be introduced, last for several years, and then fade away. For the best shopping strategy, purchase a style that is near the beginning of its "fashion life," rather than at the end.

Read, look, and listen carefully to what is said about the new fashions. You will soon be able to tell the difference between a fashion that will be around for a long time and a fad that will quickly fade from popularity.

Look for some key words that are used to describe a new style. If words and phrases, such as "latest," "newest," "direct from Paris," "the BIG news is . . .," or "keep your eye on . . ." are used, the style may not be fashionable for long. These same words are useful when an advertiser wants to appeal to people who wear status symbols. It is very important to some people to wear whatever is the newest style. If words like "classic," "traditional," or "always in fashion" are used, you know it is not a fad. These words can also be used to describe very expensive items that are status symbols, such as fur coats and expensive cars.

There is nothing wrong with buying something because it is new or classic, a fad or a status symbol. You should, however, know what you are buying and why you have decided to buy or make it. Then you will not have wasted your money.

LABELS AND HANGTAGS

Advertising will not tell you everything you need to know about a product. All of the information you gather from looking, reading, and trying on a garment will help you decide if you should buy it. But many of the things you need to know before making a final decision will come from carefully reading the labels and hangtags that are attached to the garment.

Labels: Mandatory Information

At one time the clothes that everyone wore were made from natural fibers. The most common fibers were cotton, wool, silk, and linen.

People knew what to expect from these fibers and how to take care of them.

Then the world of modern chemistry appeared. Fibers now had names like "nylon," "spandex," "polyester," and "acetate." People did not know what these were or how to care for them. Clothes were marked and advertised in such a way that consumers often thought they were buying one thing and ended up with something quite different.

- **The Textiles Fibers Product Information Act.** In 1958, Congress approved the TFPI Act. The purpose of this law is to protect consumers against misbranding or false advertising concerning the fiber content of any textile product. Similar laws have been enacted by Congress to cover products made from wool and from fur.

Every garment must now have one or more labels that give the consumer specific information. This information is **mandatory**, or *required by law.* These labels should be attached to the garment in places where they are easy to find. Usually, this is at the center back of a garment—at the neck of a shirt, sweater, or blouse, and at the waist of pants and skirts. Sometimes you will find them in the inside lower front seam of a jacket or in the side seams of lingerie.

These labels can be glued, sewn, printed, or stamped on the fabric. They can even be attached to the outside of the garment as long as they are put on in such a way that they will not come off until you, the purchaser, decide to take them off.

However, most labels remain permanently attached to the garment. If the garment will remain in a package until after it is sold, the fiber content label can be affixed to the package only.

- *Essentials of the Act.* According to the TFPI Act, there are five pieces of mandatory information that must appear on labels in the garment:

1. *Fiber Content.*

    Any fiber that makes up 5 percent or more of the garment by weight must be listed. The generic names that you learned about in Chapter 16 are required. The label may list "Polyester" or "Dacron Polyester," but it may not list just "Dacron," which is a brand name.

2. *Percentage of Fiber Content by Weight.*

    The fibers must be listed in descending order by percentage. This means that the fiber present in the greatest amount is listed first. Fibers present in an amount less than 5 percent are listed last, as "Other Fibers." If a garment is made of only one fiber type, the label must say so. It can say "100% Cotton" or "All Cotton."

3. *Identification of the Manufacturer.*

    This label identifies who is responsible for the product. Either the name of the manufacturer or the store, the registration identification number, or the trademark name for the product is written on the label. The registration identification number is assigned to a manufacturer or store by the U. S. Government's Federal Trade Commission. A **trademark** is a *symbol, design, word, or letter that is used by manufacturers or retailers to distinguish their products from those of the competition.* Trademarks are registered and protected by law so that no one can use someone else's trademark.

4. *Country of Origin.*

    The label must state *where the garment was manufactured,* such as "Made in India" or "Made in Hong Kong." Since December 1984, all textile products manufactured in the United States must carry a label stating "Made in U.S.A."

5. *Care Requirements.*

    Information on how to take care of the garment is regulated by the Care Labeling Rule, issued by the Federal Trade Commis-

This label gives information on fiber content and weight, brand name, country of origin, and care requirements.

sion. You learned about these guidelines in Chapter 18.

There are two additional pieces of information that may be included as labels in the garment. However they are not mandatory.

- *Size* can be included as part of the brand label, or it may be printed on a small separate label.
- *A union label* tells you that the garment was made in the United States by people who belong to a certain union, such as the International Ladies' Garment Workers' Union (ILGWU).

Hangtags: Voluntary Information

Hangtags are labels that literally hang from the garment. They can be attached with a string, a thread, a strip of plastic, or a safety pin. Before you wear the garment, you remove these labels. Hangtags may repeat some of the information that appears on labels within the garment. However, the information that is present on the hangtags is *voluntary,* given freely and not regulated by law.

It is useful to know where hangtags and labels are usually found, since there may be more than one of each type on a garment.

Hangtag Information. Manufacturers' hangtags may include the following information:

1. *The trademark or brand name of the manufacturer.*

   This can take the form of the **logo**, or *symbol,* for the product or its manufacturer. Sometimes the information on this hangtag also appears as a label that is sewn into the garment.

2. *The trademarks, brand names, or logos for the fibers.*

3. *Information about the construction of the fabric.*

   This information may tell whether the fabric is a stretch fabric or a knit fabric.

4. *Information concerning any warranty or guarantee that applies to the garment or its fabric.*

   A **warranty** is a *pledge or assurance that the product will meet certain standards.* A few organizations, such as the International Fabricare Institute, maintain testing laboratories that issue warranties or seals of approval. These pledges guarantee that the product will live up to the standards set by that particular laboratory. Some manufacturers also issue their own warranties. The Monsanto Company issues a "wear-dated" warranty. It guarantees that the consumer will receive a refund or a replacement garment if the original garment does not provide normal wear for a specific period of time.

Hangtags can also be a miniadvertisement for the product, with words like "classic," "comfortable," "easy care," or "As Seen in *Seventeen Magazine*." Sometimes the manufacturer includes other information, such as the size and the manufacturer's suggested retail price, on the hangtag.

Stores usually attach separate hangtags with information that is important to the store, such as size, price, stock number, and department number. Stores may also attach a hangtag or label with their name or logo.

Shopping with friends is a way to compare value. But care must be taken not to buy on impulse.

COMPARISON SHOPPING

How do you recognize a good bargain, or even a fair price, when you see it? You can learn how to be an educated shopper by doing **comparison shopping**. This means *to look at quality, price, and design to compare value.*

Comparison shop at home by reading, watching, and listening to advertisements and by studying mail-order catalogues. Then, once you are in a store, you will be able to compare the merchandise with the information you already have.

Examine the quality and take note of the price. Read the labels and the hangtags. They are valuable sources of information concerning the manufacturer, the fiber content, cost of the garment, and much more.

Recreational Shopping

Have you and your friends ever gone shopping "just to look" and then one of you decides to buy a belt or a scarf? The next thing you know, everyone has bought something.

Recreational shopping, which is *window-shopping or shopping just for fun,* may be an activity among your friends. However, it is very hard for many people to "just look" and not buy.

Instead, use recreational shopping as an opportunity to get ideas about what to sew or how to combine things you already have in your closet.

Impulse Buying

Sometimes recreational shopping leads to a great many **impulse**, or *sudden,* purchases. Store displays are specifically designed to catch your attention. An entire outfit is often displayed, complete with accessories, so that you are tempted to buy everything, rather than coordinating one new item with items already in your wardrobe. This is how our closets fill up with fads, "good buys," status items, and a variety of accessories that we do not really need.

Consider Your Alternatives

The second step in developing a good shopping plan is to consider your alternatives and examine their consequences. Your alternatives are the options or choices that you have to achieve your goals. In this case, your goal is to find the best way to carry out your wardrobe plan.

YOUR RESOURCES

You should look at your *resources,* or the means you use to achieve your goal. Your resources include such things as how much money you have to spend, your sewing skills, and the time you have available to shop or sew. An older brother or sister who will hand clothing down to you is also considered a resource.

Money

If you do not think you have enough money to spend, review the decision-making process and examine your alternatives. You could decide to do without a few things on your list. Perhaps you really need only one new shirt, instead of the three that are on your list. You could shop for multi-purpose garments.

For example, if you need both a raincoat and a warm winter coat, you might shop for a raincoat with a zip-out lining. You could reexamine the garments that are already in your wardrobe. Perhaps you can discover new ways to mix and match them to create new outfits.

If you do not already have a part-time job, you could go out and get one. Then you would have more money to spend on the items in your wardrobe plan. Remember, however, that the type of job you get may mean that you would need more or different clothes than you own.

You can also make the money you have go further by shopping very carefully. By reading and listening to advertisements, as well as comparison shopping, you can learn how much things cost. Then you will be able to recognize a bargain when you see it. You could also make your money go farther by buying merchandise on sale or at a store specializing in lower prices.

Skills

You could learn to sew. Sewing usually saves money. It also makes it easier to get the style you want in the color you want. People who sew tend to have clothes that are made from better quality fabric than they could afford to buy in ready-to-wear. Sewing experience also helps you to better evaluate ready-to-wear garments.

Your sewing skills can be used to restyle and update the clothing that is already in your closet, as well as improve the appearance and the fit of any ready-to-wear garment you purchase. You can change the length of the hem, take in or let out seams, or make minor alterations. You can change buttons or add trim for a new look. Chapter 14 suggests many ideas for redesigning and recyling clothes.

Time

If your time is limited because of commitments to family, work, or school activities, a well thought-out wardrobe plan is essential. You probably do not have time to shop "just for fun." You need to know exactly what you are looking for before you go into a store. If you like to sew, stick to classic styles and easy-to-sew patterns. Think about setting aside some time during school vacations to make your clothes. Save any hand sewing, such as putting in a hem or sewing on buttons, to do when you are watching your favorite television program.

Chapter 19 Review

Summary

A good shopping plan can save you time and money. First, you need to gather information that will help you make an informed decision. Three sources of information are advertisements, labels and hangtags, and comparison shopping. Information ads provide many details about a product. Image ads appeal to your fantasies or promote an image. Labels and hangtags include both mandatory and voluntary information. After gathering information, you should consider your alternatives. Money, skills, and time are resources that can help you achieve your goals.

Questions

1. Identify the four steps involved in developing a good shopping plan.

2. What are the advantages of developing and following both a wardrobe plan and a shopping plan?

3. Describe the differences between the information that appears in an information ad and in an image ad.

4. How do ads on radio and television, in magazines, and in newspapers differ?

5. Why should you purchase a style that is near the beginning of its "fashion life"?

6. What is the purpose of the Textile Fiber Products Identification Act?

7. List the five pieces of information that must appear on labels attached to all ready-to-wear garments.

8. What type of information usually appears on a manufacturer's hangtag?

9. How can comparison shopping help you to gather information?

10. How can sewing skills be used to expand your wardrobe plan?

Activities

1. Find examples of information ads and image ads in magazines, newspapers, or catalogues. Analyze the ads for the amount of information given that would help in making a shopping decision. What desires or dreams do the image ads appeal to?

2. Collect several manufacturers' hangtags. Evaluate each one for the type of information presented. Are any of the tags only advertisements?

3. Design a label for a garment. Include all the mandatory information that is required. Design a second hangtag that has additional information to supplement the garment label.

You Be the Expert

You often go to the mall on Saturdays with a group of friends. Many of you end up buying something that you don't really need, something that is too expensive, or something that you don't like when you get home. How can you change you and your friends' behavior?

20 Shopping — Where, When, How

TERMS TO LEARN

*annual percentage
    rate*
boutique
C.O.D.
finance charge
inventory
irregulars
lay-away
money order
outlet
seconds

The third step in developing a good shopping plan concerns making your own decisions about what to buy. We have covered part of this step in Chapter 11, when we learned how to develop a wardrobe plan.

But there is another part to this third step. It is knowing *where* to shop, *when* to shop, and *how* to pay for your purchases. We will be devoting all this chapter to these important activities.

After reading this chapter, you will be able to:

- explain the plans you should make before you begin shopping,
- identify the types of stores where goods can be purchased,
- explain the different types of store sales,
- describe the many ways you can pay for your purchases.

Where to Shop

The idea of "going shopping" sounds fun. But have you ever spent a whole day running around from store to store and accomplishing nothing? The stores were crowded, your feet hurt, and nothing looked right.

This probably happened because you omitted a very important step in the process of shopping: taking the time to do some planning and preparation before you left home.

GETTING READY TO SHOP

First, if you have not already done so, you should decide what you plan to buy and where you plan to shop.

Make a List

On a piece of paper, list each item of clothing that you want to shop for. Then read the newspaper and magazine ads for information about styles, brand names, prices, and which stores carry what items. Next, list all the stores in your area that you could visit.

Now number your list in order of importance. You will want to shop for major items first, while you are still fresh and full of energy. The stores most likely to have these items should go on the top of your list.

Arrange the list of stores according to their locations so that you will not be going back and forth across the shopping mall or all over town. Try not to shop for too many things at one time.

Go Alone or with a Friend

Some people shop best when they shop by themselves. Their time is more organized and

they are not as tempted to make impulse purchases. Other people shop better when they take a friend or relative along. Make sure that it is a person whose ideas you respect and whose taste is similar to yours.

Go Prepared

Dress appropriately for the item you are looking for. If you are shopping for a sport coat, wear dress slacks and good shoes. You will be surprised at how different it looks with these clothes instead of with blue jeans and a T-shirt. If you are shopping for a party dress, wear stockings and bring shoes that are the same height as the ones you plan to wear.

Very few of us can match colors from memory. If you are trying to buy something to match an item you already own, either wear or bring the item with you. If it is something you have made, carry a swatch of the fabric along.

THE STORES

There are many types of stores from which to choose. They may differ in type of merchandise, prices, special services, location, sales staff, and reputation. Before you select a store, you will need to consider several things.

1. *First, consider what it is that you want to buy.*
   Different stores carry different types of merchandise. You would not expect to find a tuxedo or a prom dress in a store that specializes in casual clothes. You might look for a casual winter coat in a ski shop, but you would not expect to find a dress coat there.

2. *The amount of money you have available will influence the stores you select.*
   Stores known for their special sales or for offering quality goods at lower prices are good choices if your funds are limited.
   Some stores specialize in certain price

ranges — low, medium, or high. Other stores offer a range of prices within each category.

3. *The special services a store offers are another consideration.*

   Some stores provide free parking or free delivery. Other stores offer alteration or gift wrapping services.

4. *The location of a store can also be a factor.*

   If you do not have a driver's license and access to a car, you must wait until someone else can take you. You can choose a store near a bus route or within walking distance.

5. *The type of sales staff a store employs can influence where you decide to shop.*

   Many stores employ sales personnel who are knowledgeable and helpful. They will welcome your questions, help you find just the right item for your needs, and assist you in making a wise selection.

6. *The store's reputation is important.*

   Find out which stores are known for quality merchandise, a fair return policy, and honest labeling. A store may sell goods that are not perfect, as long as these goods are clearly marked as such.

Department stores usually offer a multitude of styles and sizes to choose from.

Department Stores

Department stores are large stores that carry a wide selection of many different types of merchandise. Of all the different types of stores, department stores usually offer the most extensive choice of merchandise in many styles, colors, sizes, qualities, and price ranges.

This merchandise is grouped into areas, or *departments*, according to the specialty. Departments may be organized by size and sex, such as the Men's Department, the Boys' Department, the Junior Department, and the Teen Department. They can also be organized by fashion and price categories, such as "Designer," "Budget," or "Better Dresses." Some may have special departments, such as "Career."

Department stores carry many other things besides clothes. For example, they can sell appliances, sporting goods, electronic equipment, luggage, and housewares.

Department stores offer many special services, such as gift wrapping, deliveries, restaurants, cleaning and alteration departments, beauty salons, repair departments, a bridal registry, interior decoration services, and fashion consultations. They also sponsor events, such as fashion shows and in-store demonstrations, that are designed to sell products and educate customers. Most department stores mail out catalogues several times a year.

Because some department stores have many branches, they can buy large quantities of merchandise from the manufacturer at a lower price. These savings are often passed on to the customer.

Sometimes department stores will have a manufacturer make items exclusively for them. The department store will then put their own name on the items. This is known as *private labeling*.

Department stores usually have their own credit cards. Many of them also honor national credit cards.

Specialty Stores

A store that carries only a limited range of merchandise is known as a *specialty store*. It may specialize in clothing for a particular group of people, such as children's wear, women's clothes, menswear, or petite or large sizes. Or it may carry a particular type of merchandise, such as skiwear, hats, tuxedos, or bridal gowns.

Boutiques are *a type of specialty store featuring very fashionable or unique designs that are higher priced.* Boutiques appeal to customers looking for designer clothes, a special "look," or unusual items.

Specialty stores are usually small stores, owned by one or a few people. The atmosphere and the service are more personalized than in other stores. The salesperson that waits on you may also be the owner. If you return an item, some specialty stores will not give you a cash refund. Instead, they will give you credit toward another item in the store. Be sure to ask about this point before you buy something.

Discount Stores

Discount stores have changed over the past few years. When they first became popular, these stores usually had merchandise piled high on tables. There were very few salespeople, no dressing rooms, and long lines at the registers. You had to pay for everything in cash. If you knew how to shop for quality merchandise, you could get some very good bargains.

Today, most discount stores have become more like specialty stores or department stores. Clothing is hung on racks. There are window and floor displays, as well as dressing rooms. Some discount stores now let you pay by check or credit card.

All of these services mean that prices may not be discounted as much as they used to be. In order to get a bargain, you must shop carefully and be able to recognize good quality.

Factory or Manufacturer's Outlets

An **outlet** store *sells only the brands of merchandise that are produced by the manufacturer or the factory that owns it.* Three types of goods are sold here: *overruns, seconds,* and *irregulars.*

When a manufacturer produces more of a certain style than can be sold to stores, it is called an *overrun,* or excess merchandise.

Irregulars are *goods that do not pass inspection because they have a small imperfection,* such as a pull in the fabric, an uneven color, or a mislabeled size. These are flaws that will not affect the wear of the garment.

Seconds are *garments with more serious flaws,* such as one sleeve being longer than the other or the buttonholes being sewn in the wrong place.

Because outlet stores are usually located next to the factory, they may be in an industrial area that is hard to find. Sometimes several manufacturers will get together and open an outlet store.

You must pay cash in most outlet stores. Sometimes they accept a check, but they almost never take credit cards. You may not be

Before buying irregular clothing, carefully check out what the garment's flaws really are.

able to try on the garments, and you cannot return anything that you buy. If you are a good shopper and very familiar with certain brands, you may do very well at this type of store.

Catalogue and Mail-Order Stores

When most of our country's population lived in rural communities, people ordered many of their goods through catalogues and mail-order stores. As people began to migrate to the cities, this method of buying goods lost its popularity. In the 1970s, when gasoline was scarce and expensive, people rediscovered this method of shopping. In the 1980s, catalogue shopping grew in popularity, with thousands of catalogues available nationally.

Shopping by mail or by phone is easy and convenient. You save time and money on gasoline. You will, however, have to pay a shipping charge. If you order by phone, you may also have to pay for a long distance call. Some mail-order stores have a toll-free 800 number. Mail-order stores accept major credit cards. If you charge an item, there is usually no problem in getting credit if you return the item.

There are also several disadvantages to shopping by mail. You may not be exactly sure what the product looks like. If you are ordering clothes, you do not have a chance to try them on before you order. It is important to carefully read the written information about the product so that you will know what you are ordering. Also read the fine print in the catalogue concerning policies about returns and guarantees.

Never send cash through the mails with your order. If it is lost or stolen, you will have no proof that you sent it. Instead, pay by credit card, check, or C.O.D. You will learn about the advantages and disadvantages of these types of payments later on in this chapter.

Shopping by phone and mail is convenient if you know exactly what to buy.

Variety Stores

A *variety store* is one that sells many different types of products. Examples of variety stores are drugstores, supermarkets, five-and-dimes, and some all-purpose department stores.

Because clothing is only one of many types of items carried by a variety store, you will probably find a limited selection. Clothes are often sold prepackaged, so that it is sometimes difficult to see what you are buying.

Variety stores can be convenient sources for items, such as stockings, underwear, belts, scarves, and other accessories. These stores usually do not offer credit.

Bazaars, Flea Markets, and Fairs

These types of retail locations are becoming more and more popular. Usually, many different people rent booths in a large area and sell merchandise. The booths can be located indoors in a school, shopping mall, church, or club, or out-

Shopping by Mail

Mail-order shopping is one of the fastest growing industries in the country. It accounts for over $30 billion in sales each year. Many people find that they can save time by ordering merchandise from catalogues and advertisements. Often, they are able to choose from a greater selection of products or to find items that might not be available locally.

To use mail-order shopping successfully, follow these tips:

- Read the catalogue carefully before ordering, to familiarize yourself with the merchandise.
- Be aware of shipping and return policies so that you know when to expect delivery and how to return unsatisfactory products, if necessary.

- Look for Petite-Small-Medium-Large-X Large size ranges rather than numbered sizes, which require a more accurate fit.
- Select easy-fitting styles, such as dropped shoulders, roll-up sleeves, and elasticized or drawstring waists.
- Choose basic colors, such as navy, gray, wine, brown, red, black, and white. You will avoid being surprised about less specific colors, such as "teal" or "slate."
- Be sure to include all the required information to avoid delaying your order.
- Pay only by check, money order, or credit card. Don't send cash through the mail.
- Keep a record of your order. Merchandise must be shipped within 30 days, or you can cancel the order and obtain a refund.

doors in a parking lot or field. They may sell used clothing or new merchandise that has been purchased directly from a manufacturer.

Garage sales and tag sales may be held by one or more families. They may sell used clothing, hats, shoes, purses, and jewelry at very low prices.

In order to be a successful shopper at these outlets, you must be aware of prices and quality. You should know what a similar item would cost you in a department store or a specialty store. Just because something is being sold at a flea market or garage sale does not make it a good buy. You must pay cash in these places, and you cannot return what you buy.

Thrift Shops

Thrift shops are stores that carry secondhand or used clothing and household items. Thrift shops may be owned by an individual or by an organization, such as a church group or an organization founded to support various charities.

Some of the clothing in thrift shops may have been worn many times. But, if you look carefully, you may also find garments that are almost new, particularly party clothes or special one-of-a-kind items.

The clothing in these stores is very inexpensive. Thrift shops do not give credit, and they do not let you return the clothes you buy.

When to Shop

When you walk into a store at the beginning of August, it is well stocked with new fall merchandise. The styles are exciting, the colors are fresh, and the fabrics are different from what you have been wearing for the past several months. You are probably tempted to buy all the new clothes that you will need for school right away.

THE MAJOR SELLING SEASONS

Although new merchandise arrives all the time, stores have several major selling seasons, or periods when the majority of new things appear. These seasons are spring, fall or back-to-school, and Christmas or holiday. Stores begin to promote spring clothes in February, fall clothes in July, and Christmas items by the beginning of November.

This store is taking advantage of the back-to-school or fall season to promote their new arrivals with a sale.

If dressing in the latest fashion is important to you, then you will probably want to buy new clothes at the beginning of the season. This is the time when stores have the best selection of the newest merchandise. If getting a good price is more important to you than having the latest styles, you will probably want to wait until the stores have sales.

SPECIAL SALES

Stores have sales at special times during the year. If you need a new item, but can "make do" with what you have a for a little while, you might want to wait and buy it on sale. For example, winter coats go on sale in October for Columbus Day. Bathing suits and other hot weather clothes go on sale right after the Fourth of July. Many items go on sale after Christmas so that the stores can make room for new spring merchandise.

To judge if a sale is valid, there are a few guidelines to follow. Be familiar with the price and quality of the same or similar merchandise. Just because a store marks an item as "sale," it does not necessarily mean it is a bargain.

Check the item for flaws. Is it a little flaw that will not be noticed or can be easily mended? Or is it a big flaw that will interfere with how the garment is worn? Think about how often you will wear the item. Ten percent off on a garment you will wear many times can be a better bargain than 30 percent off on a garment you will seldom wear. A bargain is not a bargain if you never wear it.

Seconds or irregulars can be sold by stores other than factory or manufacturer's outlets. They should be clearly marked so that you know you are not buying perfect goods. If the store labels the items "As Is," you ar buying seconds or irregulars.

With sidewalk sales, price should not be the only determining factor. Check on quality, flaws, and for frequency of use.

Terms to Know

Stores use many different terms to describe their kinds of sales. *Clearance sales* occur when a store wants to move out merchandise to make room for new stock, or when a store has decided to no longer carry a particular item.

Special purchases are items that the store has bought from the manufacturer at a special price. This special price was probably given because the store bought a very large quantity of the item. It may also have been because the manufacturer is discontinuing the style or had many items left over that were not sold to other stores.

Inventory sales occur once a year when a store "takes **inventory**." The store *compares its written stock records with what is actually on sale* in the store by physically checking and counting all items. Some stores have sales before inventory time so that there are fewer items to count. Other stores have sales right after they have taken inventory, when they know exactly what merchandise is in the store.

Holiday sales are timed to match a special day, such as Election Day or Washington's Birthday. Many people do not have to work or go to school on these days and are free to shop. Stores can also create their own holiday sales, such as an Anniversary Sale or a Founder's Birthday Sale.

Holiday sales are a tradition for many stores. The customers know that the store has the same sale at the same time every year. They plan on buying merchandise at these sales.

THE TIME OF DAY

Stores are usually crowded during the times when most people are free to shop. They will be particularly busy at lunchtime, during the early evening hours, on Saturdays, and on big sale days.

If you can arrange it, shop at "off" times, like the late morning, early afternoon, or late evening. You will find that the salespeople have more time to give you individual attention then.

Avoid shopping when you are tired. Either nothing will look right, or you will settle for something you really do not want just so you can go home.

How to Pay

There are many ways to finance your purchases. If you understand the advantages and disadvantages of each method, you will be able to choose the ones that are best for you. With some methods, you pay cash before you receive the merchandise. With other methods, you "borrow" the money, receive the merchandise, and pay later. No matter which method you choose, you still need money in the end.

CASH AND CHECK PURCHASES

Cash is often the simplest and quickest way to pay for your purchases. All stores take cash. If you pay cash, it is easy to keep track of what you spend because you cannot spend more money than you have. There are no extra finance costs for paying cash, like there are when you use credit.

Paying by check is the same as paying cash. Your check represents the money you have in the bank. An advantage to paying by check is that you do not have to carry a large amount of cash with you.

Some stores, however, will not accept checks. They may have had bad experiences with people who wrote checks for money they did not have. Before accepting your check, stores will usually ask for several pieces of identification, such as a driver's license or a credit card, as proof that you are who you say you are.

CREDIT PURCHASES

When stores allow you to buy on credit, they are letting you borrow money against your ability to pay in the future.

Advantages and Disadvantages

There are several advantages to purchasing an item on credit, rather than paying by cash or by check.

1. It is fast and convenient. You usually do not have to show identification, as when paying by check, and you do not need to carry large amounts of cash.

2. Since you do not have to pay right away, you can buy something even if you do not have the money. This is particularly convenient if you need an expensive item of clothing, such as boots or a winter coat.

3. It is easier to return or exchange an item. A credit is simply made to your account.

However, there are also several disadvantages to paying by credit.

1. Any bills not paid when due are subject to extra charges.

2. It is easy to spend more money than you have or can possibly pay back.

3. Because it is so convenient, you may find yourself shopping only at stores where you have a charge account. When you get into this habit, you may not be taking advantage of sales or lower prices at other stores. Also, you may no longer be comparing the quality of merchandise in different stores.

CREDIT CARDS

Credit or charge cards can be issued by a local store; by a bank, such as MasterCard or Visa; or by a credit card company, such as American Express or Diner's Club.

Before a store, bank, or credit card company will give you a card, you will be asked to fill out

Credit and store charge cards are now used by the majority of clothing stores.

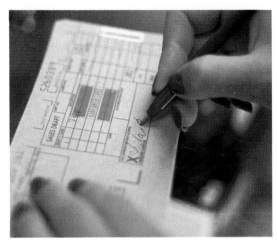

Charging items is very handy, but you must be able to pay the bill eventually.

an application form. Information such as your age, where you live, how much money you earn, what bank accounts you have, and what other charge cards you own will indicate if you are a good credit risk.

In order to have a credit card in your own name, you must be 18 years of age or older. Some stores and credit card companies will let younger teenagers use their parents' credit cards, provided that permission has been given.

Charges

In return for taking a chance on your ability to pay, a store or bank usually adds a **finance charge**. This is usually 1½ percent of your monthly bill for a total interest rate of 18 percent per year. The maximum interest rate that may be charged is controlled by state law. The finance charge is applied only if you do not pay the full amount of your bill within a specified time. This time is usually 30 days after the billing date.

According to the *Truth in Lending Law*, you must be given the following information in writing by the card issuer:

1. the cost of the finance plan in dollars and cents,
2. the percentage of interest you will be charged each month,
3. *the percentage of interest you will be charged each year,* called the **annual percentage rate**.

In addition to the finance charge, the issuer of the card may charge an annual fee for servicing your account. This service or subscription charge must be paid even if you pay the full amount of your bill within the specified time.

Types of Accounts

Many large department stores offer two different types of credit accounts. With a *Regular* or *30-Day Account*, you are expected to pay the entire bill each month. The full payment is due within 30 days after the billing date. If your payment is late, the store may charge interest.

With a *Revolving Credit Account*, you have the option of paying all or part of your bill. If you pay the full amount, there will be no finance charge. If you make only a partial payment, a finance charge will be added to your next month's statement. However, you must pay a minimum amount, usually 10 percent of the total, each month.

Sometimes a store, bank, or credit card company specifies a credit limit, also called the *line of credit*. This is the maximum amount the customer can owe on the credit card account at any one time.

Statements

Each month you will receive a *statement,* or bill, that tells you about the status of your account. This statement will list:

- charges you made since the last statement,
- the amount of your last payment,
- any credits or returns,

- the amount of your previous bill,
- the amount that is owed on the current bill,
- the billing date.

In addition, the statement includes any finance charges, information on the finance rates, and your line of credit.

Billing Problems

What happens if you do not agree with the charges on your bill, or if you have a problem with the merchandise? The *Fair Credit Billing Act* contains the following provisions relating to monthly statements and credit purchases:

- You must notify a creditor in writing about an error in your statement within 60 days. The creditor (which is the store, bank, or credit card company) must respond within 30 days to your inquiry and must resolve the problem within 90 days.
- If you use a nonstore credit card to make store purchases, you are still protected if the product or service is faulty.
- You do not have to pay the amount in question until the problem is resolved.

Credit Card Safety

When using a credit card, always take care to prevent loss or theft. Be sure your card is returned to you after each credit purchase. Keep a record of your credit card number. If your credit card is lost or stolen, notify the bank or store immediately.

LAY-AWAY PURCHASES

When you purchase an item on the **lay-away** plan, you give the store a *down payment to reserve the item for you.* This down payment may be 10 percent of the total price or it may be a small amount, such as $5.00. Then you agree to pay the store a certain amount of money each week or month until the total amount is paid. Once the store has received all its money, the item is yours.

The advantage to this method of payment is that you do not pay any finance charges, although sometimes there is a small service charge. The disadvantage is that you have to wait several weeks or months until the item is yours, even though you have partially paid for it. In addition, the store has the interest-free use of your money.

Lay-away purchases can be a good way to pay for an item you would not use immediately, such as a winter coat that you see in the store in August.

MAIL-ORDER PURCHASES

When you order an item by mail, there are several ways you can pay for it. You should never send cash through the mail because it can easily be stolen. In fact, many companies specifically state that they will not accept cash.

Instead, you can send a check or a money order. **Money orders** are *similar to checks and can be purchased from a post office or a bank.* They are used by people who do not have a checking account and want to send a payment through the mail.

C.O.D. PURCHASES

C.O.D. stands for *cash on delivery.* When the package arrives, you give the money for your purchase to the delivery person, who may be a mail carrier or a representative of a shipping company. Many stores will not ship C.O.D. Those that do may have special requirements, such as a minimum purchase amount and a down payment. Sometimes there is also a delivery charge.

Summary

You need to plan your shopping before you leave home. There are many types of stores that differ in type of merchandise, price range, special services, location, and reputation. These include department stores, specialty stores, discount stores, factory or manufacturer's outlets, catalogue and mail-order stores, variety stores, bazaars, flea markets, fairs, and thrift shops. Each type of store has advantages and disadvantages. Stores also have different selling seasons and types of sales. There are several ways to finance your purchases—cash, check, credit card, lay-away, money order, or C.O.D.

Questions

1. List at least four factors that you should consider when deciding where to shop for clothes. Explain briefly why each is an important decision.

2. Identify five types of clothing stores, and describe the differences in their merchandise and service.

3. Why might you find prices lower in a department store or a discount store than in a specialty store? What can a specialty store offer you that the other two might not?

4. What are the advantages and disadvantages of shopping by mail?

5. Why must you be particulary careful of the quality of merchandise that you purchase from a flea market, garage sale, or thrift shop?

6. What guidelines are helpful when buying merchandise that is "on sale"?

7. Describe the advantages and disadvantages of buying on credit.

8. Identify the following terms: lay-away, money order, and C.O.D.

Activities

1. Visit three different types of stores in your community. Compare three similar items in each store. List the differences in quality and price for each item. At which store would you purchase each item. Why?

2. Interview four friends or relatives about their favorite place to shop. What advantages are mentioned about each store?

3. Obtain an application for a credit card. What is the annual finance charge? If you did not pay a monthly bill of $200, how much interest would you be charged? If you paid the same amount of interest each month, what would be the annual cost?

You Be the Expert

In August you are shopping with a friend who decides to purchase a summer outfit and a winter coat on the lay-away plan. Your friend asks your advice about the purchases. What advice would you give?

21 Evaluating Your Selection

TERMS TO LEARN

compromise
cost per wearing
overlock seam
pills
quality
trade-off

Since your earliest school days, teachers have been grading your work. Grades have appeared on the math tests you took, on the book reports you wrote, and on the term papers you handed in. Each grade was the result of the teacher's careful evaluation of many things, such as the quality of the information you wrote, how well your report fulfilled the assignment, and how the material was presented.

The fourth step in a good shopping plan is to evaluate your selection when you are thinking about buying it. You should give it a grade, based on how well it rates according to your personal evaluation scale. The item that gets the best grade is the one you should buy.

After reading this chapter, you will be able to:

- give examples of different size categories in clothing,
- evaluate the fit and appearance of a garment,
- judge the quality of the fabric and the workmanship,
- describe compromises and trade-offs that can be made.

Meeting Your Needs and Wants

Imagine that you are in the sportswear department of a store, surrounded by racks and racks of garments. How are you going to decide which garments to try on? And once you have tried some of them on, how are you going to know which choices are good ones for you at this time in your life?

QUESTIONS TO ASK

When a garment catches your eye, stop and ask yourself some questions.

Where does it fit into your personal wardrobe plan? Do you really have any place to wear the garment? Does it go with anything else in your wardrobe? Do you need to buy new accessories in order to wear the item?

Is the price within your budget? Is the garment worth what it costs? What is the **quality**, or *superior characteristics*? What type of care does it need? How does it fit you?

What image does the garment project? If the garment does not represent the image you want to show the world, you will probably never be comfortable wearing it. Leave it in the store and let it send out personal messages for some other person.

Are you thinking about buying the item just because you feel like buying "something"? Every once in a while, people have a need to buy something just to make themselves feel good. It is a way of giving yourself a treat. Learn to recognize these impulse purchases for what they are and restrict them to small, inexpensive items, such as a scarf, a belt, a lipstick, or a pair of socks.

Clothing Sizes

Did you ever have the experience of buying something in a hurry without trying it on? When you got it home, you found out it did not fit—even though it was marked as "your" size! Did you think that you had suddenly lost weight, grown taller, or that the garment was mismarked? Most likely, it was none of these things.

HOW A SIZE CAN DIFFER

The major pattern companies, in cooperation with the National Bureau of Standards, joined together to develop standard body measurements that are the basis for all pattern sizes. That is why a pattern in a particular size from one pattern company fits you almost the same as a pattern in that same size from another company.

This is not true with ready-to-wear clothes. A size 10 from one manufacturer may not fit the same way as a size 10 from another manufacturer. In fact, you might find that you wear a smaller size in more expensive clothes and a larger size in less expensive clothes.

Because each manufacturer has its own sizing standards, it is essential that you try on every garment before you purchase it. Even if you already own several garments from that manufacturer and are satisfied with the way they fit, the style of a garment can change how it looks and feels on you.

The standard measurements used by a manufacturer may be influenced by production costs. If the manufacturer cuts a size 10 garment so that it is a little bit smaller, production costs are reduced.

A savings of even 1″ (2.5 cm) of fabric per garment can amount to hundreds of yards of fabric and hundreds of dollars of savings when a manufacturer is cutting for mass production. Economizing on the amount of fabric used is one way that manufacturers can sell at a lower price. For example, a size 10 dress that sells for $18.99 will probably be much smaller than a size 10 dress that sells for $100.00.

SIZE CATEGORIES FOR FEMALES

Female clothing has sizes or numbers that represent a combination of body measurements, body proportions, and height.

Teenage Sizes

Most teenage girls wear either a Misses or a Junior size. *Misses* sizes are even-numbered (4, 6, 8, 10, 12, 14, 16) and designed for a well-proportioned and developed figure. *Junior* sizes are odd-numbered (3, 5, 7, 9, 11, 13, 15) and cut for a trimmer, shorter-waisted figure. *Petite* categories are sized for females under 5'4" (1.63 m) who have a small body structure. Larger sizes (14 to 22) are also available in many stores.

Special Teen departments carry sizes for the developing preteen and teen figure. These may be marked as junior/misses sizes (3/4 to 15/16). *Girls* sizes are for preteens who have not begun to mature.

If you are unsure of your size, refer to Chapter 23 to learn how to take your measurements. Then you can compare your actual measurements with the size measurements listed in the pattern catalogue charts. Although ready-to-wear sizes do not exactly match pattern sizes, you can get a good idea of what sizes to begin trying on in a store.

Skirts, Pants, and Tops

Skirts and pants are sold by size or by the waist measurement. A size 25 pants means that

it has a 25″ (63.5 cm) waist measurement. Sweaters, t-shirts, and other loose fitting garments can be sold in petite, small, medium, and large sizes. Generally, a "petite" is equal to size 6 to 8, a "small" is 8 to 10, "medium" is 10 to 12, and a "large" is 14 to 16.

SIZE CATEGORIES FOR MALES

Male clothing comes in *Men's, Teen Boys',* and *Boys'* sizes. Special sizes have also been developed for *Tall Men, Short Men, Stout Men, Husky Boys,* and *Slim Boys.*

Jackets, Pants, and Shirts

Jackets and *suits* are sized by chest measurement and length. A size 38 means that the jacket will fit a man with a 38″ (96.5 cm) chest. A size 38-Short means that the jacket will be 2″ (5 cm) shorter than the standard size 38. A size 38-Long is for a taller man with longer arms.

Pants are sized by the waist measurement and the inseam measurement. The inseam is the inside leg measurement, from the crotch to the hem edge of the pants. Size 28/31 has a 28″ (71 cm) waist and a 31″ (79 cm) inseam.

Shirts are sized by the collar size and the sleeve length, such as 14/32 (36/81 cm). The collar size is the measurement of your neck, plus ½″ (1.3 cm). The sleeve length is measured from the base of your back neck, across the shoulder, around the outside of your slightly bent elbow, to the wrist bone.

Other Sizings

Some garments are sold in *small, medium, large,* and *extra-large* sizes. Generally, in men's sizes a "small" is size 34 to 36, a "medium" is size 38 to 40, a "large" is size 42 to 44, and an "extra-large" is size 46 to 48.

Evaluating Fit

No matter what size is marked on the label, the only important factor is how the garment fits you. When you try on a garment, be sure to look at yourself in a full-length mirror. Look at both the front view and the back view. Are there any wrinkles and bulges that indicate a poor fit? Many people buy their clothes a little bit snug with the idea that it will make them look slimmer. The opposite is true. Too-tight clothing can make you look pounds heavier.

When shopping for clothes, take time to evaluate fit, quality, care required, and price before making your final decision.

Always check for appearance and fit in front of a full-length mirror.

this without any strain across the shoulder blades. Sleeves should not ride up and become uncomfortably short.

3. *Now raise your arms straight up over your head.*

   The armholes should feel comfortable. Jackets and coats should not feel tight in the shoulder area. Blouses, shirts, and sweaters should not come untucked. When you lower your arms, dresses should fall back in place comfortably, with little pulling and tugging.

4. *Sit down.*

   Make sure the garment does not strain and pull at the hip, stomach, or thigh area when you sit. Pay attention to the waistline of pants and skirts. It should remain slightly loose and comfortable and not gap at the center back.

5. *Now stand up and bend over, as if you were going to touch your toes.*

   You may not plan on doing aerobic exercises in your clothes, but you might have to lean over to pick something up or tie your shoes. Even formal party clothes can be subjected to some fairly strenuous dancing.

   The garment that passes all these tests is one that fits well and will be comfortable to wear.

STEPS TO TAKE

Use the box feature FITTING CHECKPOINTS to evaluate your garment.

1. *First, stand straight to check the overall appearance.*

   Notice the seams, hem, and special design features.

2. *Next, try the "stretch test."*

   Bend your arms in front of you at shoulder height. Shirts, jackets, dresses, and blouses should be roomy enough so that you can do

Evaluating Quality

The price you pay for a garment is not necessarily an indication of its quality. Many other factors can influence the price, such as the number of details, the trim, the brand name or the designer's name, and the store where it is being sold. A high-priced garment can be of poor quality; a low-priced garment can be of high quality. Quality in a garment means two things: *good fabric* and *good workmanship*.

Fashion Focus

Fitting Checkpoints

One of the most important considerations you will make about every garment is the fit. Proper fit is important for both appearance and comfort. Here are some basic fitting guidelines to follow:

1. *Collar or Neckline.* It fits close to the neck without binding or gapping
2. *Shoulders.* Armhole seam lies at edge of shoulder, unless designed otherwise
3. *Chest and Back.* Fit smoothly with room for movement; closing does not pull or gap
4. *Sleeves.* They are loose enough to raise arms and long enough to cover wrist bone when arm is bent
5. *Buttons and Buttonholes.* They do not pull or strain as you move
6. *Jacket or Coat.* It fits comfortably over other garments
7. *Waistline or Waistband.* It feels comfortable without pulling or binding; tops can be tucked in
8. *Hip Area.* Skims body smoothly without pulling or forming extra folds; crotch does not wrinkle or bind
9. *Zipper.* Opens and closes smoothly
10. *Pleats and Gathers.* They hang vertical and unbroken
11. *Pants Leg.* Falls straight from hipline without wrinkles
12. *Hemlines.* They are parallel to the floor, meet evenly at openings, and are the right length for your body proportions and current fashion

THE FABRIC

Here are some pointers in evaluating the fabric.

1. *Examine the fabric.*

    Is the color even throughout the garment? If there is a design printed on the fabric, are the colors printed so that they appear in the right place? Are there any snags or pulls? Have little **pills**, or *balls of fiber*, begun to form on the surface of the fabric?

2. *Crush a corner of the garment in your hand to see if the fabric wrinkles easily.*

    This will indicate how much the garment will crease or wrinkle during wear. It will also show if the fabric will require pressing. If the fabric is a stretchable woven or knit, pull on it to see how much it stretches. Does it return to the original shape?

3. *See if the garment is cut so that the fabric is "on grain."*

    In Chapter 16, you learned about grain lines in fabric. A garment that is cut on grain will look better and wear longer than one that is cut off-grain. Seams will hang straight without twisting to one side. The hemline will hang evenly. If the garment is cut off-grain or the fabric is printed off-grain, the design lines of a plaid or a stripe will not match.

4. *Evaluate if the fabric is suitable for the way you plan to wear the garment.*

    A fragile fabric, such as a chiffon, would not be a good choice for a shirt that you planned to wear for sports activities.

THE WORKMANSHIP

Quality workmanship means careful sewing, using appropriate techniques. For example, if the fabric is loosely woven and frays easily, the garment should be lined or the seams should be

Examine seams to see that they are smooth, flat, and unpuckered.

finished. Look for these features in checking on the workmanship of a garment.

• *The stitching on a well-made garment should be even and secure, in a color thread that matches the fabric.* Avoid garments that are sewn with clear nylon thread. The heat of an iron could easily melt it.

• *If your garment has a stripe or a plaid, the fabric design should be matched throughout the garment.* See that the fabric center and side seams and design areas, such as pockets, collars, and bands, are not mismatched design-wise.

• *Seams should be smooth, flat, and unpuckered.* There should be no ridges showing on the outside of the garment.

• *Check the seam allowances on the inside of the garment.* They should be at least ½" (1.3 cm) wide unless the garment is made with special, narrow overlock seams. An **overlock seam** is *a special combination of stitches that joins the fabric and finishes the edges in one operation.* These overlock seams are often found on knit garments. If the fabric ravels, the seams should be finished to prevent fraying.

• *Darts should point to the fullest part of the body.* Darts, like seams, should be pressed smooth and flat, with no puckers. There should not be a "dimple" at the tip of the dart.

• *Facings should lie smooth and flat against the body.* When you look at the garment from the outside, the facings should not show.

• *A collar should have smooth curves and sharp corners.* It should cover the neckline seam, and the edges should lie flat so that you do not see the undercollar. The collar area should be finished nicely on the inside so that you can wear the collar open as well as closed.

• *Fasteners, such as buttons, snaps and hooks and eyes, should be securely sewn in place.* Make sure the zipper opens and closes easily, and that the stitching is neat and secure. Buttonholes should be sewn with tight, even stitches. They should be large enough for the button to slip through easily, but not so large that the garment will unfasten while you are wearing it.

• *Trims should be sewn on securely.*

• *Hems should be straight and even.* The hem stitches should not cause the garment to pull or to pucker. In fact, the stitches should be invisible from the right side of the garment, unless the hem is topstitched in place. Look at the hem allowance on the inside of the garment. It should be an even width and stitched along the edge if the fabric ravels.

• *Give the garment a final check for imperfections,* such as spots, grease marks, lipstick stains, lost belts, broken belt loops, or small rips. These are usually the result of a careless shopper trying on the garment.

Evaluating Care and Price

The last two major evaluating tests focus on garment care and garment price.

GARMENT CARE

The type of care that a garment requires can be an important factor in your decision to buy.

Things to Look For

Can the garment be washed or will it need to be dry cleaned? Does the fabric have to be ironed? In Chapter 18 you learned about the new guidelines for permanent care labels. Specific information about washing, drying, bleaching, and dry cleaning are now included on the labels.

Remember that the type of care that a garment requires is affected by the properties of the outer fabric, the lining, the interfacing, and trim. A garment made of washable fabric cannot be laundered if the trim is "dry clean only."

Also check the garment label or hangtag for any fabric finishes that affect care. In Chapter 17, you learned about the advantages of wrinkle-resistant and stain-resistant finishes.

Cost of Care

You will also want to consider how much it costs to take care of a garment. Cost depends upon two things:

• The first is how often you will have to clean the garment.
• The second is how much that method of cleaning costs in terms of *time* and *money.*

Fashion Focus

Cost Per Wearing

Your clothing investment consists of more than just the purchase price of a garment. The cost of care must be added to the price as well. A more expensive garment may turn out to be a better investment in the long run than a less expensive one. Why? Because the number of times that you wear the garment reduces the average cost per wearing, making it a better choice.

Here are the factors that make up the **cost per wearing** of a garment:

- cost of buying or sewing the garment
- cost of dry cleaning or laundering
- amount of use

Then use this equation to determine cost per wearing:

purchase price
+ cost of care

total investment ÷ number of wearings = cost per wearing

For example, you are considering buying a jacket that costs $50.00. Since it can be worn over many outfits in your wardrobe, you expect to wear it 40 times during the year. It will require dry cleaning twice, at a cost of $3.00 each time.

Purchase price	$50.00
Cost of care	6.00
Total	$56.00 ÷ 40 = $1.40 cost per wearing

A sweater you would like to buy costs only half as much as the jacket, and it is washable. Laundry costs will be only $.50. However, the sweater coordinates with only one outfit that you have, so you will be able to wear it only 10 times during the year. Although the sweater is less expensive than the jacket, the actual cost per wearing will be greater.

Purchase price	$25.00
Cost of care	.50
Total	$25.50 ÷ 10 = $2.55 cost per wearing

When making your clothing decisions, don't just think about the initial cost of a garment. You must also consider the value of its usefulness to you.

Light-colored fabrics show soil more easily than dark colors. For example, a white jacket or coat would require more frequent cleaning than a dark brown or navy jacket. However, do not allow dark colors to become too soiled, or they will be difficult to clean.

Generally, dry cleaning costs are much higher than laundry costs. A jacket may cost several dollars to dry clean, but only pennies to wash.

The method of cleaning that you prefer also depends upon your values. For some people, hand washing is easy and convenient. Others prefer only machine washable items. If time is scarce or laundry equipment is not available, then dry cleaning may be preferable in spite of the cost. A garment that needs to be pressed each time you wear it will cost more in terms of time than a garment that does not wrinkle.

GARMENT PRICE

A garment gets extra points for being a good value if it is priced within your budget. Also, think about how much the garment costs versus how many times you are going to wear it. (Refer to the box feature COST PER WEARING.) It would be foolish to spend all your money on a dress or suit that you will wear only a few times when what you really need is a new coat.

Do not be tempted into buying something that you do not really need or want just because the sign says SALE. As we discussed in Chapter 20, there are all kinds of sales. Some are better bargains than others.

Shoes

Shoes are an important and special part of your wardrobe. The style of shoe that you choose can greatly affect the overall appearance of an outfit. Since shoes are expensive, you want to make sure that you select shoes which are comfortable, attractive, and a good value.

Shoes have both a number and a letter size, such as 8A or 7½B. The number refers to the length of the foot. Shoes are numbered in full and half sizes. A size 8½ shoe is longer than a size 8 shoe, but shorter than a size 9 shoe. The letter refers to the width of the foot. An A size is narrower than a B size. A very narrow size would be AAA. A very wide size would be EEE.

SHOPPING FOR SHOES

There are several guidelines to follow when you are shopping for shoes.

- *First, do not go shopping for shoes early in the day.* Make sure that you have walked around for several hours. Feet swell during the course of the day. You want to try on shoes when your feet are the largest so that they will always be comfortable.

- *You should have your feet remeasured every time you buy shoes.* Be sure that both feet are measured because no one has two feet that are exactly the same size. Always buy the size that fits the larger foot. If necessary, you can use pads or innersoles to improve the fit on the smaller foot.

- *Buy shoes according to fit, not size.* Earlier in this chapter, you learned that a "standard" size 10 may not fit the same from manufacturer to manufacturer. The same is true of shoes. One manufacturer's size 9 shoe may not be the same as another manufacturer's size 9 shoe. Never buy shoes that feel too tight or too small. No matter what the salesperson may tell you, your feet will break before the shoes break in. You will not be able to look or be at your best if your shoes do not fit properly.

A pair of shoes is usually a large investment. Follow the above guidelines carefully.

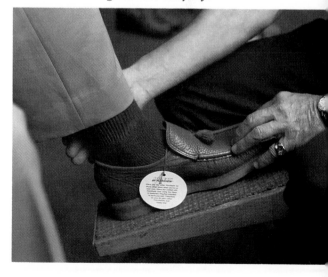

Compromises and Trade-Offs

It is not always possible to find shoes or garments that look good, fit well, have high quality, cost the right amount, and are compatible with your needs and wants.

Fortunately, there are some compromises and trade-offs that you can make. A **compromise** is *a settlement or give-and-take between two points.* A **trade-off** is *an exchange of one thing for another.*

The one thing you absolutely cannot compromise on is fit. If the garment requires *more* than a simple alteration, such as changing a hem length or moving a button, to make it fit properly, it is not a good buy. The only exceptions are tailored garments, such as suits and trousers, that may need minor alterations by the store's tailor or dressmaker.

OPTIONS TO CONSIDER

1. *Your first option is to trade quantity for quality.*

   Purchase one expensive, well-made shirt or pair of shoes, rather than two cheaper and perhaps not as well-made items. Limit your wardrobe to just a few colors so that everything you purchase will coordinate. Instead of a different pair of shoes for every outfit, you may need only several pairs.

   Limit your fad purchases to inexpensive accessories or items bought on sale. That way you can update your wardrobe with some of the latest fads, but still have most of your money left over for your basic wardrobe needs.

2. *Your second option is to develop sewing skills that will help you improve the quality of the garments you buy.*

   Seams can be restitched. You could repair a ripped side seam or reinforce a pants seam. Threads that are hanging can be clipped off or pulled through to the wrong side with a needle.

   Hem lengths on pants, skirts, and sleeves can be changed to make them more flattering or more fashionable. Shortening a garment is usually no problem. However, if the garment needs to be lengthened, check to be sure there is enough fabric and that the original fold line will not show once the garment is let down.

   Loose trims can be repaired. Missing buttons, snaps, and hook and eyes can all be replaced. Sometimes replacing cheap buttons with ones of better quality can improve the whole appearance of a garment.

   Be careful about buying a garment that has a spot or a stain. If you ask, a store will sometimes try to remove it for you so that you can be sure it will come out. If you buy a garment with a spot that is marked "As Is," you cannot return the garment if the spot does not come out.

3. *Your third option is to use your sewing skills to make garments.*

   Then you can end up with a better quality garment, in exactly the style and color that you want. You will probably save money and may even save time. In any event, you will be much more content in a garment that is the result of your own skills and talents.

Your final decision should be based on the evaluation of many factors—style, color, fit, quality, care, and price—plus your personal needs, wants, and values. By asking questions and answering them honestly, you will make wise clothing selections.

Chapter 21 Review

Summary

Before purchasing a garment, you should evaluate it according to fit, quality, care, price, and whether it fits into your wardrobe plan. Different size categories are available for both males and females. When trying on a garment, move about to check its fit. You should evaluate the quality of both the fabric and the workmanship. You should also consider the price of the garment, how often you will wear it, and the cost of care. Shoes also need to be carefully evaluated. Some compromises and trade-offs can be made, such as trading quantity for quality or using your sewing skills.

Questions

1. What are at least five questions that you should ask yourself when buying a garment?
2. Describe the basic size categories for females and for males. What other special size categories have been developed?
3. What are the two measurements used to size men's shirts and pants?
4. Why should you stretch and bend when trying on clothes?
5. Explain the statement: "Price is not an indication of quality."
6. What characteristics should you check when evaluating fabric quality?
7. What specific areas should you check when evaluating workmanship?
8. How is cost per wearing determined?
9. List guidelines for purchasing shoes.
10. Describe three options to consider when making a compromise or trade-off in clothing. What clothing factor should never be compromised?

Activities

1. Look through magazines and catalogues for advertisements listing special size categories. How are the categories described?
2. Evaluate the fabric and workmanship of several garments in different price ranges in a store. How does the quality differ? Are the best fabrics and workmanship always on the more expensive garments? Share your evaluation with the class.

3. Compute the cost per wearing of four garments that you have purchased or would like to purchase. Contact a local dry cleaner for current dry cleaning costs. Use 25¢ for laundry costs. Which garment has the lowest cost per wearing?

You Be the Expert

You are working part-time in a boutique. A customer asks your assistance in evaluating the fit of an expensive garment. What steps could you suggest for checking the fit?

22 | *Shopping for Others*

TERMS TO LEARN

accessories
costume jewelry
disability
fine jewelry

Have you ever had the experience of buying someone a gift of clothing that you liked so much that you wanted to keep it for yourself? Yet, after you gave it as a gift, you never saw the other person wear it! Did you stop and ask yourself why? Perhaps the style, the color, the size, or something else about it was not suitable for the person to whom you gave it.

Shopping for others means that we must forget about what pleases us and think about the other person. In order to make successful purchases, we need to have some knowledge about others' wants and needs, as well as carefully observe their preferences of styles and colors.

After reading this chapter, you will be able to:

- identify the important considerations to make when shopping for friends and family members,
- select suitable clothing for children,
- choose clothing gifts that will be pleasing to the elderly,
- describe the special clothing needs of people who are temporarily or permanently disabled.

Shopping for Friends and Family

Sooner or later, you will find yourself shopping for a friend or another member of your family.

Just as no two members of a family have exactly the same taste in foods, no two members will need or want exactly the same clothes.

Even best friends do not have exactly the same taste in clothes. Although many groups of friends dress in similar styles, each member of the group has personal tastes and individuality.

When you are shopping for others, it is also important that the item be returnable. If it is the wrong size, or the receiver wants a different color, there will be no problem returning it. Just be sure to keep the sales receipt.

DIFFERENT NEEDS AND WANTS

Before shopping, think about the other person's needs and wants. By being a careful listener, you may pick up clues to a person's desires. You may hear comments, such as, "I sure wish I had a new belt to go with these pants...", or "I need to get a new shirt to replace my old blue one."

Lifestyle, Interests, and Hobbies

But sometimes you have no clues, or you may want to purchase a gift that will truly be a surprise. Then you must consider the person's lifestyle. As you learned in Chapter 5, clothing needs are influenced by one's occupation and activities. Even the type of community where the person lives has an influence.

Some of the best gifts take into consideration the person's interests or hobbies. By selecting such a gift, it shows that you have taken time to think about the person's real interests – and to find a gift that is suited just for him or her.

Some interests have very obvious clothing needs. For example, a swimmer might like a new beach towel or mat. A tennis player could use a racquet cover, a jogger a new pair of shorts.

Other hobbies may have clothing needs that are not so obvious. A gardener would appreciate a special pair of garden gloves or a wide-brimmed sun hat. A person who makes pottery might like a sturdy, washable apron.

Physical Condition

The person's physical condition can be a factor in selecting the right type of clothing. You would not want to buy a blouse with lots of tiny buttons for someone who had arthritis. When someone breaks an arm or a leg, clothes that are particularly easy to get in and out of will be needed. Later in this chapter, we will discuss clothing needs for the disabled. A **disability** is *some type of condition that hampers a person in some way.* Remember that some disabilities are permanent; others are temporary, and even some people with permanent disabilities can function better than others in the same situation.

STYLES AND COLORS

You should always consider other people's tastes in clothing.

What styles do they like to wear? Are they interested in the latest fashions and fads? Or do they prefer more traditional styles? Remember that the garment or accessory is going to be worn by your friend or relative, and not by you.

However, you do not have to limit your selection to duplicates of clothing that the person already wears. Sometimes, a gift that is just "a little bit different" is greatly appreciated. Perhaps you see another side to the person's personality. Perhaps the person needs just a little encouragement to wear a certain style or color. But avoid giving any gift that is greatly different from a person's taste in clothing. Otherwise, the gift will end up never being worn.

Make a note about other people's favorite colors. You might also want to write down the colors of some of the basic items in their wardrobe, such as their winter coat or favorite sweater.

It is particularly nice to give a friend or a relative a gift that coordinates with something that they already own. For example, you could choose a scarf that matches their coat, or a shirt to be worn with their sweater.

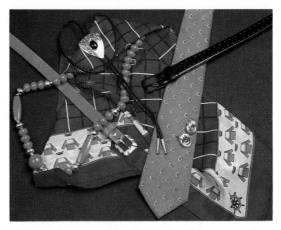

Accessories can add color and style to an outfit.

SIZES

It is important to know the sizes of the people you are shopping for. If the garment is the wrong size and has to be returned, you will be wasting valuable time – whether it is your time or the other person's time. It is a good idea to keep a small index card in your purse or wallet that lists family members' sizes. Be sure to include shoe, stocking, and belt sizes. Check from time to time to make sure that no one's size has changed.

ACCESSORIES

Accessories include items such as *scarves, shoes, hats, belts, socks, jewelry, sunglasses, ties, and handbags.* They are the small items that can add polish to an outfit. The fact that they are small does not mean that they are always inexpensive. It is possible to spend more money for a pair of boots than for a coat. Some acces-

sories, such as a narrow black leather belt, are classics. Others, such as fluorescent socks, are fads.

Jewelry

There are two types of jewelry – fine jewelry and costume jewelry.

Fine jewelry is usually made from *gold, silver, or platinum and may contain precious and semiprecious stones.* Diamonds and emeralds are examples of precious stones. A garnet or a turquoise is a semiprecious stone. Fine jewelry is expensive. Because it is expensive, the designs are usually very classic.

Costume jewelry can be *made from anything.* Plastic, metal, feathers, leather, wood, and other unusual materials can be used. Some costume jewelry is designed to look like fine jewelry. Instead of real gold or silver, it is made from a metal that is plated or coated with gold or silver. Semiprecious or fake stones are used in place of precious ones.

But, whatever kind of jewelry you are buying, a piece of jewelry is always a thoughtful gift, whether you are treating yourself or someone else.

YOUR RESOURCES

Price is an important consideration when you are shopping for others. If you are buying someone a present, do not spend more than your budget will allow. Extravagant gifts usually make the receiver feel uncomfortable. If the purchase you are making is not a gift, ask another family member how much should be spent on the item, or how much the family budget has allowed. Be sure to stay within the allocated budget.

If you need a gift, consider sewing or making it instead of buying it. A gift that is crafted or sewn with a special person in mind will be particularly appreciated because you put your own time and talents into creating it. A gift can be adapted to that person's lifestyle and tastes.

Shopping for Children

More growth and change occur in a human being's body during the infant and toddler years than at any other time in our lives. In the first months, a baby's tiny hands can barely hold on to a parent's finger. These hands soon develop so that they can fasten buttons and tie shoelaces by the time the child starts school.

Infants who can only lay in their crib and kick soon learn to roll over and to crawl. Then they learn to stand, to walk and, eventually, to run and climb. All children, particularly babies and toddlers, have clothing needs that are very different from adults.

Society did not always recognize these different needs. Until the 1900s, children were dressed like miniature adults. They wore scaled down versions of the dresses, suits, hats, shoes, and stockings that their parents wore. Today,

children's wear is a separate and very important part of the clothing industry. Clothes are specifically designed to meet the special needs of children.

CHILDREN'S SIZES

Have you ever noticed that a baby has a large head, narrow shoulders, and no waistline? In fact, anything resembling a waistline usually does not develop until a child is between four and six years old. That is why styles such as rompers, overalls, and one-piece dresses that hang from the shoulders are so popular.

Children's clothing sizes are classified according to body size and weight. The common size groupings are *Infants*, *Toddlers*, and *Children's*.

1. *Infants* clothes are sized either by weight, or by age. Some items are labeled by a weight range, such as "8 to 10 pounds" or "12 to 18 pounds." Other clothes are marked by age in months, such as "6 months," "9 months," "12 months," "18 months," or "24 months."

Light, soft but durable, easy-to-wash clothes are best for active children.

Fashion Focus

Sewing for Kids

It can be fun to sew for young children. They like bright colors and do not care if the sewing is perfect. Plus, they enjoy wearing clothes that are decorated with interesting trims and designs.

- Be sure all trims, bows, laces, and buttons are sewn on securely.
- Use hook and loop fasteners instead of buttons and buttonholes. This makes it easier for young children to dress themselves. If desired, decorative buttons can be sewn on the outside of the garment, on top of the fasteners.
- Add colorful knee patches to overalls. Cut the patches in the shape of a large flower, ball, or teddy bear.
- Add large patch pockets to garments. Children love having a place to store their special treasures!

2. *Toddlers* sizes have a T with the number: 1T, 2T, 3T, and 4T. Size is based on the child's chest, waist, and height measurements. Toddler-size clothes include extra room to accommodate bulky diapers.

3. *Children's sizes* are represented by the numbers 2, 3, 4, 5, 6, and 6X. They are also based on chest, waist, and height measurements. Children's sizes do not include a "diaper allowance."

Children's clothes should always be bought large. For example, for a baby's first birthday, purchase an "18 month" or "24 month" size outfit. A two-year-old toddler will probably wear a size 3T or a size 4T.

Older children also grow very quickly. They grow taller much faster than they grow wider. Therefore, look for garments with deep hem allowances that can be lengthened easily. Shoulder straps should be extra long so that the buttons can be adjusted as the child grows.

EASE OF DRESSING

Have you ever struggled to get a pullover sweater on an infant? If so, you will understand how important it is that a child's clothes be easy to put on and take off. Baby's and toddlers diapers and clothing are changed several times a day. Pants should have gripper snaps on the inside leg seam so that diapers can be changed easily. One-piece garments that fall from the shoulders, and shirts and sweaters that button up the front or on the shoulder all make it easier to dress the child.

Toddlers take great pride in learning to dress themselves. Garments with large neck and armhole openings are the easiest for them to manipulate. Pants with elastic waistlines are easier to pull up and down for toilet training than pants with shoulder straps. Large buttons, snaps, and zippers with over-size pull tabs are good choices. Hooks and eyes, laces, and tiny buttons are usually too complicated for the toddler to manage alone.

WEARABILITY AND SAFETY

Because children like to run, crawl, and climb, their clothes must be able to withstand the wear and tear of active play. Fabrics should be tightly woven or knitted. Denim, corduroy,

broadcloth, and firmly knitted fabrics are all good choices. Special features, such as reinforced seams or reinforced knees, will help extend the garment's life.

When shopping for babies and toddlers, look for shoulder straps that crisscross in the back. This design keeps the straps from sliding off the shoulders. Shoulder tabs on shirts are another good way to keep up straps.

It is very important to think about safety when buying clothes for children. Because infants and young children like to put things in their mouths, be careful of loosely sewn buttons and trims that the child could swallow. Avoid garments with flowing sleeves or long hemlines. These could easily get caught during play, and the child could get hurt.

As a result of the *Flammable Fabrics Act,* certain products, such as mattresses and children's sleepwear, must be treated with special flame-retardant finishes so that they will not burn quickly. (Refer to the box feature in Chapter 5, FLAMMABILITY FACTS.)

COLOR AND TEXTURE

Have you ever wondered why young children are so fond of toys like teddy bears? It is because these toys are warm and comforting to cuddle and touch. The same thing is true about clothes. Children like clothes that have texture. They particularly like fabrics that are soft and pleasant to touch, such as corduroy, flannel, terry cloth, cotton velveteen, and quilted fabrics.

Most children prefer bright, bold colors, especially the primary colors. In fact, red and yellow are the first two colors a baby can recognize. Bright colors tend to stimulate children. They are also "safe" colors because they make children more visible on dark nights or rainy days. Pale or light colors will show dirt more quickly than medium to dark colors.

Older people's daily lifestyle is often informal. They may prefer a gift of leisure clothes or an item associated with their hobbies.

EASY CARE

Clothes that are easy to care for may not be important to the child, but they will certainly be appreciated by the parent. Some children go through a stage where they develop a particular attachment to a favorite item of clothing. Everyone is happier if it is something that can be cleaned quickly and returned to the child.

Because small children lead active lives, their clothing requires frequent laundering. Certain stains, such as grass, formula, and some foods and juices, will need special treatment.

When you are buying a garment, check the hangtags and labels carefully for fabric and care information. If you are sewing the garment, read the label on the end of the fabric bolt. Look for words such as "permanent press," "soil-retardant," "stain-repellent," "colorfast," and "shrink-resistant."

Shopping for the Elderly

The elderly, too, have clothing needs that are quite special. Often, they have less need for new additions to their wardrobe because of a restricted lifestyle or because they already have enough clothes to meet their needs.

However, everyone, regardless of their age or their situation, has a need for the psychological lift that a new item of clothing provides. A sweater or robe in a favorite color, or a pretty pin for a coat lapel might be a good choice. Look for a tie in a print that matches the person's hobby, such as bird print for a bird watcher, or a stamp design for a stamp collector. Museum gift shops are a good place to shop.

THEIR VALUES, NOT YOURS

When you are shopping for the elderly, be sure that you select articles of clothing that reflect their needs and values, not yours. Unless the elderly person has made a special request for something that is "in fashion," avoid buying anything that is a fad. Observe the person's wardrobe carefully. Choose a style and color that is harmonious with items that the person already owns.

PHYSICAL CONCERNS

Did you ever notice an elderly person wearing a heavy coat on a warm day? Many people develop poor circulation as they get older. As a result, they usually prefer warmer climates, warmer rooms, and warmer clothes than younger people. Lightweight clothing that can be layered on or off is particularly appreciated. Warm slippers, attractive sweaters, dresses with jackets, flannel shirts, and garments with longer sleeves are other good choices.

Be sure to purchase the right size. Shopping can be extremely tiring for people of all ages. Walking long distances, carrying packages, and dealing with the crowds can be difficult, too. Even if the person is in excellent health, your consideration in purchasing the proper size will be greatly appreciated.

A THOUGHTFUL GIFT

An older person may be particularly appreciative of a gift you have made yourself. Most older people have developed a special regard for the time and effort it takes to make something. They are often more touched by a handmade gift than a younger person would be.

Shopping for the Disabled

Almost everyone is disabled at some time in their lives. We usually think of a disability as a permanent handicap that is the result of a birth defect, an illness, or an accident. However, a disability can also be temporary, such as a broken arm or a broken leg. Some people become disabled as a result of declining health in their older years.

Whatever the cause, the disabled person is usually restricted in his or her physical movements. This person might be in a wheelchair, wear a cast or a brace, use crutches or a walker, or have limited functioning of some parts of the body. People with special needs often find that many common clothing styles are uncomfortable or too confining for them.

CLOTHING REQUIREMENTS

In general, clothing for people with special needs should be well made because restricted movements can put great strain on certain areas of the garment. Disabled people also want to be as self-sufficient as possible, whether this means being able to dress with little assistance or being able to take care of their own wardrobe.

Washable, easy-to-care-for clothes are appreciated. Garments that wrap and tie or that fasten in the front are easier to put on and take off than other styles. Garments with an elasticized waist or no waistline at all will be more comfortable for people who must sit for long periods of time. People who use crutches often have problems keeping their blouse or shirt tucked in. Overblouses, shirts with long tails, or long

Simple Alterations for the Disabled

Simple alterations made in clothes for disabled persons will enable them to be more self-sufficient when dressing, as well as adding to their comfort. These adjustments may take the form of an easier type of fastener or a minor styling change to allow for a cast or brace.

- *Elastic.* Insert elastic at waistlines to help keep garments in place. Or add a casing with a drawstring or elastic to make skirts and pants more comfortable.
- *Large Hooks.* Replace small hooks and eyes with large metal hooks and bars or special coat-size hooks and eyes. For an adjustable waistline, sew on two bars to accommodate weight changes or provide added comfort.
- *Hook and Loop Tape.* This tape, with tiny hooks on one strip and loops on the other, can be pressed together and pulled apart very easily. Use in small pieces to replace snaps or buttons. Use in longer strips to replace a zipper or provide an adjustable closing. Apply at seam of pants or sleeve to permit easier dressing over a cast or brace.
- *Buttons.* Use large, flat buttons and enlarge the buttonholes to allow for easier fastening. Sew on buttons with elastic thread at cuffs and other openings to eliminate unbuttoning.
- *Zipper Pulls.* Fasten a large metal or plastic ring, or a fabric or ribbon loop to the zipper pull tab to make it easier to grasp and pull up or down.
- *Additional Zipper.* Add a zipper at the shoulder seam or in a raglan sleeve seam to allow the garment to be pulled over the head more easily. An extra-long zipper can be inserted in the in-seam of pants.

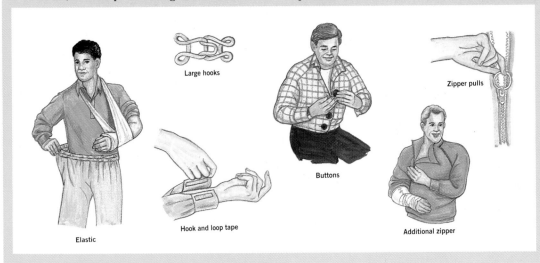

Large hooks

Zipper pulls

Buttons

Hook and loop tape

Additional zipper

Elastic

loose-fitting sweaters are good solutions. Choosing clothes that are one size larger can provide added comfort and ease of dressing.

CHOOSING THE RIGHT FABRIC

Select fabrics that are both easy to clean and comfortable to wear. Washing fabrics that require little or no ironing are the best choice. Printed fabrics do not show stains or soil as easily as solid colors. Fabrics should be colorful and attractive. As you learned in Unit 1, people feel better about themselves when they are dressed attractively.

Since many disabled people are physically confined in one position for long periods of time, comfortable fabrics are a necessity. Avoid choosing very heavy fabrics. They are too bulky and uncomfortable. Instead, choose two or more layers of lighter weight clothing for warmth. Stretch and knitted fabrics offer some stretchability for added comfort. Avoid clingy fabrics that tend to reveal casts and braces. Do not choose a scratchy fabric that may irritate the skin.

A disabled person who perspires heavily will be extremely uncomfortable if the fabric does not absorb the perspiration or allow it to evaporate. Natural fibers, such as cotton, linen, and wool, along with rayon, are absorbent fibers.

One hundred percent nylon and 100% polyester fabrics are not good choices because they do not absorb moisture. However, a blended fabric, such as polyester and cotton, will absorb moisture and stay wrinkle-free. Read the garment label to check the fiber content.

CUSTOMIZING A GARMENT

If you have some good sewing skills, there are many things you can do to make clothes for

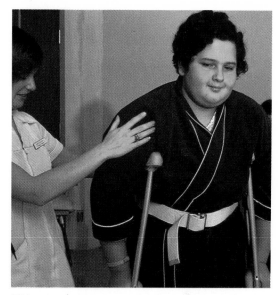

This disabled person needs garments that are comfortable and which help mobility.

a disabled person more comfortable to wear. For example, crutches and braces often rub against a garment. The extra strain on the fabric causes the garment to tear or wear out quickly. You might reinforce the areas of strain by adding a fabric patch or fusing an extra layer of fabric to the inside of the garment.

A person wearing a leg brace or a cast may have trouble getting a pant leg on over the cast. People with acute arthritis or restricted movement often find fasteners difficult to handle. (See the box feature SIMPLE ALTERATIONS FOR THE DISABLED for some simple alterations to help make dressing easier.)

Visually impaired people have trouble matching and identifying colors. You might try stitching small thread knots to the inside of the garments. One knot could mean red, two knots blue, and so on.

Shopping for others can be challenging, rewarding, and interesting. It will give you an opportunity to become a better shopper, not only for them but also for yourself.

Summary

When shopping for others, you must consider the other person's needs, wants, and personal preferences as well as your own resources. Gifts that are crafted or sewn are particulary appreciated by others. Children have special clothing needs. Children's clothes should be bought large. Other considerations include ease of dressing, wearability, safety, color, texture, and ease of care. Both the elderly and the disabled want clothing that meets their special needs of comfort and fit. You can use your sewing skills to customize garments for a disabled person.

Questions

1. Name at least four considerations that should be made before buying clothing for another person. Explain why each one is important.

2. Why are accessories good gifts for others?

3. Why might a person appreciate a handmade gift over a purchased one?

4. Since children grow very quickly, what guideline should you follow when choosing sizes of children's clothes?

5. Why is ease of dressing a major consideration in the design of children's clothing? What design features help with this process?

6. What health and lifestyle factors influence the clothing needs of the elderly?

7. List several simple adaptations that could be made in garments to make it easier for disabled persons to dress themselves?

8. What types of fabrics are most suitable for persons with restricted movement? What fabrics are not suitable?

Activities

1. Make up a list of gifts that you could buy or make for a friend or relative. Consider the person's interests and hobbies, likes and dislikes, favorite colors and styles. Show your list to the person and discover how accurate you are in your evaluation.

2. Bring several types of children's clothing to class. Evaluate the design and fabric of each garment for ease of dressing, wearability, color, texture, and ease of care.

3. Order catalogues from companies that provide clothing for disabled persons. Analyze the special features of the garments. How might these features be added to commercial patterns or ready-made garments?

You Be the Expert

You are a salesperson in a local gift shop. A ten-year-old child has $9.00 to buy a gift for a grandparent. What suggestions could you give your customer?

23 *Sewing Selections*

TERMS TO LEARN

circumference
design ease
figure type
notions
serger
wearing ease

Developing your sewing skills is a bit like learning to play the piano. Anyone can learn to play the scales. But, if you are willing to spend some time at it, you can learn to play anything from a simple, one-handed melody to a complex sonata. How well you play depends on your talents and the time you spend practicing.

Anyone can learn to sew. You can begin by learning simple skills or sewing on a button, putting in a hem, or repairing a ripped seam. You can progress and learn how to sew easy projects, such as running shorts, a T-shirt, pillows, or a wall-hanging. Then you can develop your skills and sew more advanced projects, such as a tailored jacket or a silk shirt.

After reading this chapter, you will be able to:

- select projects that match your skills, interests, and available time,
- choose patterns that fit and look well on you,
- select suitable fabrics and notions,
- make wise consumer decisions regarding sewing equipment.

Decisions

Every journalism student learns about the five "W's": *Who, What, When, Where,* and *Why.* These are the questions that must be answered in the first paragraph of every good news story. These are also good questions to ask yourself when you decide to sew.

WHO?

Whom are you going to sew for? You may decide to sew for yourself because you need something new or you cannot find exactly what you want in the stores.

You may decide to sew for another person because you cannot afford to buy a gift, or because a handmade gift would especially please that person.

WHAT?

What are you going to sew? You could make something to wear, such as a robe, a scarf, or a shirt. If you are unsure of your sewing skills, a good way to begin is by making something for the home. Items, such as pillows, place mats, and curtains, have long, straight seams and do not require any complicated fitting techniques. These are also good projects on which to try out new sewing skills, such as appliqué or patchwork.

WHEN AND WHERE?

When and where are you going to sew? How much time you have available for sewing will influence how detailed your sewing project should be. But sometimes you might have a lot of free time and no place to sew.

Ask yourself some questions. Do you have a sewing machine at home, or do you have to finish all your sewing projects during your home economics class? Could you use a classroom sewing machine after school or during study periods? Do you have a relative or friend who will let you use their machine?

If a machine is not easily available to you, pick simple projects and organize your time so that you can learn and enjoy sewing.

WHY?

Why have you selected a particular pattern and a particular fabric? Will the resulting garment go with other items in your wardrobe? Impulse sewing can be just as bad as impulse buying. You can end up wasting your money and your sewing time on a closet full of clothes that you never wear.

When you select your pattern, it is a good idea to choose one that will teach you a new sewing technique. For example, if your first sewing project was a T-shirt, your next project might be a simple shirt with a collar. Do not get carried away by the success of your first project and decide to make a blazer! Take the time to build upon your sewing skills. Avoid overwhelming yourself with too many new techniques at one time.

Selecting a Pattern

When selecting a pattern, you should consider several factors. Be sure the pattern style is flattering to your body shape. Select a pattern that matches your sewing skill level. Finally, choose a pattern in the correct size and figure type in order to get the best fit.

THE PATTERN CATALOGUE

How do you go about finding a pattern? You start by looking through the pattern catalogues. Each company that manufactures patterns produces its own catalogue. Pattern catalogues are divided into sections to make it easy for you to find the styles that you want. For example, you will find sections marked for dresses, for sportswear, and for easy-to-sew styles. You will also find sections for special categories, such as larger sizes, children and toddlers, men and boys, home decorating, crafts, gifts, and accessories.

Most garments are both photographed and sketched in the catalogue. By studying both the photograph and the sketch, you will have a good idea of exactly what the finished garment will look like. You will also get ideas for accessories to use with the finished garment.

Pattern catalogues are available in fabric stores that sell patterns. Your home economics classroom and your local public library may also have copies for you to look at. In addition, most of the pattern companies publish a magazine several times a year that features a selected group of their patterns. You can subscribe to these magazines or buy them at the newsstand.

The Right Style

A key to successful sewing is the selection of a pattern in a style that is flattering and pleasing to you. But how can you tell from a drawing on a catalogue page what the finished garment will look like on you? One way is to pay careful attention to the styles of items you already own. Which ones are flattering to your figure and enjoyable to wear?

If you do not already own a garment in the style you are planning to sew, visit a store and try on several versions in ready-to-wear. Look in the mirror and analyze the overall effect. If you are not pleased with the way the garment looks, would the style be more flattering if it were looser, or more fitted, shorter or longer?

Consider all the things you learned about line and design in Chapter 12. These design principles are important, whether you sew or buy your clothes. One advantage of sewing is that you can customize your clothes to suit your tastes and your body proportions.

CLUES ON THE PATTERN ENVELOPE

The pattern envelope will give you information about how the finished garment should look. Carefully examine the sketch or the photograph on the front of the envelope. Note the fit of the garment through the shoulders, at the waist, and at the hips. Is it fitted to conform to the curves of the body, or is it full and loose

Choose a project that is equal to your sewing skill. Most patterns note sewing difficulty.

Pattern catalogs provide measurement charts to help you determine which figure type and size to buy.

	BOYS'				TEEN-BOYS'			
Size	7	8	10	12	14	16	18	20
Chest.........	26	27	28	30	32	33½	35	36½
Waist.........	23	24	25	26	27	28	29	30
Hip (Seat).....	27	28	29½	31	32½	34	35½	37
Neckband.....	11¾	12	12½	13	13½	14	14½	15
Height	48	50	54	58	61	64	66	68
Shirt Sleeve....	22⅜	23¼	25	26¾	29	30	31	32

	MEN'S (height approximately 5'10")							
Size	34	36	38	40	42	44	46	48
Chest.........	34	36	38	40	42	44	46	48
Waist.........	28	30	32	34	36	39	42	44
Hip (Seat).....	35	37	39	41	43	45	47	49
Neckband.....	14	14½	15	15½	16	16½	17	17½
Shirt Sleeve....	32	32	33	33	34	34	35	35

GIRLS'

Girls patterns are designed for the girl who has not yet begun to mature. See chart below for approximate heights without shoes.

Size...............	7	8	10	12	14
Breast	26	27	28½	30	32
Waist...............	23	23½	24½	25½	26½
Hip	27	28	30	32	34
Back Waist Length....	11½	12	12¾	13½	14¼
Approx. Heights	50"	52"	56"	58½"	61"

MISSES'

Misses' patterns are designed for a well proportioned, and developed figure: about 5'5" to 5'6" without shoes.

Size	6	8	10	12	14	16	18	20	22	24
Bust	30½	31½	32½	34	36	38	40	42	44	46
Waist	23	24	25	26½	28	30	32	34	37	39
Hip	32½	33½	34½	36	38	40	42	44	46	48
Back Waist Length	15½	15¾	16	16¼	16½	16¾	17	17¼	17⅜	17½

fitting? Also note the type of fabric used in the photograph or indicated in the sketch. Is it shown in a heavyweight or a lightweight fabric? Is it shown in a print, a plaid, or a stripe? These are clues to help you choose your fabric.

The back of the pattern envelope is illustrated on page 377 in the *Sewing Handbook*. It tells you many things you need to know in order to make good buying and sewing decisions. For example, information about the style and the fit of the pattern is found in three different sections. Small line drawings will show you what the back of the garment looks like. A garment description tells you about any design details, such as style of sleeve, pockets, topstitching, and zippers, as well as whether it is a loose-fitting or tight-fitting garment. Finished garment measurements, such as "width at lower edge" or "finished back length," will give you an idea of the proportions of the finished garment.

In order to make these measurements meaningful to you, measure and record the lengths of several different jackets, dresses, or pants in your wardrobe. Also measure the bottom **circumference** or *distance around,* of several different styles of pants and skirts. You can use these measurements as a guideline for interpreting the measurements listed on the back of the pattern envelope. You will know right away if pants legs that are listed as "20″ (.5 m) at the lower edge" are slimmer or fuller than the brown pants you already own.

YOUR SEWING SKILLS

Most of the pattern companies market a special category of easy-to-sew patterns. These categories have special brand names that tell you something about the skill level required to sew the pattern. Look for names such as "Easy," "Fast & Easy," and "Jiffy." Some easy-to-sew patterns are even marked as Level I, Level II, and Level III to help you progress in your sewing skills.

Easy-to-sew patterns usually have fewer pattern pieces, simple-to-follow layouts, and easier construction techniques. Read the description in the catalogue or on the sewing envelope for clues about sewing difficulty.

YOUR MEASUREMENTS

To determine your correct pattern size and figure type, first take your body measurements. You will want to record your height and your circumference measurements—bust or chest, waist, and hips. Females will need to take their back waist measurement. Males should take their neck measurement. For accuracy, have someone help you measure.

Ideally, you should take your measurements over your undergarments, not over your clothes.

If necessary, you can take them over snug-fitting clothes. Remove sweaters, belts, jackets, or other bulky items.

Use a flexible 60″ (1.5 m) plastic-coated measuring tape. The tape measure should be held snugly, but not tightly around the body. Be sure that the tape measure is parallel to the floor. Tie a length of string or round elastic cord around your middle. It will roll into your true waistline position. Be sure to write down each measurement as it is taken.

Pattern Size Measurements

You will need to take these measurements for pattern size:

- *Bust/Chest.* The tape measure should be straight across your back and over the fullest part of your bust or chest.
- *Waist.* Measure exactly where the string or cord has settled.
- *Hips or Seat.* Measure over the fullest part of your hips. For most females, measure 7″ to 9″ (18–23 cm) below the waist. For most men, measure 8″ (20 cm) below the waist; for Teen Boys, 7″ (18 cm) below the waist; and for Boys, 6″ (15 cm) below the waist.
- *Neck* (for males only). Measure around the base of your neck. This measurement, plus ½″ (1.3 cm), is the neckband, or collar, size.

Figure Type Measurements

You will also need to take these measurements to determine your figure type:

- *Height.* Be sure to be in bare feet. Measure from the top of your head to the floor.
- *Back Waist Length* (for females only). If you bend your head forward, you will be able to locate a very prominent bone at the base of your neck. Measure from this bone down your center back to the waistline string or cord.

YOUR FIGURE TYPE

Figure types are *size categories determined by height and body proportions.* In order to determine your figure type, you will need to look at three pieces of information—your height, your back waist length (for females), and your body proportions. Now compare this information with the male or female charts on page 266, or check it with the Figure Type or Size Charts that appear in the back of the pattern catalogues.

YOUR PATTERN SIZE

Once you have determined your figure type, the next step is to determine your pattern size within that figure type. Compare your bust or chest, waist, and hip measurements with the ones that are listed on the chart on the pattern envelope back. Make sure that you are looking only at the measurement within your figure type category. Find the measurements that come closest to yours. That is your pattern size.

Since few people are a perfect size, your measurements might not exactly match one of the sizes. If your measurements fall between two sizes, select the smaller size if the design is full or loose fitting. Select the larger size if the design is closely fitted.

If you are choosing a pattern for pants or a skirt, you should select your pattern size by your waist measurement. However, if your hips are large in proportion to your waist, choose the pattern by the hip measurement.

Pattern Ease

All patterns have a certain amount of ease, or wiggle room, built in to them. If your garments fit you as tightly as a well-wrapped package, you would not be able to sit down, bend over, or stretch in your clothes.

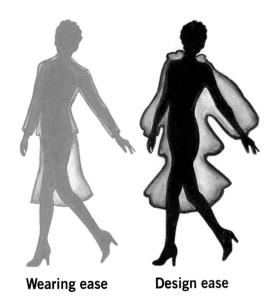

Wearing ease　　**Design ease**

Wearing ease concerns wearing comfort. Design ease *concerns the fashionable silhouette of the garment.*

This extra ease, known as **wearing ease,** is *the amount of fullness needed for movement and comfort.* The garment is larger than your body to give you the space to move about in your clothes. The only garments that do not have this wearing ease are special items, such as bathing suits and exercise wear made of stretch fabrics.

There is a second kind of ease that is built into a garment. This is called **design ease.** It is *the extra fullness built into the clothes by the designer to create a particular style or silhouette.* Some designers prefer their clothes to have a very loose-fitting silhouette. Others like their clothes to fit snugly against the body. The picture and the description on the pattern envelope will give you clues as to the amount of ease. See the *Sewing Handbook,* page 376 for additional information about patterns.

Female

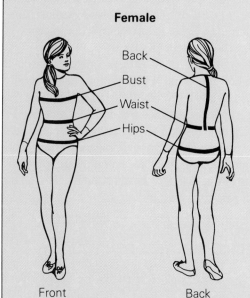

Back
Bust
Waist
Hips

Front   Back

Male

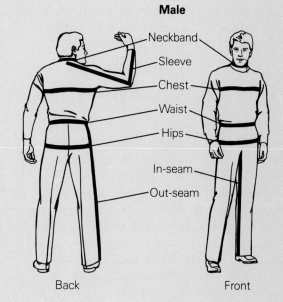

Neckband
Sleeve
Chest
Waist
Hips
In-seam
Out-seam

Back   Front

Depending on the garment you're buying, you will need to take different measurements to determine your size.

In a man's shirt, for example, neck and sleeve measurements are most important. For a woman's dress, the measurements needed to find the right size are bust, waist, and hips.

To find out what size you wear, take your measurements according to the following instructions. Then compare your measurements to those on a size chart. Most clothing stores have size charts available.

How to Measure

Measuring to check your size is not difficult. Remember to stand naturally, and to hold the tape taut, but not tight.

Height   Stand against the wall (barefoot). Have another person make a mark level with the top of your head. Measure from this point to the floor. For pants and skirt measurements, it is best to wear shoes.

Bust or chest   Measure over the fullest part of the bust or chest, with the tape straight across the back.

Waist   Measure the smallest part of the natural waistline.

Hips   Measure at the fullest part of the hips in a straight line around the body.

Back   Measure from waist to neck.

In-seam   Place pants that are correct length on a flat surface. Measure along inner seam from the bottom of one leg to where the two legs meet.

Out-seam   Measure from waist to point where pants bottom breaks slightly on shoe.

Neckband   Measure around the fullest part of the neck for neckband size, adding ½″ (1 cm) for wearing ease.

Sleeve   Bend arm up. Measure from base of neck across center back to elbow, across elbow crook, and up over wrist bone.

Selecting Fabric

Once you have selected a pattern, the next step is to choose a suitable fabric. You will want to select one that is compatible with both the pattern style and your sewing skills.

FABRIC SUITABLE FOR THE PATTERN

How do you know which fabrics would be best for your style of garment? Take another look at the back of the pattern envelope. The *Suggested Fabric List* is a guideline for which fabrics to choose. If the suggested fabrics are denim, poplin, or corduroy, then you know you should choose a firmer fabric. If the suggested fabrics are jersey, tricot, or crepe, then you know you should choose a soft, drapeable fabric. Canvas would be excellent for a sturdy duffle bag, but wrong for a ruffled blouse.

The pattern envelope suggests fabrics that would be suitable for your project.

Sometimes a pattern is designed only for knit fabrics. You will need to be sure that the knit you are considering has the right amount of stretch for your pattern. All "knits only" patterns have a *Stretch Gauge* on the pattern envelope. The Stretch Gauge shows how much the knit must be able to stretch in order to be a good choice for the pattern.

If your pattern has *gathers,* grasp the fabric to see how it drapes. If your pattern has *pleats,* crease a small section of the fabric between your fingernails to see if it will hold a pleat.

The Suggested Fabric List will also tell you if certain fabrics are not suitable for the design. Sometimes stripes, plaids, or obvious diagonal fabrics would look very unattractive if made up in a particular design.

FABRIC SUITABLE FOR YOU

The fabric you select should be right for your tastes and your lifestyle. Pick a color and a texture that is personally flattering and that coordinates with items you already own. Choose a fabric that is appropriate for the occasions when you plan to wear the garment. For example, even if the pattern envelope says that the dress or shirt can be made in denim, that would not be a suitable fabric choice if you planned to wear the garment to a wedding.

Look for quality fabric. In Chapter 21, you learned how to evaluate fabric for quality. These same guidelines are even more important when you are sewing because you have to work with the fabric as well as wear it. A good quality fabric is a pleasure to sew.

Be sure that the fabric is woven or knitted on *grain.* The color should be even without any streaks or spots. Any pattern design should be printed on grain. Check for wrinkle resistance and stretchability. Read the end of the fabric bolt for information about fibers and finishes and for care instructions.

FABRIC SUITABLE FOR YOUR SKILLS

The type of fabric you choose will also depend upon how much sewing experience you have had. If you are a beginning sewer, you will want to choose a fabric that is easy to sew. Your best choice is a medium weight, firmly woven or knitted fabric. A small all-over print is a good choice because any small sewing mistakes often do not show.

There are certain fabrics that require special sewing techniques. These fabrics are not good choices for beginning sewers:

- *slippery fabrics,* because they are hard to handle as you cut and stitch,
- *loosely woven fabrics,* because they can easily ravel and will require special seam finishes,
- *both sheer fabrics and thick, bulky fabrics,* because they are hard to pin, sew, and press,
- *fabrics with a one-way design,* because all the pieces must be laid out in the same direction,
- *pile fabrics,* such as velvet or corduroy, because they require a special layout and special pressing techniques,
- *stripes and plaids,* because they must be matched at all seam lines and design points, such as collars, cuffs, and pockets.

HOW MUCH TO BUY

The label or hangtag at the end of the fabric bolt will tell you the width of the fabric. Most fabrics are 36″ (.9 m), 45″ (1.1 m), or 60″ (1.5 m) wide. The *Yardage Chart* on the back of the pattern envelope will list how many yards or meters of fabric you will need for your size. Do not buy a fabric that is narrower than the ones listed on your pattern envelope. For example, if the Yardage Chart lists only 45″ (1.1 m) or 60″ (1.5 m) fabric, do not buy fabric that is 36″ (.9 m) wide. Some of the pattern pieces for that style are probably too large to fit on a narrower piece of fabric.

It is important to know if a fabric wrinkles easily. Here is a way to test it. Also, be sure to use the stretch gauge on the pattern envelope before purchasing knit fabric.

The Yardage Chart may indicate that extra fabric is required for fabrics with a nap, pile, shading, or one-way design. With these fabrics, all of the pattern pieces must be cut so that the pile or design runs in the same direction. Otherwise, the finished garment will look like it has been cut from two different shades of fabric or that part of the fabric is upside-down.

To check, fold the fabric so that part of it is turned upside-down. Stand back and look carefully for color variations and design direction. Corduroy, velveteen, and many knits need a one-way layout.

If you have selected a stripe, a plaid, or any other fabric design that requires matching, you will need to purchase extra yardage. The best way to determine how much extra fabric you will need is to actually lay out your major pattern pieces on the fabric at the store. Then you will not get home and find out that you have too little fabric or waste your money by buying too much. Most stores will let you do this, but be sure to ask a salesperson for assistance.

Measurement Conversion Chart

When You Know	Multiply by	To Find
inches	2.5	centimeters
feet	30.0	centimeters
yards	0.9	meters

One final decision concerns the price of the fabric. Multiply the cost of the fabric per yard or meter by the amount that you are going to buy. Does the total amount fit into your budget? Remember that you will also need some money to buy items, such as thread, buttons, zippers, and interfacing. It does not make good budgeting sense to spend more money on fabric than you would pay for the finished garment in ready-to-wear.

SELECTING NOTIONS

Notions are *the small items, such as zippers, snaps, buttons, trims, thread, and seam tape, that go into your garment.* Most of the notions you need to buy are listed under the section marked *Notions* on the back of the pattern envelope. Items such as thread, hooks and eyes, snaps, and shoulder pads are included. If you need a zipper, the length will be given. If you need buttons, the size and the quantity will be listed.

Some notions, such as lining, interfacing, trim, and elastic, are purchased by the yard or meter. Because the amount you need to buy may depend on the pattern size, these notions will be listed in the Yardage Chart.

You should always buy your notions when you buy your fabric. Then you will be sure that you have everything you need, the colors will match, and all items will require the same type of care. Buttons, tapes, trims, and interfacings

should have care requirements that are compatible with the care of the fabric. You will not be able to wash a garment if you put on buttons or trim that are dry clean only.

Color is very important when choosing notions. *Thread* should be the same color as your fabric. If you cannot find the exact color, choose one that is a shade darker. Thread looks lighter after it is stitched. *Trims* should match exactly. If you cannot find trims that match, select a contrasting color instead. *Interfacings* and *linings* should not show through on the right side of the garment. Test them in the store by draping a piece of your fabric over the lining and interfacing that you are considering.

The *weight* of your fabric will also affect your choice of notions.

- Heavy-duty threads are available for sewing on heavy fabrics.
- Zippers are available with metal or polyester coils. A lightweight, polyester coil zipper is a better choice for a lightweight fabric.
- Interfacings come in many different weights. You will want to select an interfacing that is either the same weight or slightly lighter in weight than your fabric. Otherwise, your finished garment will be either too stiff or too limp.

Selecting a Sewing Machine

If you are fortunate enough to be shopping for a sewing machine, there are several things you should consider.

1. *Purchase a machine that suits your needs.*
   Do not get carried away and buy a machine that has more features than you will

Technology

The Serger

The newest development in sewing machines is the **serger,** or *overlock machine.* Although sergers have been used for many years in the garment industry, sewing machine manufacturers now offer sergers for home or school use.

A serger stitches at twice the speed of an ordinary sewing machine. It is designed to do three steps at once:

- stitch the seam,
- trim off the extra fabric in the seam allowance, and
- finish the fabric edge with an overcast stitch.

To do this, sergers use two, three, or four spools of thread, depending on the model. Knife blades trim off the fabric as it is stitched. Needles and loopers form the stitches over the fabric edge as it passes through the machine.

Overlock sewing can be used to seam and hem fabric in one easy step. It can stitch overcast seams or finish the fabric edges on conventionally stitched seams. Narrow rolled hems can be made quickly on clothing, scarves, curtains, napkins, and tablecloths. Decorative seams on garments such as sweaters, sweatshirts, and lingerie can be stitched with embroidery thread, fine yarn, metallic thread, or even narrow ribbon.

However, the overlock machine does not replace a regular sewing machine. This is because there are some things it cannot do. For example, it cannot be used to make buttonholes, to put in a zipper, or to topstitch.

Pattern companies are now making patterns specifically designed for overlock sewing. Look for them in the pattern catalogs.

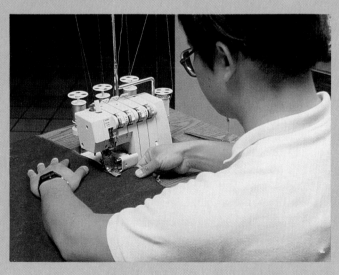

When purchasing a sewing machine, be sure to compare the special features and warranties of different brands and models.

need or use. That would be like buying a limousine when what you really need is a small economy car.

2. *Purchase the sewing machine from a dealer with a good reputation.*

Ask people who sew what kind of machine they have, where they bought it, and how they like it.

3. *Bring swatches of your own fabric with you to the store to test the machine stitching.*

Be sure to include any fabrics that have been difficult for you to sew. Sit down at each of the machines you are considering buying, and sew on these fabrics. You will learn more about the quality of the machine by sewing on your own fabric than by using the store's demonstration fabric.

4. *Find out what warranties the manufacturer offers and what warranties the dealer offers.*

Ask the dealer if someone will teach you how to operate the machine after you have bought it. Some dealers offer this service free of charge.

5. *Ask about service fees and policies.*

Sewing machines are like automobiles: they all need a tune-up now and then.

No matter what sewing machine you buy, it is important to understand how it operates. Read the *Sewing Machine Manual.* It will tell you how to use the machine properly. Information, such as needle size, tension adjustments, and suggested stitch lengths and widths for various fabrics, are included in the manual. The manual will also describe special features or techniques that will make sewing easier.

Refer to the *Sewing Handbook*, page 356, for more information on operating a sewing machine.

Chapter 23 Review

Summary

When selecting a sewing project, consider the five W's: who, what, when, where, and why. A pattern should be flattering to your body shape and match your sewing skill level. For the best fit, choose a pattern in the correct size and figure type for your own measurements. Select a fabric that is suitable for both the pattern style and your sewing skills. Certain fabrics require special sewing techniques and are not good choices for beginning sewers. Purchase your notions at the same time as your fabric. Selecting a sewing machine or a serger is a major purchase that deserves careful consideration.

Questions

1. List the five W questions to ask yourself about a sewing project. Why is each one important?

2. What clues are given on the front and back of a pattern envelope about how a garment should look?

3. How do you determine your figure type? How do you determine your pattern size within a figure type?

4. Explain the difference between wearing ease and design ease in patterns.

5. What is the purpose of the *Suggested Fabric List* on the back of a pattern envelope? Are you restricted to using only those fabrics listed?

6. What are three considerations that you should make when selecting fabric?

7. List at least three types of fabric that a beginning sewer should avoid using.

8. Why should notions be purchased at the same time as your fabric?

9. List the five guidelines for purchasing a sewing machine.

Activities

1. Look through pattern catalogues and select patterns that would be suitable for beginning sewers. Identify which features make each pattern easy-to-sew.

2. Collect illustrations of garments from fashion magazines. Write a description of each garment, such as would be found on the back of a pattern envelope. Include information about style, fit, and design details.

3. Visit a local fabric store. Compute how much it would cost for the pattern, fabric, and notions to make a garment. How does this cost compare with a similar ready-to-wear garment?

You Be the Expert

You are working in a fabric store. A customer asks your advice about selecting corduroy fabric for a beginning project. What advice would you give?

24 Consumer Rights, Protection, and Responsibilities

TERMS TO LEARN

arbitration
consideration
hidden costs
kleptomania
standards
toxic

At one time, a sweater that you bought in a store did not have any labels or hangtags. You could not tell what fibers the sweater was made from, or whether to wash or dry clean it. If you took a chance on washing the sweater and it shrank, it was your loss. Fortunately, this "consumer nightmare" does not exist any more. Today, consumers are protected by rules and regulations.

After reading this chapter, you will be able to:

- understand how to help keep the costs of products down by being a considerate and responsible shopper,
- explain how industry and government regulations protect the consumer,
- describe the responsibilities that consumers have in order to get the most satisfaction from purchases,
- explain what to do when a product does not live up to expectations.

Consumer Behavior

Your behavior as a shopper can affect the price of clothing. Someone must pay for cleaning and repairing clothes that are damaged by careless customers. Someone must pay for items that are stolen by shoplifters. Someone must pay for the salaries of store personnel who spend their time handling customer exchanges and returns. These *expenses for customer carelessness, theft, and returns* are known as **hidden costs**. The cost is passed on to you, the customer, in the form of higher prices.

However, there are many things that you can do to help control these hidden costs. Showing consideration for other customers and store personnel will improve conditions for everyone.

DAMAGED MERCHANDISE

If a seam is ripped, a hem is torn, or a garment has stains on it, the retailer will have to lower the price of the garment. You might find a dress with a missing belt on sale as a result.

However, it may cost you more in time and energy to find a new belt than you have actually saved on the price of the dress. In addition, the retailer will raise the price on other items in the store in order to make up the difference.

Guidelines to Follow

If you are going to be a thoughtful shopper, there are a few guidelines to follow:

- Always be careful when you try on clothes.
- Do not try to squeeze into a garment that is too small for you. This is how zippers are broken, buttons lost, and seams ripped.
- When pulling a garment over your head, be careful makeup does not stain the fabric.
- Always take off your shoes when trying on

any garment that you step into. The garment will stay clean, and you will not run the risk of getting your heel caught in the hem.
- Be careful that your jewelry does not snag the fabric.
- Do not remove any labels, hangtags, or price tags. It costs the store time and money to replace them.
- Do not let a garment fall on the fitting room floor where it might become wrinkled and dirty. Put it back on the hanger with any belt, scarf, or other accessory.
- Do not leave any garments in the fitting room. Return them to the salesperson or checker.

SHOPLIFTING

Shoplifters are responsible for the fact that retailers in North America lose over $10 million worth of merchandise every day. More and more effort is being made to insure that shoplifters are caught, arrested, and convicted. Shoplifting is a crime that can result in a stiff fine, legal supervision, a jail sentence, and a police record that lasts a lifetime.

People shoplift for many reasons. Some people shoplift because they cannot afford to buy some of the things that they need or want. A few people shoplift as a result of a personality disorder called **kleptomania**. They have *an abnormal and persistent impulse to steal.* Some people shoplift because of peer pressure from within a group involved in this illegal behavior.

Whatever the reason, shoplifting is stealing. It costs everyone money. The store that loses merchandise because of shoplifting must raise its prices. The higher prices cover the cost of the stolen items, plus the increased costs of higher insurance premiums, security guards, television monitors, and security systems.

Because shoplifting is on the increase and retailers cannot afford to absorb the losses,

All stores should clearly post their policies about returns, exchanges, and the acceptance of credit cards and checks.

many stores no longer take a lenient attitude toward shoplifters. Additional security guards, as well as increased security systems, are used to apprehend shoplifters. Hidden cameras are used to survey shopping areas. Merchandise is often electronically tagged. These large tags can only be removed with special equipment at the cashier's desk when you pay for the item. Small tags may be hidden in a pocket or seam allowance. If someone were to try to take an item out of the store with one of these tags still attached, a special alarm would go off.

EXCHANGES AND RETURNS

Another hidden cost is the extra expense a retailer may have to absorb if you return an item many days or weeks after it was purchased. When this happens, the returned item may have to be put on sale because the selling season is over or the store does not have any more items like it.

Always exchange or return items promptly. Some stores have a limit of 7 or 10 days from date of purchase for returns. You will save your-self time, energy, and money if you shop carefully. Be sure of sizes and colors before you buy. Check for fit, evaluate quality, and compare prices to avoid making exchanges and returns.

SHOWING CONSIDERATION

Shopping often brings out the worst in people because they are tired, rushed, or frustrated in their search for items. However, being rude or discourteous toward salespersons or other customers never solves the problem. Instead, try to show **consideration**, which is *thoughtfulness, or helpfulness, toward others whenever you are shopping.*

Always be pleasant to a salesperson when describing what you are looking for. If you must complain about an item or service, state the problem clearly and firmly, but never yell. Wait in line for your turn for a dressing room or to pay. If other customers try to cut in line ahead of you, tell them nicely that you are ahead of them. If you are with a group of friends, try not to block the aisles or talk and laugh too loudly.

Consumer Rights and Protection

In 1962, President John F. Kennedy delivered a special consumer message to Congress. It was brought about because of mounting problems that consumers were having with certain goods.

CONSUMER RIGHTS

President Kennedy's message was the inspiration for new legislation and amendments to existing legislation, all designed to protect the consumer. This legislation established that all consumers have four basic rights:

- *The Right to Safety.* To be protected against the manufacturing and selling of goods that are hazardous to one's health, life, or limb.
- *The Right to Be Informed.* To be protected against false advertising, labeling, or highly misleading information about products, and to be given the facts needed to make a good choice.
- *The Right to Choose.* To have as much access as possible to a variety of goods and services at a reasonable price.
- *The Right to Be Heard.* To be assured that consumers' interests will get a sympathetic hearing by the government and that the laws protecting consumers' rights will be enforced.

Two other consumer rights were later added by President Richard Nixon and President Gerald Ford:

- *The Right to Redress.* To have corrected any wrong done to the consumer in the marketplace;
- *The Right to Consumer Education.*

CONSUMER PROTECTION

Federal, state, and local legislation has been passed to protect consumers. Federal laws cover all consumers. State and local legislation varies in coverage. Many of these laws and regulations are designed to help you know exactly what you are buying and to give you a better, safer product. Government agencies are responsible for enforcing the laws and establishing health and safety rules. Private groups have also been formed to assist consumers.

Government Regulations

The United States Government has established federal laws and regulations relating to fibers, fabrics, and textile products.

- In Chapter 15, you learned about the *Textiles Fiber Products Identification Act* of 1958. It specifies what information should appear on the labels of the textile products that you buy. It was revised in 1984 to include additional information about country of origin.

- In Chapter 18, you covered material about *Care Label Ruling,* which was enacted in 1972, expanded in 1981, and revised in 1984. It specifies the *type* of care information and the *wording* to be used on permanent care labels attached to garments and other textile products.

- *The Wool Products Labeling Act,* revised in 1980, states that the manufacturer must identify the type of wool and the fiber content of the item. The manufacturer must also indicate whether the wool is new or recycled.

New wool is wool that has never before been woven or knitted into fabric. *Recycled wool* is wool that is obtained by shedding a previously manufactured wool product back into fibers. Then the fibers are remade into fabric.

The Wool Act was expanded in 1984 to include the country of origin.

- *The Fur Products Labeling Act* of 1952 states that the manufacturer must indicate the type of fur, its English name, its country of origin, and whether the fur has been dyed or otherwise altered.

- *The Flammable Fabrics Act* of 1953 prohibits the sale of fabrics that burn faster, easier, and more intensely than other fabrics. One of the major accomplishments of this law is the development of standards for flame-retardant sleepwear for children. These standards also apply to fabric sold by-the-yard that is intended for use in children's sleepwear and apparel. There are also flammability standards for rugs, carpets, and mattresses. Even vinyl plastic films used for wearing apparel are covered by the Flammable Fabrics Act.

- *The Hazardous Substances Labeling Act* protects consumers from the use of **toxic,** or *poisonous,* substances in products. For example, lead is highly poisonous. It can be dangerous to a young child who may tend to put many things in his or her mouth. Therefore, all paints and surface coatings used in children's wear, such as painted T-shirts and athletic jerseys, must be free of lead.

There are other federal regulations designed to protect you financially. You learned about some of them in Chapter 20.

- *The Consumer Credit Protection Act* requires that institutions, such as banks, credit card companies, and retail stores, clearly explain all the terms of a credit agreement. They also provide you with various types of protection if someone steals your credit card and uses it to make any purchases in your name.

- *The Consumer Product Warranty and Federal Trade Commission Improvement Act* requires that all warranties be written in clear and simple language. They must be posted on, or close to, the product when you purchase it.

Industry Standards

Although federal legislation does require that manufacturers make products that meet certain standards, many retailers and manufacturers set up their own quality standards that go beyond what is required by law. **Standards** are *specific measurements or models to which similar products are compared.*

Sometimes these quality control tests are conducted on behalf of a manufacturer who wants to make certain claims about the product. Sometimes they are conducted for a retailer who wishes to double check the claims made by the manufacturer.

Some very large companies have their own product testing laboratories. Others use the services of an independent testing company. A group of manufacturers in an industry may also get together and establish standards of its own.

The major pattern companies did just that when they worked together to establish *Standard Sizing.* A set of body measurements was developed for each pattern size. All the major pattern companies now use these standard measurements when they produce their patterns.

Consumer Agencies and Organizations

Some government agencies are responsible for enforcing laws that affect consumers.

The *Federal Trade Commission*, or FTC, has a Bureau of Consumer Protection. It handles consumer problems relating to advertising, price fixing, credit, and fraud.

The *Office of Consumer Affairs* recommends consumer protection and education to the president of the United States.

The *Food and Drug Administration,* or FDA, enforces laws and regulations for cosmetics, as well as for food and drugs.

Technology

Textile Testing

Textile testing has played an important part in the improved performance and quality of textile products. Laboratory testing requires special scientific equipment and closely controlled conditions to assure accuracy of results. Each test is conducted on several samples of fabrics or garments to determine an average result.

Here are a few of the tests that relate to consumer use of textiles:

- *Appearance after Repeated Launderings.* This test is used to evaluate the performance of permanent press fabrics and wrinkle-resistant finishes. Samples are washed in automatic washing machines using different water temperatures and washing cycles. The samples are dried using different methods and then evaluated.
- *Shrinkage.* Different washing and drying methods are used to determine the amount of shrinkage or change in size after one or more launderings.
- *Colorfastness to Light.* A Fade-Ometer® is a special machine used to expose fabrics to high intensity light that can cause fading. In only a few hours, tests can be

conducted that equal the natural fading that takes place over a long period of time.
- *Flammability.* Fabrics are tested to determine if they will ignite easily and to measure their rate of burning.

The *United States Postal Service* handles complaints about mail-order shopping.

Private consumer groups include the *Better Business Bureau,* which helps to settle customer complaints through voluntary **arbitration**. This is *the settlement of a dispute by a person or panel that listens to both sides and issues a decision.*

Other consumer groups are organized by interested citizens at the national, state, and local levels. They may focus on certain consumer issues of interest to their membership.

Consumer Responsibilities

If you are going to be a smart consumer, you cannot rely on government regulations, industry standards, and consumer groups to guarantee that all your purchases will be wise ones. You are the only person who can know your own personal needs and wants.

RESEARCH THE PRODUCT

It is the manufacturer's and the retailer's responsibility to provide you with information that is clear and accurate and not misleading. It is your responsibility to read that information before you purchase an item. In many cases, you will not want to rely only on what the manufacturer claims or the salesperson tells you. You will want to do some research on your own.

For example, if you are going to buy a sewing machine, you should visit several dealers and

When you are making a major purchase, it is wise to gather as much information about it as possible.

try out various machines. But, before you do that, you should do some research.

1. Ask friends and relatives who sew about their recommendations.

2. Go to the library and look up "Sewing Machines" in the *Reader's Guide to Periodical Literature.* It will give you the names of any magazines, as well as the date and the page numbers, that have published articles on purchasing a sewing machine. The librarian will be glad to help you find them. Also look in *Consumer Reports.* It is a magazine that specializes in providing information and advice about many consumer goods and services.

3. Ask your Home Economics teacher and Extension Home Economist to let you look through their collection of sewing publications for additional articles. Make a list of your needs and wants in a sewing machine and take it with you when you visit the dealer. That way, you will not get confused or sidetracked when you get into the store.

4. Before you purchase a major item, such as a sewing machine, it is also a good idea to contact your local office of the *Better Business Bureau* or *Chamber of Commerce.* Ask if there are any complaints against the dealer from whom you are planning to buy your machine. You want to be sure that you are buying from a reputable dealer who will give you good service.

UNDERSTAND STORE POLICIES

It is your responsibility as a consumer to understand the store's policies before you purchase an item. If you are using a lay-away plan or a credit card, be sure that you have read and understood the terms for payment.

Find out about the store's return policy. It should be posted in the store. If you cannot find it, ask. Can you return the item? How long after you have bought it? Will you get cash or credit?

Save Receipts and Warranties

It is your responsibility to keep the sales receipt, all the hangtags, and any warranties that come with your purchase.

The sales slip is your proof of where you bought the merchandise and how much you paid for it. If you must return the item for any reason, you will need to show the sales slip.

The warranties and hangtags will give you valuable information about the performance of your purchase.

ACT IN GOOD FAITH

If there is something wrong with your clothing purchase, return it promptly to the store for credit, exchange, or cash refund. When you do this, you should act in *good faith,* in a way that is fair and reasonable. This means you should not expect the store to take back merchandise if you have not followed the instructions on the care label. For example, if the care label said "dry clean only," but you went ahead and washed the sweater, then it is your fault if the sweater shrank.

Good faith means that you should have reasonable expectations about the wear and performance of a garment. If your new bathing suit fades after two wearings, it is reasonable to return it. If it fades after two months of frequent wear, it is not reasonable to return it.

You should also take care not to abuse the store's return policy. Always be honest about your reason for a return. Store personnel deal with refund problems every day and have experience in handling complaints. If it is a manufacturing problem, the store may return the item to the manufacturer for credit. Otherwise the store absorbs the refund costs.

It is always wise to save sales slips, charge statements, and warranties, especially on important purchases.

COMPLAIN EFFECTIVELY

You have a right to expect that the item you buy will perform properly. An umbrella should not leak. The heel should not come off your shoe the first time you wear it. If there is a problem with any item that you have purchased, do not be shy about making your complaints heard. If you approach the problem in a direct and mature manner, your chances of receiving satisfaction are greatly improved.

There are some simple procedures to follow:

1. *Take your complaint directly to the store where you purchased the merchandise.*

   Bring the item and the sales receipt with you. Explain your problem politely to the salesperson. If the salesperson cannot help you, ask to speak to the department manager or the store owner. Some department stores have a Customer Service Department or an Adjustment Department. If you have acted in good faith, your complaint will usually be resolved. After all, stores do not want unhappy customers.

The telephone book is a good place to find a manufacturer's or store's address.

2. *If the problem is not solved, write a letter to the store.*

Address the letter to the store owner, the store president, or the head of the Customer Service Department. Write to the person by name. If you do not know his or her name, call the store and ask the telephone operator. Enclose photocopies of your sales receipt and any cancelled checks. Photocopies can be made for a small fee at many libraries, post offices, stores, or printing companies. Never send the original documents.

An effective complaint letter should contain all of the following:

- your name and address;
- the name, job title, and address of the person to whom you are sending the letter;
- a clear explanation of the problem including how the product or service is defective;
- the name and address of the store where the item was bought or the service was arranged, and the purchase date;
- specific information, such as style number, catalogue number, order number;

- the steps you have taken to resolve the problem;
- what you believe should be done about your problem.

3. *Contact the manufacturer if the store does not give you satisfaction.*

Write to the manufacturer's Customer Relations Department and enclose a copy of your letter to the store, plus a copy of your sales receipt. If the problem still remains unsettled, write directly to the president of the company. You can obtain the company's address and the president's name from reference books at your public library. Ask the librarian for assistance.

4. *If none of the above work, contact a consumer protection agency for advice.*

You will find them listed in the telephone book. Look in the white pages under the name of your city, county, or state. If your local newspaper or radio station has a consumer reporter or an action line, you might also get in touch with them. Because manufacturers and retailers do not like bad publicity, it may force them to deal immediately with your complaint.

You could also contact your Better Business Bureau. It has information about the dependability of businesses and can help settle disputes between consumers and businesses. Your local Chamber of Commerce may also have an Ethics Committee to help settle disputes.

Legal assistance can be obtained from a lawyer or a legal service. Less serious complaints can be settled in a small claims court where you present your own case before a judge.

Shopping is a three-way process. It involves the customer, the manufacturer, and the retailer. It is to everyone's benefit that all are satisfied with the goods that are bought and sold.

Chapter 24 Review

Summary

Damaged merchandise, shoplifting, exchanges, and returns are extra expenses for retailers that can affect the price of clothing. Federal, state, and local legislation help protect consumers. Some of these laws and regulations cover the labeling and safety of textile products. Many manufacturers and retailers set their own quality standards. A variety of agencies and organizations also benefit consumers. In turn, consumers have certain responsibilities. You should research the product before buying, understand store policies, save receipts and warranties, act in good faith, and know how to complain effectively about a problem.

Questions

1. Describe the guidelines that a considerate shopper should follow when trying on clothing in a store.

2. How does shoplifting affect the prices that you pay for merchandise?

3. How long should you wait before exchanging or returning an item?

4. List the six consumer rights guaranteed to you under law. Explain what each one means.

5. Identify four consumer protection acts in the area of clothing and textiles. Explain the areas of the textile industry that are governed by each.

6. List three government agencies that enforce consumer laws.

7. Why should you save sales receipts, hangtags, and warranties?

8. What procedures should you follow when making a complaint about a product?

9. What information should a complaint letter contain?

Activities

1. Choose a consumer item that you would like to buy if finances permitted. Research the item, using consumer magazines, catalogue comparisons, and visits to retail stores. Which brand and model would you buy? Why?

2. Set up a file box where you can save sales slips, hangtags, and warranties for items that you have purchased. Be sure to write the name of the item on each related piece of information that you save.

3. Write a letter to a store about a problem with a garment that you recently purchased. You have already taken your complaint to the salesperson who told you that nothing could be done about the problem.

You Be the Expert

You are shopping with a friend who suggests that you both shoplift some merchandise. Your friend says, "Even if we're caught, nothing will happen to us!" What reply could you give?

6

The Workplace

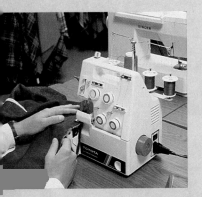

25 *Careers and You*

The careers that interested us in the past do not always match the skills we develop as we grow older. There may be careers that we are not even aware of that would suit us perfectly. Fortunately, a person who is in high school today does not have to decide what he or she wants to "be" for the rest of his or her life. This is a time to explore many different fields before eventually choosing a career. Even then, many people change careers during their lifetime.

After reading this chapter, you will be able to:

- describe the wide variety of career opportunities that are a part of, or related to, the clothing industry,
- understand how to put your talents, skills, and experiences to work in discovering the careers that interest you,
- identify the education and training that are needed for these types of jobs,
- explain how career objectives can change over the course of your lifetime.

Changes in Careers

When your great-grandparents were young, they could look forward to living until the average age of 55. They probably planned on having only one career. For girls, it was usually motherhood. For boys, it was usually a career similar to the one that their father had chosen. There was little thought to changing careers during their lifetime. Today, there is a wide variety of career opportunities for both men and women. Both sexes are accepted as teachers, fashion designers, lawyers, salespersons, and computer programmers, for example. Talents and interests are more important than gender in developing career goals.

In recent years, our **standard of living** has increased. This is *the goods and services we feel are necessary in order to maintain a certain level of living.* In order to afford and maintain this higher standard of living, just about all of us will have to work all or most of our adult lives. Many families cannot maintain their desired standard of living with one income.

Today, it is not unusual for both husband and wife to work. If the family has children, balancing work and family responsibilities become very important for parents. Single working parents have the added stress of juggling all responsibilities by themselves. Good management of time and other resources is vital for such families.

CAREER TRENDS

Many changes have occurred in the work force since your great-grandparents were young adults.

- *Longer career spans.* People are living longer. If you are a female, you can expect to live to an average age of 83. If you are a male, you can expect to live until age 76. That means that people are not only living longer, they are working longer. With the elimination of a mandatory retirement age for many jobs, people are choosing to work past age 65.

- *Increased technology.* We live in a highly technological world. New discoveries and developments are happening almost daily. As a result, there will be certain jobs ten years from now that are unthought of today. It is possible that some of the skills you need for a job today will be **obsolete,** or *no longer useful,* in twenty years.

- *More than one career.* Unlike your great-grandfathers, many people will have more than one career during their lifetime. Technological changes will make some people's skills obsolete. They may have to learn new skills, either related to their current job or in a completely different field, in order to continue in the work force. Many people will return to school or start a second career after they have retired from the first one.

- *More women in the work force.* Years ago, women worked only when it was a financial necessity. The jobs they held were limited to certain ones that were considered women's work. Today, many women work not only for the money, but also for the feelings of satisfaction, self-fullfillment, and status that they get from their careers.

Some women work throughout their lives. Others drop out of the work force when they have a child. Some mothers return to work when their children are young, while others may not work outside the home until their children are older. Child care arrangements have become a very important consideration for many families. Some companies now offer child care facilities for their employees.

- *Increased job flexibility.* More and more people desire job flexibility because of personal interests or family responsibilities. Part-time jobs enable a person to more easily take college courses, become involved in special activities, or care for children. Some people have jobs that allow them to work at home. At-home work offers advantages such as flexible hours and being able to supervise children's activities. Some people have a job-sharing arrangement in which one person works in the morning and the other person in the afternoon. Parents may try to arrange their work hours so that one parent is always home with the children.

In today's world, it is no longer necessary to make decisions while still in high school that will lock you into a lifetime career. However, it is still a good idea to explore as many opportunities and work experiences as possible. It will help you discover the jobs that you enjoy and are good at. After all, you will spend the greater part of your adult life at work. Wouldn't you prefer to be doing work that is satisfying and enjoyable?

Career Opportunities in the Clothing Fields

Mary Clayton is a computer programmer, Roger Fox is an artist, Jane Martex is a teacher, and Sam Thwait is a chemist. What do they all have in common? Each of them has a job in an industry that is related to the clothes you buy, sew, and wear.

When we think of a person who has a career in the clothing field, we tend to think of a fashion designer or a buyer for a store. But there are many more career opportunities. The clothing field is really made up of five interconnecting areas: the *textile industry,* the *apparel industry,* the *fashion field,* the *education field,* and the *communications industry.*

THE TEXTILE INDUSTRY

The textile industry is made up of all the people and companies that contribute the materials that are ultimately used to make the clothes we wear, the linens we use, the upholstery we sit on, and the carpeting we walk on. Did you know that every roll of 35 mm film you buy for your camera has a little piece of black velvet inside to help protect it from the light? How many other uses can you think of for textiles?

The textile industry begins with the people who produce the fibers. Farmers grow the plants that provide the cotton fibers. Ranchers raise the sheep that provide the fleece for wool. Scientists who work for chemical companies develop fibers that are eventually spun into yarns.

Mills take the natural and synthetic yarns and convert them into fabric. Designs are dyed, printed, knitted, or woven into the fabric in endless variations. Fabrics are treated with special finishes that increase the fabric's performance, such as permanent press or stain-repellent finishes. Other finishes, such as glazing or napping, enhance the fabric's appearance.

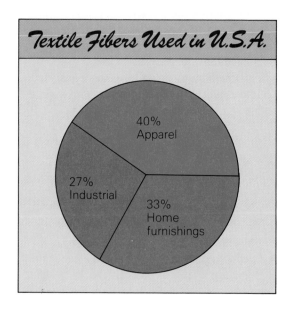

Textile Fibers Used in U.S.A.

40% Apparel

27% Industrial

33% Home furnishings

Many steps are involved in the production of fabrics.

Finished fabric may be sold to a designer or manufacturer to be cut and sewn into finished products, such as shirts, towels, curtains, or even automobile seats. Fabric is also sold to fabric stores where you can buy it by the yard and sew it into whatever you wish.

It takes many jobs to make all of this happen. Jobs in the textile industry include machine operators, machine technicians, engineers, chemists, and computer programmers.

In Chapter 26, you will learn more about textile industry jobs.

THE APPAREL INDUSTRY

Take a look at the clothes you and your classmates are wearing. Someone designed the garment, selected the fabric, drafted the pattern, sewed the garment together, and sold it to the store. Someone at the store, in turn, sold it to you. All of these people and the companies they work for are part of the **apparel**, or *garment,* **industry**.

The processes of designing, manufacturing, and selling apparel offer job opportunities for people of every skill level, from stock clerk to pattern maker to merchandise manager. There are also many career opportunities in the service industries that are concerned with the care and repair of apparel. These include dry cleaners, laundries, and alteration and repair services.

You will learn about job opportunities in design and manufacturing in Chapter 26. In Chapter 27, you will learn about the variety of jobs in retailing and the service industries.

THE FASHION FIELD

Goods are produced by the textile and apparel manufacturers. Then these goods are sold to the retailer who sells them to you, the customer. People who work in the fashion field present these goods in an attractive and pleasing way. They promote items that are very new and "in fashion," or show you new ways to wear familiar styles. Their aim is to get you to buy new clothes.

This display artist designs and lays out a large department store's newspaper ads.

This department store display artist must possess a great deal of creativity and be well informed of current fashion trends.

Jobs in the fashion field include fashion illustrators, display artists, photographers, models, copywriters, stylists, and fashion coordinators. These are the people who are responsible for the "look" of newspaper and magazine advertisements, window displays, catalogues, and fashion shows.

There are fashion jobs in all the clothing areas, particularly in retailing and apparel manufacturing. Textile companies also employ fashion experts. Their job is to report to the company about current fashion trends and to predict new ones. This helps textile companies identify needs and uses for new fibers and fabrics. In order to be successful in a fashion job, a person must have a good eye for line, design, and color, as well as an interest in things that are new and different.

In Chapters 26, 27, and 28, you will learn more about careers in the fashion field. They are many and varied.

THE EDUCATION AND COMMUNICATION FIELDS

The education and communication fields have something in common—both are concerned with giving information to people. Your home economics teacher is an educator in the clothing field. So is the person who teaches sewing at your local fabric store, the instructor who teaches pattern drafting at a vocational school, and the extension home economist who may have worked with you in 4-H.

The consumer education field includes people who work for manufacturers, retailers, government agencies, and trade associations. Their job is to help people learn how to get the greatest satisfaction from the goods and services they purchase. Many of the companies involved in the home sewing area, such as sewing machine manufacturers and pattern companies, employ consumer education specialists.

Technology

The Textiles and Apparel Industries

The combined textiles and apparel industries make up one of the largest industries in the nation. It includes the production and manufacture of fibers, fabrics, clothing, furs, hosiery, hats, and other accessories.

Here are some facts to consider about the industries in the United States:

- over 2 million people are employed
- 80% of employees in the apparel industry are women
- textile sales exceed $50 billion a year
- retail apparel sales are $97 billion a year
- over 40% of the apparel sold is imported from other countries

The *textile industry* is made up of fiber and fabric producers. The largest percentage of the total fiber used in the United States goes into clothing. The remainder is used for home furnishings and for industrial uses. Twenty years ago, most clothing was made from natural fibers. Today, the majority of fibers used in apparel fabrics is man-made, or manufactured.

The *apparel industry* consists of about 30 very large manufacturers and many smaller companies, some employing fewer than 100 people. A great deal of labor is required to manufacture clothing. Few tasks are automated. Because of frequent fashion changes, large quantities of any one style are seldom produced.

Imports are posing a serious threat to both the textiles and apparel industries in the United States. For example, more than 50% of all sweaters and woven shirts are now imported. As a result, employment is down significantly in some states. The average wages in the United States are over $5 an hour in the apparel industry and over $6 an hour in the textiles industry. In contrast, the hourly wages are $1 in Hong Kong, $.50 in Taiwan and Korea, and only $.16 in China.

Today, the textiles and apparel industries compete with goods made in over 100 countries. They are part of a global market that did not exist 25 years ago. Due to improved shipping and trade, geographic location has far less importance than it once did. Less developed countries of the world are developing their own textiles and apparel industries in the world market.

Significant questions now face the textiles and apparel industries in the United States. How will they continue to operate successfully in the global market? How can they compete with lower priced imports? Should import quotas be established to protect jobs and prevent companies from going out of business? Should consumers be able to buy merchandise as cheaply as possible? Imports are a very complex issue that even affect international relations between countries.

Technical school or college courses are necessary for some jobs in textiles and apparel.

People in the communications field are often informal educators. As you learned in Chapter 19, an advertisement that was designed to make you want to buy a product can also teach you many things about that product, even if that was not the main purpose of the ad. In Chapter 28, you will learn more about jobs in the communications and education fields.

Your Interests and Skills

Do you remember the story *Alice in Wonderland?* Alice followed the White Rabbit down the rabbit hole without a second thought. She encountered an unusual collection of characters and had many different adventures before finding her way home again. Sometimes the process of finding out about the jobs and careers that match your skills and interests can make you feel a little bit like Alice following the White Rabbit down the rabbit hole! Finding a job that fits yourself first means knowing yourself and developing your skills and interests.

KNOW YOURSELF

The first step is to find out who you are and what interests you. Take the time to really think about the classes you take. What subjects do you do well in? What subjects are difficult for you? What subjects are easy for you? Are there some classes that you enjoy even though you must work hard at the subject?

Think about how you spend your **leisure time**, which is *free or spare time.* What activities are satisfying to you? Do you like group activities, or activities that you do alone? Do you get along with all types of people? What talents do you have? Can you sew, do you take great photographs, have you decorated your room in a unique and attractive way?

Do not limit yourself to the activities you are doing right now. Think about what you did in grade school or junior high school. Did you sell the most boxes of cookies or candy for your school or Scout troop? Perhaps you have a special gift for salesmanship. Remember that no one is "average" in everything. There are always some things you do better than others. If you have trouble identifying them, remember that you may not have discovered all of them yet!

Other people's judgments of our talents and personality can greatly influence how we see

Knowing how to sew can be the first step to many apparel industry jobs.

subjects. Learn as much as you can about line, design, and color.

Where could all this lead you? Fashion illustrator, costume historian, fashion designer, and fashion coordinator are just a few of the jobs that require knowledge of clothing and art.

Get involved in after-school activities that will help you learn and grow. If you are interested in writing, volunteer to work on the school newspaper or yearbook staff. Many people, at some point in their careers, have to make presentations to a group. It could be a small group of co-workers or a large group of consumers. Any experience you can get in being in front of an audience, whether as a member of the Debating Club or as an actor in the school play, will help you later on.

ourselves and the goals we set for ourselves. You will have to be the judge of how much you let other people's opinions limit you. A friend, a teacher, or a family member may help you recognize your strengths and weaknesses.

Remember, however, that they may only see certain parts of your personality. They may only see those characteristics that fit in with their own lives. *You are the one person who knows all your wishes and dreams.*

In Chapter 3 you will find material on self-image, decision-making, and values which you may want to review. You may also wish to review Chapter 1 on needs and wants.

DEVELOP YOUR SKILLS AND INTERESTS

Once you have identified some of your skills and interests, you can begin to develop them. Suppose you are interested in fashion and you like to draw. It would be a good idea to take as many art and clothing courses as you can.

Begin with the home economics and art courses offered in your school. Then, find out if any fabric stores or art museums in your area offer special courses on Saturdays or after school. Visit art exhibits and read about these

Part-Time Experience

It is a good idea to try and test out your interests in the job market. Part-time jobs can give you a taste of what it is like to work full-time in a particular field. For example, if you think you might like a career in retailing, get a part-time or summer job as a salesperson or a stock clerk. You will learn about how a store functions and about the rewards and problems of running a store. You will also have the opportunity to learn something about the type of people who choose careers in retailing. If it is a small store, they might let you work on the window displays. You may discover some talents that you did not know you have!

Remember that volunteer work can be just as valuable a source of experience as a job that pays a salary. Think about offering your services as a guide at a local art museum, to teach younger children how to sew, or to help a charity with its benefit fashion show.

LEARNING BY ASKING

Learn as much as you can about the jobs that interest you. If there are people who have these jobs in the places where you work, observe what they do and ask them about their background. Talk to family members, your friends, parents, older brothers and sisters, and anyone who has a job that interests you.

Find out what the job really involves. What does the person do on an average day? How long are the hours? Is it a standard eight-hour-a-day job or does the person work weekends, evenings, and overtime? Does the job require traveling? Where? Are the trips long or short, frequent or occasional, in the United States or abroad? Where will you find opportunities in this field? Will they be in a city, in the suburbs, or in a small town?

Evaluate what you see and hear. Ask yourself these questions:

- Would this type of job be satisfying to me?
- What talents do I have that this job requires?
- Could I do it well?
- What education or training would I need?

A job in retail sales can lead to other positions in the apparel and fashion fields.

Education and Training

Many jobs require special training. Some jobs, such as salesperson or model, require only a high school education. Additional training is given on-the-job by the employer. If this *on-the-job training is part of a formal program,* it is often called an **apprenticeship program**.

Various jobs require a degree from a vocational school, a junior college, or a four-year college. Sometimes, a certain degree is not absolutely necessary, but it will help you get a head start on your career.

Whether or not you need to attend a vocational school for technical training may depend on the companies in your community and the types of training programs they offer. If you are interested in a particular type of job, do some research.

Call the Personnel Department of a company that employs people in that type of job and ask them about their educational requirements. Then talk to a counselor at the vocational school. Find out where their graduates are employed and what type of assistance in finding a job the school gives to its graduates.

Some jobs, such as pattern maker or textile machine technician, require some vocational school training. Other jobs, such as copywriter, retail merchandise manager, or public relations specialist require a general college degree. Jobs such as a home economics teacher, a textile chemist, or a plant engineer require college degrees that specialize in certain subjects.

Flexibility

One of the most important traits you can bring to the work place is flexibility. **Flexibility** is *the willingness to adapt oneself to new opportunities and situations.*

JOB CHANGES

The career you are aiming for now may not be the one that you have in 20 years. You will find that every job you take can open doors to possibilities you never thought about.

You may learn about a new job. You may decide to go back to school to change careers or get a college degree. You may even find an employer who is willing to pay for your schooling.

Some large companies have **tuition refund plans** that make it possible for you to work and go to school at the same time. If the courses you wish to take or the degree you wish to earn meet with the company's approval, *the company will pay all or part of the cost of going to school after work.*

OUTSIDE FACTORS

Flexibility also means that you recognize outside factors that may limit or shape your career opportunities. For example, if you live in a small Western town and want to be a fashion designer, you should realize that most designers work in New York or Los Angeles. If you are not willing to move to these cities, it will be much harder for you to become a designer. You will have to be more creative about how you apply your skills.

You might develop a small business designing items for a boutique. You might design cos-tumes for a local theater group. You might open your own custom dressmaking business.

If you have family financial responsibilities, you may hesitate to choose a career that requires additional education beyond high school Think about attending school in the evening or getting some type of financial aid to help you out.

BEING YOUR OWN BOSS

Many people, at some point in their career, have to decide whether to work for someone else or to start their own business. Such a decision depends, to a large degree, on the person's flexibility and willingness to take a risk.

Being your own boss can mean doing anything from owning and operating your own factory, to being a free-lance writer or artist, to working as a self-employed tailor, dressmaker, or store owner.

You need to develop many skills and talents in order to be successful in your own business. For example, a dressmaker or tailor needs to have good sewing skills. He or she should also keep up-to-date on new developments in fabrics, sewing machines, notions, and sewing techniques that produce better and faster results.

You also need to know how to market and advertise your products or skills, where to go for financial advice, and how to keep business records.

In Chapter 29, you will learn about the types of businesses and the talents, interests, personality characteristics, and knowledge that one must have to run a business successfully in today's world.

Exploring and learning about all of these job opportunities can be exciting and rewarding. Having a job that you enjoy and are good at contributes as much to your positive self-image as how you look or how you feel.

Chapter 25 Review

Summary

Many changes are occuring in the work place such as longer career spans, increased technology, multiple careers, more women workers, and job flexibility. A wide variety of career opportunities exists in the different areas of the clothing field: textiles, apparel, fashion, education, and communication. When deciding on a career, you should consider your own interests and skills. You can learn about careers through part-time jobs. Additional education or training is required for many jobs. One of the most important traits you can bring to the work place is flexibility.

Questions

1. What were the career opportunities for young adults 75 years ago?

2. Describe four trends that are occurring in the work place.

3. What is the purpose of each segment of the clothing field: textile industry, apparel industry, fashion field, education field, and communication industry? How are the areas interrelated?

4. Why is it helpful to analyze your interests and skills when considering job and career possibilities?

5. Give two examples of how school activities or volunteer work can help you prepare for a future career.

6. What can you learn from a part-time job?

7. Where can you get additional training for jobs? Give examples.

8. Why is flexibility an important personal trait of any worker?

Activities

1. Read the want ads from a variety of newspapers to find job announcements related to the clothing field. Create a display of the listings in each of the career areas.

2. Interview a person who works in some aspect of the clothing field. Ask about job responsibilities, likes and dislikes, career experiences, and educational background. What advice would the person give to someone who is interested in entering this field?

3. List part-time or summer jobs in your area that offer experience in the textile or apparel field. If you have held such a job, describe what you learned about the field. Would you like to work full-time in this area?

You Be the Expert

Your cousin is a salesperson in a clothing store. Although she likes working with new fashions, fabrics, and colors, she is unsure if she wants a career in retailing. What other types of jobs could you suggest?

26 | *Design and Manufacturing*

TERMS TO LEARN

assembly line
knock-off
market research
pattern grading
piecework
sales analysis
sweatshop

Do you have a good eye for details? Do you like to tinker with machinery? Do you have a good sense of line, design, and color? These are only a few of the many talents and interests that can lead you to a career in design and manufacturing in the textiles and apparel industry.

After reading this chapter, you will be able to:

- explain the designer's and stylist's role in creating the fashion look of clothing and fabrics,
- understand the part that research and development play in discovering new fibers and methods for producing fabrics,
- recognize the role of production and manufacturing in making fabrics and producing garments,
- identify the responsibilities of marketing experts and sales representatives for selling the finished products.

Textiles and Apparel

The many jobs in the textile and apparel industries are like the links in a chain you may wear around your neck. It takes many links to form a necklace. When one of those links breaks, the whole necklace is weakened.

The same is true of the textile and apparel industries. A designer could have a great idea for a garment, but that idea may never become a reality. The technology might not exist to make the fabric or to produce the garment at a reasonable price. Once the garment is manufactured, if the workmanship is not good quality, or if the sales representatives do not sell it to the right markets, the product will not be successful.

The Textile Industry

The textile industry is concerned with the development and production of fibers and fabrics. It is one of the oldest and largest industries in America. When we think about textiles, we tend to think only about items such as clothing and home furnishings. But do you know that the covering on a tea bag, the strings on a tennis racket, the napped surface on a paint roller, and even the artificial turf on the football field are products developed by the textile industry?

THE EARLY YEARS

As you learned in Chapter 7, the first textile factory in the United States was built in the late 1700s. Most of the early factories were built in New England. They were located near railroad lines and rivers, and seaport cities, such as New York and Boston. Many of these factories were mills that spun and wove natural fibers into cloth. Raw materials would be shipped to the mills, made into cloth, and then cut and sewn into garments.

After the Civil War, people started to build mills and factories in the South in order to be closer to where the fibers were grown. Then the finished fabric was shipped North to be made into garments.

TODAY'S LOCATIONS

The South for years has been the center of textile manufacturing, as well as research and development, for most of the industry. Textile mills tend to be located near small urban communities. However, the many phases of the industry that are involved with design, sales, and market research are in the Northeast. Most of the major textile companies have sales and marketing offices located in or near New York City.

The Apparel Industry

The shirt you just bought because the style is really "in" this year, the special clothing you wear for playing sports, and even the gloves you wear to keep your hands warm are all products of the apparel, or garment, industry. It is an industry that is fast-paced, constantly changing, and very complex.

The "heart" of the garment industry is in New York City. Most of the major manufacturers have design and marketing offices there. Los Angeles has become the headquarters for the garment industry on the West Coast.

Although many manufacturing facilities are located in these two urban areas, you will find individual manufacturers located in many other cities, suburbs, and small towns throughout the United States. Cities such as Chicago, Dallas, Denver, and Atlanta have developed apparel marts where manufacturers have showrooms and sales offices.

HOW IT OPERATES

Most manufacturers produce two *lines*, or collections, of clothes per year. These lines are produced at least six months ahead of a season. Clothes shown to the buyers and the press in the spring will be in the stores in the fall. Clothes shown in the fall will be available in the stores the following spring. It takes many people to produce a line – designers, stylists, pattern makers, production managers, cutters, sewers, finishers, pressers, inspectors, models, stock clerks, shipping clerks, and showroom personnel.

The garment industry is also a very risky business. Ideas about what is fashionable can change very quickly from season to season and are very difficult to predict. Although some companies have been in business for many years, others seem to go in and out of business almost overnight. Manufacturers can make a large profit one season because their line is "hot" and sells very well. But if they guess incorrectly about what will sell the next season, they could lose a great deal of money.

CONDITIONS IN THE EARLY FACTORIES

Until the late 1700s, most garments were made by tailors or dressmakers, or sewn at home by the female members of the family. Gradually, garments came to be mass-produced.

At first, a manufacturer would employ women who lived close to the textile mills in New England to sew the garments at home. These women did **piecework**, which means *they were paid so much per piece or garment, rather than being paid by the hour.*

Later, these women were employed in factories to make the garments. These factories were sometimes called **sweatshops** because they were *dark, airless, uncomfortable, and unhealthy places* to work. Most of the workers were women and children.

Henry Ford developed the idea of the **assembly line** for the automobile industry. It was soon introduced into other industries, such as the garment industry. When a garment is made on the assembly line, *each worker specializes in a certain part of a garment's construction.*

For example, on a shirt, one person may stitch the sleeve, another person may attach the collar, another may sew the button holes, and a fourth person will put on the buttons. Special sewing machines can be designed for each of these separate tasks.

Unions paved the way for better working conditions and higher pay in the garment industry.

THE ROLE OF THE UNIONS

At one time, the average garment worker labored 10 to 12 hours per day, six days per week. The wages were so low that workers often took extra work home to do at night and on Sundays. Conditions in the early garment factories were so bad that workers began to organize into unions.

The purpose of the unions was to obtain better working conditions, better pay, and benefits, such as medical insurance, sick pay, and vacation pay for the workers. Unions worked hard to get laws passed that would give workers these things. Today, by law, a person who is paid an hourly wage works no more than 40 hours per week at his or her regular wage. For any additional hours, he or she is paid overtime pay, which is one-and-a-half to two times the regular hourly wage.

The ILGWU and ACWA

Most garment workers today belong to a union. The largest union in the garment industry is the International Ladies' Garment Workers' Union (ILGWU). It is for workers employed in the manufacture of women's and children's clothing. Members of the Amalgamated Clothing Workers of America (ACWA) work in the men's and boy's clothing industry.

As a result of the intense efforts of the unions, American garment workers are among the best paid in the world. Their wages allow them to maintain an average standard of living. However, many manufacturers have chosen to have their clothes made in other countries where the cost of labor is cheaper.

The ILGWU puts a union label in every item that is made by its members. This union has sponsored an advertising campaign to remind people to look for the union label, which shows that the clothes were made here in America.

Careers in Design

A *designer* is a person who is creative enough to have new ideas and practical enough to know how to turn those ideas into a product. A *stylist* is a person who takes other peoples' ideas and puts them together in a way that looks fresh and original.

FABRIC DESIGNERS AND STYLISTS

Are you interested in new things? Are you interested in new ways of doing familiar things? Do you have a talent for combining colors in fresh and attractive ways? Are you interested in the technical methods of production? If so, you may be interested in a career as a fabric designer or stylist.

A *fabric designer* works very closely with the research department of a textile company to develop new weaves, patterns, prints, and colors. A good fabric designer has the ability to predict trends very far in advance. Fabric designers are working today on fabrics that will appear in the stores one to two years from now. Clothing designs are often inspired by the new fabrics that are created by the fabric designers.

In some companies, the fabric designer and the fabric stylist are the same person. In other companies, a *fabric stylist* spots trends by visiting stores, talking to research people, and traveling to other parts of the world to see what is selling there. The stylist then reports back to the textile designers with recommendations for color combinations and print designs.

Both a fabric designer and a fabric stylist must understand the technical aspects of fabric construction and have good art training. Some knowledge of clothing construction is also valuable since most of the fabric designs will probably be made up into garments by a manufacturer or a home sewer. The best source of training is a specialized two-year technical school or a four-year college.

This apparel designer and her assistant examine new fabric combinations.

APPAREL DESIGNERS AND STYLISTS

Do you like to work with fabric? Are you constantly looking for ways to change your personal clothing to give it a new "look"? Do you have a talent for sketching? Are you a good observer of how other people live and dress? Are you a naturally curious person? If so, you may be well suited to a career as an apparel designer.

An *apparel designer* develops original ideas for clothing or translates other people's ideas into clothing for a particular market. The designer is inspired by many things, such as travel, movies, theater, art exhibits, historical clothing, and the work of other designers.

Being a fashion designer is a high pressure job. He or she works against many deadlines to develop fresh, new ideas for a collection of garments that must please many people.

The fashion reporters must like the collection enough to write about it. The retailers must like it enough to buy the clothes for their stores. The customers must like the clothes enough to purchase them from the stores.

A designer turns out at least two collections a year, sometimes three or four. There is a saying in the garment industry that "a designer is only as good as his or her last collection."

Not all apparel designers work in a situation where they develop completely new ideas for clothing. Some designers, also known as *fashion stylists,* translate other people's garment ideas into clothing for a special market within a specific price range. These *less expensive copies* are called **knock-offs**. For example, a well-known fashion designer may introduce a new and innovative design that is very expensive to produce. A moderate-priced apparel manufacturer may employ a fashion stylist to produce a similar look at a price the manufacturer's customers can afford.

The stylist has many design options. For example, the original design might be made in silk; the stylist could choose polyester. The original design might have 12 very rare buttons; the stylist could use 8 less expensive ones. The original design might have a jacket that was lined; the stylist could make an unlined jacket.

If you are interested in a career as an apparel designer or a fashion stylist, you will need special training in a two-year or four-year technical school or college. There you will learn sketching, sewing, draping, and pattern-making skills.

Do not expect to get a job as a designer right away. Most designers and stylists begin their careers in positions such as sketcher, sample maker, or design assistant, which may mean bringing coffee and picking up pins when you first start. Most aspiring designers work many years for many different companies before they make it as a successful designer.

Careers in Research and Development

The research and development areas are the backbone of the textile and apparel industries. These are the people who develop new fibers, new weaves and patterns, new dyes, and new quality-control tests. They also develop the equipment to make it all happen.

A career in research and development requires a four-year college degree in chemistry, physics, or one of the engineering fields. Many research and development people also obtain a Master's or a Doctor's degree in their field.

Textile chemists search for new textiles that will bring us greater comfort and wear.

TEXTILE CHEMISTS

Textile chemists are responsible for creating new fibers, new dyes, and new finishes. A textile chemist may work alone, as part of a team, or as the manager of a team of researchers working on a special project. A good textile chemist is patient and accurate. He or she must have a creative mind and a talent for problem solving. Fibers such as rayon, nylon, and polyester, as well as water-repellent and permanent press finishes, are the result of the textile chemist's work.

LABORATORY TECHNICIANS

Once a new fiber or a new finish is discovered, tests are developed to see how the new product will perform. A *laboratory technician* works with the textile chemist to develop and carry out these special tests. These tests include how well a new fiber will take and keep a particular dye, how strong a fiber is, and how it will react to special finishes.

ENGINEERS

Someone must develop new equipment, keep it in good running condition, and measure its performance and effectiveness. The engineers who do this are a very important part of the research and development area, in both the textile and the apparel industry.

An *industrial engineer* makes sure that all the operations in the plant are running smoothly and efficiently. He or she develops procedures for testing the efficiency and measuring the costs of existing equipment and methods. A good industrial engineer is always trying to develop better production methods while maintaining the company's standards of quality.

A *mechanical engineer* is responsible for maintaining and developing the plant's equipment and machinery. The industrial and the mechanical engineer often work together to improve methods of production.

An *electrical engineer* is responsible for the plant's general operating systems. This includes the electrical and the cooling systems.

Careers in Production and Manufacturing

The production and manufacturing areas of both the apparel and textile industries offer a wide variety of job opportunities. Although some jobs require technical or college degrees for advancement, others do not require any education beyond high school.

TEXTILES

Textile mills need skilled *machine operators* for the many pieces of equipment that prepare and spin the fibers into yarn, weave or knit yarns into fabric, and apply the required finishes. *Quality control experts* are also needed. These people are trained to carefully examine the finished products for flaws. Skilled *mechanics* are needed to work with the mechanical engineers to keep all the machinery in top running condition.

Most of the workers in a textile mill are paid an hourly wage. At many mills, the workers are expected to join a union.

APPAREL

The apparel industry has many different types of production jobs. The *sample maker* or the *design assistant* works closely with the designer to develop the sample garment. This garment may be changed and reworked many times until the designer and the marketing manager feel that the design will sell. The garment will then appear in the designer's fashion show.

Then a *pattern maker* develops a master pattern in the manufacturer's standard size. This master pattern is then "graded" up and down into the other sizes. **Pattern grading** is *the art of converting a pattern from one size into many other sizes.* Pattern measurements change from one size to another, and the shape of the neckline curve is different for every size. Pattern grading used to be done entirely by hand. Today, the large apparel manufacturers use computers to convert the patterns into many sizes.

Next, a layout must be developed. This is like doing a giant jigsaw puzzle. All the pattern pieces must fit onto the smallest amount of fabric possible. When a manufacturer is producing many hundreds of garments, a savings of a few inches of fabric per garment can add up to a lot of money. This, too, used to be a hand operation, but now is done by computers.

Spreaders stack layers of fabric on a table so that many garments can be cut out at the same time. *Markers* transfer the outline of the pattern pieces to the fabric. *Cutters* operate machines that will cut through layers of fabric as much as 1′ high and 60′ long. Then *sorters* number the pieces and gather them into bundles.

Now the pieces must be assembled into a garment. Some manufacturers do all their own production work. Others send the pieces to *contractors,* who specialize in sewing certain types of garments. The contractor or the manufacturer employs *sewers* who operate industrial sewing machines.

Each sewer handles only one or two parts of a garment. *Finishers* complete any hand sewing, such as buttons. *Pressers* iron the garments, which are checked by *inspectors.* Finally, the garments go to the *stock clerks* and *shipping clerks.* Some production workers are paid an hourly wage. Others are paid by piecework, for instance, how many sleeves they sew or how many buttons they attach. Training is given on the job or through a vocational school program. Many production workers belong to a union.

Technology

Manufacturing Garments by Computers

There are many steps involved in manufacturing garments. With today's technology, a system called CAD/CAM can save time and reduce costs. CAD/CAM means "Computer Aided Design/Computer Aided Manufacturing."

Pattern Design. The individual pattern pieces can be drawn on the computer's display screen. If the designer or the pattern maker changes one pattern piece, the computer will adjust all the pattern pieces. For example, if the neckline is changed on the garment, the computer will adjust the collar and facings, too.

Grading. Using a special digitizing table, information about the shape of the master pattern is entered into the computer. Then the computer automatically grades the pattern pieces to the different sizes.

Layout. A cutting marker is created by moving the pattern pieces around on the display screen. The computer automatically checks the grainlines, the direction of the nap, and even matches plaids. Then a high-speed machine, called a plotter, prints the marker on paper.

Cutting. A computer can control the knife used to cut out stacks of garments. The speed of the knife is adjusted to match the thickness and the number of layers of fabric to be cut. The computer even tells the knife when to sharpen itself.

Assembly. Computerized sewing machines, or "robots," stitch the garments together. A computer-operated "railroad" can move garments from one type of sewing machine to another.

In the past, garment production depended almost entirely on human labor. Today, computers are used in most phases of garment production.

aders begin the job of stacking fabric, but they check for irregularities.

A sorter *is putting out fabric in bundles for delivery to another department.*

Careers in Marketing

Marketing is an overall term for the process of buying and selling goods. People with jobs as market researchers, sales analysts, advertising and promotion specialists, and sales representatives all have careers in marketing. Marketing plays an important role in both the textile and apparel industries.

MARKET RESEARCH AND ANALYSIS

How much is the customer willing to pay? Is it important that the garment be washable? What blends of fibers do consumers like best? What fabric finishes are most desired? Should the line include shirts that coordinate with the pants? What colors will sell best in different parts of the country? How can a manufacturer predict how many garments to make?

In order to run a successful business, it is helpful to the manufacturer to know something about the market and be able to answer questions like these. That is where market research and sales analysis come in.

Market research is *the study of consumer needs and attitudes.* For example, if a manufacturer is considering hiring a "name" designer to develop a special line of clothes, the market research department might conduct a survey. They could find out which customers would want to buy designer clothes and what "names" would appeal to them. Market research can also track the type of advertising that people respond to most.

Sales analysts help stores and manufacturers discover what the public likes.

Sales analysis is *the study of what has sold in the past in order to predict what will sell in the future.* A careful analysis of sales can give a manufacturer information about what styles, colors, and fabrics have traditionally sold best in different sections of the country. Information about which sizes and styles sell best can be determined from sales. How to organize production and shipping schedules so that the goods are in the stores when the customers want to buy can also be provided.

Both textile manufacturers and apparel manufacturers can use this information to help develop new products. This information is also particularly helpful to a manufacturer in planning how to spend money on advertising.

A career as a *market researcher* or a *sales analyzer* requires a college degree that includes courses in psychology, statistics, and general marketing. A graduate degree in business is often helpful.

SALES REPRESENTATIVES

A *sales representative* sells a company's products to its customers. A sales representative may work for a fiber company, selling fiber to manufacturers who will convert it into fabric. The fabric manufacturer may hire sales representatives to sell the finished fabric to apparel manufacturers. Apparel manufacturers, in turn, may employ sales representatives to sell finished garments to retail stores. In addition, many manufacturers of items employ sales representatives to sell these goods directly to the fabric stores.

Sales representatives are an important communication link between the manufacturer and the market place. They report back to the manufacturer with information, such as market conditions, requests for future products, and the activities of the competition.

There are two types of sales representatives. *Manufacturer's sales representatives* work exclusively for one manufacturer. *Independent sales representatives* work for several different firms that do not manufacture competing products. For example, an independent sales representative might represent a button company, a fabric company that makes lace trim, and a fabric company that makes velvet.

It is important for sales representatives to be able to get along with all types of people, to have a neat and pleasant appearance, and to have an aptitude for mathematics. Since most sales representatives are paid a salary, plus a percentage of every sale, the amount of money they make can vary from year to year.

There is a great deal of pressure to make a sale. Most sales representatives travel extensively. Many are away from home from Monday to Friday. Others are away from home several weeks at a time. Some people find such a schedule exciting, but others find it lonely. A college degree is helpful, but not necessary, for a career as a sales representative.

Careers in Computers

Some historians and sociologists believe that three major discoveries in the history of mankind significantly changed how we live and work. The first was primitive man's discovery of fire. The second was when man developed the alphabet so that he could read and write. The third was the development of the computer.

More and more of the jobs that were once done by hand are now accomplished faster and easier by computers. People with knowledge of computers are in great demand in many industries. *Computer programmers* are needed to develop the *information systems,* also called *programs* or *software,* that result in the computer being able to perform various tasks. In addition, *technicians* skilled in operating and repairing computers are needed in all areas of the textile and apparel industry.

Careers in computers is the fastest growing field in the textile and apparel industry.

can be set up and threaded in minutes, rather than hours. Computer graphics can even show the designer or the researcher what the finished design will look like without the need for an actual sample.

COMPUTERS IN RESEARCH AND DEVELOPMENT

The painstaking job of developing a new fiber, a new dye, or a new fabric weave is made much easier by the use of computers. For example, there is a computerized piece of equipment called a *spectrophotometer.* It can analyze the color of one item, such as a chip of paint, and tell you what formulas to use to exactly reproduce that color in a variety of yarns and fabrics. Another machine has been developed that applies complicated colors and patterns to fabrics by using thousands of tiny dye jets individually controlled by a computer.

Complicated designs can be developed for patterned fabrics, laces, and embroideries. Using sophisticated computer programs, looms

COMPUTERS IN MANUFACTURING

As you learned earlier in this chapter, some manufacturing functions, such as pattern grading and developing the cutting marker, can be done faster and easier with the aid of the computer. The cutting machines used to cut out all the garment pieces can also be operated by a computer. Even sewing machines can be computerized. They are custom-designed to perform a specific function, such as sewing collars, embroidering, or tucking. Besides sewing faster, these machines can adapt quickly and easily to a change in fabric, stitch length, or type of stitch with the help of a computer.

Computer-operated robots can move garments along the assembly line from one spot to another. They can even pick the finished garments off the assembly line and organize them for packing and shipping.

Computers can be used to help garment manufacturers determine the cost of a finished garment. Computers can even help them decide what changes need to be made in order to produce the style at a price the customers can afford.

COMPUTERS IN BUSINESS

More and more retailers and manufacturers are finding computers beneficial in the day-to-day operations of a business. Computers can be used to keep track of inventory, maintain accounting records, analyze sales and store files, and keep accurate lists of suppliers. Computers with word processors are replacing the typewriter in many offices.

A store's cash registers can be linked to its computer system so that when a sale is rung up, that item is automatically deducted from the store's inventory list. Eventually, systems will be developed so that information about each item sold at a store will be fed back to the manufacturer's computer. The manufacturer will know instantly which goods are selling in the marketplace.

If you are interested in a career in computers, you will need some special training. The minimum type of training you would need is a degree from a vocational school with a specialized program in computers. Some large computer companies train their employees. However, they usually prefer to hire someone with a college degree in business, mathematics, or computer science. In the future, more and more people who have careers such as designers, chemists, writers, and market researchers will find it impossible to work effectively without some knowledge of computers.

The fields of design and manufacturing offer a wide range of career opportunities. They are good fields for you to explore. After all, everyone needs clothes!

Chapter 26 Job Listings

Fabric Designer
Fabric Stylist
Apparel Designer
Fashion Stylist
Textile Chemist
Laboratory Technician
Industrial Engineer
Mechanical Engineer
Electrical Engineer
Machine Operator
Quality Control Expert
Mechanic
Sample Maker
Pattern Maker
Spreader
Marker
Cutter
Sorter
Sewer
Finisher
Presser
Inspector
Stock Clerk
Shipping Clerk
Contractor
Market Researcher
Sales Analyzer
Manufacturer's Sales Representative
Independent Sales Representative
Computer Programmer
Computer Technician

Chapter 26 Review

Summary

Careers in design and manufacturing exist in both the textile and apparel industries. Designers and stylists develop original ideas or translate other people's ideas into new designs and styles. Textile chemists, laboratory technicians, and engineers work in the area of research and development. Many different types of production and manufacturing jobs are available in textile mills and the apparel industry. Marketing jobs include market research, sales analysis, and sales representatives. A growth area is in the field of computers.

Questions

1. What is the major function of the textile industry and the apparel industry?
2. What factors determined the location of early textile factories? Why were factories relocated in the South?
3. Name five job categories involved in the production of a line of clothing.
4. Describe the assembly line method of constructing a garment.
5. What sources of information are used by designers and stylists for developing fresh ideas?
6. What modifications can be made in a "knock-off" garment to make it more affordable?
7. Explain why the research and development areas are considered the backbone of the textile and apparel industries.
8. What information can market research and sales analysis provide to manufacturers?
9. Describe the role of computers in the textile and apparel industries.

Activities

1. Create a flow chart that lists all the steps required in the production of a shirt—from fiber to fabric to finished product. Show where research and development, as well as sales and marketing, influence the process.

2. Examine pictures of expensive or moderately expensive garments in fashion magazines. Brainstorm suggestions on how a "knock-off" of these garments could be made.

3. Research the history of the ILGWU or the ACWA. How did salaries, benefits, and working conditions in garment factories prior to the unions compare with those afterwards? Identify current issues that could be a concern to workers today.

You Be the Expert

A friend dreams of becoming a fashion designer but does not want to move to New York City. What suggestions for designing opportunities in other parts of the country could you give your friend?

27 Retailing

Whether you live in a very large city, a very small town, or somewhere in between, it is possible for you to have a career in **retailing** or *selling goods to customers*. Retail stores come in all sizes, from small operations where the owner manages the store and does the buying, to large department stores with hundreds of employees who all have specialized jobs.

After reading this chapter, you will be able to:

- describe the responsibilities of salespersons and stock clerks who handle and sell merchandise,
- explain the buyer's and merchandise manager's role in choosing the items that are available in the store,
- explain how fashion coordinators, display artists, and advertising managers work together to develop the "look" of the store,
- describe how customer service representatives and other workers represent the quality of service that a store provides its customers.

Types of Stores

Department stores are stores that group certain merchandise into special areas or departments. These departments can be organized by size, by price, or by fashion categories.

Most department stores have *branches*. These branch stores are smaller than the main store and are often located in the suburbs. Some department stores also have branches located in different cities and different states than the main store. The buyers work out of the main store and purchase goods for both the main store and all branches. A buyer then works with a department manager in each branch to determine what sizes and colors will sell best in that branch. Advertising and promotional themes are also developed in the main store and used for all the branches.

A **chain** is *a large retail company with stores in many cities and towns all over the country.* Chains have a headquarter office where all the buying, merchandising, and promotional decisions are made, but they do not have one main store. Chain stores may not carry exactly the same goods in all their stores. Because they have so many stores, chains can afford to buy some goods only for stores in certain regions.

Specialty stores are stores that carry one particular type of merchandise, such as shoes, lingerie, or fabric. Specialty stores can be owned by an individual or group of individuals, or be part of a chain.

Boutiques are a type of specialty store. Instead of carrying one type of merchandise, they carry a variety of merchandise that is carefully chosen to appeal to a particular type of customer. A store that carries expensive designer clothes, a store that carries trendy young fashions, and a store that specializes in clothes for the working mother-to-be are all examples of boutiques. Some boutiques are part of a chain, but most boutiques are individually owned.

Careers in Selling

A job as a *salesperson* or a *stock clerk* is a good way to begin a career in retailing. You will learn how a store operates from "the ground up." This knowledge is a valuable basis for all retail jobs.

It is possible to get both full-time and part-time work as a salesperson or stock clerk. The workday is not necessarily nine-to-five. Stores are open in the evenings, as well as on Saturdays and Sundays. This provides flexibility that many people appreciate, particularly if they have school or family obligations. Many high school students find that these jobs are good for after school and during the summer. Some adults have these as second jobs during times when additional money is needed. Most stores provide on-the-job training.

SALESPERSONS

A good *salesperson* is a very important employee in a store. He or she is the person directly responsible for selling the merchandise to the customer. If you are waited on by a pleasant, courteous salesperson who is familiar with the store's stock, you will be much more likely to make a purchase.

Even if the store does not carry what you need, you will probably think well of the store and return another time. If you are waited on by a rude, unpleasant, and lazy salesperson, you will probably go to another store the next time you need to buy something.

The most successful salespeople enjoy working with the customers.

A good salesperson enjoys working with people and makes a real effort to become familiar with the store's merchandise. He or she has a desire to be helpful and often goes out of the way to assist a customer.

A good salesperson is also a good communicator. If something is wrong with one of the items in stock, or if customers are requesting an item that the store does not carry, a good salesperson lets the buyer know about it. This helps the buyer to do his or her job better.

Basic arithmetic skills are important. Salespeople write up receipts, ring up sales on cash registers, and sometimes handle credits and exchanges. Physical stamina is also important because most salespeople spend many hours standing on their feet.

STOCK CLERKS

Stock clerks provide the behind-the-scenes support to the salespeople. When new merchandise arrives in the store, it goes straight to the store's receiving room. It is **inventoried**, which means that *the items are carefully counted and recorded, and then checked against both the packing slip and a copy of the buyer's order.* Any damaged merchandise is set aside for the buyer to examine and possibly return to the manufacturer.

Next, all merchandise is tagged. Two types of tags are attached: the sales tag, which has the price, inventory number, and any other information the store needs; and the security tag, which is removed by the cashier or salesperson when you pay for your purchase. Then the tagged merchandise is delivered to the proper department to be hung on racks, displayed on counters, or put on shelves. All of this is the responsibility of the stock clerk.

The stock clerk, along with the salesperson, is responsible for keeping the stock that is displayed for sale neat and tidy. Bins and counters must be straightened out. Garments that have been tried on by customers must be put back on hangers, zippered and buttoned, and rehung on the racks. A good stock clerk is conscientious, careful, and reliable.

WAGES

Most salespeople and stock clerks are paid an hourly wage. Sometimes, a salesperson is paid a **base salary**, or *minimum salary,* plus a **commission**, or *percentage of the purchase price on every sale.*

Employees of a retail store are usually entitled to an *employee discount.* This means that they are able to buy items in the store at a lower price than the customer pays. Most stores put a limit on the total amount an employee can spend and still be entitled to a discount. This limit is usually based on a percentage of the employee's salary.

"Made in the U.S.A."

Since 1984, Federal law has required that all apparel and home fashions be clearly labeled with their country of origin. Until then, only foreign textile products had to be labeled.

The purpose of the legislation is to promote the sales of American-made garments, sheets, towels, and other fabrics for the home. The "Made in the U.S.A." labels help consumers more easily identify American-made products. The law was sought by a coalition of fiber and fabric producers, labor unions, and clothing manufacturers.

Each separate item must be labeled, including items sold in packages, such as underwear. If the labeling is not visible through the package, then the package must also be labeled. The one exception is socks which can be labeled just on the package.

The law also requires that mail-order companies must identify in their catalogues which items are manufactured in the United States and which in foreign countries.

people will want to buy six months from now? If you can answer "yes" to these questions, a career in buying may be a career for you.

BUYERS

A *buyer* is responsible for selecting and purchasing the clothes and other items that are sold in a store.

Buyers are always planning for the future. Right now, they are purchasing the clothes that will be in their stores six months from now. Success on the job depends on how well the buyer can predict what you will want to buy many months from now.

In order to accomplish this, buyers do a great amount of research. They read all the fashion

Buyers must be aware of what the competition is selling, and must search out new items.

magazines and fashion publications that report on new styles and trends. A buyer travels to market several times a year. **Market** is *the place where designers' and manufacturers' showrooms are located.* A buyer who works for a large store or group of stores may travel to market at least once a month.

A buyer for a fabric store or a knitting shop goes to market to order fabrics and notions, or yarns and needlework kits. Some buyers travel overseas several times a year to purchase new and unusual merchandise from foreign countries.

Although buyers plan very far ahead, they must still pay careful attention to what customers are purchasing in their store today. This is how buyers decide which sizes to order, which colors will sell best, and what type of customer their store attracts. Customers may be conservative or fashion-conscious, young or older, concerned about price, or conscious of designer names.

Buyers used to rely on handwritten records and their own instinct for most of their information about what sells. Today, many stores have sophisticated computer systems that can tell a buyer, on a moment's notice, how well a particular style is selling. These systems can predict, based on early sales figures, how many of an item the store can expect to sell. This helps the buyer to keep track of the inventory and to know when to reorder an item.

The buyer decides when to put old stock on sale in order to make room for new merchandise. It is also the buyer's responsibility to keep the salespeople informed and excited about new merchandise. Many buyers have regular meetings with the sales staff to acquaint them with new merchandise, to share fashion information, and to get feedback about merchandise on the selling floor.

Part of a buyer's time is spent researching the market, selecting merchandise, and working with the salespeople. The rest of the time is spent on paper work. A buyer must keep track of what is selling, check inventory records against buying orders, and determine how much money is left in the budget to buy new merchandise. Some stores have *assistant buyers* who place orders for merchandise and help supervise the sales staff.

MERCHANDISE MANAGER

A *merchandise manager* oversees the operation of several departments within a store. Usually, the departments are somehow related. For example, one merchandise manager may be responsible for all the "budget" departments, which may include the moderately priced dress, coat, sportswear, and shoe departments. Another merchandise manager may supervise the expensive designer departments or the men's departments. Another manager may be responsible for all the accessory departments, such as jewelry, scarves, handbags, hats, and luggage.

Each merchandise manager has several buyers reporting to him or her. The merchandise manager coordinates the departments to make sure that they do not compete with one another. For example, the sportswear buyer and the dress buyer might both want to carry the same type of two-piece dresses in their departments. The merchandise manager makes sure that each department has its own "look" so that the two departments each retain their image.

The merchandise manager assists the buyer in developing budgets and establishing prices. Often, the merchandise manager accompanies the buyer on buying trips. This is particularly important when the buyer is new to the job.

The merchandise manager checks that the sales and promotional events in each of the departments relate to the overall activities of the store. A buyer may be promoted to a merchandise manager.

REWARDS AND DRAWBACKS

Many people think that a career as a buyer or a merchandise manager is very glamorous. Sometimes it is. Most buyers do much traveling to markets in the United States or to foreign countries. Some people find this very exciting. Others find travel extremely tiring and do not like to be away from home so much.

Buyers and merchandise managers both work long hours. They are often expected to be at the store in the evenings, on Saturdays, and on some holidays. Remember, stores are often the busiest when everyone else is not working. Since they are paid a weekly salary, rather than an hourly wage, merchandise managers do not receive overtime pay.

Buyers and merchandise managers are expected to dress well. If you enjoy fashion, that can be exciting. However, when you start your job as a buyer and you are not making very much money, a large percentage of your salary may be spent on clothes. To compensate for this problem, many stores give a larger employee discount to buyers and merchandise managers than to salespeople or stock clerks.

A job as a buyer or a merchandise manager includes many glamorous aspects, such as travel, the opportunity to meet interesting people, and the chance to work in a fast-paced environment. It also involves long working hours, as well as paperwork and budgeting.

SKILLS NEEDED

In order to become a buyer, you must have a college, junior college, or fashion merchandising degree. In addition, buyers must have a keen eye for fashion, some mathematical ability, and a lot of energy. They also must be able to get along well with all kinds of people. Most department stores and chains have special training programs for buyers.

Careers in
Fashion Promotion

Do you like to write? Do you have a flair for drawing? Do you have a talent for putting things together in pleasing, but unusual, combinations? Are you challenged by doing things differently each time, rather than learning the one "right" way to do something? If you can answer "yes" to any of these questions, you should explore the possibility of a career in fashion promotion.

Fashion promotion is *all the ways that manufacturers and retailers try to get your attention so that you will want to buy their product.* There are many ways to promote a product. Eye-catching window displays are designed to make people stop and notice the store. Other displays inside the store are planned to attract your attention to certain merchandise. Clever words and illustrations make a store's advertisements stand out from all the others.

Special theme promotions, such as "Our Birthday Celebration" or "Spring in January," are put together to attract more customers to the store. Fashion shows and in-store demonstrations may be organized as a part of these theme events, or they may be organized separately.

Sometimes a store will sponsor an outside event, such as a Halloween parade, a marathon, or a charity function, to promote good will. It is hoped that people will associate the store's name with an activity that benefits the community.

All of these activities require the talents of many different people. Although each person has special responsibilities, they must all work closely together to promote the store and its merchandise.

The *promotion director* is responsible for developing and planning special events for the store. Theme promotions, community activities, fashion shows, and personal appearances by designers and demonstrators are scheduled through the Promotion Department.

It is the promotion director's job to make sure that the store is organized and ready for each event. This might mean ordering staging for a fashion show, hiring caterers for a special luncheon, finding clowns for a parade, or arranging for a store full of tulips in January. In addition, the Promotion Department is responsible for details, such as organizing publicity for an upcoming event, handling any special invitations that are required, and notifying other departments in advance about these events.

In order to have a successful career as a promotion director, you must be creative and organized. You will probably start as a copywriter or a general assistant in the Promotion Department. Working on a fashion magazine is also good training.

THE FASHION DIRECTOR

Every store has a fashion personality, or an image, that it presents to its customers. The *fashion director* and staff of *fashion coordinators* are called the *Fashion Office.* They are responsible for seeing that everything the store does reflects this personality.

The Fashion Office is responsible for fashion shows presented by the store. It plans the theme for the show, borrows the clothes from various departments, accessorizes the outfits, hires the models, and writes the commentary.

It is the fashion director's job to be the person with the most knowledge about upcoming fashion trends and to share that knowledge with everyone in the store. The opinions of the fash-

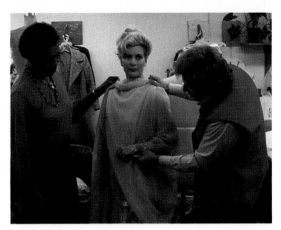

The fashion director and her fashion coordinators set a store's fashion image.

ion director determine how the entire store looks and what it sells. The Advertising Department consults with the fashion director when it develops an ad. The Display Department works with the fashion director when it is planning displays. Buyers consult with the fashion director before they go to market.

The fashion director is also the store's representative to those people who make and report fashion news, such as designers, manufacturers, and the fashion reporters.

In order to become a fashion director, you must have a real flair for fashion. Fashion directors are expected to look very fashionable. A good fashion director is very objective. He or she must be able to evaluate the importance of a trend, whether or not he or she personally likes it. A degree from a two- or four-year program that emphasizes business and fashion is important.

There are many paths to becoming a fashion director. You could begin as an assistant in the fashion office or the promotion department and work your way up. Or you could start as an assistant buyer or work at a fashion publication. The important thing is to get yourself a starting job where you can learn as much as possible.

RETAIL ADVERTISING PERSONNEL

A store's advertising does not just "happen." There are three different areas of responsibility that must all work together to produce the advertising—the *advertising manager,* the *copywriter,* and the *commercial artist.*

The advertising manager supervises the store's total advertising program and develops an advertising plan for the store. The plan includes any newspaper, radio, and television advertisements that the store will run. The advertising manager determines where these ads will appear, the size of each ad, when and how often they will run, and how much money will be spent.

The advertising manager works with the fashion director to develop the "look" of the ad, with the buyer to make sure the department will have the merchandise featured in the ad, and with the copywriter and the commercial artist who will actually design the ad.

Just like the fashion director, no one becomes an advertising manager right out of school. A two-year or four-year college degree is usually required. Courses in English, business, and advertising are valuable. Then, the person must get some on-the-job experience in a junior position with an advertising agency or the advertising department of a retailer or manufacturer. Many advertising managers began their careers as copywriters.

A *copywriter* must have a real flair for writing. A good ad is one that makes the product sound as attractive as possible and also gives information about the product. A good copywriter is one who can do this in as few words as possible.

In order to become a copywriter, you must enjoy writing, have a good knowledge of grammar, and be well read. A high school degree is required.

Although some education after high school is helpful, it is not always necessary for a beginning job. However, if you hope to advance to a management position, such as advertising manager, some additional education beyond high school is necessary.

A *commercial artist* draws the illustrations for newspaper and magazine ads. Some commercial artists work directly for the store. Besides doing artwork for advertisements, they may also design posters, inserts for charge account bills, and special invitations. Other commercial artists are **free-lance**, which means that *they are self-employed and sell their work to many different companies.* A store may hire a free-lance commercial artist because it does not have enough work to keep a full-time artist busy or because the artist may have a particular "look" to his or her work.

In order to become a commercial artist, you must take courses in commercial art. These courses should include figure drawing, fashion illustration, and perspective, as well as some technical art courses.

Display artist assistants get on-the-job training in large department stores.

THE DISPLAY DIRECTOR AND ARTIST

The way a store's windows are decorated and how merchandise is displayed in departments or highlighted near the elevators and escalators are all forms of advertising.

A store displays a garment in an eye-catching manner. It hopes that you will want to buy not only the garment but also the shoes, the belt, the scarf, and other accessories that are shown with it. All these displays are the work of the *display director.*

A store may employ one display artist or a display director with a staff of many artists. These people plan, build, and arrange the store's displays.

The display director works very closely with the fashion director to make sure that the displays reflect the fashion image of the store. The fashion office checks that each garment is shown with the "right" accessories.

The display director also works closely with the advertising department. Very often, a store will feature the same merchandise in its advertisements, windows, and in-store displays. This gives the fashion message greater impact.

A *display artist* must be very imaginative and creative. He or she must be able to draw or sketch out ideas, and then be able to translate those ideas into three-dimensional objects. Garments must be draped and hung in a pleasing manner. Accessories and props must be added to form an attractive arrangement.

In order to become a display artist, you should have some courses in art and design, such as fashion illustration, perspective, and color. A high school degree is required.

After that, most of what a display artist needs to know comes from on-the-job training. You might begin as an assistant in the display department of a large store. You might also get a job as a salesperson in a small store or boutique that would let you acquire some on-the-job experience.

Behind the Scenes Careers

There are many more skills needed behind the scenes to help make a retail store run smoothly. *Maintenance workers* help keep the store neat, clean, and in good physical condition. *Security workers* protect the store against shoplifters. They are also on call to handle any emergencies, such as a shopper who is taken ill, or an accident that occurs in the store.

A retail store needs people to work in its *administration* and *personnel* departments. Some of these jobs require people with college degrees in business, finance, and personnel. Other jobs are *clerical* or general assistant positions that require a high school degree and some clerical skills.

If you are particularly skilled at getting along with people and have a good sense of detail, you might enjoy a job as a *customer service representative*. A customer service representative handles customer complaints, merchandise returns, and billing questions. Often, the person who comes to a customer service representative is upset. How he or she is treated may make the difference between keeping or losing a customer for the store.

If you have a talent for sewing, you might consider a job as an *alterations expert*. Many stores offer this service to their customers. If you are interested in a career as a tailor or a dressmaker, a job in the alterations department is a good place to polish up your skills.

Retail Service Industries

The retail service industries include dry cleaners, laundries, and alteration and repair services. These services can be located in a separate store or as part of another store. For example, sometimes a dry cleaner offers a repair and alterations service. Or, a dry cleaner and a laundry may be combined into one store.

DRY CLEANERS AND LAUNDRIES

These service stores can be individually owned or part of a chain of stores. If the dry cleaner or laundry is part of a chain, garments are usually sent from all the various store locations to one central plant for dry cleaning.

Individually owned stores often advertise that they do their cleaning "on premises." This means that the garments are cleaned right in the store. Prices in such a place may be a little higher, but if a belt or a button is missing from a garment, it is usually easy to find because the garment never left the store.

In a chain of service stores with one central location, jobs will be broken down into specialties, such as *sorter, spotter,* or *presser.*

A *sorter* separates the clothes into groups that can be cleaned together. *Spotters* examine the clothes for stains. Because a general cleaning will not remove certain types of stains, many stains must be specially treated before the clothes are cleaned. *Pressers* operate the machines that iron the clothes after they have gone through the cleaning process. In a small, individually owned store, one person may perform all of these tasks.

To work as a *dry cleaner* or *laundry worker,* you must have some knowledge about fabrics and how to operate the equipment. You will need a high school or vocational school education and some on-the-job training.

A dry cleaner has a good knowledge of fabrics and how best to clean them.

ALTERATIONS AND REPAIR

Alteration and repair services include *dressmakers* and *tailors*. Some dressmakers and tailors will custom-make garments for you in addition to doing alterations. Others specialize only in alterations and repairs.

To become an alterations and repair specialist, you must know how to sew. You must also have a knowledge of fashion in order to alter garments so that they do not look out-of-date. Clothing construction courses in high school or at a vocational school are a necessity.

Many department stores, specialty stores, and dry cleaners employ one or more alteration and repair specialists. These stores are good places to get on-the-job training. You might begin by doing simple jobs, such as hems and

replacing buttons, and progress to more complicated alterations.

Many tailors and dressmakers prefer to go into business for themselves. They become part of the rapidly growing group of self-employed people, known as entrepreneurs. In Chapter 29, you will learn about the rewards and drawbacks of working for yourself.

Think about getting a part-time or summer job in a retail store while you are still in high school. It might give you a head start on everyone else! Your first job can be the beginning of a career in retailing or a stepping stone to many other careers in the apparel and textile fields.

Chapter 27 Job Listings

Salesperson
Stock Clerk
Head of Stock
Department Manager
Buyer
Assistant Buyer
Merchandise Manager
Promotion Director
Fashion Director
Fashion Coordinator
Advertising Manager
Copywriter
Commercial Artist
Display Director
Display Artist
Maintenance Worker
Security Worker
Administration
Personnel
Customer Service Representative
Alterations Expert
Dry Cleaner
Laundry Worker
Sorter
Spotter
Presser
Dressmaker
Tailor

Chapter 27 Review

Summary

Salesperson and stock clerk are entry-level jobs in retailing. Buyers and merchandise managers are responsible for selecting merchandise for the store. Fashion promotion jobs include promotion director, fashion director, fashion coordinator, advertising manager, copywriter, commercial artist, display director, and display artist. Many behind-the-scenes jobs are needed to help a retail store run smoothly. Retail services include dry cleaners, laundries, and alteration and repair services.

Questions

1. What is the difference between a department store and a chain store?

2. Why is the job of a salesperson such an important one in retailing?

3. What career advancement could be considered by a person who has had sales or stock clerk experience?

4. Describe the computer's role in assisting buyers to make reordering and purchasing decisions.

5. Why is it necessary for departments within a store to report to a merchandising manager?

6. What career preparation and experience is necessary for the job of a fashion director?

7. How do the display director and the advertising director work together to create the store's image? What skills are needed for each position?

8. Why is the job of a customer service representative such an important one to the retailer?

Activities

1. Write two scripts about a salesperson waiting on a customer. In one, depict a salesperson's friendly, pleasant manner. In the other, depict an unpleasant and rude attitude. Have classmates act out the scenes.

2. Pretend that you are a buyer. Predict a clothing fad that might be popular a year from now. Sketch or describe the outfit. Include information about possible colors, fabrics, accessories, and prices.

3. Create a theme promotion for a department store. Plan and design an advertising slogan, promotional campaign, and merchandise displays that could be used throughout the store.

You Be the Expert

You have been a salesperson in a large department store for two years. Your boss offers you an opportunity to enter the store's training program for buyers. However, you have thought of applying for a position in fashion promotion. What should you consider in order to make the best decision?

28 | *Communications and Education*

TERMS TO LEARN

certification
client
curator
curriculum
portfolio
secondary school
seminar

Suppose you have just invented the world's most practical jacket. How is anyone going to know you have this wonderful product? If you find ways to let your potential customers know about this exciting product and how to use it, then your chances for success are much greater.

After reading this chapter, you will be able to:

- explain how fashion promotion experts help manufacturers, magazines, and advertising agencies,
- define the editor's, writer's, illustrator's, photographer's, and model's role in the communications industry,
- explain how consumer education specialists teach the public how to use a product,
- list the types of teaching opportunities available with a home economics education degree.

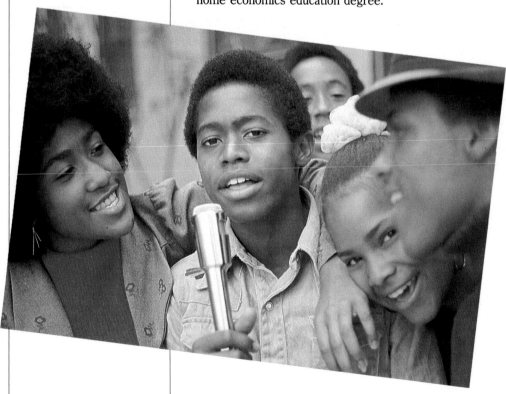

Fashion Promotion

The field of fashion promotion includes all the activities conducted by a retailer or manufacturer to get the public interested in a fashion product or service. In Chapter 27, we explored retail careers in fashion promotion. You learned about the role of the Promotion Director, the Fashion Director, and their staffs.

A retail store is not the only place where these jobs can be found. Other areas of the textile and apparel industries, such as at manufacturers, fashion publications, and advertising agencies, may employ such specialists.

WORKING FOR A MANUFACTURER

Many large fiber and fabric companies and apparel manufacturers employ *fashion promotion specialists.* These specialists are concerned with any project that involves the company's fashion image. They may work closely with the advertising department to develop the fashion look of the ads. They may share their knowledge of what is going on in the fashion market with the design and production departments.

Fashion promotion specialists might also serve as the company's representative to the fashion press and appear on television. They may provide press releases and fashion photographs for publication.

WORKING FOR A FASHION PUBLICATION

Fashion publications and consumer magazines want to attract more readers and more advertisers. Fashion promotion specialists are very important in helping the magazine to do this.

Have you ever noticed a listing in your favorite fashion magazine of a special event cosponsored by the magazine and several retailers around the country? Perhaps such an event has been scheduled for a store in your city or town. Events such as make-over sessions, career programs, or wardrobe coordination seminars are organized and presented by the magazine's fashion promotion department.

The promotion department may also research and publish *fashion trend reports.* These reports predict the styles, colors, and fabrics that the magazine's readers will be wearing next season. These reports are developed as a service to the magazine's advertisers.

WORKING FOR AN ADVERTISING AGENCY

Often, a manufacturer or a retailer will not have its own advertising department. Instead, it will employ an outside advertising agency. The manufacturer or retailer will be the agency's **client** or *customer.* One agency may have many clients. Sometimes these clients have similar needs; sometimes they have very different ones.

If the client is very large, or the agency has several clients in the fashion field, it may employ one or more fashion promotion specialists full-time. More often, however, the agency employs fashion promotion specialists on a free-lance, or consultant, basis.

This means that the promotion specialist is hired by the agency just for a specific project. The project might be to assist in designing an advertising campaign or to write a leaflet that will help consumers use the product better. Or the specialist might organize special programs to introduce a new product to consumers and the fashion press. Free-lance fashion promotion specialists usually have had previous experience working full-time for a manufacturer or a publication.

Careers in Communication

Fashion writers, editors, illustrators, photographers, and models are all involved in communicating the fashion message. This message can be communicated by advertisements, catalogues, magazine and newspaper articles, or radio and television programs.

FASHION WRITERS AND EDITORS

There are many different kinds of *fashion writers*. In Chapter 27, you learned about being a copywriter in the advertising department of a store. A good advertising copywriter may also write copy for catalogues. However, a slightly different style of writing is required. Advertising copy is written to make you interested enough in the product to want to come into the store. Once you are in the store, the salesperson will answer any questions you may have.

Catalogue copy is written so that you will get enough information about the item to order it without having to go to the store. A *catalogue copywriter* is more precise and detailed when writing catalogue copy.

There are other jobs for fashion writers besides that of an advertising copywriter. Some large newspapers employ a *fashion reporter* on their staff. A reporter may write articles about fashion trends and new developments in textiles, interview designers, and review fashion collections.

Magazines have editorial departments that put together the stories you read in the magazine. The *fashion editor* assigns these stories to various fashion writers. The fashion editor also develops and supervises any photography that accompanies the story. Many fashion editors begin their careers as fashion writers.

The two most important talents for a good fashion writer are a flair for writing and an endless curiosity. A college degree in journalism can be very helpful. Courses in English, art history, fashion design, and retail marketing will give the fashion writer extra insight into the areas that he or she is writing about.

FASHION ILLUSTRATORS

A *fashion illustrator* specializes in drawing the human figure. Fashion illustrations are usually drawn in a stylized manner. This means that the figures are taller, with longer arms and legs, and have more elegant faces than real life drawings of people. The fashion illustrator must also be able to use texture and shading to indicate different types of fabrics. The fashion illustrator's work is used in advertisements, catalogues, pattern envelopes, posters, and anywhere that fashion art is needed.

To be a fashion illustrator, you will need to take special art courses, including figure drawing and fashion illustration. Courses in textiles

This fashion illustrator works at preparing catalogue sketches for a pattern company.

are also helpful. Some fashion illustrators have a degree in commercial art. Others have a degree in fine arts or in home economics from colleges that offer fashion illustration courses.

FASHION PHOTOGRAPHERS

The *fashion photographer* is a very important person in the world of fashion communication. Just as every fashion illustrator has his or her own style, every photographer has his or her own style, too. Some photographers may be known for their natural-looking photos. Other photographers may be known for a very decorative style.

Sometimes, the photographer is asked to accurately translate the ideas of the fashion editor or the advertising department into a photograph. At other times, the editor or the advertising department gives the photographer only a very general idea. It is the photographer who then creates the mood of the photograph.

Some photographers have special training under experienced photographers. Others learn by reading and doing. Courses in art and photography are always helpful.

Fashion photographers learn about trends from market researchers and sales analysts.

If you are interested in a career in fashion photography, you can begin now by taking many pictures. Volunteer to take photos for the school newspaper, the yearbook, or a charity fashion show. Get as much practice as you can. The idea is to develop a **portfolio**, or *collection of your work.*

Many aspiring photographers begin with a job as an assistant to an established photographer and learn as much as they can from that person. Others have another full-time job and pursue their photography on a part-time basis until they get enough assignments to support themselves.

FASHION MODELS

Did you ever look at a beautiful or handsome face smiling at you from a magazine cover and think how glamorous it must be to have a job as a model? That glamorous image is the result of a lot of hard work.

There are two types of models. *Photography models* pose for advertisements, catalogues, and the fashion pages of newspapers and magazines. *Runway models* wear clothes in fashion shows produced by designers, manufacturers, or retailers. Some models do both runway and photography work.

Many people want to model, but it takes much more than having a pretty or handsome face. A photography model must photograph well. Not everyone who is good-looking has this ability. All models must have a certain type of figure and wear clothes well. A runway model must have the type of posture and graceful walk that makes clothes look attractive as the model moves.

Models must have good health and plenty of stamina. They may spend hours in front of a camera, often under hot lights, or be required to change clothes very quickly many times during a fashion show.

Models must have a certain talent for acting. If a photographer is shooting bathing suits on a cold beach in January, the models must be able to make you believe that it is a warm and sunny July day!

Models must devote a large amount of time to taking care of their physical appearance. They must spend their own money on makeup, hair-care, and accessories. All of this effort may still not be enough if the model does not have the certain "look" that advertisers and fashion editors want. This "look" could be outdoorsy or athletic, sophisticated or romantic, youthful or mature. This "look" can change from season to season.

The largest modeling agencies, the ones that represent the models you see in the major fashion magazines, are located in Chicago and New York. They are constantly on the lookout for new talent. Other agencies in smaller cities are looking for models for local photography or fashion shows.

There is a lot of competition for only a few modeling jobs. Even the most successful models usually last only a few years. Either younger or better looking models come along, or their special "look" is no longer needed.

Careers in
Consumer Education

There is often much more to be learned about a product and its uses than can be included in the copy for an advertisement, a catalogue page, or a hangtag. Many companies employ *consumer education specialists* to teach people, in an informal way, about the product. Pattern companies, fiber and fabric companies, apparel manufacturers, sewing machine and sewing equipment manufacturers, and some large retail chains employ consumer education specialists. Even some educational institutions have consumer specialists.

THE CONSUMER EDUCATION SPECIALIST

A career as a consumer education specialist includes a wide range of responsibilities. The reply you receive to your letter to a pattern company, the sewing leaflet your teacher shares with you on "How to Match Plaids," and the demonstration given by a sewing machine representative at your local fabric store may be the work of the consumer education specialist.

Consumer education specialists also represent their companies at trade shows, speak at meetings and conventions, and act as a support group for the sales staff. An active consumer education department often provides that slight edge over the competition that a sales representative needs to make the sale.

In order to become a consumer education specialist, you must have a college degree, preferably in home economics. Some consumer education specialists work at the company's main office and travel occasionally by plane to other cities. Others have full-time traveling jobs. They usually work within one region, or within a limited geographical area, and travel by car. These consumer education specialists present programs in stores, work with the sales staff, and make radio and television appearances. A consumer education specialist who travels full-time must be very independent, organized, and a good self-starter.

An effective consumer education specialist pays careful attention to what consumers are saying and reports back to management. The specialist can often help spot and correct a

Technology

Fashion Videos and Computer Programs

Modern technology is being used to entertain, inform, and educate consumers in stores, at home, and in school.

More and more stores are using fashion videos to introduce their customers to the newest merchandise in stock. Some videos feature the latest fashions from designers around the world. Others show how to accessorize or mix-and-match garments to expand your wardrobe. Whether entertaining viewers with music and script or showing step-by-step techniques, these videos try to motivate customers to buy the featured items.

Some cosmetic companies have special computer programs that will analyze a customer's hair, skin, and eye color. Then the computer recommends the shades of makeup that would be most flattering. The display screen might even provide a "face map" to show where to apply the cosmetics.

Computer programs are also available for home and school use. One program analyzes individual measurements and recommends styles that enhance specific body shapes. Other computer programs focus on clothing selection, color analysis, basic sewing techniques, or consumer skills.

In the future, you might be able to feed your measurements into a computer which would produce a pattern designed just for you. Or you might stand in front of a video camera and "see" yourself in a variety of garments without actually trying them on!

Now, through computer technology, you can tell ahead of time what you will look like in a new hair style or outfit.

problem before it embarrasses the company and costs a large sum of money. The consumer education specialist also lets management know about any customer's needs that are not being met. This information can help the company develop or sell new products.

In addition to a degree in home economics, a successful consumer education specialist must be a good communicator. He or she should be able to write well, speak effectively, and have a pleasing appearance. Courses in consumerism, public speaking, and journalism are also particularly helpful for a position as a consumer education specialist.

Careers in Education

When you think of a career in education, you probably think first of the teachers whom you have every day in school. Teaching at a high school, junior high school, or middle school is one way to have a career in education. But there are many others. You could be a vocational school teacher, a college professor, an adult education teacher, a teacher at a sewing school, or an extension agent. You might also work for a museum or a university as a costume historian or a textile restorer.

The requirements and responsibilities of each of these careers in education are slightly different. However, they all share several things in common. A good teacher knows his or her subject thoroughly, has a desire to share that knowledge, and is an effective communicator.

HIGH SCHOOL/JUNIOR HIGH/ MIDDLE SCHOOL TEACHERS

Have you ever thought about how *home economics teachers* became teachers? They have a degree from a college or university that offers home economics. In addition, they have taken some additional education courses in order to be certified as a teacher. That means that they have a teaching license. **Certification**, or *official approval*, is required for teachers in all public schools and most private schools. Teachers in many states take courses every five years to renew their certification. In some states, teachers must take competency examinations.

Home economics is taught in *high schools* and *junior high schools*, which are often referred to as **secondary schools**. Middle schools and grade schools may offer home economics in the upper elementary grades.

At one time, home economics clothing teachers only taught sewing techniques. Today, the clothing courses that you take cover a wide variety of topics.

Knowledge of fibers and fabrics, as well as consumer education, are also important. Understanding clothing needs of individuals and families, using clothing resources, and dealing with problems related to clothing are other topics that may be included in the **curriculum**, or *course of study*.

Your home economics teacher keeps up-to-date in all these areas by reading, attending in-service workshops and professional meetings, and by taking courses.

VOCATIONAL SCHOOL TEACHERS

Vocational school training teaches you a particular skill or group of skills that will prepare you to get a job in a particular field. You might go to a vocational school to learn to be a pattern maker, a fashion illustrator, a textile machine technician, or a commercial sewing machine operator. A *vocational school teacher* often has some industry work experience. In most states, the teacher is expected to have a college degree or a vocational certificate offered through state universities.

COLLEGE TEACHERS

In order to be eligible to teach clothing and textile courses on the college level, you must have both an undergraduate degree from a four-year college and a graduate degree. Some *college teachers* also find it helpful to have some industry, business, or secondary teaching experience in their chosen field.

A *college professor* is a teacher who has done additional, specialized research or study in a chosen field and has received a Master's or Doctoral degree.

In addition to teaching classes, college teachers and professors are expected to do research and write articles for scholarly publications. This helps enhance the status of the college or university.

ADULT EDUCATION TEACHERS

An *adult education teacher* usually is someone who has an excellent reputation and a great deal of knowledge and skill in a particular field. A college degree is usually not required. Teaching adult education can be a lot of fun. Students take the courses because they are interested in the subject and really want to learn.

Most adult education courses are taught in the evenings at the local high school, adult education center, or community college. A career as an adult education teacher is usually a part-time one.

After-work and weekend courses can be taken in subjects that will open up industry jobs.

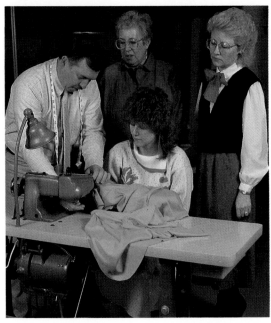

SEWING CLASS TEACHERS

Fabric and sewing machine stores may sponsor their own sewing classes. A *sewing class teacher* could work exclusively for one store or teach courses in several different stores. He or she is usually paid according to the number of hours spent teaching. Sometimes the teacher conducts a series of classes taught over several weeks, such as a tailoring course. At other times, he or she may teach a short one- or two-hour **seminar**, or *workshop*. Usually a seminar focuses on a very specific topic, such as "Sewing on Silk" or "Fitting Pants."

A sewing class teacher must be a highly skilled sewer and be able to communicate those skills to other people. It is not necessary to have a college degree, but some fabric stores prefer one.

THE EXTENSION SERVICE

The U.S. Department of Agriculture has a division called the *Cooperative Extension Service*. Cooperative Extension has state offices in every state and local agents in almost every county. The county extension agents develop information and present workshops on a wide variety of topics, such as nutrition, housing, agriculture, and clothing. They write material for leaflets and newspapers. They work with 4-H and other youth groups, homemaker groups, and other local organizations. They may have their own radio or television program. Many county extension agents have home economics degrees and are called *extension home economists*.

Almost every state has an *extension clothing specialist*, who is affiliated with the state's land grant university. The extension clothing specialist trains the extension home economists and develops a wide variety of programs on textile and clothing topics. In addition, the extension clothing specialist prepares bulletins and pamphlets, conducts workshops, and may also teach college courses and do consumer research.

The requirements to become a state clothing specialist are the same as for college educators. Some business or teaching experience may be considered an asset.

COSTUME HISTORIANS AND TEXTILE RESTORERS

A *costume historian* learns about the history of societies and cultures by studying the clothing worn by its members. A *textile restorer* repairs and reconstructs damaged textiles that have historic or artistic value.

A costume historian might work for a museum or a university as the **curator**, or *person in charge*, of its costume collection. A costume historian might also work for a historical preservation society, such as Colonial Williamsburg. The costume historian's job would be to select costumes that are historically accurate, help keep them in good condition, and locate additional items of clothing for the collection.

A textile restorer cleans, mends, and reconstructs items, such as tapestries, historic costumes, or intricate handmade laces and trims. If a museum or university has a very large textile collection, it would employ a textile restorer. He or she would work closely with the costume historian.

Textile restorers may also be hired by a museum, university, or historical society for a particular project, but not work there permanently. They are also employed by fabric companies that specialize in restoration work. These fabric companies often work with clients all over the world.

In order to become a costume historian or a textile restorer, a college degree is required. A Master's degree or some advanced coursework at a specialized school is also necessary. Course work includes art, history, sociology, textile science, fabric construction, and clothing construction.

Careers in fashion promotion, communications, consumer education, teaching, and extension all have one requirement in common. You must be able to get your message across effectively to other people. A good communicator has many different career opportunities in the textile and apparel fields.

Chapter 28 Job Listings

Fashion Promotion Specialist
Fashion Writer
Fashion Reporter
Fashion Editor
Fashion Illustrator
Fashion Photographer
Photography Model
Runway Model
Consumer Education Specialist
Home Economics Teacher
Vocational School Teacher
College Teacher
College Professor
Adult Education Teacher
Sewing Class Teacher
Extension Home Economist
Costume Historian
Textile Restorer

Summary

The field of fashion promotion includes all activities conducted by a manufacturer, retailer, advertising agency, or fashion publication to get the public interested in a fashion product or service. Fashion writers, editors, illustrators, photographers, and models are involved in communicating a fashion message. Consumer education specialists, teachers, and extension agents help educate the public. Costume historians and textile restorers help people learn about clothing of the past.

Questions

1. What responsibilities do fashion promotion specialists have with manufacturers, fashion publications, and advertising agencies?

2. What two important talents should a fashion writer possess?

3. If you are interested in a career in fashion illustration or photography, what can you do while you are in high school to develop the necessary skills?

4. What are some of the demands that make modeling such hard work? Why is modeling so competitive?

5. Describe the responsibilities of a consumer education specialist. What personal qualities are necessary for this career?

6. What opportunities are available for a teaching career in clothing and textiles?

7. What training is required for teaching in each educational area?

8. If you have an interest in history, what jobs are available in clothing and textiles?

Activities

1. Write copy for two different types of ads for the same garment. One should be an image ad for a fashion magazine; the other an information ad for a catalogue. Which type of copy is harder to write? Why?

2. Gather information about modeling fees. How much can a top model earn per hour? Per year? How do these earnings compare with the average modeling fees? What percentage of models earn the highest rates?

3. Interview two teachers at your school. Find out what they like and dislike about the teaching profession. What type of training and credentials do they have? How did they become interested in the profession?

You Be the Expert

A friend wants to become a model in order to earn lots of money and travel to glamorous places. What could you say to help your friend gain a more realistic understanding of a modeling career?

29 *Entrepreneurs*

TERMS TO LEARN

consignment
entrepreneur
marketing
market research
merchandising
promotion
regulations
target audience

An **entrepreneur** is *a person who organizes and manages his or her own business.* If there are any risks—like loosing your shovel in a snowbank or not making enough money on the car wash to cover the cost of soap and water—the entrepreneur must take the responsibility. On the positive side, however, the entrepreneur gets to keep any profits.

After reading this chapter, you will be able to:

- identify the types of businesses you might consider starting,
- interpret regulations that may affect the type of business you choose,
- explain how to conduct market research, establish production techniques, and determine quality standards for your goods and services,
- demonstrate how to promote and sell your product.

Types of Businesses

A person who is in business for himself or herself can have almost any type of business. Many entrepreneurial businesses are small businesses. They may be so small that the owner is the only employee or so large that the owner employs many people. Just remember that every large business had to start out as a small business!

Every business sells something. What you sell could be an item that you make, or it could be a service that you perform.

The free-lance illustrator, sewing school teacher, fashion photographer, and copywriter that you read about in the other chapters of this Unit are all examples of people who might be self-employed. This means that they work for themselves. They sell a product, such as photographs or fashion sketches, or a service, such as teaching sewing or writing ads, to many different customers. Or you might own a store, such as a boutique or a fashion store, and sell items that other people manufacture.

How you conduct your business depends on the size and the type of business you have.

SMALL BUSINESSES WITH A SHOP OR OFFICE

Many small businesses, particularly those that sell goods and services provided by other people, are located in a shop or an office. Your goal might be to own a laundry, a custom clothing store that employs several dressmakers and tailors, or a gift shop that sells handcrafted items.

Some other examples of a small business are a boutique, a specialty store, a fabric shop, a yarn and needlework store, a repair shop, or a store that specializes in recycled clothing.

The entrepreneur who begins this type of business must be prepared to put in long hours at the store or office, particularly when the business is just beginning. A new store usually requires the constant attention of its owner. It often takes time for the owner to find and train a store manager that he or she has complete confidence in.

AN IN-HOME BUSINESS

Many successful entrepreneurs began their businesses in their homes. Some people work out of an extra room or their basement. Others work at a corner of their dining room table. If you always meet your clients or customers in their office, then you may only need enough space to keep records and make phone calls in your home.

Sewing alterations and custom dressmaking are two examples of businesses that can be conducted successfully from the home. You would need space for your sewing machine and sewing equipment and a place where customers can try on their garments.

Many people conduct small businesses from their kitchen or a spare room in their home.

A wardrobe consultant who meets with clients at their homes or at a store might maintain office space at home. A cosmetic representative or a fabric representative who sells through visits or parties given at other people's homes would need at-home office space for writing reports and keeping records. A fashion illustrator or copywriter might also choose to work at home. Since they would probably have meetings at their clients' offices, the home workspace could be very simple and functional.

Parents with small children may choose to work at home. This arrangement lets the parent be near the child while still earning a salary. It solves any babysitting problems if a child gets sick. It also provides the flexibility in working hours that families with small children often need.

Some people, however, find that working at home is difficult. There can be many distractions. Small children may interrupt frequently, even when there is someone else there to supervise them. Friends may call to chat. It takes discipline to work at home.

The successful home-based entrepreneur will not be distracted by household chores that need to be done or by an invitation to go shopping. Working at home can also be lonely. Some people work better when there are other people around with whom they can share ideas.

SMALL MANUFACTURERS

Many small manufacturing businesses begin as an at-home operation. Later on, if the business grows, the owner might decide to move into a separate factory or workroom. Different types of products can be manufactured at home. These include accessories, such as scarves, hats and belts, and children's clothing and toys.

Items for the home, such as pillows, wall-hangings, picture frames, and quilts, are other successful products. You do not even need to make the entire item. You might consider decorating, customizing, or personalizing a product that someone else manufactures. Or you could make craft kits that the customer finishes.

There are many different ways to sell products, whether they are manufactured at home or in a factory. The first way is to manufacture a quantity of the item and then get retailers to sell it for you. You could sell the items to the stores at a wholesale price, the price the store owner pays the manufacturer. The store now owns the items and can sell them at any price it wishes.

You could also sell the items on **consignment**. This means that *the store owner will put the items on sale in the store.* The manufacturer still owns the items and only gets paid when someone buys them. Then the store owner and the manufacturer each get a percentage of the price. If the items do not sell, the manufacturer does not make any money and must take back the goods. Crafts and special one-of-a-kind garments are often sold on consignment.

A second way for an entrepreneur to sell his or her products is at a *craft fair.* Many organizations sponsor these craft fairs. Sometimes you pay for your booth and keep all the profits you earn. At other times, you must give the organization that runs the fair a percentage of your sales. Sometimes retailers shop these fairs in the hopes of finding new and unusual items to carry in their stores.

MAIL-ORDER BUSINESSES

Many entrepreneurs began their careers with a mail-order business. Suppose you have designed and made a special line of bibs for babies.

Instead of selling your bibs through local stores, you might consider taking out advertisements in magazines that are read by the parents of new infants. You could keep a small inventory of bibs on hand and make more as you receive orders.

Many mail-order businesses send out direct mail pieces to potential customers. A direct mail piece can be anything from an elaborate catalogue to a simple letter with a sketch of the item. One of the advantages of direct mail is that you can send information to a *very specific audience,* or **target audience**. Suppose you designed and made a special knapsack for bikers. If you obtained a list of all the people in your area who belong to Bicycle Clubs, you could mail information directly to them. There are companies that sell or rent such lists to mail-order businesses.

Small Business Management Techniques

In order to be a successful entrepreneur, you must learn to do more than create a product or offer a service. You must learn how to manage your business.

COSTS AND PROFITS

Good record keeping is essential to a well-run business. You must know what your costs are in order to set your prices and make a *profit,* the amount of money that is left over after all your bills have been paid.

Some costs, such as rent, the price of raw materials, and the cost of advertising, are easy to determine. Other costs, such as the time you

put into the business, are more difficult to determine.

Every entrepreneur should include his or her personal salary as part of the cost to run a business. This may not seem to be a chief consideration now, while you are still in school, but if you were supporting yourself and paying for your own rent and food, it would be very important.

As a business grows, it is not necessary for the owner to do all the record keeping. Many entrepreneurs hire an accountant, and sometimes a lawyer, to work for them for a fee. These fees become part of the entrepreneur's costs to run the business.

Often, a person who is very creative will go into business with a partner who is business-oriented. Each person can handle the parts of the business that match his or her talents. The creative person might design the product, write the advertising, and handle the public relations.

A growing business requires careful accounting practices, inventory control, and cost analyses.

The business-oriented person might keep records, set prices, and work with the wholesalers, the retailers, and the sales representatives.

REGULATIONS

There are local, state and Federal **regulations**, or *laws,* that may affect the type of business you operate.

• *Protecting Your Business Name.* If you do business under a name other than your own, you should protect it by registering it. You can register the name in your county and your state. That way, no one else can call their business by the same name as you do. Check with your local County Clerk's Office.

• *Sales Tax.* Many countries and states have a sales tax on certain items. If you sell any of these items directly to the public, you must collect the sales tax from your customers and pay it to the county and/or the state. This must be done whether the product is sold by mail order, at a craft fair, or through your own store. Your local County Clerk's Office can give you information about county and state sales tax regulations.

• *Licenses.* If you are planning to manufacture certain products or provide certain services, you may be required to take out a license. For example, in some states you need a license to make and sell certain kinds of stuffed items, such as toys and quilts. Your local Department of Public Health can usually give you information about required licenses.

• *Zoning Laws.* A person cannot decide to build a dry cleaning store any place he or she wants, or to set up a manufacturing operation in the basement of a house. Most communities have zoning laws that set aside certain areas as commercial, or business, areas and others as residential, or home and apartment, areas.

There are even zoning laws that restrict some areas to certain types of businesses or certain types of housing. Zoning information is obtained from the town's Building Inspector.

• *Labeling.* In Chapters 18 and 24, you learned about government regulations regarding care labeling. Both large manufacturers and small manufacturers must comply with these regulations.

Merchandising

The product or service you sell and the way you merchandise it is very important to the success of your business. **Merchandising** includes *all the decisions that go into the selling of a product.* These decisions include what you will sell, who you will sell it to, how you will produce it, how you will package and ship it, and what price you will charge.

MARKET RESEARCH

Market research means *investigating the potential market for a product or a service before you begin to produce it.* Have you ever heard the expression "an idea whose time has come"? Market research will help you decide if the time and place are right for your idea.

Large companies spend many thousands of dollars on market research. They conduct elaborate consumer surveys. They keep sophisticated records of their own and their competitors' sales. They are continuously on the lookout for a consumer need that is not being filled.

A small business, or someone thinking about going into business, usually does not have thousands of dollars to spend on market research.

This entrepreneur, who sells products at craft fairs, must keep accurate records, make decisions about inventory, and determine selling price.

However, spending a lot of money is not necessary. A business that starts small usually begins by selling to a small market. Otherwise, you might spend all your money on advertising to a large market and not get enough orders back to cover your costs. You might also get more orders than you could handle. Even if your product is a success, your business might fail.

Begin by finding out if there is a need for your product. Is your idea one that everyone could use or would it be of interest to only a very special market? How would you reach that special market? Talk to some of the people who might be your potential customers.

Find out who your competition would be, and how much it charges. Look in the Yellow Pages of the telephone directory. Check out the advertisements in your local newspaper. Visit area stores to find out how much they are charging for similar items or services. If you are thinking of designing and making a special item, you might even visit area craft fairs to see what items sell best.

Are people interested in buying items that are knitted, crocheted, quilted, beaded, or hand-sewn? Are they buying items for children, for the home, or for themselves? Are people willing to pay what you would have to charge in order to make a profit?

Think about how the product or service you offer might be just a little bit different from the ones already on the market. Will it be less expensive, personalized, of better quality?

PRODUCTION

Another important consideration is how you are going to produce your product. Are you going to produce one-of-a-kind originals or many copies of the same item? Because it takes longer to produce each individual item, one-of-a-kind products are usually more expensive than mass-produced items.

Do you have enough time to personally make every item you are going to sell? Or do you need

Bags and Belts Co.

Students at the Henry James Memorial School in Simsbury, Connecticut, have been successful entrepreneurs right in their home economics class!

Under the leadership of their home economics teacher, the students ran a small business of making and selling canvas belts and bags. The students, while improving their sewing skills, also learned how to operate a business. They were involved in all aspects of the business from production and quality control to sales and profit-sharing.

First, the students researched the market in their community to learn what fashion accessories were popular. They did comparison shopping at local stores to check on styles of products and prices. The students decided to limit their merchandise to two items—a small tote bag and a ribbon belt, both popular with students and adults in their community.

A field trip to a local factory helped determine production procedures. The students observed assembly-line methods but decided that each person would make two items from start to finish.

Jobs were then defined, interviewed for, and appointed. The group decided on the company name "Bags and Belts," and labels were printed to go on each bag and belt.

A hangtag was designed with information on fabric content, washing instructions, and price. A quality control center was established in each class. Two students checked each piece of merchandise before it could be sold. An advertising campaign was planned to begin well before the sale date.

"Bags and Belts" held a two-day sale as part of a school-wide fair. The students learned about retailing, accounting, guarding against theft, and sales techniques. Before the afternoon of the second day, all the bags and belts were sold.

to have a group of people to work with you? Remember that your time is limited. There are only 24 hours in a day!

As an example, suppose you plan to open an alterations business that specializes in hems. Figure out how long it takes you to complete an average hem. Then figure out how many hours a week you can devote to your business. Divide your available number of hours by the time it takes you to sew a hem. That will tell you how many hems you can agree to do each week before you need to hire someone else to help you out.

Suppose it takes you 30 minutes to complete a hem and you can devote 15 hours a week to your business. That means you could agree to take in 30 hems a week. If you agree to do more, you would have to hire some help.

Perhaps you have designed a very special pillow. Several stores have given you very large orders. How will you meet their delivery date? You could try to produce them yourself or you could get a group of friends together to help you mass-produce them.

You would choose the fabric and the colors. Then someone else could be the cutter, cutting out lots of pillows at one time. The next person could be the sewer. A fourth person could clip the corners, trim the curves, and turn the pillows right side out. A fifth person would stuff the pillows, and a sixth person could hand-stitch them closed.

A group working like this on an assembly line works very fast and can produce many more pillows than if each person did one pillow from start to finish.

In order to determine your production costs, you will need to know several things. First, you will need to know how much you will pay for raw materials. Raw materials include items such as fabric, thread, zippers, yarn, needles, beads, and other trimming.

Next, you will need to determine how much you will pay yourself or someone else to produce the item. Remember that your time is worth as much as someone else's and there is no point in being in business for yourself if you are not going to get paid.

Then you will have to decide what you are going to do about packaging and shipping your product. Will you need labels? Will you need hangtags? Will it need a special package or wrapper? Even if you are selling at craft fairs, you will probably find that people expect some kind of bag in which to put their purchases. All of these expenses go into the total cost of producing a product.

QUALITY STANDARDS

It is very important, particularly in a new business, to maintain your standards of quality. Your customers expect a certain level of quality. If you disappoint them, the result will be no more business. You cannot afford a reputation as a person who sometimes does shoddy work or sells inferior merchandise.

Many new businesses fail because they expand too rapidly. In order to meet the demand for their product, they sacrifice quality for quantity. Sometimes it is better to limit the amount you produce or the number of customers you handle until you have carefully examined ways to expand your business.

Marketing

Marketing is concerned with *all the various ways to advertise, promote, and distribute a product.* Some businesses use only one method, such as direct mail, to market a product. Other businesses use a combination of techniques. An entrepreneur could sell some items on consignment, some at craft fairs, and some through ads in carefully selected publications.

SALES

An entrepreneur could act as his or her own salesperson. If calling on customers is not one of the entrepreneur's talents, or if he or she does not have the time, someone else can be hired to do the selling.

An entrepreneur might also use the services of an independent sales representative. He or she would choose a sales representative that carries a variety of products and calls on the types of stores that would sell the product. Free-lance people, such as photographers and illustrators, often use agents to get work for them. This leaves the photographer or illustrator free to create.

The agent makes money by receiving a commission on every job. A dressmaker might advertise for customers and also have people referred to her by the local fabric store. An alterations expert might develop a business arrangement with a specialty clothing store and still maintain his or her own customers.

PROMOTION

Promotion is *a form of advertising that you do not pay for.* If the local newspaper writes an article about your business, that is promotion. If an organization mentions your business in its newsletter, that is promotion. If a store refers its customers to you, that is also promotion. Promotion is particularly important to a new entrepreneur who may not have a large budget for advertising.

Promotion should be an important part of your business. You want to let people know that you exist. You want to inform not only the peo-

Entrepreneurs can hire independent salespeople to call on customers.

ple who are your potential customers, but also the people who will be able to help you spread the word to other potential customers.

Suppose you custom-design handmade leather belts. You might ask your local fabric store to display some belts that you designed to complement their model garments. The store may be willing to do this, particularly if you purchase some of your supplies from them. It will make the store's garments look special and will give you some extra publicity.

Evaluation

Going into business for yourself may seem like a very attractive idea. If you are looking for a very small business that will help you earn extra spending money, it can be fairly easy to start one. If you are looking for a business that will support you full-time, that is much harder. Over 90% of the small businesses that are started each year do not succeed. That is because people do not do their homework. It is important that you learn all you possibly can about a business before going into it full-time.

Find out everything you need to know about running a business—record keeping, marketing, taxes, advertising, insurance, licensing, and zoning regulations. Any experience you can get now, while you are still in school, will be invaluable later on.

Start small, maintain control, build a reputation—then expand. Most businesses fail because of bad management, not because of bad ideas.

KNOW YOURSELF

The first step toward good managment is to know yourself. Before you decide to become an entrepreneur, ask yourself some questions. Do you get along well with other people? If your answer is "no," stay away from service-oriented businesses. Do you have enough initiative? Do you have enough self-confidence? Are you willing to take risks? Why are you going into business? It might be for fun, for profit, or for self-fulfillment. Can you handle stress and pressure? Because you are the one making all the decisions, you get to take all the credit when things go well. You also get to take all the blame when things go wrong. All of the joys, problems, and decisions belong to you alone.

There are many advantages and disadvantages to being your own boss. You should examine them carefully to decide if this is the career path for you. For most people, a major advantage is that you are your own boss. No one tells you what to do, how to do it, or what hours to keep. You are the one who chooses how you use your time.

You must, however, be the type of person that is called "self-motivated." That means in order to work and do a good job, you do not need a great deal of praise and direction from other people. Another advantage is the satisfaction that can come from developing a product or a service that people want or need.

Being an entrepreneur provides you with the opportunity to take risks. For many people, this means a feeling of excitement that might not come from working for someone else. Another major advantage is that if you are successful, you will be financially rewarded for that success.

DISADVANTAGES

The disadvantages of being in business for yourself include an uncertain income. You cannot depend on a regular salary to pay your expenses. You will need some money for start-up expenses.

That money will probably have to come from your savings or from a loan. Taking out a loan means that you will have to pay interest in addition to all your other start-up expenses. You must be prepared for unexpected events and emergencies. If you get sick, who will run the business and how will you pay your bills?

Another disadvantage is that most people who work for themselves work longer hours than people who work for someone else. This is particularly true when your business is just getting started. A final disadvantage is that there is always the risk of failure.

There are many organizations that will give you advice and assistance. The Small Business Administration, the Service Corps of Retired Executives (SCORE), and your local Chamber of Commerce are just a few of them.

Finally, make a personal examination of your talents and capabilities, as well as your goals and ambitions. Start with something you already know and do well. You can always expand your business to include other products or services as you grow and develop your skills.

Chapter 29 Review

Summary

An entrepreneur can conduct business in a variety of ways—in a shop or office, at home, as a small manufacturer, or by mail order. Business management of costs and profits is essential for success. Both large and small businesses must comply with many regulations. Entrepreneurs must merchandise and market their products. Production methods, quality standards, promotion, and distribution are very important. You should examine the advantages and disadvantages of being your own boss carefully to decide if this is the career path for you.

Questions

1. List five or more examples of businesses that could be started by an entrepreneur.

2. Identify at least four clothing and textile-related businesses that could be operated in a private home.

3. What are some of the expenses that must be paid before a business makes a profit?

4. Name five regulations or laws that may affect a small business.

5. Describe how an entrepreneur should conduct market research before deciding whether to sell a product or service.

6. Why are quality standards important to business success?

7. What are several ways to promote and distribute a product developed by an entrepreneur?

8. What are some personal qualities that an entrepreneur should have to be successful?

9. What are the advantages and disadvantages of being self-employed?

Activities

1. Make a list of your special interests, talents, abilities, and job experiences. For each item on your list, identify a product or service that you could sell.

2. Visit a local crafts store and discuss with the owners how they conduct their business. Do they accept merchandise on a consignment basis? If so, which items sell best?

3. Choose a textile product that could be made and sold at your school. Estimate the cost of materials, marketing, and other expenses. Determine a selling price for the product in order to produce a profit.

You Be the Expert

Your older sister makes lots of gifts for relatives and friends. Some people have asked if they could buy some of her items, but she doesn't know how to set up her own business. What advice could you give her?

30 | *Finding the Job for You*

TERMS TO LEARN

courteousness
cover letter
interview
job application
reliability
résumé

If someone asked you why you wanted to get a job, you might think the answer was very obvious: to make money. That is certainly one goal, but there are others. The kind of work you do in the summer or part-time during the school year can help you decide what type of career you would like to have in the future.

After reading this chapter, you will be able to:

- describe the process of finding the right job,
- demonstrate how to write an effective résumé and cover letter,
- explain how to conduct yourself at an interview,
- list characteristics that help on-the-job success.

What Do You Want to Do?

In the previous chapters of this Unit, you learned about a variety of careers in design, manufacturing, retailing, communications, education, and entrepreneurship. There are ways you can gain experience and knowledge while you are still in high school that will give you a head start on many of those careers.

The job you get now can help you make some important decisions about the work you want to do in the future. For example, if you are interested in a career as a buyer in the apparel industry, try to get some experience as a salesperson in a department store or a boutique. If you want a career in communications, you might try to get a part-time job at the local newspaper. If you would like to become a designer, think about working for a local manufacturer or tailor to learn about clothing design and construction. A job in the alteration area of a dry cleaner or a department store can teach you the details of how clothes are made.

These experiences can help you learn first-hand what it would be like to work in a particular job on a day-to-day basis. While working, you can see how your own interests and skills fit in. You can talk to fellow workers about their jobs. You can observe the advantages and disadvantages of certain careers and compare them with your own personal likes and dislikes. You may discover that a job which appears to be very glamorous to an outsider is actually filled with routine tasks and long hours.

Always think of your first job as a stepping-stone. This attitude will help you decide if you want—or more importantly, do not want—to choose a particular career. Although you will probably begin at an entry-level position, your

A stock clerk's job can be the first step in a merchandising career.

first job can help you advance to the career you want.

For example, a job as a salesperson or a stock clerk can provide knowledge about how a store operates, what customers are interested in buying, and experience in working with other people.

This knowledge can help you succeed in a career in retailing. But, you may decide that you want to switch fields. You may want to change from retailing to manufacturing, or from manufacturing to advertising. Your first job will still give you valuable experiences for whatever job or career you finally select.

Where to Look

Finding just the right job can be fun, but you must do some research to be successful. Make an appointment to see your school's guidance counselor. Besides giving you some good advice, your counselor may be able to give you some tests to help identify your special skills and interests.

Tell everyone you know—friends, relatives, teachers, and parents of friends—that you are looking for a job. Word of mouth is sometimes the best way to get one.

Local businesses, particularly stores and factories, often post job notices and "Help Wanted" signs. If they do not, call or write to the personnel department of the local businesses and ask for an interview.

Check the "Help Wanted" section of the classified ads in your local daily newspaper. Sunday is usually the day with the largest number of classified ads. Check the weekly community newspapers. Small local businesses often use these to advertise part-time job opportunities.

Read these ads very carefully, as there can be different ways to list the same job. Watch for clues that will help identify entry-level jobs. Words and phrases such as "trainee," "we will train," "you will learn," "growth opportunity," "entry-level position," and "must have a desire to learn" are all clues. Part-time jobs may be listed in a separate section or scattered throughout the ads.

Employment agencies are another resource for finding full-time jobs. Some agencies will want a fee or a percentage of your salary if they find you a job. Sometimes you are responsible for paying the fee, and sometimes your employer is. Be sure to find out who pays the fee before you take a job that is offered to you through an agency.

If you are looking for a summer job, you might register with an agency that specializes in temporary jobs. This means you work for the agency, and it sends you to work at a different company every week. One week you could be working as a receptionist, the next week as a typist, and the third week in a company's mailroom. The company pays the agency that you work for, and the agency then pays you.

Your Résumé and Cover Letter

A **résumé** is *a written summary of who you are and what you have done.* You will give or send it to the person you hope will hire you. Since it will represent you when you are not there to speak for yourself, it should be as professional-looking as possible.

WRITING A RÉSUMÉ

A résumé must be typed on plain white, 8½″ x 11″ paper. If typing is not one of your skills, ask someone to type it for you. The résumé should not have any spelling or grammatical errors. Proofread it yourself, and then ask someone else to read it also.

Your résumé should contain the following:

1. *Name.* Give your full name.
2. *Address and Phone Number.* Give your complete address and the phone number where you can be most easily reached.
3. *Education.* List the school that you are attending and your grade level.
4. *Work Experience.* List any and all jobs you have had. Your most recent job should be listed first. Include a brief description of the work you did and the dates you were employed. Include experiences such as paper routes, babysitting, and volunteer work. These will show that you are a responsible person.
5. *Interests and Skills.* List any special skill that will help you get the job that you want. If you are applying for a sales job in a fabric store and are an avid sewer, say so. If you can type, have a driver's license and access to

a car, or know how to do alterations, say so. Include any special interests such as art, photography, carpentry, music, or computers.

6. *Activities and Honors.* If you belong to any clubs or organizations, have received any special awards, or have been elected to any class offices, list them.

7. *Age.* List your age and/or birthdate if you are under 18. In most states, a person under 18 years must obtain a work permit. You also must have a social security card, whether you are 18 years or not. The guidance office in your school can tell you how to obtain them.

8. *References.* List two or three people, along with their addresses and phone numbers, who will give you a good recommendation. Be sure to ask permission from these people before you use their names.

Your résumé should be complete, but short. One page is ideal. Do not go over two pages in length.

WRITING A COVER LETTER

Every résumé that you send to a business or company should have a cover letter to go with it. The **cover letter** *requests a meeting, or interview, and mentions that you are enclosing your résumé.* It should be typed and, if possible, sent to the person who handles employee applications at the company. If you cannot find the name of such a person, send your letter to the company's Personnel Director. For smaller businesses, send it to the owner or manager.

Be sure to mention any skills or experiences that would make you particularly valuable to that company. This information is an important part of your cover letter, even if it is already in your résumé.

Job Applications

A **job application** is a company's own record of every person who applies for a job. Even if you send a cover letter and a résumé, you will probably have to fill out a job application.

Read the application carefully before you begin to fill it out. Be sure that you understand the directions and each of the questions on the application. If you are not sure of any question, ask for assistance.

Unless your handwriting is extremely neat, you should print the information on a job application. Bring an extra copy of your résumé with you. You may need to include information that the résumé contains, such as the names, addresses, and telephone numbers of your references.

The Interview

After reading your résumé, cover letter, and job application, a company personnel person may want to interview you. An **interview** is *a meeting to discuss the details of the job and the qualifications of the person seeking the job.* The first rule of a good interview is to relax. Just remind yourself that if the company was not already impressed with you, they would not be giving you an interview.

POINTS TO REMEMBER

Be on time for the job interview. There is no excuse for being late. If you do not know where the company is, allow plenty of time to get there.

Lifestyle

Dressing for a Job Interview

When you are interviewed for a job, it is important to make a good impression. The way you dress for the interview gives messages to the employer about what kind of employee you might be.

Dress for the interview, not for the job. On the job you might wear blue jeans or a uniform. For the interview, you should wear good clothes, the type you might wear to someone's home for a special dinner. Dress conservatively. This means no extreme outfits, heavy makeup, or elaborate hair styles. Choose colors and styles that flatter you and make you feel good.

Before you leave for the interview, make sure that:

- your clothes are neat, clean, and pressed,

- your shoes are polished, and
- everything you have on is in good repair with no loose buttons, ripped seams, or hanging hems.

Personal grooming is important, too. Remember to use a deodorant and, if necessary, a mouthwash or a breath freshener. Hands should be clean and scrubbed, including under the fingernails. Hair should be clean and brushed. If you have a dandruff problem, don't wear dark colors. Avoid wearing strong perfume or cologne.

By having confidence in your appearance, you can relax and focus on discussing the job during the interview.

The interviewer may offer to shake your hand when you enter his or her office. Respond by looking at the interviewer in a friendly way and returning the handshake with a firm grasp. Do not sit down until you are invited to do so. Place any items you may have brought with you on the floor. Do not put your things on the interviewer's desk. Although it is important to be relaxed, do remember to sit up straight and look directly at the interviewer when talking.

Answer with more than a "yes" or "no" when the interviewer asks you a question. Always try to tell something about yourself, such as, "Yes, I enjoy working with people. I've worked as a summer camp counselor for two years." Above all, answer the questions honestly.

If you are especially interested in a job, do a little research about the company before your interview. Read the business section of your local daily newspaper. Go to your local library and ask the librarian for assistance. This background information will help you to know what questions to ask during the interview. It will also show that you are interested in the company.

When the interview is over, be sure to thank the person for taking the time to see you.

FOLLOWING UP

Thank you letters are always good manners. This is true whether you are thanking someone for a gift or for taking the time to interview you. When you get home, type or neatly write a letter to each of the people who interviewed you.

Thank them for seeing you and mention that you are very interested in working for the company. Remind them about anything that makes you particularly qualified, such as your previous jobs, your typing skills, or your interest in fashion and sewing. Sometimes the "little extras," such as a follow-up letter or a phone call, will help you get the job.

On-the-Job Success

Once you have been hired, your goals will change. Now, you concern should be to do your job well. Success will make you eligible for a raise or even a promotion to a better job. Certain personal qualities, such as the ability to get along well with other people and good communication skills, will help you to succeed.

PERSONAL QUALITIES

Personal qualities are those that reflect your inner self. They influence how other people feel about you and respond to you. Important personal qualities for any job are reliability, punctuality, the ability to get along with people, good communication skills, and a willingness to learn. These traits are valued by all employers.

- **Reliability.** This trait is very important to job success. It means that *you are dependable,* and the company can be sure that you will do your work. If your employer gives you a task to do, you will do it without constantly being reminded. You will do the best job you can.
- **Punctuality.** You should always be at work when you are supposed to be. Punctuality means that you arrive on time and do not leave early. You don't take extra minutes for lunch or breaks. You don't socialize or loaf on the job. Time is money to your employer. If you are constantly late, you risk being fired.
- **Ability to get along with people.** A good employee is friendly, cooperative, and helpful to others. One important aspect of getting along with others is **courteousness.** This means being *polite, considerate toward others, and pleasant to be around.* A person who is rude—whether to the employer, to customers, or to coworkers—is a troublemaker and will not be welcome.

- **Good communication skills.** The basic communication skills of reading, writing, and speaking are important in every job. There are always sales slips to fill out, customers to speak to, reports to write, and instructions to follow. Take the time to develop these skills while you are in school.
- **Willingness to learn.** You should take an interest in your job, be willing to learn about new areas, and accept other assignments. Saying "It's not my job" will not make you very popular with your employer. Instead, develop a positive attitude. By trying to do the job better each day, you will become a more valuable employee.

To help you succeed on the job, you must be willing to learn about new areas and accept other assignments.

ADVANCEMENT

Important personal qualities will help you to do your job well. Eventually you may seek a promotion or another job.

When you have mastered the job you are doing, find out about other jobs which interest you in the company. What skills do the people in these jobs have? Do you have these skills? If not, think about how you can develop them.

Perhaps you can take an extra course in school. You could tell your employer that you are interested in a job with more responsibility. For example, if you are working as a stock clerk in a small retail store, you might want to became a salesperson. If you are a salesperson, you might want to assume some of the responsibilities of an assistant manager.

Your employer may be willing to give you "on the job" training, or pay toward schooling after work. All businesses want to promote people who can qualify for other jobs.

Employers look for leadership skills in their employees. A good leader can get the job done and help others work together. Leadership skills can be learned and developed. They do

not come from a job title. Activities at school and work can help you develop these skills. Learn to organize and manage tasks, listen to other people's ideas and concerns, solve conflicts, help carry out group activities or projects, and build a sense of teamwork within a group.

LEAVING A JOB

It is best to have another job lined up before you leave a job. Most employers prefer to hire someone who is already working. Be sure to give your present employer reasonable notice before you resign. Two weeks is considered standard. Also, maintain good relations with your employer until you leave. He or she may be asked to provide a reference about you to potential employers.

Learn to look at each job as a stepping-stone to your career goal. Examine the job's potential to find out how it can be used to take you where you want to go in the world of work.

Chapter 30 Review

Summary

Gaining experience and knowledge about jobs can help you decide what you want to do. There are many different ways to locate a job. A good résumé and cover letter can help you obtain interviews. Prepare ahead for an interview, which is an opportunity for you to learn more about a job and for the employer to learn more about you. Certain personal qualities, such as reliability, punctuality, ability to get along with people, good communication skills, and a willingness to learn can help you achieve on-the-job success.

Questions

1. What kind of insights can be learned about a career by working in an entry-level job in a related field?

2. What would be the benefits of telling as many people as possible that you are looking for a job?

3. When deciding to use the services of an employment agency, what should you keep in mind about its fees?

4. List the eight categories of information that should be contained in a résumé.

5. Why is it important for you to read a job application form through completely before filling out any portion of the form?

6. What preparation can you do before a job interview that will help you to speak with confidence about yourself and the company?

7. What personal qualities can help you to succeed on the job?

8. When leaving a job, what guidelines should you follow?

Activities

1. Write a personal résumé, summarizing your present level of experience.

2. Write a cover letter for a specific job. Express the personal qualifications that will give the prospective employer an understanding of how your abilities meet the job requirements.

3. Contact local employment agencies and gather information on their general policies for placing high school students, their fees, and any required legal contracts.

4. Locate two magazine pictures that show appropriate job interview clothing and two that show inappropriate dress. Explain the reasons for your choices.

You Be the Expert

A friend has applied for a position at a specialty store where you work. What recommendations could you give that would help your friend prepare for the interview?

Effective Sewing Handbook

Getting Ready to Sew

354

Basic Construction

392

Special Sewing Techniques

427

UNIT I

Sewing for fun or for profit is a skill that takes practice to develop. Just as in any sport, you have to first learn the fundamentals before you can become an expert.

- You need to use right equipment that is in good working condition.
- You need practice at each level before you advance to the next.
- You need to understand the various steps of layout and construction.

Your efforts will be well rewarded as you develop a skill that you can use throughout life.

- Use your sewing skills to construct an entire wardrobe.
- Use your sewing skills to repair a well-loved pair of pants.
- Use your skills to design a special gift for a friend or to decorate your room.
- Perhaps you may even use your skills to develop your own business or establish a career in textiles and clothing.

CHAPTER 1

Get Organized

Whether you are sewing at home or in the school laboratory, always take time to get organized. Too often, rushing to begin a sewing project results in mistakes or wasted time. It is frustrating to suddenly discover that your scissors are not sharp, or that you do not have the right color of thread. It is discouraging to rip out stitching because you forgot to read the directions on the pattern guide sheet.

Organization involves several areas of sewing:

- Arranging your sewing area.
- Gathering needed equipment and supplies.
- Planning your activities.

ARRANGING YOUR SEWING AREA

A pleasant, well-arranged, well-lighted place to work has a lot to do with the enjoyment of sewing.

Your Machine

- Be sure you know how your sewing machine works.
- Test the stitching on fabric scraps, and be able to refer to the instruction manual.
- Keep your machine in good working order—free from lint and dirt, and regularly oiled.

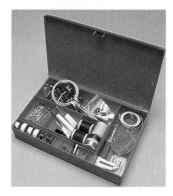

Your Cutting Surface

- A surface for cutting out fabric should be large enough to hold the full width of a piece of folded fabric.
- If you do not have a large table at home, then it is better to cut on the floor where the fabric will be flat.
- Avoid cutting on a bed. Your fabric will shift because the cutting surface is not firm and the results will not be accurate.

Your Ironing Board

- Set up your ironing board and iron near the sewing machine so you will not be tempted to sew without pressing.
- A full-length mirror makes it easy to check fit as you sew and iron.

At home, you may be fortunate to have a special sewing area where the sewing machine and equipment are always available. If not, be sure to store all your sewing equipment together so it will be easy to set up each time that you sew.

At school, many students are sharing the same equipment throughout the day. To correct any equipment problems, report them to your instructor as soon as possible.

GATHERING EQUIPMENT AND SUPPLIES

A few basic supplies and equipment are needed by the beginning sewer. Start by purchasing a few basic items of the best quality you can afford. Good tools make sewing easier, but the most expensive tools are not always the best for you. As your skills and interest increase, you can add more specialized tools and equipment. Be sure to keep your tools well cared for and they will last a long time.

Before you begin a project, be sure you have all the necessary notions and supplies. The recommended size and quantity of fasteners and trims are listed on the pattern envelope for your convenience.

Storing Equipment

There are many inexpensive and attractive ways to store your sewing equipment and supplies.

- Cardboard and plastic boxes can store a variety of materials.
- Be sure to label each box so you can easily identify the contents.
- Most sewers save extra fabric, buttons, trims, and notions for use in future projects.
- Store little items in small boxes before placing in your larger box.
- Bundle tapes and trims with rubber bands or string.
- Roll or fold up pieces of fabric.

If you follow these guidelines, all your supplies will be kept neatly together for use at any time.

PLANNING ACTIVITIES

It is important to plan your activities before you begin sewing.

The Pattern Guide Sheet

- Always read the pattern guide sheet thoroughly so that you clearly understand the various steps of layout and construction.
- Tips, such as laying out all pattern pieces on the fabric before cutting, insure that you will have enough fabric for all the pieces.
- Carefully follow the step-by-step directions of the guide sheet so that you avoid having to rip out and redo.

Pressing and Fitting

- Stop to press after each step of construction, because it may be impossible to carefully press a certain

area after other seams have been stitched.
- Fit as you go along. It is much easier to make a few minor adjustments during construction than to wait until the end and discover you have to make a major alteration!

Double-Checking

Always take a moment to double-check your steps. Ask yourself some questions:
- Are all the pattern pieces properly laid out before I start to cut?
- Are the fabric pieces pinned together correctly before I start to stitch?
- Are the seams and darts pressed smoothly before I stitch the other seams?
- Does each section fit properly before I continue on?

Questions such as these will help you achieve satisfaction and success with your project.

"Haste makes waste" is an old saying. In sewing, this is often true. By taking a few minutes to get organized before you begin a project, you will end up saving time and effort all along the way.

Sewing Safety

Equipment
- Keep pins in a pin cushion, never in mouth or clothes.
- Keep shears and scissors closed when not using.
- Pass a sharp object, handle first, to another person.
- Keep all tools and supplies in your sewing box when not in use.

Sewing Machine
- Keep the sewing machine cord out of people's way.
- Use a slow speed when learning how to use the machine.
- Keep your fingers away from the needle.
- Do not lean your face too close when stitching in case the needle breaks.
- Stitch carefully over pins.

- Unplug the cord from the outlet and then disconnect the cord from the machine when not in use.
- Close the sewing machine carefully or replace its cover when you are finished sewing.

Iron
- Don't touch a hot iron except on the handle.
- Keep your fingers and face away from steam.
- Locate the iron cord so that the iron will not be accidentally pulled off the ironing board.
- Rest the iron on its heel when not in use.
- Unplug the iron when finished. Empty any water in it. Let the iron cool and then store properly.

CHAPTER 2

The Sewing Machine

The most important and expensive piece of sewing equipment is the sewing machine. Just like a computer, a tape recorder, or a motorcycle, a sewing machine is a piece of fine equipment.

You should understand the parts of the sewing machine that you are using at school or at home. By becoming familiar with the parts and their use, you will be able to operate the machine more effectively and avoid certain problems that may occur if you are not familiar with the machine.

BASIC PARTS

All sewing machines operate in a similar manner. However, there are differences among various makes and models. Study the illustration on page 360 and then identify the corresponding parts on your machine.

The Instruction Manual

Study the instruction manual that comes with your machine. The manual will show the various parts of the machine and explain what they do. Directions are included for operating the machine and any accessories. Information about caring for the machine is also included. Always refer to the instruction manual whenever you have a specific question or problem with your machine.

CHOOSING SEWING MACHINE NEEDLE AND THREAD

Sewing machine needles are available in a variety of sizes and types. Choose the needle according to the type and weight of fabric that you are sewing. For convenience, always keep an assortment of needles with your supplies.

Needle Sizes

Needle sizes range from 9 (for delicate fabrics) to 18 (for heavyweight fabrics). The lower the number, the finer the needle.

- Size 9 or 11 is used for fine, lightweight fabrics, such as chiffon and voile.
- Size 14 is used for mediumweight fabrics, such as flannel and corduroy.
- Size 16 or 18 is for heavier and thicker fabrics.

Some foreign sewing machine manufacturers use a different numbering system for needles. However, the same rule applies—the lighter and finer the fabric, the finer the needle.

Types of Needles

Four types of sewing machine needles are available: *sharp, ball-point, wedge-shaped,* and *twin.*

- A sharp, or general-purpose, point is used for woven fabrics.

- A ball-point is used for knits and stretch fabrics. The slightly rounded tip allows the needle to slip between the fabric yarns.
- A wedge-shaped point is used for sewing leathers and vinyls.
- Twin, or double, needles are available for decorative stitching.

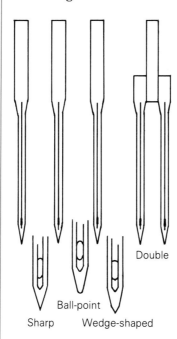

Sharp   Ball-point   Wedge-shaped   Double

Always replace a sewing machine needle when it becomes dull, bent, or burred (rough). A damaged needle can cause stitching problems and harm fabric. Some people insert a new needle when they begin a project.

Thread

The type of thread is also determined by the type and weight of your fabric. Refer to the chart on page 358 for the recommended thread, needle size, and stitch length for different fabrics.

In general, for fine fabrics use a fine needle, fine thread, and short stitches. For heavier fabrics, use a coarser needle, heavier thread, and longer stitches.

Except for special decorative stitching, always use the same type of thread in the needle and in the bobbin.

Changing Needles

These are the steps for changing a sewing machine needle:

1. *Raise* the needle to the highest position by turning the hand wheel.
2. *Loosen* the thumb screw on the needle clamp.
3. *Remove* the old needle, being sure to notice the way it was turned. The position of the needle depends on the model of your sewing machine. (The shank of a sewing machine needle has a round side and a flat side. A long groove runs down the round side. This groove protects the thread as the needle is lowered into the bobbin case. On all models, the long groove on the needle should face the side from which you thread the needle. Refer to your manual for specific directions.)
4. *Insert* the top of the needle firmly up in the needle clamp.
5. *Tighten* the screw securely.

Fabric, Thread, Needle Size, Stitch Length

Fabric	Thread	Needle Size	Stitches per Inch
Delicate: chiffon, fine lace, and silk	polyester fine mercerized cotton silk	9	14–16
Lightweight: batiste, crepe, organdy, taffeta	polyester mercerized cotton silk	11	12–14
Mediumweight: gingham, poplin, percale, linen, fine corduroy, light-weight wool, velveteen	polyester mercerized cotton silk	14	10–12
Medium-heavy: denim, corduroy, gabardine, wool-ens, sailcloth	polyester mercerized cotton silk heavy-duty	16	10–12
Heavy: canvas, coatings, fake fur, upholstery fabrics	polyester heavy-duty	18	8–10
All knits and stretch fabrics	polyester	ball-point 9–16	10–14 or special stretch stitch
Leather and suede	polyester heavy-duty	wedge	8–10
Decorative topstitching	buttonhole twist	18 or twin needle	8–12

WINDING AND INSERTING THE BOBBIN

Most bobbins must be removed from the bobbin case in order to be wound. However, some machines have a bobbin winder built into the bobbin case for easy rewinding.

Keep extra bobbins in your sewing box to avoid winding one color thread over another.

Winding

Refer to your manual for specific instructions for winding a bobbin on your machine. However, most bobbins today are wound in a similar method.

1. *Loosen* the hand wheel knob to stop the movement of the needle.
2. *Insert* the end of the thread through a hole in the bobbin.
3. *Wrap* the thread securely around the bobbin several times so that it will hold.
4. *Place* the bobbin on the bobbin winder.
5. *Hold* the end of the thread until the bobbin starts winding.

It is very important to check that the bobbin winds evenly. It may be necessary to gently guide the thread with your finger. If your bobbin winder does not have an automatic shut-off, wind the bobbin only until it is about ¾ full. Cut the thread with scissors, and remove the bobbin from the winder. Tighten the hand wheel knob.

Inserting

To insert the bobbin, open the slide plate that covers the bobbin case. For a removable bobbin case, take the case out of the machine and insert the bobbin. Be sure that the thread unwinds in the right direction. Check your manual for specific instructions. Insert the bobbin case back into the machine. For a built-in bobbin case, simply insert the bobbin directly into the case.

Pull the bobbin thread gently to see whether there is a slight tension on it. If it unwinds too easily, check the threading of the bobbin case again. Then close the slide plate.

THREADING THE MACHINE

Threading a machine may look difficult at first, but the general procedure is the same for all machines. The thread goes from the spool pin to the tension discs. Then it goes to the take-up lever and down to the needle.

The thread also must go through the various thread guides. The location of the thread guides differs from machine to machine. Study the illustration on this page and also the one in your own manual.

The Tension Discs

It is important to check the threading of the tension discs. Raise the presser foot and pull the thread gently to see if there is a slight tension on it. If the thread unwinds

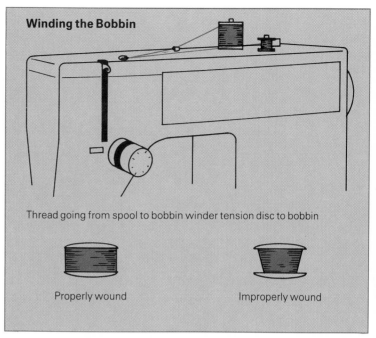

Winding the Bobbin

Thread going from spool to bobbin winder tension disc to bobbin

Properly wound   Improperly wound

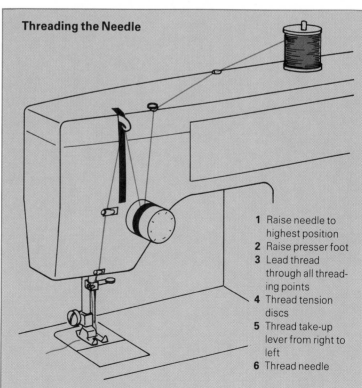

Threading the Needle

1 Raise needle to highest position
2 Raise presser foot
3 Lead thread through all threading points
4 Thread tension discs
5 Thread take-up lever from right to left
6 Thread needle

The Sewing Machine

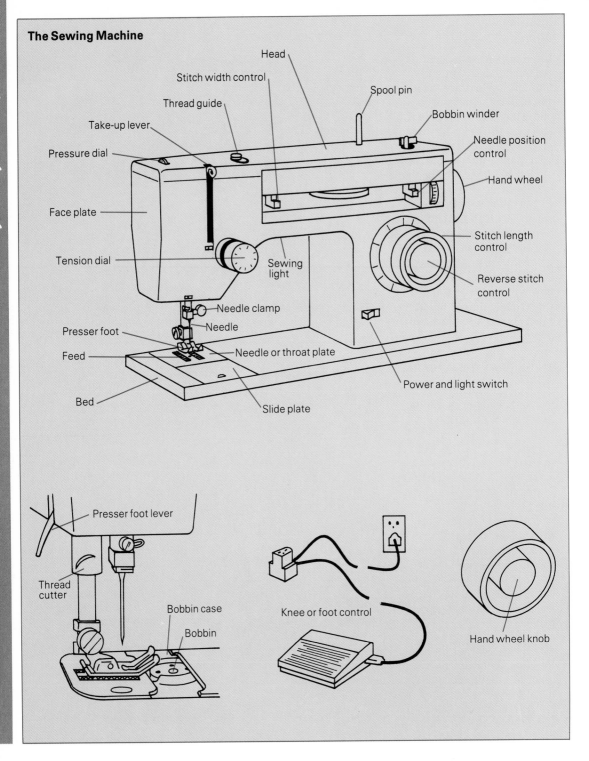

Head

Stitch width control

Spool pin

Thread guide

Bobbin winder

Take-up lever

Needle position control

Pressure dial

Hand wheel

Face plate

Tension dial

Sewing light

Stitch length control

Reverse stitch control

Needle clamp

Presser foot

Needle

Feed

Needle or throat plate

Bed

Slide plate

Power and light switch

Presser foot lever

Thread cutter

Bobbin case

Bobbin

Knee or foot control

Hand wheel knob

Parts of the Sewing Machine

Bed   Flat base of the machine that contains the bobbin and bobbin case

Bobbin   Holds the bottom, or bobbin, thread

Bobbin case   Holds the bobbin in the machine and regulates the tension of the bobbin thread; may be removable or stationary

Bobbin winder   Spindle, latch, and tension discs used to wind thread onto a bobbin

Face plate   Cover that opens for access to the needle bar and presser bar

Feed   Moves the fabric under the presser foot advancing the fabric one stitch at a time

Hand wheel   Controls the movement of the take-up lever; can be turned by hand to raise or lower needle

Hand wheel knob   Can be loosened to stop the needle from moving when winding a bobbin

Head   The main part of the sewing machine, excluding the bed, or base

Knee or foot control   Regulates the starting, running, and stopping of the machine by the amount of pressure applied to the control

Needle   Available in different sizes and types; must be inserted firmly into the needle bar

Needle clamp   Holds the needle firmly in the needle bar; loosened and tightened by a screw

Needle or throat plate   Located directly under the needle and surrounds the feed; usually has guidelines to help keep your stitching straight

Needle position control   Regulates the position of the needle from left to center to right

Power and light switch   Turns on the light and the machine

Presser foot   Holds the fabric against the feed as you stitch

Presser foot lever   Raises and lowers the presser foot

Pressure dial   Regulates the pressure of the presser foot on the fabric

Reverse stitch control   Button or lever that allows you to stitch backward

Sewing light   Illuminates stitching area

Slide plate   Covers the bobbin and bobbin case in the bed of the machine

Spool pin   Holds spool of thread

Stitch length control   Regulates the length of the stitch

Stitch width control   Regulates the width of zigzag stitching and positions the needle for straight stitching

Take-up lever   Controls the amount of thread pulled from the top spool for each stitch

Tension dial   Regulates the tension of the tension discs on the needle thread

Thread cutter   Located on presser bar for easy cutting of threads

Thread guides   Help guide upper thread from spool to needle without tangling

too easily or without any resistance, you should try once more to pass the thread around the tension discs. The thread should be placed between two of the discs, and then brought up and caught on a hook or spring on the tension discs. Remember to always thread the tension discs before you thread the take-up lever.

The Thread Guides

The location of the last thread guide on your machine tells you in which direction to thread your needle. If the thread guide is on the right, then you thread the needle from the right. If the guide is on the left, then you thread the needle from the left. If the guide is on the front of the needle bar, then the needle is threaded from front to back. Pull out at least 3″ (7.5 mm) of thread from the needle. This will prevent the thread from pulling out of the needle as it is raised and lowered.

Raising the Bobbin Thread

Now that the bobbin and needle have been threaded, bring the bobbin thread up through the needle hole in the needle or throat plate. To do this, hold the needle thread in your left hand. With your right hand, turn the hand wheel slowly until the needle enters the throat plate. Continue turning until the needle rises and brings up a loop of the bobbin thread. Pull up the loop to bring the end of the bobbin thread out. Pull both thread ends under the presser foot and toward the back of the machine so that the threads will not tangle as you start to stitch.

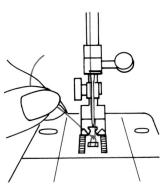

Raising the bobbin thread

ADJUSTING YOUR MACHINE

How does a sewing machine work? As the needle thread intertwines with the bobbin thread, a *lockstitch* is formed. This type of stitch does not pull out or unravel when a loop or loose thread is pulled. Look at the illustration on page 363 to see how an actual stitch is formed.

For each type of fabric that you sew, different adjustments need to be made to achieve the best type of stitch for your fabric. It is important to always pretest your adjustments by stitching on a scrap of the same fabric. Use a double thickness of fabric, just as you will when sewing actual seams.

The adjustments that need to be checked deal with *type and length of stitches, tension,* and *pressure.*

Type and Length of the Stitch

• *Type of Stitch.* Although any garment can be constructed with a straight stitch, some machines offer a zigzag stitch or a variety of other stitches for special purposes. These stitches may be regulated by controls on the machine or by separate cams, or discs, which are inserted into the machine.

• *Length of Stitch.* This varies according to the type of fabric and the purpose of stitching. The numbers on your stitch-length control are based on either the inch or metric measurement. Numbers from 6 to 20 indicate the number of stitches per inch. Numbers from 0 to 4 indicate the length of stitch in millimeters.

• *For regular stitching,* a medium-length stitch, 10 to 12 stitches per inch (2–2.5 mm in length) is recommended for most fabrics. For lighter-weight fabrics, use a shorter stitch. For heavier fabrics, use a longer stitch. For *machine basting,* use the longest stitch possible so it can be easily removed, 6 to 8 stitches per inch (3–4 mm in length). For *reinforcement stitching,* use very short stitches, 15 to 20 stitches per inch (1–1.5 mm in length) to prevent stretching or pulling in certain areas. For further information, (See MACHINE STITCHING, page 392.)

Adjusting Tension

A properly *balanced stitch* has two threads locking in the center between the two layers of fabric. Tension must be adjusted if the stitches are too tight or too loose.

Check your tension by sewing sample stitches on a double layer of fabric. Examine the stitching.

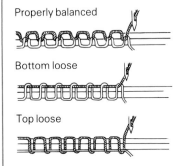

Properly balanced

Bottom loose

Top loose

If the top thread lies flat on the surface of the fabric and loops show on the top, then the top tension is too tight. Turn the tension dial to a lower number.

If the bottom row of stitching is flat along the bottom layer of fabric with loops

How a Stitch Is Formed

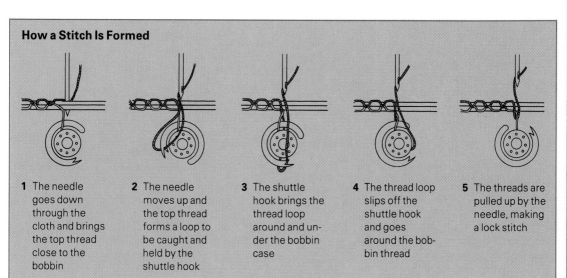

1 The needle goes down through the cloth and brings the top thread close to the bobbin

2 The needle moves up and the top thread forms a loop to be caught and held by the shuttle hook

3 The shuttle hook brings the thread loop around and under the bobbin case

4 The thread loop slips off the shuttle hook and goes around the bobbin thread

5 The threads are pulled up by the needle, making a lock stitch

showing on the surface, then the top tension is too loose. Turn the dial to a higher number.

Keep adjusting and testing until the proper balance is achieved. You can test the tension balance by pulling the fabric until the stitching breaks. If one thread breaks before the other, then the tension on that thread is tighter.

Keep in mind that bobbin tension is set at the factory and should not be adjusted unless absolutely necessary. Refer to your manual for directions.

Adjusting Pressure

For an *evenly stitched seam,* the pressure applied by the presser foot on the fabric should interact with the feed to move the two layers smoothly under the needle. If one layer of fabric feeds faster, the pressure must be adjusted.

The pressure regulator controls how firmly the presser foot holds the fabric against the feed. Some pressure is needed to grip and move the fabric ahead for each stitch. Bulky, thick, or fluffy fabrics require less pressure than flat, smooth, and thin fabrics.

When the pressure is correct, both layers of fabric feed smoothly under the needle. If one layer of fabric feeds faster than the other, the fabric will bubble or ripple. If the pressure is too great, one layer of fabric may be longer than the other layer at the end of the seam. Adjust the pressure regulator according to the directions in your manual.

USING YOUR MACHINE

It takes practice to learn to control the speed of your sewing machine. Use light pressure on the knee or foot control and experiment with slowly increasing and decreasing the speed. Learn how to start slowly, build up speed when stitching a long row of stitching, and then slow down as you approach the end.

Guidelines on Stitching

1. *Before you start to stitch,* raise the take-up lever and needle to the highest position. This will prevent the upper thread from pulling out of the needle when you start stitching. Also be sure that both threads are pulled back behind the presser foot to prevent any tangled stitches.
2. *Place* your fabric under the presser foot with the bulk of the fabric to the left of the needle.
3. *Line up* the stitching line directly under the needle.

4. *To begin stitching,* turn the hand wheel to lower the needle into the fabric. Then lower the presser foot. Gradually apply pressure on the knee or foot control to stitch at a slow, even speed.

5. *When you stop stitching,* turn the hand wheel to raise the take-up lever and needle to the highest point. Raise the presser foot. Gently slide the fabric toward the back of the machine. Do not pull the fabric forward because you could bend the needle. Clip the threads.

Stitching Straight

It also takes practice to learn to guide your fabric as you stitch. Your first rows of stitching may not be perfectly straight. Learn how to use your hands. Keep one hand in front and one hand behind the presser foot to

guide the fabric smoothly. Do not pull or push the fabric. And be careful not to let your fingers get too close to the needle!

Use the guideline markings on the needle or throat plate to help keep the rows of stitching straight. If your plate does not have markings, place a piece of masking tape ⅝″ (1.6 cm) from the needle to act as a guide for regular seams. Line up the edge of your fabric with the ⅝″ (1.6 cm) guideline. Keep your eyes on this marking. Do not watch the needle.

Stitching curves takes more practice. Draw curved lines on fabric scraps and

Correcting Stitching Problems

Problem	Possible Solution	Problem	Possible Solution
Skipped stitches	Check size and type of needle for fabric Replace dull or bent needle Rethread machine Loosen upper thread tension Check needle position		Check thread for knots or unevenness Begin stitching at a slower speed
Bunching of thread	Pull thread ends behind presser foot and hold when starting to stitch Rethread machine	Needle breaks	Stitch carefully over pins Guide fabric, do not pull Check needle position Tighten presser foot Too many layers or thickness of fabric
Puckering	Loosen upper tension Replace dull or bent needle Use same type thread in needle and bobbin Loosen pressure on presser foot Shorten stitch length	Machine jams	Check for loops of matted thread Under stitching Check bobbin for caught thread Check needle position Check machine threading
Thread breaks	Check threading of machine Replace needle Check size of needle	Machine does not sew	Check on/off switch Tighten hand wheel knob Check electrical cord Check knee or foot control

practice stitching until you can do it smoothly. Sometimes you have to stitch around a corner when you sew. For this method, see page 402.

Correcting Stitching Problems

When something goes wrong with the stitch, usually the problem can be corrected by a simple adjustment. Frequently the cause is incorrect threading. If rethreading the machine does not correct the difficulty, check your needle and tension setting. Refer to the chart on page 364 for solutions to specific stitching problems.

SEWING MACHINE ACCESSORIES

A variety of accessories are available for most machines.

- *Straight Stitch Foot.* It has a narrow opening and is used for sewing straight stitches.
- *Zigzag Foot.* It has a wide opening to allow for sideways movement of the needle for zigzag and special stitches, as well as straight stitches.
- *Zipper Foot.* It can be adjusted to the right or left side of the needle for stitching close to zipper teeth or cording.
- *Buttonhole Foot.* It has markings for measuring buttonhole stitches.
- *Blindstitch Hem Foot.* It guides the fabric for a blindstitch hem.

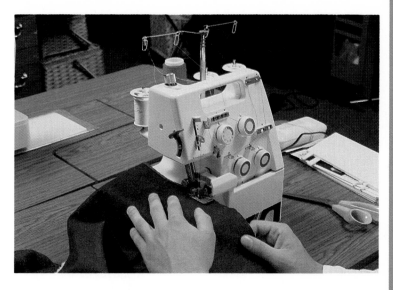

USING A SERGER

Sewing on a serger or overlock machine is a little different than sewing on a conventional sewing machine. Here are a few guidelines:

- *Thread.* Special thread is available on very large spools, called cones. These cones contain 1,000 yards or more of thread and will last a long time.
- *Tension.* To identify which tension dial controls which thread, make some practice seams using different color thread for each needle and looper. Change the dials to see what happens to the stitch.
- *Stitching.* Never sew over pins as they will damage the knives. Instead hold fabric pieces together by placing pins 1″ (2.5 cm) away from the edge. Fabric glue or basting stitches can also be used.

- *Cleaning.* As the knives trim the fabric, the cutting action creates much lint. Use the brush that comes with the serger to keep it clean and free of lint. Canned compressed air, available at fabric, sewing machine, and camera stores, can also be used for cleaning.

CARING FOR YOUR MACHINE

A sewing machine needs routine care so that it is always in top working condition. How often do you need to clean your machine? It depends on how often it is used. Lint from fabric gathers around the bobbin and the needle bar and can eventually clog the machine. Many people clean their machine before starting a new project. In the sewing laboratory, your instructor will give you guidelines.

Cleaning the Machine

1. *Disconnect* the plug.
2. *Use a soft cloth* to remove lint or fuzz from the machine base and needle bar.
3. Open or remove both the slide plate and the needle or throat plate for easy access to the bobbin case.
4. *Use a soft brush* to gently clean the bobbin and the bobbin case. If possible, remove the entire bobbin case mechanism, following directions in your manual.
5. *You may need* to use a wooden toothpick to remove chunks of accumulated lint from around the bobbin case and the feed.
6. *Wipe* away old oil with a cloth.

Oiling the Machine

Before oiling your machine, be sure to consult your manual. Each model has specific areas to be oiled. Follow the manual diagram and place one drop of oil to each location in the head of the machine and also underneath. Use only high-grade sewing machine oil. Wipe the machine carefully with a cloth to remove any excess oil or drips.

After you have oiled the machine, plug it in and stitch on a swatch of fabric for a couple of minutes to be sure all excess oil is removed. Machine oil stains and is very difficult to remove.

CHAPTER 3

Sewing Tools and Supplies

A variety of sewing tools and supplies are needed for any sewing project. These should be kept together in a special box or basket for easy use. Then they will always be easy to locate when you decide to begin a project or make a minor repair.

Sewing tools are *equipment used during the different stages of sewing.* **Sewing supplies** are *items that become a part of your garment or project.* As you know, many of these smaller tools and supplies are called *notions* and can be purchased in the notions department of a fabric store or variety store.

SEWING TOOLS

Good sewing tools help make your sewing easier. You will discover that there is a wide variety of items from which to choose.

Check with your instructor to learn what basic equipment is needed in your class work. Some tools are necessary to have—others are designed for very specialized tasks. These items can be added to your basic equipment as your skills and interest grow. Take good care of your sewing tools, and they will last for many years.

Sewing tools can be divided into six groups according to their use: *measuring, pinning, cutting, marking, stitching,* and *pressing.*

Measuring

Measuring tools are among the most important items in your sewing box. Most new measuring tools will include both standard and metric measurements. The three essential measuring tools are *tape measure, sewing gauge,* and *yardstick or meterstick.*

- *Tape Measure.* A flexible measuring tape 60″ (1.5 m) long to use for taking body measurements; keep neatly rolled in your sewing box. (1)

- *Sewing, or Seam, Gauge.* A 6″ (15 cm) ruler with an adjustable marker to use for measuring short lengths, such as hems and seam widths; set the marker for the width you are measuring. (2)

- *Yardstick or Meterstick.* A 36″ (1 m) rigid measuring tool of wood, metal, or plastic to use for measuring flat surfaces, such as checking grain lines and marking hemlines. (3)

There are also certain specialty measuring items:

- *Transparent Ruler.* Useful for measuring and marking straight lines, such as pleats, tucks, bias strips, and buttonholes. (4)

- *Hem Gauge.* A metal or plastic gauge to mark straight or curved hems. (5)

- *French Curve.* It has one sharply curved side to use

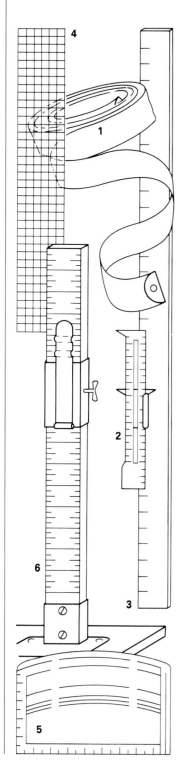

for redrawing curved areas, such as armholes and necklines, when altering patterns.

• *Skirt Marker.* A device used to measure and mark hemlines of garments with either pins or chalk. (6)

Pinning

Pins are necessary for many stages of sewing—from laying out the pattern, to holding two layers of fabric together while stitching, to marking the hemline. Pins should be sharp, slender, and smoothly finished to avoid damaging your fabric. Major pin items are the following:

• *Silk Pins.* These pins are made of stainless steel or brass; they can be used with most fabrics. (1)

• *Ball-Point Pins.* Such pins have rounded points to slip between the yarns and help prevent snagging the fabric; use for knitted fabrics. (1)

• *Ball-Headed Pins.* These pins have colorful round plastic heads to make them easier to see and to pick up. (2)

• *T-Pins.* These pins each have a large T-shaped head for use with loosely woven, bulky, or pile fabrics. (3)

• *Pin Cushions.* These are available in many different styles; some have an elastic or plastic band so they can be worn around your wrist. (4)

Always use a pin cushion to hold your pins as you work. This will prevent the frustration of spilling a whole

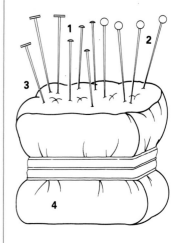

box of pins on the table or floor, and the possibility of swallowing a pin.

Cutting

Cutting tools are used for cutting out your fabric pieces, trimming, clipping, and other detail work. Be sure your sewing scissors and shears are sharp. Dull blades make it very difficult to cut accurately.

Never use your sewing tools to cut paper (other than pattern tissue), string, or other objects. At home, keep a pair of household shears handy for other cutting jobs. To have your shears or scissors sharpened, check with a fabric store or hardware store.

Shears have *long blades, and the two handles are shaped differently.* They are used for cutting out fabric. **Scissors** are *smaller tools, and both handles are the same shape.* They are used for trimming, clipping, and cutting threads.

You will need a pair of shears and a pair of scissors.

• *Dressmaker's Shears.* These have bent handles so that the fabric can lie flat on the table while being cut. This results in better accuracy than lifting up the fabric as you cut. Shears have two differently shaped handles— one fits your thumb and the other handle fits several fingers. Blades are usually 7″ to 8″ (18–20 cm) long. Left-handed shears are also available. Quality shears have an adjustable screw so you can adjust the cutting action of the blades. (1)

• *Sewing Scissors.* These have small round handles and shorter blades 4″ to 6″ (10–15 cm) long. The blades are different widths. Sewing scissors are easier to handle than shears for detail and precision work. Use scissors to trim seams, clip curves, and cut into corners. (2)

There are also certain specialty items:

• *Pinking, or Scalloping, Shears.* They are used to finish a seam edge or other raw edge on firmly woven fabrics. The zigzag or scallop design helps to prevent raveling. Do not use pinking or scalloping shears to cut out fabric pieces because the uneven edge is difficult to follow when stitching. Instead, pink or scallop the seam edges after the seams are stitched. (3)

• *Embroidery Scissors.* These are small scissors, only 3″ to 4″ (7.5–10 cm) long, with very pointed blades. Use embroidery scissors for detail work such as cutting buttonholes and ripping stitches. (4)

• *Seam Ripper.* This is a pen-shaped gadget with a small blade at one end for removing stitches. Use the blade to lift the thread away from the fabric before cutting. Be careful not to cut the fabric. (5)

• *Thread Clipper.* This has spring-action blades to clip thread ends or stitching. (6)

Cutting Tools

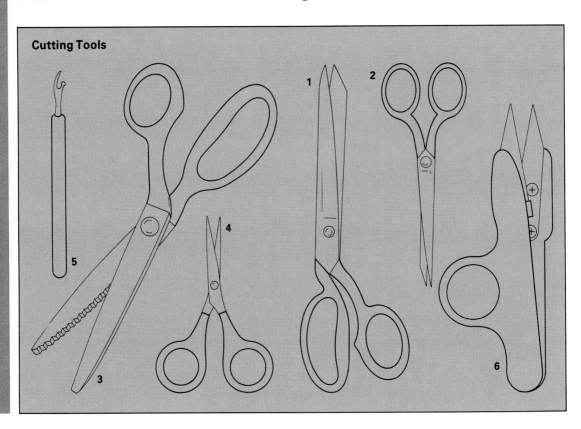

Marking

Marking tools are needed to transfer symbols and lines from the pattern pieces to the fabric. Accurate markings help make construction easier. The type of marking equipment you use depends on the type of fabric you are marking. Your sewing box should contain a *tracing wheel, tracing paper,* and *tailor's chalk.*

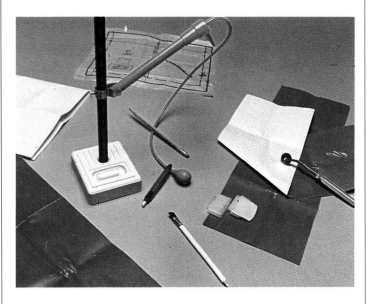

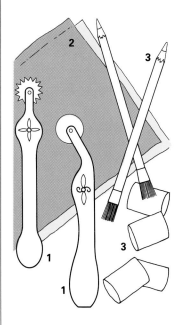

- *Tracing Wheel.* Use by running the wheel over tracing paper to transfer markings to your fabric. A sawtoothed wheel can be used for most fabrics. A smooth-edge wheel is recommended for delicate fabrics. (1)
- *Dressmaker's Tracing Paper.* This item is a special waxed carbon paper to be used with a tracing wheel. It is available in several colors.

Choose a color that is similar to the color of your fabric, but one that will still show. The tracing marks can be removed by washing or dry cleaning the fabric. (2)

- *Tailor's Chalk.* This chalk is available in small squares or in pencil form to mark fabrics. The markings can be brushed away or will disappear when pressed with an iron. (3)
- *Ordinary Thread.* It can be used to make tailor's tacks (see page 391), or thread tracings of construction lines and grain lines, on your fabric.

Stitching

Although most projects can be made almost entirely by machine stitching, some hand sewing is usually needed to complete the project. All sewing boxes need a variety of needles and at least one thimble.

- *Needles.* They are available in a variety of sizes and types. Sizes range from 1 (coarse) to 12 (fine). The smaller the number, the larger and coarser the needle. For most *hand-sewing tasks,* use a size 7 or 8 needle. For *delicate fabrics,* use a finer needle. For *heavy fabrics,* use a coarser needle.

All needles should have sharp points and smooth eyes to avoid snagging the fabric or splitting the thread. Some packages contain only one size of needles, while others contain a variety.

Different types of needles depend upon the length of the needle and the shape of the eye. *Sharps* are all-purpose, medium-length needles with a small eye and sharp point. *Embroidery* and *crewel needles* have larger eyes and thus are easier to thread. *Specialty needles* are available for heavy-duty fabrics and crafts.

Stitching Tools

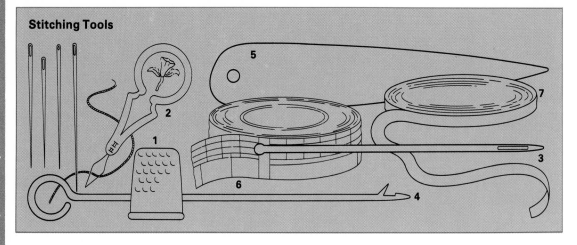

• *Thimble.* This covering will help protect your finger when sewing by hand. Made of metal or plastic, a thimble has small indentations, which help hold the end of the needle as you push it through the fabric. Wear a thimble on the second, or middle, finger of your sewing hand. Thimbles are available in different sizes. Be sure to select one that fits comfortably. (1)

When you first try wearing a thimble, it will probably feel awkward on your finger. Try wetting the end of your finger before you put on the thimble. The suction will hold the thimble firmly in place as you learn how to use the end or side to push the needle through the fabric. There are a number of specialty items available for stitching:

• *Needle Threader.* This is a small device with a thin metal wire that helps you thread a needle. (2)

• *Bodkin.* This gadget resembles a large, blunt needle and is used to pull cord, elastic, tape, or ribbon through casings. (3)

• *Loop Turner.* This tool is a long metal rod with a hook at one end used to turn bias tubing right side out. (4)

• *Pointer.* This is a wooden tool, with one pointed end for pushing out sharp corners, and a rounded end for holding seams open for pressing. (5)

• *Sewing Tape.* This tape has measured markings to use as a stitching guide. (6)

• *Basting Tape.* This tape is a narrow, double-faced tape used to hold two layers of fabric together or a zipper in place for stitching. (7)

Special Sewing Items

Here are some special notions for faster and easier sewing:

• *Disappearing basting thread* dissolves in the wash or when you iron over it with a damp press cloth.

• *Fabric marking pens* have disappearing ink so you can mark on the right side of your fabric. One type has blue ink which disappears when the marks are treated with plain water. Another type has purple ink which evaporates from the fabric.

• *Liquid seam sealant* is a colorless liquid which can be applied to fabric or ribbon to prevent the cut edges from fraying.

• *Magnetic pin cushions* hold pins securely even when tipped over. One type is shaped like a shallow bowl and can be turned upside down to pick up pins off a table. Another type has adhesive backing and can be attached to your sewing machine.

Pressing

Pressing equipment helps to give a professional finish to a garment. It is very important to always press as you sew. Three essential items needed are an *iron, ironing board,* and *press cloth.*

- *Iron.* A combination steam-dry iron gives best results. It should have a wide temperature range to use with all fabrics. Handle an iron carefully. If you drop it, the thermostat control that regulates the temperature can be damaged. Avoid ironing over pins since they can scratch the *soleplate,* or bottom, of an iron. Also, take care when using fusible interfacings or fusible webs so that the adhesive does not touch the iron. Irons should be stored empty of water. (1)

- *Ironing Board.* Select a level, sturdy board with a tight-fitting durable cover and smooth padding. A silicone-treated cover helps to prevent scorching and sticking.

- *Press Cloth.* Use this cloth to protect certain fabrics from developing a *shine,* or glossy marking, and from scorching. A press cloth can be dampened to create steam for special pressing techniques. Many different types of cloths are available. You can also use a clean cloth or handkerchief. (2)

There are a number of useful specialty items for pressing:

- *Tailor's Ham.* This tool is a firm, round cushion used to press curved areas of a garment, such as darts and curved seams. (3)

- *Sleeve Board.* This item is a small ironing board about 20″ (.5 m) long used to press narrow areas, such as sleeves, which cannot fit over the end of a regular ironing board. (4)

- *Press Mitt.* This item is a small tailor's ham that fits over your hand or sleeve board to press hard-to-reach areas.

- *Seam Roll.* This item is a long, firm tubular cushion used to press long seams and small curved areas. A seamline can be pressed without having the imprint of the seam allowances showing through on the right side of the fabric. (5)

- *Point Presser.* This has a narrow wooden surface with a pointed end used to press collar points. Other edges can be used for pressing curves and straight edges. (6)

- *Pounding Block* or *Clapper.* This item is a block of wood used to flatten seam edges in tailoring. (7)

Pressing Tools

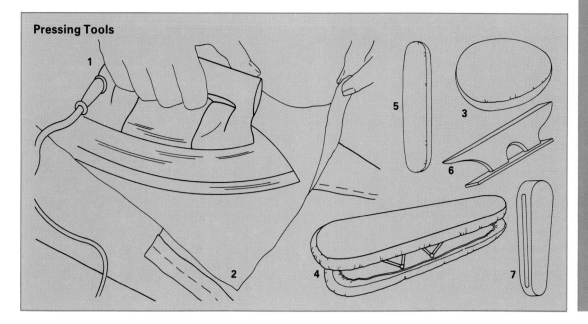

SEWING SUPPLIES

Many different items—such as thread, fasteners, interfacing, and trims—may go into a garment during construction. These items become a permanent part of the garment. The sewing supplies that you will need for a project are listed on the back of your pattern envelope.

Thread

Thread is available in a wide assortment of types and colors. A good quality thread is strong and smooth, has even thickness, and resists tangling. The type of thread you select is determined by the type of fabric you are sewing.

Thread is made from different fibers and also in different sizes or thicknesses. You should choose thread that is similar to your fabric. Try to match the fiber content so that the stretchability and shrinkage of the fabric and thread will be similar. Also try to match the fineness of the thread to the fineness of the fabric. An assortment of threads is recommended for your sewing box.

• *Polyester or Polyester/Cotton.* This thread is an allpurpose one that can be used for sewing almost all fabrics. It is strong, flexible, and has less shrinkage than other threads. It is recommended for knits and stretch fabrics because the thread has some "give" or stretchability. This

helps to prevent the seams from breaking as the garment is worn.

• *Mercerized Cotton.* This thread can be used to sew natural fiber woven fabrics such as 100% cotton or silk.

• *Silk.* Such thread can be used on silk or wool fabrics; excellent for basting delicate fabrics.

• *Heavy-Duty.* This thread is used to sew heavier fabrics and projects, such as slipcovers, that require strength and durability.

• *Buttonhole Twist.* This thread is thicker than the others, and is used for decorative top stitching and handworked buttonholes.

Special threads are available for specific sewing and crafts projects, such as *basting thread, quilting thread,* and *carpet thread.* See the THREAD CHART on page 358.

Try to match the color of thread as closely as possible to the color of your fabric. If in doubt between two shades of color, choose the darker thread. A single strand of thread will appear slightly lighter in color than it does when wound on the spool. When matching a print or a plaid, select the background or dominant color for your thread.

Fasteners

Fasteners are any items used to close a garment. They include *zippers, buttons, snaps, hooks and eyes, buckles,* and *hook and loop tape.*

- *Zippers.* These fasteners are available in a wide variety of colors, lengths, and types.

  Several types of specialty zippers are also available. These include:

  1. A *separating zipper* opens at the bottom for use on jackets, parkas, and vests.
  2. A *two-way zipper* has sliders at the top and bottom so that it can be opened from either end.
  3. A *trouser zipper* usually has metal teeth and wider tape.
  4. A *decorative zipper* has large teeth and a pull ring.

- *Buttons.* There are two basic types of buttons, *sew-through* and *shank.*

  1. A *sew-through button* has two to four holes on the face of the button for attaching with thread.
  2. A *shank button* has a metal, plastic, or fabric loop behind the button through which thread is stitched. A shank allows room for the buttonhole to lie smoothly between the button and fabric to which it is stitched.

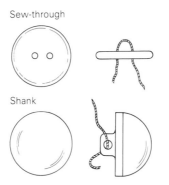

Sew-through

Shank

The size of a button is the measurement of its diameter. The recommended size and number of buttons are listed on the back of the pattern envelope. Kits are also available for covering your own fabric buttons.

- *Snaps.* These fasteners range in size from 0000 or 4/0 (small) to size 4 (large). The smaller sizes are the most useful; larger sizes are good for heavy-duty use. Large covered snaps are available for coats and suits. Snaps preattached to fabric tapes are ideal for sportswear and children's wear.

- *Hooks and Eyes.* These items are packaged with two types of eyes—*curved* and *straight.* A *curved eye* is used on edges that just meet such as the edge of a collar or neckline. A *straight eye* is used on lapped edges such as a waistband. Hooks and eyes range in size from 0 (small) to 3 (large). Larger covered hooks and eyes are available for coats and jackets. Specialty waistband fasteners with a large flat hook and bar closure are designed for use on skirts and pants.

- *Buckles.* These features are available in a wide variety of shapes, sizes, and materials. However, there are only two types of buckles: *buckles with prongs* and *buckles without prongs.* For a *buckle with a prong,* eyelets must be used. Ready-made metal eyelets can be applied with special pliers or attaching

Zippers

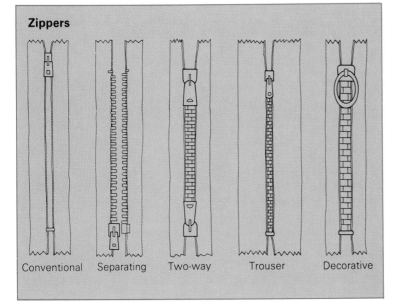

Conventional   Separating   Two-way   Trouser   Decorative

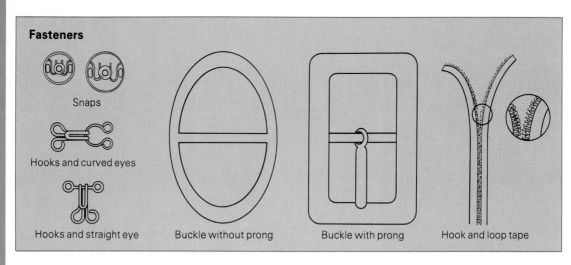

Fasteners

Snaps

Hooks and curved eyes

Hooks and straight eye

Buckle without prong

Buckle with prong

Hook and loop tape

tool, or eyelets can be hand sewn using a buttonhole stitch. Buckles can be purchased separately or in kits.

- *Hook and Loop Tape.* This fastener consists of two nylon strips, one with tiny hooks and one with looped pile. The hooks and pile intermesh when pressed together. Such tape is often used on parkas and sportswear. Available by the yard or in precut shapes, it can be stitched by hand or machine.

Tapes and Trims

Tapes and trims can be functional or decorative. They can be used to reinforce a seam, cover a fabric edge, or create a special design on the outside of a garment. Tapes and trims are available in a variety of types, widths, and colors. Some are stretchable; others are not. They may be woven, knitted, braided, or made of lace.

The choice of which type of tape or trim to use depends upon how it will be used in your garment. For areas where you want to prevent stretching, select a firm, nonstretchable tape or trim. For areas that should stretch during wear, such as a hemline, choose a stretchable tape or trim.

Some of the common tapes and trims are:

- *Seam Tape.* Woven tape or lace used to finish hem and facing edges.
- *Bias Tape.* Single or double-fold tape used for binding curved or straight edges, and for casings, ties, and trims.
- *Hem Facing.* Wide bias tape or lace used for facing hems and binding edges.
- *Twill Tape.* Firmly woven tape used for reinforcing seams.
- *Grosgrain Ribbon.* Firmly woven ribbon used for facing waistbands and belts, and for trims.
- *Foldover Braid.* Knitted braid folded in half used for binding and trimming edges.

- *Piping.* A narrow, corded bias strip of fabric that is inserted into a seam for a decorative trim.
- *Cable Cord.* Cord used as a filler for piping, cording, and tubing.
- *Ribbing.* A stretchable knitted band used to finish a neckline, armhole, sleeve, pants leg, or waistline.
- *Belting.* A very stiff band used to reinforce belts and waistbands.

Elastics

Elastic is available in several different types and widths. The type of elastic to choose will depend on whether it will be used in a casing or stitched directly to a garment.

- *Braided Elastic.* This is recommended only for casings because it narrows when stretched.
- *Woven Elastic.* It stays the same width when stretched. Thus it can be stitched directly to a garment or used in a casing.

Tapes and Trims

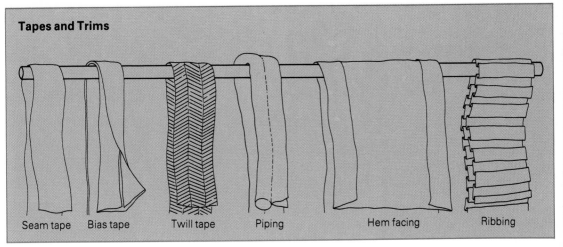

Seam tape   Bias tape   Twill tape   Piping   Hem facing   Ribbing

- *Elastic Thread.* This is a very thin covered elastic core used for shirring.
- *Special Purpose Elastics.* These are available for pajamas, lingerie, and swimwear.

Woven   Braided

Read the label when purchasing any type of elastic to be sure that it will serve the correct purpose.

Interfacings and Linings

Interfacings and linings are fabrics used on the inside of a garment. They are added to prevent stretching, give more shaping, reduce wrinkling, or finish off the inside of a garment. Both interfacing and lining fabrics must be able to receive the same care as the outer fabric.

- *Interfacings.* A piece of fabric placed between the outer fabric and facing. It is used to prevent stretching of necklines, front closings, and buttonholes. It can shape collars, cuffs, pockets, and hems. It adds crispness and stability to waistbands and belts.

Interfacings are available in a variety of types and weights. The two types of interfacings are determined by the method of application. *Sew-in interfacings* must be stitched by hand or machine to the garment. *Fusible interfacings* have a resin coating on the back and will fuse to fabric when pressed with an iron. Either type may be woven or nonwoven.

When selecting the proper weight of interfacing, consider the weight of your outer fabric and where the interfacing will be used. For most garments, choose an interfacing the same weight or lighter than your fabric. Heavyweight interfacings are recommended only for accessories and crafts.

To help you check the final effect, drape the fabric and interfacing together to see how they look and feel. Remember that fusible interfacings may be slightly crisper after fusing.

- *Linings.* Linings have two types: *lining* and *underlining.*

1. *Lining* is used to finish the inside of a jacket, coat, skirt, or pants. A lining also helps to prevent stretching and to reduce wrinkling. Many different types of fabrics are labeled as "linings." Select one that is firmly woven, slippery, and static-free.

    Linings are constructed separately from the garment and

then inserted into the garment. For skirts and pants, a lining is attached along the waistband and zipper. For coats, jackets, and vests, a lining is stitched around the facing edges. Lining hems can be sewn to the garment hem or hemmed separately.

2. *Underlining* is a lining fabric that is stitched into the garment seams and handled as one layer with the outer fabric. It is used to support and reinforce the fabric. It can also be used with sheer fabrics for opaqueness.

Fusibles

Fusibles are a new category of sewing supplies. They are a web of fusible fibers used to hold two layers of fabric together. When heat and/or steam is applied, the web melts and fuses the fabric layers together.

Fusibles can be used to hem, apply trims, hold facing edges in place, and mend fabrics. They are sold by the yard as narrow strips or wide fabric.

Before using a fusible for the first time, be sure to read the instructions carefully. Then test the application on a piece of scrap fabric before applying it.

Patterns

A **pattern** is just like a blueprint. It is *a project that contains all the instructions you will need for constructing your sewing project.* Every pattern consists of an *envelope,* a *guide sheet,* and *tissue pattern pieces.*

The *envelope* has a wealth of information about the design of the garment, fabric, and notions needed. The *guide sheet* gives you step-by-step instructions for cutting and sewing. The *tissue pattern pieces* contain many symbols to aid in construction.

Always take the time to completely read all parts of the pattern before beginning your project. Each item contains valuable information to help make your sewing easier and more successful.

PATTERN ENVELOPE

The pattern envelope contains important information on its front and back. Read both carefully.

Envelope Front

On the front of the envelope, you will find a drawing or photograph of the fashion design. Several different views may be shown to give you a wider selection of styles. Each view will show the garment made up in a fabric suitable for that style. Thus, if corduroy or a plaid fabric is

shown, you know that these fabrics can be used. From the drawing or photograph, you will be able to see how the garment fits—whether it is slim or full on the body. Additional information about fit is also stated on the back of the pattern envelope. The drawing will also show all the seams, darts, and design details.

The envelope will list the pattern number, figure type, size, and price. Sometimes a label will indicate that the pattern is Easy or For Beginners. Special features of the pattern—such as a designer fashion, a sewing lesson, or a crafts project—may be mentioned on the envelope.

Envelope Back

The back of the pattern envelope gives you more information per square inch than any other part of the pattern. You will find all the necessary information for buying the fabric, notions, and sewing supplies needed for your project.

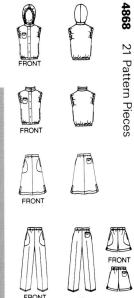

MISSES' VEST, SKIRT, PANTS & SHORTS

Very loose-fitting unlined vest has collar with concealed zipper for attached hood, front snap or buttoned closing, extended shoulders, elasticized armhole and lower edge. A-line skirt 2" (5cm) below mid-knee, pants and shorts have elastic waistline. All have side pockets and pockets with flaps. Skirt and shorts: hem slits. Purchased tops. **NOTIONS:** Heavy Duty Hammer On Snaps or Buttons; Five ½" (13mm) and Three ⅜" (10mm) for Vest, One ⅜" (10mm) for Skirt, Pants or Shorts. **Vest:** Three Packages of ¼" (6mm) Bias Tape doublefold and 2⅜ yds. (2.20m) of ¾" (20mm) Elastic. **Hood:** 12" (30cm) Zipper and ⅝ yd. (0.60m) of ¼" (6mm) Elastic. **Skirt, Pants or Shorts:** 1 yd. (1.00m) of ¾" (20mm) Elastic. **FABRICS:** Broadcloth, Chino, Poplin, Ltwt. Denim, Kettlecloth, Ltwt. Twill and Pinwale Corduroy. Ciré for Vest Hood and Pockets. Obv. diag. - unsuitable. One-way designs - use nap fab. and layouts. Allow extra fab. to match plaids or stripes.   *with nap, shading, pile or 1-way design. **w/o nap, shading, pile or with 2-way design. **Finished lengths will be found above cutting layouts.**

BUST	31½	32½	34	36	38
SIZE	**8**	**10**	**12**	**14**	**16**
VEST					
35" */**	2⅛	2⅛	2⅛	2⅜	2⅜
44/45" */**	1⅝	1⅝	1⅝	1⅝	1¾
60" */**	1⅜	1⅜	1½	1½	1½
CONTRAST (Hood and Pockets)					
44/45" Ciré	½	½	½	½	⅝
INTERFACING					
18, 22" Fusible	⅞	⅞	⅞	⅞	⅞
36, 45"	⅜	⅜	⅜	⅜	⅜
SKIRT					
35, 44/45" */**	1¾	1¾	1¾	1¾	1¾
60" */**	1¼	1¼	1¼	1¼	1¼
PANTS					
35, 44/45" */**	2½	2½	2½	2½	2½
60" */**	1½	1½	1½	1⅝	1¾
SHORTS					
35" */**	1⅛	1¼	1¼	1½	1½
44/45" */**	1⅛	1¼	1¼	1¼	1¼
60" */**	⅞	⅞	1	1	1
Width at lower edge					
Skirt	50	51	52½	54½	56½
Pants (each leg)	15¾	16¼	17	18	19
Shorts (each leg)	25½	26	26¾	27¾	28¾

BUST	80	83	87	92	97
SIZE	**8**	**10**	**12**	**14**	**16**
VEST					
90cm */**	2.00	2.00	2.00	2.20	2.20
115cm */**	1.50	1.50	1.50	1.50	1.60
150cm */**	1.30	1.30	1.40	1.40	1.40
CONTRAST (Hood and Pockets)					
115cm Ciré	0.50	0.50	0.50	0.50	0.60
INTERFACING					
46, 56cm Fusible	0.80	0.80	0.80	0.80	0.80
90, 115cm	0.40	0.40	0.40	0.40	0.40
SKIRT					
90, 115cm */**	1.60	1.60	1.60	1.60	1.60
150cm */**	1.20	1.20	1.20	1.20	1.20
PANTS					
90, 115cm */**	2.30	2.30	2.30	2.30	2.30
150cm */**	1.40	1.40	1.40	1.50	1.60
SHORTS					
90cm */**	1.10	1.20	1.20	1.40	1.40
115cm */**	1.10	1.20	1.20	1.20	1.20
150cm */**	0.80	0.80	1.00	1.00	1.00
Width at lower edge					
Skirt	127	130	133	138	143
Pants (each leg)	40	41	43	46	48
Shorts (each leg)	65	66	68	70.5	73

BUTTERICK PATTERN SERVICES, NEW YORK, NEW YORK

- *Description.* Mentions the silhouette or fit of the garment, the design features of various parts of the garment, and any special construction details that cannot be shown in the sketch.

- *Number of Pattern Pieces.* Usually the fewer the number of pattern pieces, the easier it will be to make the garment.

- *Views.* Shows the design lines and construction details of all the views.

- *Body Measurements.* Lists measurements for all sizes for which the pattern is designed. Use these measurements to compare with your own body measurements for size selection and pattern adjustments. The actual pattern pieces will measure larger to allow for movement and comfort.

- *Yardage Chart.* Lists the amount of fabric needed for different views, sizes, and fabric widths. The terms "with nap" or "without nap" appear after each fabric width. "With nap" refers to fabric with nap, pile, or a one-way design. This means that all pattern pieces must be turned in one direction on the fabric. These layouts sometimes require more fabric than cutting "without nap" layouts. Yardages for any lining, interfacing, or trims may also be listed on this chart.

- *Garment Measurements.* Includes the circumference of the hemline at the lower edge and the finished back length or side length. Use these measurements for making pattern adjustments.

- *Suggested Fabrics.* Recommends types of fabrics that could be used for this style of garment. Special fabric information will tell you if extra fabric is needed for matching plaids and stripes or if stretch fabric must be used. It will also note if the pattern is not suitable for stripes, plaids, or diagonal fabrics.

- *Notions.* Lists the quantity and recommended sizes of additional sewing supplies such as thread, buttons, tapes, and zippers.

- *Pattern Company.* Includes the name and address in case you want to write for more information.

Guide Sheet

The guide sheet gives you step-by-step information for cutting, marking, and sewing the fabric pieces together. General information and cutting layouts are printed on the front side of the guide sheet. Sewing directions are printed on the reverse side and may extend to two or more pages.

General Information The front side will include line drawings of front and back views. A diagram of all the pattern pieces will make it easier for you to recognize and sort the various pieces. Information about how to lengthen and shorten pattern pieces and how to fold your fabric for layouts is included.

Useful tips are given for preparing fabric, cutting, and marking. The most important symbols on the pattern pieces are illustrated and explained. A fabric key shows how shading is used to indicate fabric layers and the printed or reverse side of pattern pieces.

Cutting Layouts The diagrams show you how to arrange the different size pattern pieces on various widths of fabric. Select the diagram that matches your own combination of design view, pattern size, fabric width, and with or without nap layout. Circle this cutting layout for easy reference.

Read any special notes or instructions before you begin to cut. A separate cutting layout may be included for interfacing or lining.

Sewing Directions Step-by-step sewing directions appear on the reverse side of the guide sheet. For patterns with several garments or views, the directions may continue on another sheet. A fabric key will show how shading and texture is used to indicate the right and wrong side of fabric and any interfacing or lining. Some construction details may be enlarged to clearly show the specific sewing procedure.

Always keep your sewing guide handy so you can refer to it throughout construction. Complete each direction. Then go on to the next.

PATTERN PIECES

The various lines and symbols on the pattern pieces serve as guides during cutting and sewing. Learn to recognize and understand these symbols. In addition, each pattern piece is marked with the pattern brand name, pattern number, figure type, and size. A number or letter and a specific name, such as collar or sleeve, will identify each piece. The number of fabric pieces to be cut will also be printed on the pattern piece. Some pattern pieces will have many markings and symbols; others will have only a few.

PATTERN PREPARATION

Follow these simple steps:

1. *Remove* the entire pattern from the envelope.
2. On the guide sheet, *circle* the layout diagram that you will be using.
3. *Select* the pattern pieces that are needed for the particular view you are sewing.
4. *Fold* the rest of the pattern pieces and put them back into the envelope.
5. *Cut apart* any pattern pieces that are printed on one large piece of tissue paper. Do not trim away the extra tissue paper from around the pieces. This will be cut off as you cut out the fabric.
6. *Write* your name on all the pattern pieces, guide sheet, and pattern envelope.
7. *Smooth out* the pattern pieces. Press with a cool dry iron, if necessary. Wrinkled pattern pieces make it very difficult to cut fabric accurately. Always handle the pattern pieces carefully so that they do not tear.

BUTTERICK 4868

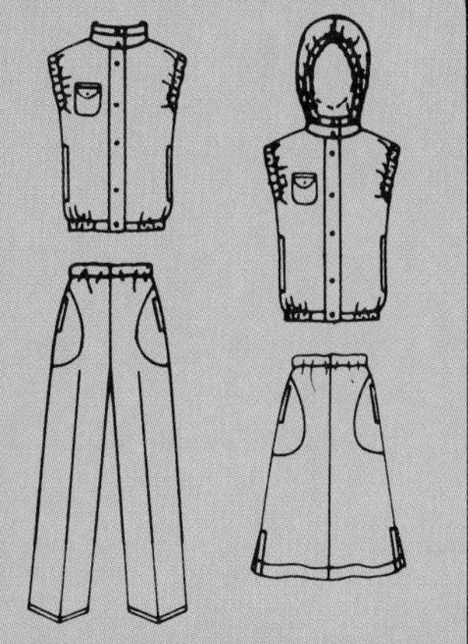

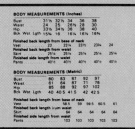

Pants

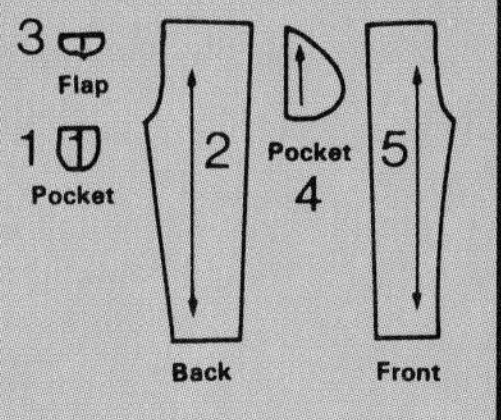
3 Flap
1 Pocket
2
Back
Pocket 4
5
Front

Skirt

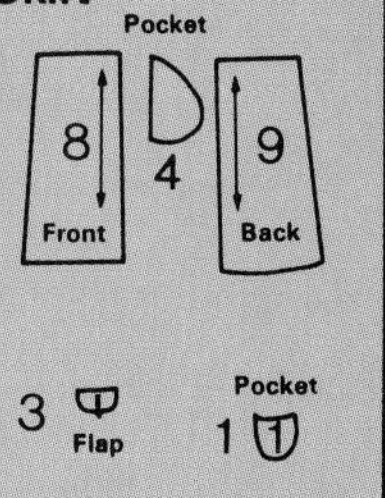
Pocket
8
Front
4
9
Back
3 Flap
Pocket
1

Vest

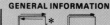

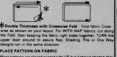

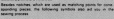

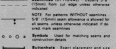

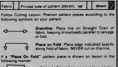

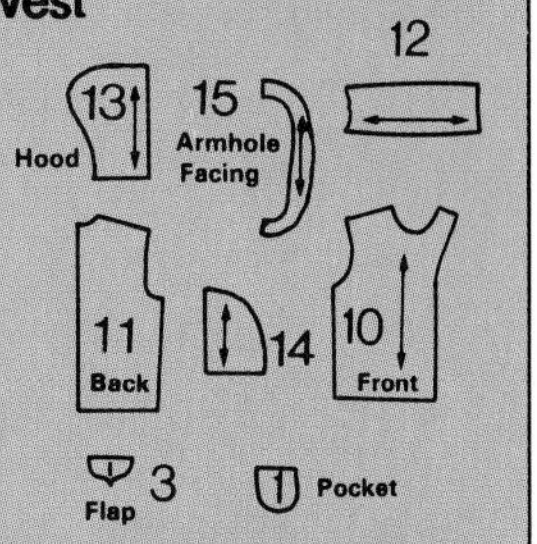
13
Hood
15
Armhole
Facing
12
11
Back
14
10
Front
3
Flap
Pocket

BODY MEASUREMENTS (Inches)

Bust	31½	32½	34	36	38
Waist	24	25	26½	28	30
Hip	33½	34½	36	38	40
Bck Wst Lgth	15¾	16	16¼	16½	16¾
Finished back length from base of neck					
Vest	23	23¼	23½	23¾	24
Finished back length from waist					
Skirt	25¼	25¼	25¼	25¼	25¼
Finished side length from waist					
Pants	40½	40½	40½	40½	40½

BODY MEASUREMENTS (Metric)

Bust	80	83	87	92	97
Waist	61	64	67	71	76
Hip	85	88	92	97	102
Bck Wst Lgth	40	40 5	41 5	42	42 5
Finished back length from base of neck					
Vest	58.5	59	59.5	60.5	61
Finished back length from waist					
Skirt	64	64	64	64	64
Finished side length from waist					
Pants	103	103	103	103	103

GENERAL INFORMATION

PREPARE PATTERN

Select pattern pieces needed

Compare your measurements with the pattern measurements for your size printed on the back of the envelope Increase or decrease size of pattern if necessary.

Lengthen or shorten pattern at adjustment lines or where indicated on pattern

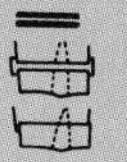

Adjustment lines

To Lengthen - Slash between Adjustment Lines. Place on paper - spread amount needed.

To Shorten - Crease along Adjustment Line. Make a fold half the amount needed.

PREPARE FABRIC

Pre-shrink fabric if necessary. Press.

FIND CUTTING LAYOUT

Find layout(s) needed by Garment or View Chosen, Fabric Width and your Size. For WITH NAP fabric use WITH NAP layout.

POSITION FABRIC

Position fabric as indicated on layout. If layout shows

...**Single Thickness** - Place fabric right side up

...**Double Thickness** - Fold with right sides together

...**Combination of Single and Double Thickness** - Arrange fabric as shown in layout, allowing enough fabric for each portion before cutting

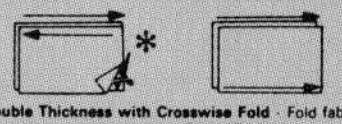

* **Double Thickness with Crosswise Fold** - Fold fabric Crosswise as shown on your layout. For WITH NAP fabrics, cut along the Fold, then keeping the fabric right sides together, TURN the upper layer around to assure Nap, Shading, Pile or One Way designs run in the same direction

PLACE PATTERN ON FABRIC

Most patterns are placed printed side UP, but if shown shaded, they are to be placed printed side DOWN.

CUTTING LAYOUTS SHADING KEY

Fabric		Printed side of pattern placed: up		down	▨

Follow Cutting Layout. Position pattern pieces according to the following symbols on your pattern.

Grainline: Place line on Straight Grain of fabric, keeping arrowheads parallel to selvage or fold.

Place on Fold: Place edge indicated exactly along Fold of fabric. NEVER cut on this line.

If a **"Place On Fold"** pattern piece is shown on layout in the following manner

...first cut other pattern pieces in layout (allowing fabric where piece is shown), then fold fabric and cut piece on the fold.

*open fabric Right Side Up, cut ONE on a single layer of fabric.

CUT PATTERN PIECES

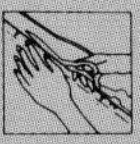

Cut all pieces along the cutting line (heavy black outline), cutting all notches (▾ shaped symbols) outward, or if desired, snip center of notch, through edge of pattern and fabric

Keep pattern attached to fabric until all sewing symbols and markings are transferred to the fabric

MARK SEWING SYMBOLS

Besides notches, which are used as matching points for corresponding pieces, the following symbols also aid you in the sewing process

Seamlines (OPTIONAL) - Usually 5/8" (15mm) from cut edge unless otherwise indicated

NOTE: For patterns WITHOUT seamlines - 5/8" (15mm) seam allowance is allowed for all seams, unless otherwise indicated. If desired, mark seamlines

Symbols - Used for matching seams and construction details

Buttonhole - Exact placement and size needed

Button Placement - Indicates button placement

All other lines, such as Centers, Foldlines, Placement Lines, Stitching Lines are clearly identified on pattern

Transfer all Sewing Symbols to Fabric before removing pattern. Markings needed on right side of fabric should be Thread Traced

FABRIC CUTTING LAYOUTS

NOTE: All fabric layouts are for with or without nap fabric unless otherwise specified.

Pants USE PIECES: 1,2,3,4 and 5

35" (90 cm)
44/45" (115 cm)
ALL SIZES

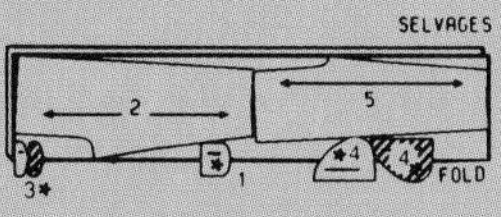
SELVAGES
2
5
4
3
1
FOLD

60" (150cm)
FOR SIZES
8-10-12-14

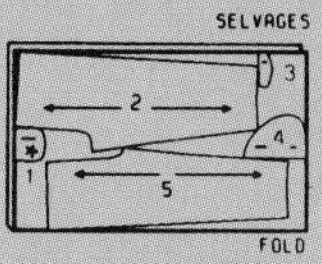
SELVAGES
2
3
4
1
5
FOLD

60" (150cm)
FOR SIZE 16

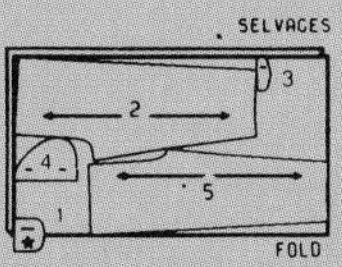
SELVAGES
2
3
4
5
1
FOLD

Skirt USE PIECES: 1,3,4,8 and 9

35" (90 cm)
44/45" (115 cm)
ALL SIZES

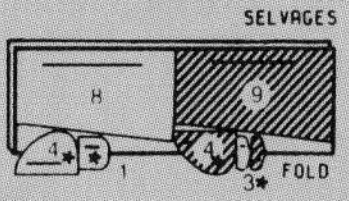
SELVAGES
8
9
4
1
3
FOLD

Continued

60" (150cm)
ALL SIZES

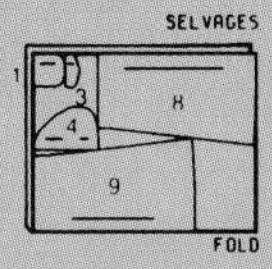
SELVAGES
1
3
8
4
9
FOLD

Vest USE PIECES: 1,3,10,11,12,14 and 15

35" (90 cm)
FOR SIZES
8-10-12

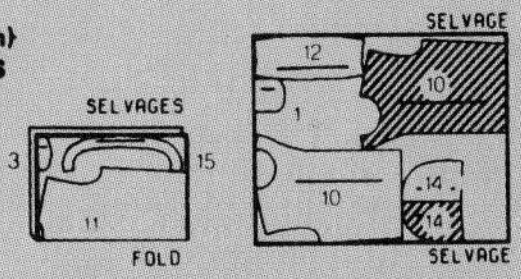
SELVAGES
3
15
11
FOLD
SELVAGE
12
10
1
10
14
SELVAGE

35" (90 cm)
FOR SIZES
14-16

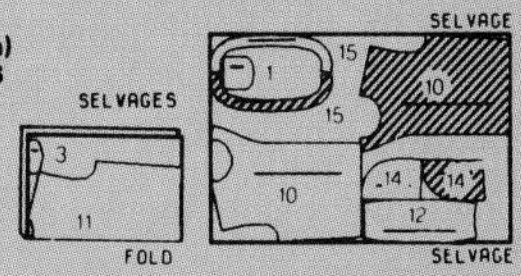
SELVAGES
3
11
FOLD
SELVAGE
15
10
15
10
14
14
12
SELVAGE

44/45" (115 cm)
ALL SIZES

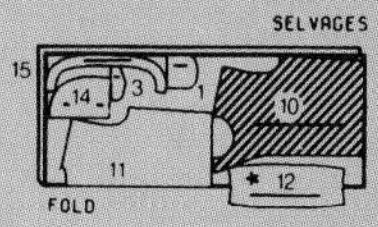
SELVAGES
15
14
3
10
11
12
FOLD

Continued

60" (150cm)
ALL SIZES

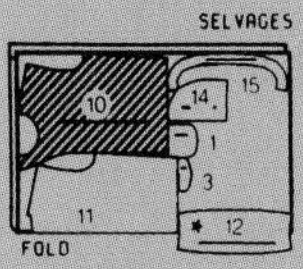
SELVAGES
10
14
15
1
3
11
12
FOLD

Interfacing USE PIECE: 10

18", 22" (45, 56 cm)
ALL SIZES

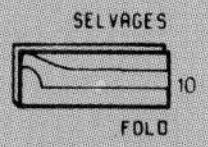
SELVAGES
10
FOLD

36", 45" (90, 115 cm)
ALL SIZES

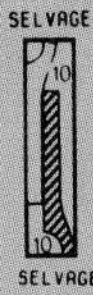
SELVAGE
10
10
SELVAGE

Contrast USE PIECES: 13 and 14

44/45" (115 cm)
CIRÉ
ALL SIZES

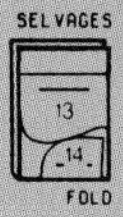
SELVAGES
13
14
FOLD

Major Marking Symbols

Dots, squares, and triangles

Stitching line, or seamline

Dart

Placement line

Fold line

Buttonholes

Grain line

Cutting line

Notches

Adjustment line

Hemline

Center front and center back

- *Grain Line.* A heavy solid line with arrows at both ends. It appears on all pattern pieces not cut on a fold. When placing pattern pieces on your fabric, the grain line arrow must run exactly parallel to the selvage unless otherwise noted.

- *Cutting Line.* A heavy line that outlines the pattern pieces. Sometimes a symbol of scissors is printed on the line to tell you the proper direction for cutting. Occasionally, a cutting line is within the pattern. This is used to indicate a shorter hemline, a lower neckline, or a lining cut from the same pattern piece. Such a cutoff line will always be labeled.

- *Stitching Line, or Seamline.* This line is indicated by a broken line. It is usually ⅝" (1.6 cm) inside the cutting line. Sometimes it is marked by the symbol of a sewing machine presser foot. Others have arrows showing in which direction to stitch to prevent stretching fabric.

- *Notches.* Diamond-shaped symbols that extend beyond the cutting line. They are used for matching seams and joining garment pieces. Always cut around them so that they are clearly marked. When two or more notches are grouped together, cut them as one large block.

- *Dots, Squares, and Triangles.* These are used to help match and join garment sections, especially in areas that are gathered or eased.

- *Dart.* Darts are indicated by dots and two broken lines for stitching.

- *Fold Line.* A solid line showing where fabric is to be folded to form a finished edge, e.g., a hemline or cuff.

- *Buttonholes.* They are marked by a solid line that shows the exact location and length of the buttonhole.

- *Center Front and Center Back.* A solid line indicating where the center of the garment is located. If brackets are located on the center front or center back line, they show that the pattern piece is to be placed on a fold of fabric.

- *Adjustment Line.* Double parallel lines show where the pattern piece can be lengthened or shortened. Sometimes this information is printed at the hemline.

- *Placement Line.* A single solid, or broken line showing the exact location of pockets, pleats, zippers, and trims.

- *Hemline.* A solid line indicating the finished edge of the garment and the depth of the hem.

PATTERN ADJUSTMENTS

Before you lay out any pattern pieces on your fabric, always check to see if any adjustments are needed in the pattern. Once the fabric is cut, it is too late to add any extra inches to any part.

Compare your own personal measurements with the body measurements listed on the pattern envelope. Measure yourself accurately with a tape measure. For a fitted garment, your measurements should correspond very closely to the body measurements for your pattern size.

Thus, if your waistline is 1″ (2.5 cm) larger than the pattern size, you will have to increase the pattern pieces at the waistline a total of 1″ (2.5 cm). For loosely fitted garments, minor differences in measurements can be overlooked. For length adjustments, compare back length or finished length measurements.

Understanding Ease

Pattern sizes are designed for the body measurements listed on the pattern envelope. However, no garment, except for a body suit or swim suit, will measure exactly the same as those body measurements. The actual pattern pieces will always measure larger to allow for *ease*. This is *the extra amount of fabric needed for you to move about in a garment*—to walk, run, and sit—*without pulling or straining.*

"Wearing ease" is the amount of fullness added to a pattern to allow for movement and comfort. For fitted garments, most patterns have the following amount of ease: about 1″ (2.5 cm) at the waistline, 2″ to 2½″ (5–6.5 cm) at the hips, and 2½″ to 4″ (6.5–10 cm) at the bust or chest. For fuller garments, designers have added extra fullness to create a particular style or silhouette. This ease is called "design ease."

What Adjustments Are Needed?

Few people have the exact same measurements as those listed for the pattern sizes. Make a chart listing your own measurements and the pattern size measurements for bust or chest, waist, hip, and back or side length. If any measurements are not the same, mark the plus or minus difference on your chart. Now you know where you have to make adjustments and how much to take in or let out.

Some measurements are not listed on the pattern envelope. For these you will have to measure the actual pattern pieces. Be sure to measure only from seamline to seamline. Do not include any darts, pleats, tucks, or overlapping edges. For total width, you have to measure both the front and back sections and then double the amount. For length, measure only from seam allowance to hemline. Do not include the hem allowance. Remember that these measurements also include ease.

Adjustment Guidelines

Adjustments can be made in length or in width. Lengthwise adjustments are made at the adjustment line on the pattern or at the hemline. Width adjustments that are 2″ (5 cm) or less can be made along the side seams. Larger adjustments require cutting and spreading or overlapping the pattern pieces. For these, please refer to an alterations book or a detailed sewing book.

Personal Chart			
	My Own Measurements	Pattern Measurements	+ or −
Bust │Chest			
Waist			
Hip			
Back or side length			

Remember, adjustments for length and for width must be done on both the front and back pattern pieces. It is very important to be accurate. If you make an error of just ¼″ (6 mm) at the side seam of a pants pattern, it will become a 1″ (2.5 cm) error when all four seam allowances are added up!

For all adjustments, follow these steps for best results:

- Make any length adjustments by shortening or lengthening pattern.
- Make any width adjustments by increasing or decreasing pattern width.
- Check that grain line remains straight.
- Redraw any darts or design details.
- Complete the same adjustments on both the front and back pattern pieces.

Adjusting Length

These are the easiest adjustments to make. Many patterns have adjustment lines printed on the pattern pieces. Other patterns are lengthened or shortened at the lower edge.

To Lengthen a Pattern Cut the pattern apart at the adjustment line. Place paper under the opening and spread the pieces the necessary amount. Keep the cut edges parallel across the entire opening. Check with a ruler. Be sure that the center front line and grain line arrow are straight. Tape the pattern pieces in place. Re-

draw the cutting line along the outer edge. Redraw any darts or design details if necessary. For pants, first adjust the crotch length and then adjust the overall length.

To lengthen at the *lower edge* of a pattern, tape paper to the lower edge. Measure down the necessary amount and draw a new cutting line parallel to the lower edge. Extend the cutting lines along side edges.

Lengthen

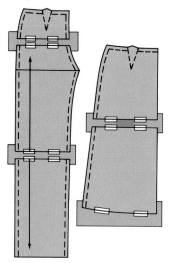

To Shorten a Pattern Measure up from the adjustment line the necessary amount to be shortened and draw a line. Fold the pattern along the adjustment line and bring the fold up to exactly meet the newly drawn line. Check the grain line. Tape the fold in place. Redraw the cutting lines and any darts or design lines.

To shorten at the *lower edge* of a pattern, draw a new hemline above the original line. Redraw cutting lines.

Shorten

Adjusting Width

An adjustment of 2″ (5 cm) or less can be made along the side seams of a garment. Because a garment has two side seams and four side-seam allowances, the amount to be adjusted on the front pattern piece is ¼ the total amount. For example, to increase the waistline by 1″ (2.5 cm), you will add ¼″ (6 mm) to the side seam of the front pattern piece and ¼″ (6 mm) to the side seam of the back pattern piece. Thus, each side seam will be increased ½″ (1.3 cm), and the total garment will be increased 1″ (2.5 cm).

To Increase the Width Tape paper along the pattern piece edge. Measure out ¼ the necessary amount at the area to be widened.

For a *waistline,* redraw the cutting lines and side seams tapering up from the waistline to the armhole, or down from the waistline to the hipline. Extend the waistline seam to the new side seam. For a garment with a waistband, you must make the same adjustment on the waistband pattern.

Cut the waistband apart at the side seam markings and increase each side ½ the needed amount.

For a *hipline*, any adjustments should be carried down to the hemline to retain the original shape of the skirt or pants. Measure out ¼ the necessary amount at the hipline and at the lower edge of the pattern. Redraw the cutting lines and side seams. Above the hipline, taper the lines in to meet the original waistline.

For *pants*, the pattern should measure at least 1″ (2.5 cm) more than your thigh measurement. Add ¼ the amount to each leg seam. Extend the line straight down to the hem edge.

To Decrease the Width For a *waistline*, measure in ¼ the necessary amount at the waistline seam. Redraw cutting lines and side seams tapering up from the waistline to the armhole or down to the hipline. For a waistband, make adjustments at the side seam markings. Fold out ½ the necessary amount at each side.

For a *hipline*, measure in ¼ the necessary amount and redraw the cutting lines and side seams. Taper the lines up to the original waistline and straight down to the hemline.

For *pants*, take in ¼ the amount on both the inside seam and the side seam for a small thigh measurement. Redraw the cutting lines and seam lines straight down to the hemline.

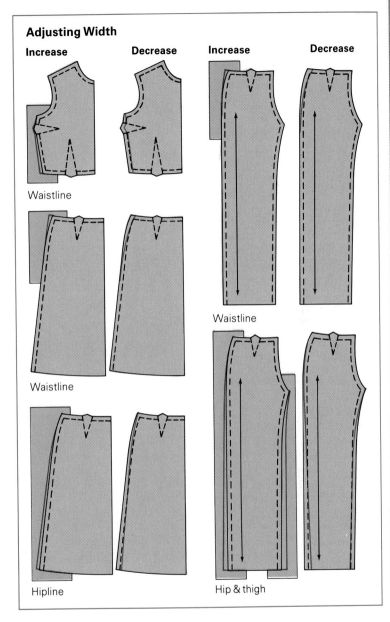

Adjusting Width

Increase   Decrease   Increase   Decrease

Waistline

Waistline

Waistline

Hipline

Hip & thigh

Bodice Adjustments

Bust Darts When fullness created by the bust darts is not in the right place, you need to raise or lower the darts. Mark the new point of the bustline. Cut out the un- derarm dart as shown. Tape paper under the opening in the pattern. Slide the dart section up or down until the dart is in line with the new bust point mark. Tape the pattern piece in place. Redraw the cutting line.

Narrow or Broad Shoulders

On the back bodice, draw a vertical line from the shoulder seam, beginning halfway between the shoulder dart and armhole, and extending down to the lower edge of the armhole. Continue the line horizontally just to the underarm seamline. Cut the pattern along these lines. Do not cut through the seam allowance. Place paper under the pattern.

For *narrow shoulders,* lap pattern piece the necessary amount at shoulder edge. For *broad shoulders,* spread pattern apart the necessary amount. Tape the pattern edges in place. Redraw the shoulder cutting lines. Make the same adjustment on the bodice front pattern piece.

Square or Sloping Shoulders

On the back bodice, draw a vertical line from the shoulder seam, beginning halfway between the shoulder dart and armhole, and extending down to the lower edge of the armhole. Continue the line horizontally through the underarm seam. Cut pattern apart on these lines. Place paper under the pattern.

For *square shoulders,* slide the armhole section up to raise the shoulder the necessary amount. For *sloping shoulders,* slide the armhole section down to lower the shoulder the necessary amount. Tape the pattern edges in place. Redraw the shoulder cutting lines as shown. Make the same adjustment on the bodice front pattern piece.

CHAPTER 5
Fabric

Now that your pattern is ready, turn your attention to your fabric. Although you may be eager to start cutting out the pattern pieces, it is very important do some preparation steps. These steps are necessary for the fabric pieces to go together easily. They also help to guarantee that your garment will fit properly when it is finished, and after it has been worn and laundered.

FABRIC TERMINOLOGY

Special fabric terminology is used on guide sheet layouts. These terms need to be understood in order to avoid cutting errors. In Unit 4 on fabrics, you learned that woven fabric is made of two sets of yarns that are interlaced at right angles to each other. The finished lengthwise edges of the fabric are the *selvages.* This narrow border is formed when the crosswise yarns reverse direction during weaving. Selvages are usually stiffer than the rest of the fabric. Avoid placing parts of your pattern pieces over the selvage when laying out your pattern.

A *bolt* of fabric refers to fabric rolled or folded onto a cardboard or metal form. Most fabrics are folded so that both selvages are on one end and the center fold is at the other end of the bolt.

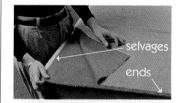

Grains

In sewing terms, the direction in which the yarns run is called the *grain.*

• *Lengthwise Grain.* It runs in the same direction as the selvage. This is the same direction as the lengthwise yarns on the loom. Thus, it is usually the strongest and sturdiest direction of the fabric. Most garments are cut with the lengthwise grain running vertically, or up and down, for more strength and durability during wear. Directions referring to "straight grain" or "grain line" mean the lengthwise grain.

• *Crosswise Grain.* This runs across the fabric from one selvage to the other. It is the same direction as the crosswise yarns of the fabric. In most fabrics, the crosswise grain usually has a slight amount of give or stretch.

• *Bias Grain.* It runs diagonally across the fabric. Bias is any direction other than lengthwise or crosswise grain. Fabric cut on bias grain has more stretchability than fabric cut on straight grain.

- *True Bias.* This is created by folding the fabric at a 45° angle so that the crosswise grain is parallel to the selvage. True bias has the most stretch.

Look at your own fabric and find the lengthwise grain, crosswise grain, and true bias. Try stretching the fabric in the different directions. Is there any difference in the stretchability?

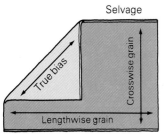
Selvage

True bias

Crosswise grain

Lengthwise grain

Selvage

For nonwoven fabrics, such as felt and interfacing, the grain lines are not visible. However, most nonwovens do have different amounts of stretchability in different directions. Gently stretch your fabric to check. The lengthwise grain is the direction with the least amount of stretch. The crosswise grain is perpendicular to the lengthwise direction.

Knitted Fabric Terms

Knitted fabric is made up of rows of loops. The lengthwise chain of loops, called *wales or ribs*, corresponds to the lengthwise grain. The crosswise rows of loops are called *courses.* The amount of stretch in either direction depends upon the type of knit. In most knits, the crosswise loops have the most stretch.

PREPARING YOUR FABRIC

Both woven and knitted fabrics need to be preshrunk and straightened before you start to cut out your pattern.

Preshrinking makes sure that your fabric will not shrink after the finished garment is washed or dry-cleaned. *Straightening* makes sure that the garment will hang properly on your body.

If the crosswise yarns are not at right angles to the lengthwise yarns, the fabric is said to be *off-grain,* or *crooked.* This may happen during the finishing process or when the fabric is rolled onto the bolt. If the fabric is not straightened before the pieces are cut out, the garment may pull or twist to one side of your body, and the hemline may hang unevenly.

Straightening Fabric Ends

The first step is to check the fabric ends. When fabric is cut from the bolt in a store, it is often not cut straight. Uneven edges make it difficult to check the straightness of the grain.

If you can clearly see the individual crosswise yarns, cut along one yarn from selvage to selvage. If not, clip the selvage and pull one crosswise yarn, gently pushing the fabric along the yarn. The pulled yarn will leave a mark that you can use as a cutting line. If your yarn breaks in the middle of the fabric, cut up to the broken point, then pick up the end of the yarn and continue pulling.

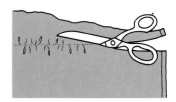

Some firmly woven fabrics can be straightened by tearing the fabric. Clip through the selvage and grasp each side of the cut edge. Tear firmly but carefully. This method is quick, but it can also be dangerous. Tearing can pull the fabric off-grain and sometimes the fabric may suddenly split along the lengthwise grain.

For knitted fabrics, straighten the ends by cutting along one crosswise row of loops. Knits do not have a thread that can be pulled. Instead, baste across the fabric, following one row of loops. Then use the thread basting as a cutting line.

Preshrinking Fabric

It is best to preshrink all your fabrics. *Preshrinking* also helps to remove some fabric finishes that cause stitching problems on lighter-weight woven and knitted fabrics. The method you choose depends upon how you plan to clean your finished garment. Check the fabric care instructions.

For *washable fabrics,* simply wash your fabric in the machine with other clothes. For fabrics that may ravel easily, first machine zigzag or hand overcast the raw edges. Dry either in a tumble dryer or lay flat, being sure to keep the edges square.

For *hand-washable fabrics,* fold the fabric and place in hot or warm water for 30 minutes.

Fabrics to be *dry-cleaned* should be taken to a professional dry cleaner or a self-service dry cleaner for preshrinking.

Be sure to also *preshrink* any *zippers, trims, tapes, interfacings,* and *linings* that will be used in your garment. The only exception is *bias tape,* which should not be preshrunk. Tapes and trims can be left wrapped on their cardboard, which should be bent slightly to allow for any shrinkage, and placed in hot water for 30 minutes.

Straightening Fabric Grain

Check to see if your fabric needs to be straightened. Fold fabric in half lengthwise and match selvages accu-rately. If the crosswise ends match exactly and are at right angles to the selvage, the fabric is straight. The fold will be smooth and wrinkle-free. If the edges do not match or the fabric puckers when you try to line up the edges, the fabric is not straight.

Straight

Off-grain

To straighten the fabric, pull the fabric on the true bias as shown. Open up the fabric and pull the two opposite corners that are too short. Ask someone to help you since two people can do it more easily than one. Refold the fabric to check if you have pulled enough.

Fabric may be slightly off-grain because it was pulled or stretched as it was rolled on the bolt. These fabrics can be easily realigned by pulling. However if the yarns became off-grain during the finishing process for permanent press fabrics, the grain cannot be straight-ened. The grain is locked in position permanently by the finish, and the fabric will have to be used as is.

Pressing Fabric

Press your fabric to remove all wrinkles. Fabric that is wrinkled cannot be cut accurately. Check to be sure that the center fold can be pressed out of the fabric. If the fold does not press out with a steam iron and a damp press cloth, the fold will not come out with washing or dry cleaning. This sometimes occurs with knits and permanently finished fabrics. You will have to plan a special cutting layout to avoid the fold line.

THE PATTERN LAYOUT

Locate and circle the cutting layout for your particular view, size, and fabric width. Be sure to use the "with nap" layout if your fabric has a nap, pile, shading, or a one-way design.

Knitted fabrics should also be cut using the "with nap" layout. The cutting guide will show you exactly how to lay out the pattern pieces so that all the pieces will fit on the minimum amount of fabric.

Finding the Right Side

For many fabrics, the right side is very obvious due to the nap, pattern, or print. However, for other fabrics, the right side may be difficult to determine. One clue is the

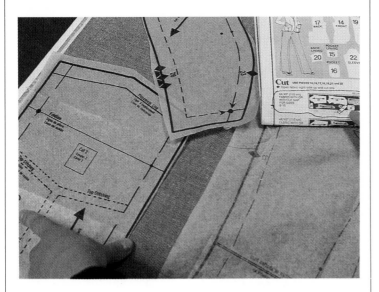

way the fabric is folded or rolled on the bolt. Cottons and linens usually have the right side out on the bolt. Wools and most other fabrics are folded with the right side toward the inside.

Fold back one edge and compare the two surfaces. The right side may have a more pronounced weave, more nap, a brighter and clearer print, or be shinier. However, some plain weave fabrics are the same on both sides. For knitted fabrics, stretch a crosswise cut edge. The edge will usually roll to the right side of the fabric.

If you are undecided, pick the side that you like best. Then be sure to keep the same side throughout, so the finished garment will not have any differences in color or sheen. To help identify the sides, you can mark the wrong side of the fabric with chalk marks.

Folding the Fabric

The cutting guide will show exactly how to fold your fabric. For most layouts, the fabric is folded with the right side in. The pattern pieces are placed on the wrong side of the fabric so that it will be easier to transfer markings. This also helps to protect your fabric from soil or dirt as you handle the fabric pieces. However, stripes, plaids, and prints should be folded with the right side out. This makes it easier to match the fabric design. When cutting a single layer of fabric, place the fabric right side up.

Your fabric may be folded *lengthwise, crosswise, double,* or *partial:*

• *Lengthwise Fold.* Fold fabric in half lengthwise with right sides together. Match the selvages and ends.

• *Crosswise Fold.* Fold fabric in half crosswise with right sides together. Match cut ends and keep the two layers of selvage even along each side. For *napped fabrics,* the nap must run in the same direction on both layers. Cut the fabric along the crosswise fold and turn the top layer around end to end. Match all edges.

• *Double Fold.* Fold fabric twice along the lengthwise grain, right sides together. Usually the selvages meet in the center. This layout is often used for knitted fabrics.

• *Partial Fold.* Fold fabric on lengthwise grain, right sides together, only wide enough to fit the widest pattern piece.

Lengthwise fold

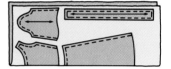

Crosswise fold

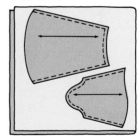

Partial fold Double fold

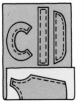

Special Layouts

• *Napped Fabrics.* Place all pattern pieces facing in the same direction. For a richer color in corduroy and velvet, lay out the pattern so the nap or pile runs up the garment. Use a "with nap" layout.

• *Plaids.* Plaids can be even or uneven, depending on the repeat of the lines. *Even plaids* are the same in both the vertical and horizontal directions. Use a "without nap" layout. For *uneven plaids,* use a "with nap" layout so that all the pattern pieces are laid in the same direction. Use the dominant line of the plaid for the center front and center back. Match plaids at side seams and sleeves.

• *Stripes.* For *even stripes,* use a "without nap" layout. For *uneven stripes,* use a "with nap" layout. For *vertical stripes,* place the dominant stripe at center front, center back. Match stripes at side seams and sleeves. Stripes will chevron on bias seams.

• *Directional Prints.* Use a "with nap" layout. Match designs at seamlines.

• *Border Prints.* Place all pattern pieces on the crosswise grain. Match hemline markings to the lower edge of the border design. Place other pieces in the space available above design.

Pattern layouts may require extra fabric depending upon the size of the fabric design.

Always place the largest pattern pieces on the fabric first, being sure that the dominant lines or designs are placed attractively on the body. Fold the fabric along the dominant line of a plaid or stripe. The dominant design of a print is usually placed at the center front and above or below the hipline.

Match stripes, plaids, and prints by placing corresponding notches of the pattern pieces on the same line or design of the fabric. Be sure to match at the seam line, not at the cutting line. To be sure that both layers of fabric are perfectly matched, pin the layers together along the dominant stripes before pinning the pattern in place.

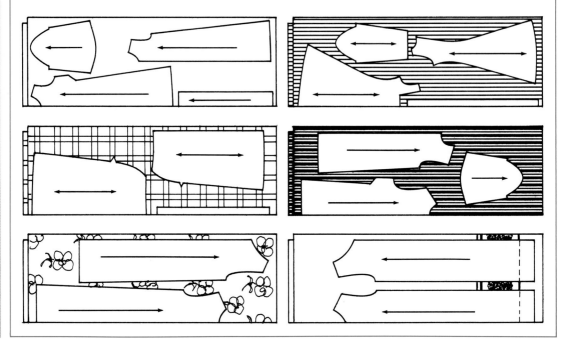

Smooth out any wrinkles by pulling both layers of fabric at the ends or at the sides. Do not try to smooth out only the top layer with your hand. This will cause the two layers to be off-grain. When the grain lines are straight, pin the two layers together along the edges. This prevents the fabric from shifting as you lay out the pattern pieces.

Always work on a large hard surface so that the full width of fabric can be laid out without any fabric hanging over the sides. In school, use a long cutting table. At home, work on a large table, folding cutting board, or the floor. Do not use the bed because your fabric can easily shift on a soft surface.

For long lengths of fabric, fold up the extra length and place it at the end of the table or on a chair at the end of the table.

Pinning the Pattern Pieces

Check all pattern pieces to be sure that any length or width adjustments have been made on both the front and back pattern pieces. Lay out all the pattern pieces in the same position as shown on your circled cutting layout. Most pattern pieces are placed printed side up on the fabric. Pattern pieces that are shaded on the layout should be placed with the printed side down.

Each pattern piece has the grain line indicated by an arrow or a "place on fold" bracket. It is critical that

every pattern piece be placed exactly on the proper grain line. Never try to tilt or angle any pattern piece in order to fit it into a smaller space. The result will be a great mistake because that section of your garment will not hang properly.

Start with the large pattern pieces to be placed on the fold. Place the fold line on the pattern exactly along the fabric fold. Pin about every 6″ to 8″ (15–20 cm) along the fold. Smooth the pattern away from the fold and pin diagonally into the corners. Pin the remaining edges of the pattern about every 6″ (15 cm). Pin every 3″ (7.5 cm) on curves and slippery fabric. Place the pins at right angles to the edge, being

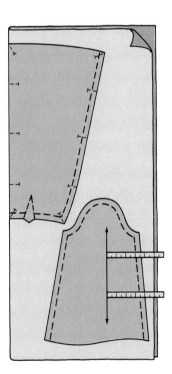

sure that the points do not go past the cutting line.

Next, pin the pattern pieces that have a grain line arrow. Place a pin at the end of each arrow, pinning through all fabric layers. Measure carefully from the point of each arrow to the edge of the fabric. If the measurements are not exactly the same, unpin one end and shift the pattern. Repin and measure again. Repeat until the grain line is straight. Smooth out the pattern in all directions from the grain line arrow and pin diagonally into the corners. Finish pinning every 3″ to 6″ (7.5–15 cm) along all the edges of the pattern.

After the pattern is pinned in place, count the number of pieces on the circled cutting layout. Then count the pieces pinned to the fabric to be sure that you have not forgotten any pieces. If any pattern pieces are to be cut more than once to create four or more layers, be sure that you have left the proper amount of space. If two pieces are to be cut from a single fabric layer, you must reverse the pattern when cutting the second piece. If a piece extends beyond the folded edge of the fabric, cut the other pieces first. Then unfold the fabric and cut the remaining pattern piece.

Finally, double-check your layout. Are all the pieces positioned correctly? Are the grain lines straight? Are there any special instructions for certain pattern pieces?

CUTTING ACCURATELY

After you have pinned all the pattern pieces to your fabric, you can begin to cut. Use bent-handled shears and cut slowly and accurately. Never use pinking shears. Cut with long, even strokes without closing the blades completely. Hold your fabric flat on the cutting surface with your other hand. Use the tip of the shears around the notches. Cut double and triple notches together with one long edge across top.

Cut directionally with the grain line. Some patterns have a symbol printed on the cutting line or stitching line, which shows in which direction to cut and stitch. If in doubt, cut from the widest point to the narrowest point.

After cutting out a garment, leave the pattern pieces pinned to the fabric until you make the construction markings and are ready to sew. Save all fabric scraps. You will need them for testing marking methods, stitch tension, pressing temperatures, and for cutting a bias binding or buttonhole strips.

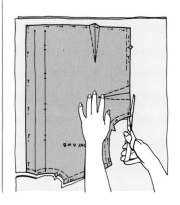

MARKING METHODS

The lines and symbols marked along the edges and inside the pattern pieces will help you to assemble your garment. These markings should be transferred to your fabric before the pattern is unpinned. The markings must be visible as you sew, but they should never show on the outside of your finished garment. Different marking methods may be used for different fabrics and types of marks.

What to Mark

Mark all construction markings such as darts, pleats, tucks, and dots along seamlines. Placement lines for buttonholes, buttons, pockets, and any trims should be marked. You may also want to mark fold lines and center front and back lines. Seam allowances and hemlines are not marked on the fabric. Seam allowances can be measured as you stitch, using the guidelines marked on your sewing machine. Hems are measured and turned under after garment is made.

How to Mark

Markings can be transferred to the fabric with a *tracing wheel and dressmaker's tracing paper, tailor's chalk,* or *thread.* There are advantages and disadvantages to each method.

● *Tracing Wheel and Dressmaker's Tracing Paper.* This method of marking is quick and useful for most fabrics.

Use a *saw-toothed wheel* for most fabrics and a *smooth-edge wheel* for delicate fabrics. Tracing paper has a waxy surface on one side and is available in several colors.

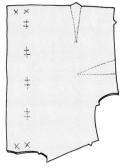

1. *Choose* a color of tracing paper that is similar to your fabric color but will still show. Test on a scrap of fabric to be sure that the markings do not show through on the right side. Use caution with light-colored and lightweight fabrics.
2. *Place* waxy side of paper against the wrong side of the fabric. Two layers of paper are needed to mark a double layer of fabric. For small areas, you can fold a paper in half. *If the fabric is folded*

right sides together, slip one paper between the pattern and the fabric, with the waxy side down. Place the other paper, waxy side up, under the bottom layer of fabric. *If the fabric is folded with the wrong sides in,* insert two layers of paper between the fabric layers, with waxy sides facing fabric.

3. *Mark* all symbols by pressing down lightly on the tracing wheel. Guide the wheel over each line or mark only once. Mark dots with an X. The end of a dart can be marked with a short line. For longer lines, use a ruler to keep lines straight.

• *Tailor's Chalk.* Chalk markings can be used on most fabrics. Mark only the wrong side of the fabric with either a flat square of chalk or a chalk pencil. Be sure that the edge or point is sharp so that the markings are accurate. Chalk markings can be easily brushed off of some fabrics, so handle carefully until construction is completed.

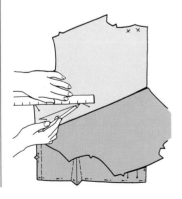

1. *Push a pin* through both layers of fabric at each symbol to be marked. Carefully loosen the paper pattern and slip it over the pins. Be careful not to pull out any pins.
2. *Make a chalk dot* at each pin on the top layer of fabric.
3. *Turn fabric* over and mark other layer at each pin.

• *Thread.* Thread can be used to transfer markings by basting or by making tailor's tacks. Both methods take extra time, but they can be used on fabrics that cannot be marked by other methods.

Other Marking Methods

• *Basting.* This is used for marking long lines such as center front and back, and placement lines.

1. Make uneven basting stitches about 2″ (5 cm) long on a single layer of fabric.
2. Clip the long stitches and carefully remove the paper pattern.

• *Tailor's Tacks.* These are not as accurate as other markings and take much more time to make. However, they can be used to mark sheer, loosely woven, or bulky fabrics. Handle the fabric pieces carefully to avoid pulling out any of the threads.

1. *Use* a double thread without a knot. Make a small stitch through the pattern and both layers

of fabric. Pull the thread through but leave at least 1″ (2.5 cm) of thread extending from the pattern.
2. *Make* a second stitch over first stitch, leaving a loop of 1″ (2.5 cm).
3. If you are marking a series of dots, as for a dart, *move* from one marking to another. At the last marking, leave a 1″ (2.5 cm) thread end.
4. *Clip* the threads between the markings.
5. *Unpin* the pattern and gently pull the thread loops and ends through the paper pattern.
6. *Pull apart* the two fabric layers as far as the loops will allow. Cut threads between the two layers.

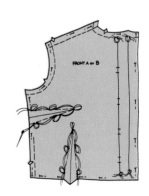

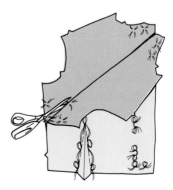

UNIT 2

The unit construction method is the simplest way of sewing garments. **Unit construction** means that *everything is completed on the smallest unit possible before you begin to sew the separate units together.*

This method allows you to work on smaller areas that are easier to handle. It also guarantees that areas are pressed before being crossed by another seam.

First, all staystitching is completed, and any darts, gathers, tucks, or pleats are stitched on each separate piece. Details such as buttonholes and plackets can be completed on small sections. Interfacings can be applied. Then all the pieces can be carefully pressed before being sewn to each other.

Try to finish a complete stage of construction each time you sew. For example, you can complete a sleeve. Or attach a pocket. Or stitch a waistband. Then the next time you begin to sew, you can start a new step instead of trying to finish a half-completed one.

These next chapters show the various techniques of basic construction. You will learn why certain procedures should be followed and how to do them. Use these step-by-step instructions along with your pattern guide sheet to learn the construction basics.

CHAPTER 6

Stitching

Sewing is a combination of machine and hand stitches. Machine stitches are used for the major seams of the garment. Hand stitches are used primarily for basting and for finishing the garment, such as hemming and sewing on fasteners.

MACHINE STITCHING

Checkpoints

- Always check your machine before you begin sewing:
  - ☐ Stitch length
  - ☐ Stitch width
  - ☐ Tension
  - ☐ Presser foot pressure
  - ☐ Needle—smooth, straight, and inserted properly
  - ☐ Presser foot—firmly tightened
  - ☐ Bobbin—inserted properly into bobbin case
  - ☐ Hand wheel knob—tightened after winding bobbin
- Practice stitching on two layers of scrap fabric to check stitch length and tension.
- Control the speed of your stitching. Always slow down as you come to a corner, curve, or end of a seam.
- Guide your fabric with your fingers. Do not push or pull the fabric.

- As you stitch, keep your eyes on the fabric edge and the guideline markings—not on the needle.
- Sew carefully over pins, which must be placed at right angles to the stitching line.
- Mistakes do happen. To rip out stitches, use a seam ripper, thread clipper, or small scissors. Cut threads about every 2″ (5 cm) along one side of the fabric. Pull the thread out on the other side, and then remove the short threads from the clipped side.

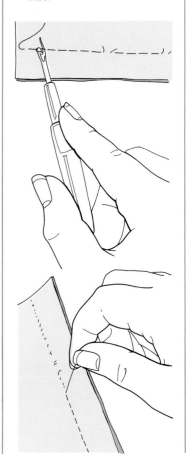

Length of Stitches

The length of the stitches depends upon the purpose of the machine stitching. Most stitching uses a medium-length stitch. Basting stitches are very long; reinforced stitches are very short.

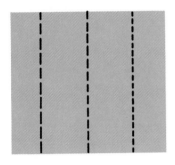

• *Standard Stitching.* This is used to stitch permanently most seams and construction details. Use 10 to 12 stitches per inch (2–2.5 mm in length) for most fabrics. Finer fabrics require a shorter stitch of 12 to 15 stitches per inch (1.5–2 mm in length). Heavy fabrics need a longer stitch of 8 to 10 stitches per inch (2.5–3 mm in length).

• *Basting Stitching.* Machine basting is used to temporarily hold two or more pieces of fabric together until the permanent stitching is completed. It can also be used on a single layer of easing, gathering, and marking guidelines. Use a very long stitch, 6 stitches per inch, (2.5 cm in length). Decrease the upper tension 1 or 2 settings to make it easier to remove the basting stitches.

• *Reinforcement Stitching.* This is used to permanently stitch fabric areas that will be trimmed or clipped close to the stitching. Use a very short stitch, 15 to 20 stitches per inch (2.5 cm in length) to hold the fabric yarns in place.

Types of Machine Stitching

Machine stitching can be used for many different construction techniques. Specific terms are used to describe each method of stitching. These terms are used frequently in sewing directions. You should learn how to do each of these techniques:

• *Staystitching.* This is used along bias and curved edges to prevent stretching as you handle the fabric. It is done after the fabric is marked and before pinning, basting, and permanent stitching. Staystitch on a single layer of fabric ⅛″ (3 mm) away from the seamline in the seam allowance. Use standard machine stitching and stitch directionally. Staystitching can act as a guideline for clipping and joining curved edges.

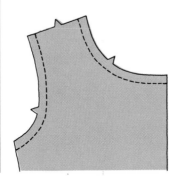

• *Directional Stitching.* This stitching is *with,* or in the same direction, as the fabric grain. It helps to prevent a seam from stretching or changing shape as you stitch. To determine grain direction, run your finger along the fabric edge. The direction that smooths the yarns against the fabric is with the grain. This is the direction in which to stitch.

Some patterns may indicate grain direction with an arrow or an illustration of a presser foot on the seamline. If you stitch from the wide part of a fabric section to the narrow part, you will be stitching with the grain in most situations. Seams on straight grain can be stitched in either direction.

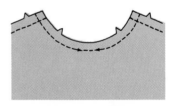

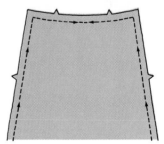

• *Stitching a Standard Seam.* A standard seam is ⅝″ (1.5 cm) wide. Almost all patterns are designed with standard seams. If another seam width is used, it will be marked on the pattern piece.

• *Backstitching.* This is used to secure the ends of a row of stitching. To backstitch, begin stitching ½″ (1.3 cm) in from the beginning of the stitching line. Stitch backward to the edge of the fabric, then stitch forward over the stitches you have just made. Continue stitching the seam and backstitch at the other end for ½″ (1.3 cm) exactly over the first stitching.

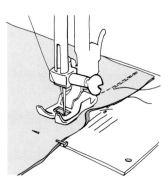

• *Understitching.* This is a row of stitching used to keep a facing or bottom layer of fabric rolled out of sight. Use standard stitching and stitch from the right side, through the facing and seam allowances, ⅛″ (3 mm) from the seam line.

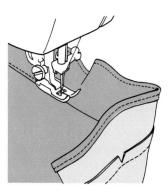

• *Topstitching.* This is a row of stitching done on the outside of a garment. It can be decorative or functional.

Topstitching is used to outline seams, secure facings, attach pockets, stitch pleats, and hold hems. Stitch from the right side of the fabric with either matching or contrasting thread. Use a slightly longer stitch length, 8 to 10 stitches per inch (2.5 cm in length). To keep the topstitching even, use the edge of the presser foot, guideline markings, or sewing tape as a guide.

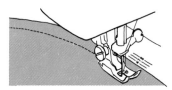

• *Edgestitching.* This is a row of topstitching placed very close to the finished edge.

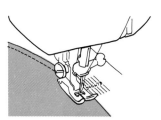

• *Stitch-in-the-Ditch.* This is a row of stitching done on the outside of a garment in the groove of a seam line. It is used to hold two or more layers of fabric together when finishing facings, collars, cuffs, and waistbands. Stitch from the outside directly in the seam groove through all layers of fabric, using standard machine stitching.

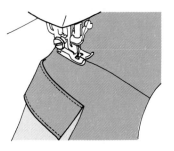

• *Zigzag Stitching.* This is available on most machines. It can be used to finish seams, stitch buttonholes, attach cording and elastic, and create decorative designs. Both the length and the width of a zigzag stitch can be adjusted—from very narrow and closely spaced for a satin stitch, to very wide and far apart for a seam finish. Some machines also offer a variety of specialty stitches. Refer to your sewing machine manual for specific directions.

HAND STITCHING

Threading a Needle

Unwind no more than 24" (.6 m) of thread. Longer lengths may tangle or knot as you sew. Use scissors to cut the thread at an angle so the end will slide through the eye of the needle easily. Biting or breaking the thread will cause it to fray and make it difficult to thread the needle.

Most hand sewing is done with a single thread. A knot is made in just one thread end. If you need a double thread, hold two ends together as you tie the knot.

Types of Hand Stitching

Hand stitches can be used for basting permanent seams, seam finishes, hems, reinforcement, and decorative stitching. Hold the fabric so that the area you are sewing is at the top, with the bulk of the fabric falling down in your lap or on a table. For most hand stitches, hold the fabric so that you will sew from right to left if you are right-handed. For left-handed sewers, just reverse and sew from left to right.

To secure the beginning and end stitches, make a small knot or take two small stitches, one on top of the other, on the wrong side of the garment.

- *Basting Stitch.* Hand basting is temporary stitching used to mark or to hold fabric layers together. Basting should be removed from the garment as soon as the permanent stitching is com-

Tying a Knot

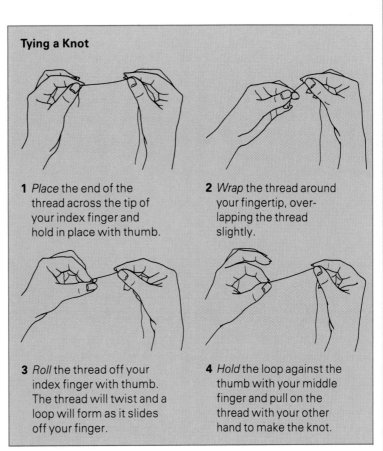

1 *Place* the end of the thread across the tip of your index finger and hold in place with thumb.

2 *Wrap* the thread around your fingertip, overlapping the thread slightly.

3 *Roll* the thread off your index finger with thumb. The thread will twist and a loop will form as it slides off your finger.

4 *Hold* the loop against the thumb with your middle finger and pull on the thread with your other hand to make the knot.

pleted and it is no longer needed. There are three types of basting stitches:

1. *Even basting* is used to hold seams together for fitting or permanent stitching, such as basting sleeves into armholes. Make stitches about ¼" (6 mm) long and even on both sides of fabric.

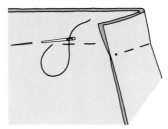

2. *Uneven basting* is used for marking or for holding hems in place for stitching. Make 1" (2.5 cm) stitches on top side of fabric and short ¼" (6 mm) stitches on the underside. To save time, take several stitches with your needle before pulling thread through.

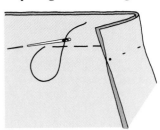

• *Running Stitch.* This is the simplest type of hand stitching. It is used for gathering, easing, tucking, quilting, and sewing seams that have little or no strain. Make tiny, even stitches ¼″ to ⅟₁₆″ (6–1.5 mm) in length.

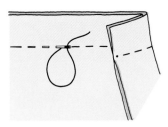

• *Backstitch.* This is one of the strongest handstitches. It is used to repair machine-stitched seams and to fasten thread ends securely.

Begin with a tiny running stitch. Then insert the needle back at the beginning of the first stitch, and bring it out again one stitch length in front of the thread. Keep inserting the needle in the end of the last stitch and bringing it out one stitch ahead. The stitches on the underside will be twice as long as those on the upper side.

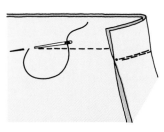

The *pickstitch* is a variation of the backstitch. It is used for the hand application of zippers and as a decorative stitch. The needle is

brought back only one or two threads to form a very tiny stitch on the upper side.

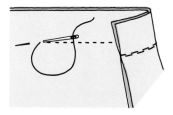

• *Slipstitch.* This is an almost invisible stitch. It is used to attach one folded edge to another piece of fabric, such as patch pockets, hems, linings, and trims.

Slip the needle inside the fold of the upper fabric for ¼″ (6 mm). Then pick up one or two threads of the under fabric directly below. Continue to take a stitch through the fold and then in the other fabric.

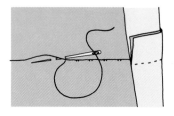

• *Overcast Stitch.* A stitch used to prevent raw edges from raveling. Make diagonal stitches over the edge of the fabric, spacing them evenly apart.

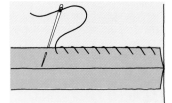

• *Hemming Stitch.* This slanted stitch is used for finishing different types of hems, especially ones with seam binding or a folded edge.

Make a tiny stitch in the garment. Then bring the needle diagonally up through the folded edge of the fabric or the seam binding. Space stitches about ¼″ (6 mm) apart.

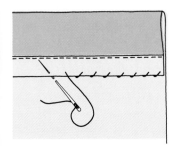

• *Blindstitch.* This is an excellent stitch for hemming and for holding facings in place. It is barely visible from the right side of the garment. It also allows movement without pulling.

Fold back the hem or facing edge about ¼″ (6 mm). Take a small stitch in the garment, catching only one or two threads. Then take a tiny stitch diagonally above in the hem or facing. Do not pull the stitches tight. Continue to form a very narrow zigzag stitch.

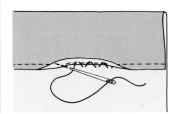

- *Catchstitch.* This criss-cross stitch is used to hold two layers of fabric together with flexibility. It can be used to hem stretchy fabrics or to attach interfacings.

Stitch from left to right if you are right-handed. Make a small horizontal stitch from right to left in one layer of fabric a short distance from the edge. Then make another horizontal stitch, just over the edge and diagonally to the right, on the other layer of fabric. The threads will cross each other between stitches.

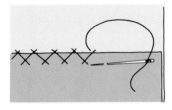

For a *blind catchstitch,* fold back the hem edge about ¼″ (6 mm). Make catchstitches between the two layers.

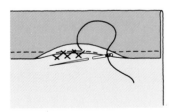

- *Cross-Stitch.* This decorative stitch is used to hold layers of fabric together. A series of cross-stitches is often used at the center back pleat of a jacket lining.

Make a series of horizontal stitches about ¼″ to ⅜″ (6–9 mm) wide, spaced as far apart as they are long, to form a diagonal design. Then reverse direction and continue making horizontal stitches at the same location as the previous stitches to form an X design.

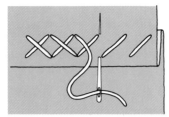

A *cross-stitch tack* is used to hold a facing edge in place at a seamline. Make a cross-stitch over the edge, being sure that stitches do not show on the outside. Continue making several cross-stitches over the first one.

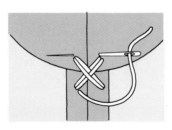

- *Buttonhole Stitch.* This stitch is used primarily to make handworked buttonholes and to attach hooks and eyes. It can also be used as a decorative finish along the edge of a garment by placing stitches farther apart. Use a buttonhole twist or double thread. Begin by inserting the needle through the buttonhole slash and bring it out on the right side of the fabric. Then loop the thread under the eye of the needle and under the point. Pull the needle out of the fabric and draw up the loop to form a knot along the buttonhole edge.

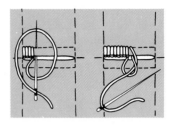

- *Blanket Stitch.* This stitch is used for making thread loops, eyes, and belt carriers. It can also be used to make bar tacks, French tacks, and a decorative finish along a fabric edge.

Stitch from left to right, holding the fabric edge toward you. Point the needle toward you and insert through the fabric from the right side. Keep thread under the needle as the stitch is pulled up.

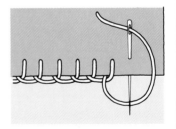

A *thread loop, eye, or belt carrier* can be made by working blanket stitches over longer base stitches. Use double thread or a single strand of buttonhole twist. Take 2 or 3 stitches the desired length of the loop, eye, or carrier. Secure the ends with small backstitches. Be sure the base stitches are long enough for your button, hook, or belt to pass through. Then with the same thread, make closely spaced blanket stitches over the entire length of the base stitches. Secure with several small stitches on the underside of the fabric.

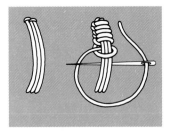

A *bar tack* is used to reinforce areas of strain, such as pocket corners, and ends of handworked buttonholes. Make several overlapping stitches the desired length of the bar tack. Work buttonhole stitches over the bar, catching fabric underneath.

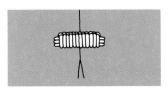

A *French tack* is used to hold a lining hem to a coat hem at a seamline. Form by working blanket stitches over several long stitches.

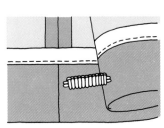

• *Chain Stitch*. This stitch can also be used to form thread loops, eyes, and carriers. Use a double thread or buttonhole twist to form a series of loops.

Secure thread with several overlapping stitches on the underside. Then take a short stitch to form a loop on the right side. Slip your thumb and first two fingers through the loop. Reach through the loop with a finger and catch the thread to form a new loop. Pull the new loop through the first loop and tighten so that the first loop forms a knot at the base of the thread chain. Keep forming new loops and sliding them down the thread evenly until the desired length. Slip the needle and thread through the last loop to end the chain. Stitch into the fabric and secure with small stitches on the underside.

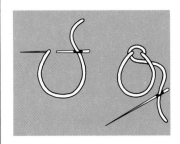

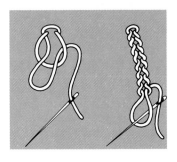

Darts

Darts are triangular folds of fabric stitched to a point. They are used to control fullness and give shape to fitted clothing. Darts should point to the fullest part of the body and end about 1″ (2.5 cm) from the body curve to which they point. The two basic types of darts are the *single-pointed dart* and the *double-pointed dart*.

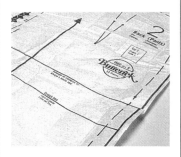

STITCHING DARTS

There are four basic steps in stitching single-pointed darts:

1. *Fold* the dart with the right sides of fabric together matching the stitching lines. Place one pin exactly at the point and other pins at the small dot markings.
2. *Stitch* from the wide end of the dart to the point.
3. *Stitch* the last two or three stitches as close to the fold line as possible. This will create a sharp point without any bubbles. Do not backstitch

because it can cause puckering at the point of the dart.

4. *Tie* the thread ends in a knot. Or simply leave 1″ (2.5 cm) thread ends, which will not pull out.

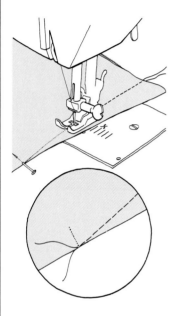

For *double-pointed darts*, start at the center and stitch to each point. Overlap the stitching lines in the center about 1″ (2.5 cm). Make one or more clips in the dart along the fold so it can be flat.

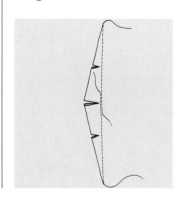

PRESSING DARTS

Always press a dart before crossing it with another seam.

1. *Press* the dart flat, as stitched.

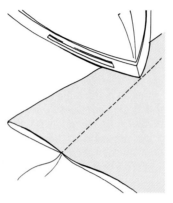

2. *Place* the dart over a tailor's ham and press it to one side.

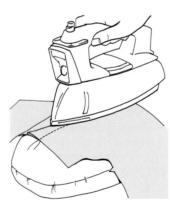

Horizontal darts are pressed downward.

Vertical darts are pressed toward center front or center back. Be careful not to crease the fabric beyond the point.

Double-pointed darts are pressed over a tailor's ham the same as single-pointed darts.

Wide darts or darts in heavy fabric should be pressed open. Refer to your pattern guide sheet. Slash the dart along fold line to within 1″ (2.5 cm) of point. Trim the slash to ½″ (1.3 cm) from the stitching line, as shown. Press the dart flat, as stitched. Then press the trimmed edges open and press the point flat.

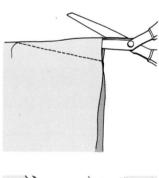

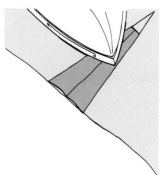

CHAPTER 8

Gathering and Easing

Gathering and easing are methods used to control fullness along a seamline.

Gathers are *soft folds of fabric formed by pulling up basting stitches to make the fabric fit into a smaller space.*

Easing is used when *one edge of fabric is only slightly larger than the other.* Easing should not create any visible folds or gathers.

A puffed sleeve is much fuller along the seamline than a set-in sleeve. The puffed sleeve has gathers to control the fullness. The set-in sleeve has the extra fullness eased into the seamline to create the curved shape of the sleeve.

GATHERING

An area to be gathered will be marked on the pattern with "gather" or "gathering line" on the seamline. The beginning and end of the gathered area will be marked by notches or dots. Usually, fabric is gathered into ½ or ⅓ of its original width. It takes more yardage to create full gathers in lightweight fabrics than in heavier ones.

How to Gather

Gathers start with two rows of machine basting. Then the bobbin threads are pulled from both ends to draw up the fabric. Finally, the gathered fabric is stitched to the shorter length of fabric.

1. *Adjust* the stitch length for 6 to 8 stitches per inch (3–4 mm in length). Loosen the upper thread tension.
2. *Stitch* the first row of basting next to the seamline in the seam allowance. Leave long thread ends. For large areas, start and stop the stitching at the seams.
3. *Stitch* the second row ¼″ (6 mm) away in the seam allowance. Leave long thread ends.

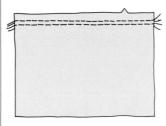

4. *Pin* the fabric edges, right sides together, matching notches, seams, and markings.
5. *Pull* up both bobbin threads from one end. Gently slide the fabric along the thread to gather half the section. Repeat at the other end until the gathered section is the proper length.

Wrap the threads in a figure 8 around a pin to secure.

6. *Distribute* gathers evenly and pin in place about every ½″ (1.3 cm).

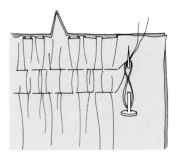

7. *Stitch* with standard stitching along the seamline, gathered side up. Use your fingers to hold the gathers evenly on both sides of the needle to prevent any folds catching in the seam.

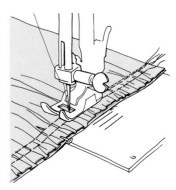

For large gathered areas, such as a gathered waistline, the seam should be stabilized to prevent stretching. This is done by stitching a piece of firmly woven tape along the seamline. (See WAISTLINES, page 448.)

For heavy fabrics, use a zigzag stitch over a narrow

cord for easier gathering. Place a thin cord on the seam allowance, ¼" (6 mm) from the seamline. Zigzag stitch over the cord, being careful not to catch the cord. Pull the cord ends to form gathers. Stitch along seamline with gathered side up. Remove cord.

Pressing Gathers

To press gathers:

1. *Press* the seam allowances flat.
2. *Lay* the garment flat on ironing board with seam allowances turned away from the gathers.
3. *Press* carefully up into the fullness with the tip of your iron on the wrong side. Hold the seam allowances taut above the gathers to prevent folds being pressed into the gathers at the seamline.

Shirring

Shirring is formed by several rows of gathering. Use only on soft or lightweight fabrics. Stitch as many rows of gathering as desired and secure each row with a knot. Then stitch over the knots in the seam allowance.

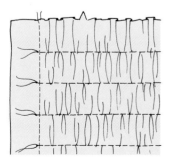

Elasticized shirring is made by using elastic thread in the bobbin. Wind elastic thread on the bobbin by hand, stretching slightly. Use a long stitch, 6 to 8 stitches per inch (3–4 mm in length). Stitch on the right side of the fabric, stretching the previously stitched rows as you sew each new row.

EASING

Easing allows fabric to be shaped over a curved area of the body. It is used most often at shoulder seams, sleeves, yokes, and waistbands. The most common eased seam is a set-in sleeve. The finished seam should look smooth, without any gathers or tucks.

Pinbasting

If one fabric edge is only slightly longer than the other, pinbaste the right sides of the fabric together with the longer side on top. Place pins every ½" (1.3 cm) to keep fullness from shifting. Stitch with the longer seam on top and gently ease in the extra fullness as you stitch.

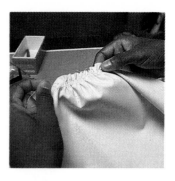

Ease Stitching

To ease a greater amount of fullness, use one or two rows of ease stitching. Follow the techniques as for gathering.

1. *Stitch* close to the seamline with long machine stitches, extending the stitching slightly beyond the markings.
2. *Stitch* a second row ¼" (6 mm) away in the seam allowance for set-in sleeves.
3. *Pin* the fabric, right sides together, with eased side up.
4. *Pull* up thread between the markings and distribute fullness evenly.
5. *Stitch* along seamline, being careful not to stitch in any folds or gathers.

CHAPTER 9

Plain Seams

A seam is a line of stitching used to hold two layers of fabric together. A plain seam is the standard seam used for most sewing. It is ⅝″ (1.6 cm) deep and is stitched with the standard stitch length for your fabric. Patterns are designed with standard seams unless stated otherwise. (For special types of seams, see page 405.)

STITCHING A SEAM

For best results, always follow these steps:

1. *Staystitch* any bias or curved areas ½″ (1.3 cm) from the cut edge.
2. *Pinbaste* fabric layers along seamline, with right sides together. Match fabric ends and notches, then pin. Place additional pins 6″ (15 cm) apart to keep edges of the fabric even. Insert pins at a right angle to the stitching line, with the heads toward the seam allowance.
3. *Raise* needle and take-up lever to their highest point. Be sure the thread ends are back behind the presser foot to prevent the thread from pulling out or jamming when you start to stitch.
4. *Position* fabric under the needle. Line up the edge with the ⅝″ (1.6 cm)

marking on the right side of the needle plate. Place the fabric about ½″ (1.3 cm) in from the end for backstitching. Turn the hand wheel to lower the needle into the fabric. Lower presser foot.
5. *Backstitch* for ½″ (1.3 cm) to beginning of the seamline.
6. *Stitch* forward slowly and evenly to end of the seam. Remove the pins as you stitch. Or if your machine allows, stitch slowly over the pins.
7. *Backstitch* ½″ (1.3 cm) to secure the end.
8. *Remove* fabric by turning hand wheel to raise the take-up lever and needle to their highest position. Lift the presser foot. Slide the fabric toward the back of the machine. Clip the threads at both beginning and end of the seam.
9. *Finish* the seam edges, if necessary. (See page 405.)
10. *Press* the seam open.

Turning a Corner

To turn a corner in the middle of a seam, pivot the fabric. Stitch to within ⅝″ (1.6 cm) of the corner and stop with the needle down in the fabric. Lift the presser foot and turn the fabric on the needle. Lower the presser foot and continue stitching in the new direction.

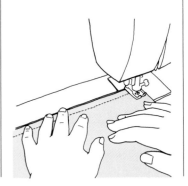

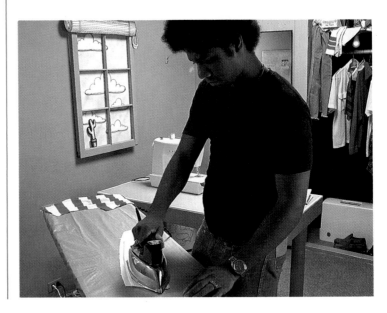

Turning a Sharp Point

To turn a sharp point, such as the point of a collar, take one or two diagonal stitches across the corner. The extra stitch makes a thinner, neater corner when the point is turned to the right side. Stitch to the corner and leave the needle down in the fabric. Raise the presser foot and turn the fabric diagonally. Lower the presser foot and make one or two stitches by turning the hand wheel. Leave the needle in the fabric, raise the presser foot, and turn the fabric to complete the corner. Lower the foot and continue stitching.

Reinforcing

To reinforce a sharp corner or point, such as a V-neckline or placket, use reinforcement stitches, 15–20 per inch (1–1.5 mm in length), for about 1″ (2.5 cm) on either side of the point. This will help prevent fabric yarns from pulling out of the seam after the fabric is trimmed and turned.

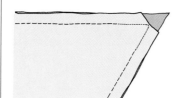

SPECIAL SEAM TREATMENTS

Some seams may need special treatment to reduce bulk in the seam allowance. Enclosed seams, such as necklines, collars, and cuffs, should lie flat and smooth. Curved seams and corners also need special treatment. There are several different ways to reduce the bulk of a seam, among them are *trimming, grading, clipping, and notching.*

Trimming

Seam allowances of enclosed seams should be trimmed to an even width, usually ¼″ (6 mm). The corner of a seam allowance should be trimmed diagonally to remove extra thickness when the corner is turned. If the corner is very pointed, make an additional diagonal cut on each side of the point, trimming to ⅛″ (3 mm).

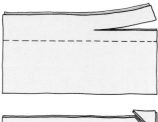

Curved seams, such as the lower part of an armhole and the center back seam of pants, are usually trimmed. Usually these areas are reinforced with two rows of stitching ¼″ (6 mm) apart, and then trimmed close to the second row of stitching.

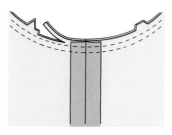

Grading

Enclosed seams in heavier fabrics should be *graded,* or *layered.* Also, seams with three layers of fabric, such as a collar stitched to a neckline, should be graded. Grading means to trim each layer to a different width to reduce bulk.

Always grade a seam so that the widest seam allowance is next to the outside of the garment. This reduces press marks on the right side. To grade, trim the seam allowance in half. Then trim the seam allowance toward the inside of the garment in half again. For three layers, trim each one slightly narrower.

Clipping

On a curved seam, the seam allowances should be clipped to allow the curve to lie flat when pressed. Clipping is done after the seam is trimmed or graded. Using the point of your scissors, make a tiny clip or snip in the seam allowance every ¼" to ½" (3–6 mm). Clip to within ⅛" (3 mm) of the seamline or up to the staystitching line. The sharper the curve, the closer together the clips should be made.

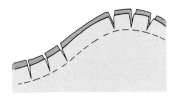

Sometimes an inward curve or corner must be clipped before stitching the seam. Stitch a row of reinforcement stitches, 15 to 20 stitches per inch (1–1.5 mm in length), just inside the seamline in the seam allowance. Clip up to the reinforcement stitches to allow the fabric to lie flat for stitching the seam.

Notching

Some curved seams have too much fabric in the seam allowance after being trimmed or graded. The extra fabric forms ripples and does not allow the seam to lie flat. These are usually outward curves, such as the edge of a patch pocket or collar, that are then turned and pressed to form an inward curve.

Notching means cutting tiny wedgeshaped pieces of fabric from the seam allowances. Notch no closer than ⅛" (3 mm) to the seamline. When pressed, the sides of the notches should meet.

PRESSING SEAMS

Seams should be pressed after they are stitched and before they are crossed by another seam. Check your pattern guide sheet to see if the seam is to be pressed open or to one side.

First, press all seams flat to blend in the stitches. Then open the seam allowances and press again. If necessary, press both seam allowances to one side. Curved seams should be pressed over a tailor's ham.

Enclosed seams in a collar or cuff should be pressed open before turning. Use a point presser or a sleeve board and press with the tip of your iron. Then turn the fabric to the right side and lay flat on the ironing board with the underside up. Roll the edge in just until the seam shows and press lightly. This helps to prevent the underside or facing from showing along the edge.

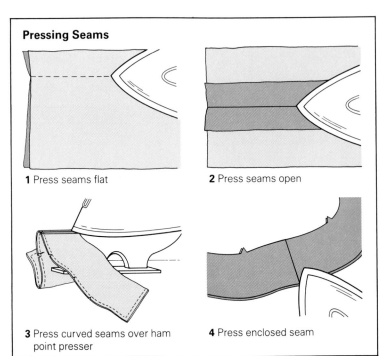

Pressing Seams

1 Press seams flat

2 Press seams open

3 Press curved seams over ham point presser

4 Press enclosed seam

SEAM FINISHES

Seam finishes are needed on woven fabrics that will ravel or fray. Sometimes seam finishes are used to give the inside of an unlined jacket, vest, or coat a neater, more professional appearance. Seam finishes are done after the seams of the garment are stitched and pressed. The method to use depends upon the type of fabric and the reason for finishing the seams. Zigzag stitching or pinking are the easiest and quickest methods to do.

Types of Finishes

• *Machine Zigzag Finish.* This is a fast and easy method for finishing fabrics that ravel. Set the zigzag setting for medium width and length. For loosely woven or heavy fabrics, use a wide-stitch width. Zigzag along the edge of each seam allowance.

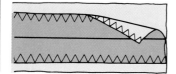

• *Pinked Finish.* Most firmly woven fabrics can be trimmed with pinking shears. However, pinking does not prevent raveling entirely. For more protection, stitch ¼" (6 mm) from each edge before pinking. Press the seam open.

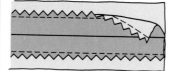

• *Hand Overcast Finish.* This method is very time-consuming, but is sometimes used for sheer or delicate fabrics. Make overcast stitches by hand over the edge of the seam allowances.

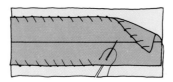

• *Hemmed Finish.* This method forms a narrow, single-fold hem along the edges of the seam allowances. It is also called a *clean finish* or a *turned and stitched finish.* This method can be used on light to mediumweight fabrics. It makes an attractive finish for unlined jackets. Turn edge under ¼" (6 mm) and press. Stitch close to folded edge.

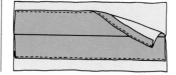

• *Bound Finish.* This finish is suitable for medium to heavyweight fabrics. It also is an attractive finish for unlined jackets and coats. Trim notches. Slip double-fold bias tape over the raw edge of the seam allowances and stitch in place.

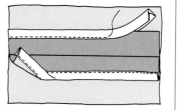

The *Hong Kong Finish* is a special bound finish. Cut 1" (2.5 cm)-wide bias strips of lining fabric. Place the bias strip and seam allowance right sides together. Stitch ¼" (6 mm) from the edge. Fold the bias strip over the edge to underside and pin it in place. Stitch-in-the-ditch exactly over the previous row of stitching. Trim the bias strip close to the stitching on the underside.

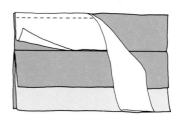

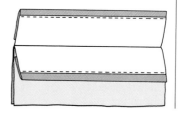

CHAPTER 10

Facings

A facing is used to finish a raw edge, such as a neckline or armhole. It may be a separate piece of fabric or cut in one with the garment. It is then turned to the inside for a smooth finish. Facings should not be visible from the outside.

The necessary facing pattern pieces are included in your pattern envelope. If you made any adjustments in the pattern, be sure to make the same changes in the facing pieces before cutting out the fabric.

TYPES OF FACINGS

There are three general types of facings: *shaped, extended,* and *bias.*

- *Shaped Facing.* This cut is the same shape as the area it will cover. It is stitched, then turned to the inside of the garment. It is also called a *fitted facing.* A separate pattern piece is given for a shaped facing.

- *Extended Facing.* This is cut in one piece with the garment and folded to the inside. It is used along a front or back opening.

- *Bias Facing.* This strip of bias fabric is stitched to the garment and turned to the inside. It is used mostly for very bulky or sheer fabrics.

Use purchased bias tape or cut bias strips from lining fabric.

Types of Facings

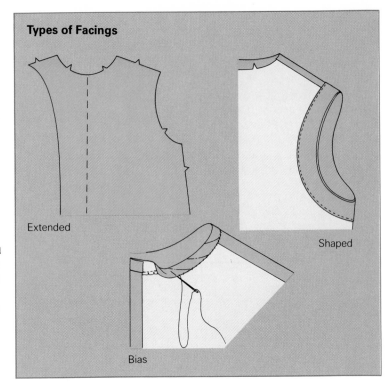

Extended

Shaped

Bias

STITCHING FACINGS

All three types of facings are attached to a garment in the same way.

Construct Facing

1. *Staystitch* the notched edge.
2. *Pin* the right sides of the facing pieces together, matching the notches.

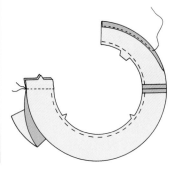

3. *Stitch* seams, trim, and press open.
4. *Finish* the outside edge of the facing with pinking or stitching. (See SEAM FINISHES, page 405.)

For a hemmed finish, first stitch a row of staystitching ¼" (6 mm) from the outside unnotched edge. This will make it easier to turn under the hem along the staystitching line.

Knitted fabrics do not require a finish. However, a row of staystitching around the outer edge will help the facings to hold their shape better. If a garment is to be lined, no edge finish is needed.

For a bias facing, no construction is necessary.

Attach Facing to Garment

1. *Pin* the facing to the garment edge, right sides together. For an extended facing, turn the facing to the right side along the foldline.
2. *Stitch* the seams. Trim or grade the seam allowances; trim the corners. Clip the curved areas.

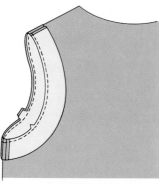

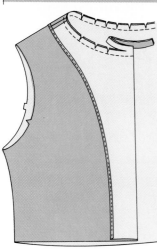

3. *Press* the seam allowances open, then press toward the facing.
4. *Turn* the facing to the inside of garment. Press along the seamline, rolling the seam slightly toward the facing side.

For a bias facing, open out one long edge of bias tape.

1. *Pin* the crease line of the tape along the seamline of the garment, right sides together.
2. *Stitch* the seamline. Trim, grade, and clip the seam allowances.

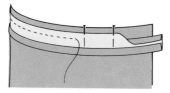

3. *Fold* the bias tape to the inside of the garment and press.
4. *Slipstitch* the edge in place.

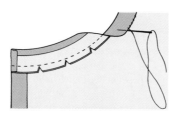

Understitch Facing

Understitching is *a row of stitches used to prevent a shaped or extended facing from rolling to the outside of a garment.*

1. *Open* out the facing flat, with the seam allowances toward the facing.
2. *Machine stitch* close to the seamline from the right side of the facing through all seam allowances. Gently pull on the fabric on either side of the seamline to keep it flat.

3. *Turn* the facing to the inside and press.
4. Or *topstitch* the garment edge from the outside, instead of understitching.

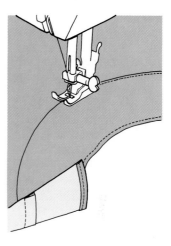

Tack Facing at Seams

The edge of the facing should be **tacked,** or *fastened,* at each seam allowance. Use a blindstitch, a cross-stitch tack, or the stitch-in-the-ditch method. (See STITCH-ING, page 394.) Or fuse the facing and garment seam allowances together with a small piece of fusible web, following the manufacturer's directions.

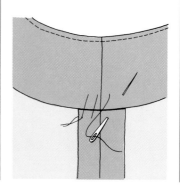

CHAPTER 11
Casings

A **casing** is *a closed tunnel of fabric that holds a piece of elastic or a drawstring inside.* Casings are used at sleeve edges, necklines, waistlines, and hemlines to help control fullness. The elastic or drawstring makes the garment adjustable. A casing is much easier to construct than a waistband or a cuff and thus is used in many beginner or easy-to-sew patterns.

There are two basic types:

- **Self-Casing.** This is formed by *folding over the edge of the garment and stitching in place.*

- **Applied Casing.** This is *made by sewing a separate strip of fabric or bias tape to the garment.* An applied casing can be sewn to the edge of a garment or inside a garment, such as a waistline casing in a jumpsuit.

Casings can also be sewn with headings. A **heading** is *a width of fabric between the casing and the edge of the garment.* A narrow heading has a more tailored appearance. A wider heading creates a ruffle edge.

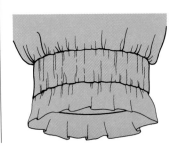

SELF-CASING

A self-casing is made similar to a hem.

1. *Turn* the raw edge under ¼″ (6 mm) and press.

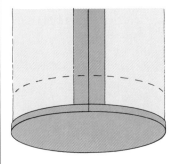

2. *Turn* the casing to the inside of the garment along the fold line and pin in place. Press the outer edge of the casing.

3. *Stitch* close to the inner pinned edge of the casing. Leave a 2″ (5 cm) opening at a side seam or center back to insert the elastic. If the casing has a header, stitch around the heading line.

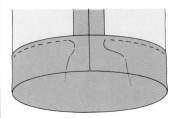

APPLIED CASING

Either a single-fold bias tape or a strip of fabric can be used for an applied casing. The length of the tape or fabric strip should be ½″ (1.3 cm) longer than the finished casing. The width of the strip should be 1″ (2.5 cm) wider than the width of the elastic. Your pattern guide sheet should include cutting instructions or a separate pattern piece for the casing. Fold in the long edges of the fabric strip ¼″ (6 mm) and press before you begin.

At Edge of Garment

1. *Pin* one edge of casing to the garment, with right sides together. Fold the back ends.
2. *Stitch* a ¼″ (6 mm) seam.
3. *Turn* the casing to the inside of the garment and press.
4. *Edgestitch* the other edge of the casing to garment.

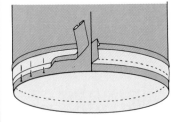

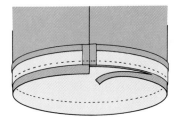

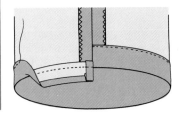

Within Garment

1. *Pin* the casing to the garment, using the placement markings on your pattern. Turn under the casing ends so the folds meet without overlapping.
2. *Edgestitch* along both long edges of the casing.

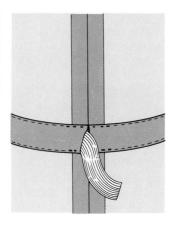

ELASTIC

Several different types of elastic are available, including special elastics for swimwear and lingerie. Your pattern will recommend the proper width of elastic to use. The elastic should be about ⅛″ (3 mm) narrower than the finished casing so it can be pulled through the casing easily. If the casing is too wide, the elastic may twist and roll inside the casing as the garment is worn.

Your guide sheet will give directions for cutting just the right length of elastic for your needs. If not, measure your body at the casing position and add 1″ (2.5 cm) for overlapping the elastic ends.

Using Elastic

1. *Pull* the elastic through the casing with a safety pin, being careful not to twist it. Leave the ends extending several inches at the opening.

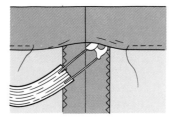

2. *Overlap* the ends ½″ (1.3 cm) and pin together. Try on the garment to check fit and adjust the elastic if necessary.
3. *Stitch* overlapped ends securely by machine.

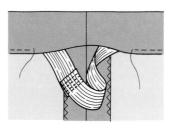

4. *Finish* the opening of a self-casing by completing the edgestitching, stretching the elastic as you stitch. Finish the opening of an applied casing by slipstitching along the folded ends.

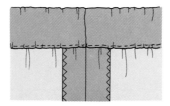

DRAWSTRINGS

Drawstrings can be made from cord, tubing, braid, and ribbon. You will need an opening in the garment to pull the drawstring through to either the outside or the inside. The opening can be either two buttonholes or a slit in a seam. The opening should be reinforced with a small piece of fabric or fusible interfacing.

Make buttonhole openings in the outer fabric before the casing is stitched. A seam opening is made as you stitch the seam. Leave the seam open between markings, and reinforce the opening with backstitching. Use a safety pin to pull the drawstring through the casing. Ends of the drawstring can be knotted to prevent it from pulling out of the casing during wearing or washing.

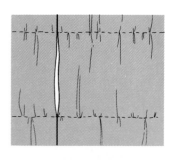

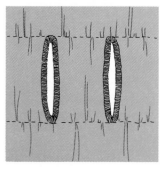

CHAPTER 12

Fasteners

Fasteners are used to help close garments securely. They include *hooks and eyes, snaps, special nylon tapes, buttons,* and *zippers.* There is a wide variety of fasteners for many different purposes. Some are decorative as well as functional. Sometimes a combination of fasteners will be used on the same closing of a garment—such as a hook and eye above a zipper, or a snap with a button.

Your pattern envelope will recommend which type of fastener is needed for your garment. Usually snaps, hooks and eyes, and buttons are attached by hand. Use a double strand of thread or buttonhole twist. Always secure the stitches with a knot or tiny backstitches.

HOOKS AND EYES

Hooks and eyes are available in a variety of sizes and types. Small hooks and eyes are used most often at necklines and waistlines. Large covered hooks and eyes are available for jackets and coats. Special heavy-duty hooks and bars are designed for waistbands on pants and skirts.

Hooks are sold with two kinds of eyes—a *straight eye* for edges that overlap, and a *round eye* for edges that meet. A thread eye may be used in place of a metal eye for a less noticeable one.

Edges That Overlap

A hook and a straight eye are used for edges that overlap. The hook is placed on the overlap side.

Hook

1. *Place* the hook on the underside of the overlap at least ⅛″ (3 mm) from the edge.
2. *Stitch* around each loop with a buttonhole or overcast stitch. Sew only to the facing fabric. No stitches should show on the right side of the garment.
3. *Slide* the needle between the fabric layers to the end of the hook. Take three or four stitches across the end of the hook to hold it flat against the fabric. Secure threads.

Straight Eye

1. *Overlap* the edges.
2. *Mark* the position of the eye by placing a pin in the fabric under the bend of the hook.
3. *Stitch* the eye in place with buttonhole or overcast stitches around each loop. Secure threads.

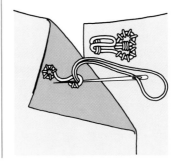

A *thread eye* should be made the same length as a metal eye. Use either a blanket stitch or a chain stitch. (See HAND STITCHING, page 395.)

Edges That Meet

A hook and a round eye are used for edges that meet.

Hook

1. *Stitch* hook in place ⅛″ (3 mm) from the edge.
2. *Stitch around* each loop with a buttonhole or overcast stitch.
3. *Stitch across* the end of the hook to hold it flat against the fabric. Secure threads.

Round Eye

1. *Match* garment edges.
2. *Position* the eye so that the loop extends ⅛″ (3 mm) beyond the edge. When hook and eye are attached, the garment edges should meet exactly.
3. *Stitch* around each loop with buttonhole or overcast stitches. Secure threads.

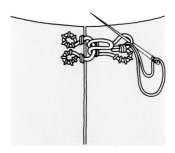

A *thread loop* can be made with either a blanket stitch or a chain stitch. (See HAND STITCHING, page 395.)

SNAPS

Snaps are used to hold over-lapping edges together where there is not much strain. They are available in a variety of sizes. Small snaps are used at necklines or cuffs. Heavy gripper snaps are used for children's clothes and sportswear. Large covered snaps are available for jackets and coats.

Snaps are made of two sections—a ball half and a socket half. The *ball half* is sewn to the overlap. The *socket half* is sewn to the underlap.

Sewing on a Snap

1. *Center* the ball half of the snap over the marking on the underside of the overlap. Be sure it is at least ⅛″ (3 mm) from the edge.
2. *Sew* three or four stitches through each hole. Use either the overcast stitch or the buttonhole stitch. Carry thread under the snap from one hole to the next. Stitch only through the facing, being careful not to have any stitches show on the right side of the garment. Secure threads.
3. *Mark* the position of socket half of snap. Overlap the edges and push a pin through the ball of the snap to the underlap. Or rub tailor's chalk on the ball and press it on the fabric.
4. *Place* the socket half over the marking. Hold in place by inserting a pin

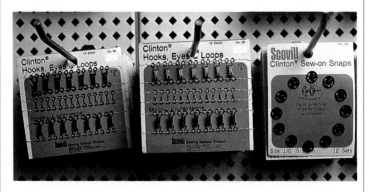

through the center hole of the socket and into the fabric.
5. *Stitch* in place in same manner as the ball half, except stitch through all the layers of fabric.

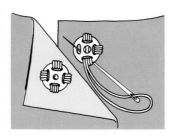

A *hanging snap* can be used instead of a hook and eye on edges that meet. It is used most often to fasten a neckline above a long back zipper. Sew the socket half to the inside of neckline. Attach the ball half of the snap to the opposite side with a thread loop, using blanket stitches.

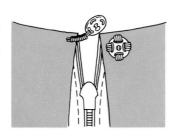

HOOK AND LOOP TAPE

Hook and loop tape is a special nylon-tape fastener. It is available in strips or precut into round or square shapes. One side has tiny hooks, the other has a looped pile. When pressed together, the two sides interlock until pulled apart. Hook and loop tape can be used on over-lapping edges. It is excellent for sportswear, children's clothes, home furnishings, and craft items.

Using Hook and Loop Tape

1. *Cut* strips to desired length.
2. *Place* the loop half on the underside of the over-lapping edge.
3. *Position* the hook half directly underneath on the underlap.
4. *Machine stitch* around the tapes.

BUTTONHOLES AND BUTTONS

Buttons and buttonholes can be used on all types of overlapping edges, such as collars, cuffs, center fronts and backs, pockets, and waistbands. They are a very strong fastener and are able to withstand much pulling and strain. Besides being functional, buttons and buttonholes can add a decorative accent to your garment.

Buttonholes should always be completed first; then the buttons are sewn in place. Traditionally, buttonholes are made on the right front side in girls' and women's garments. On boys' and men's clothing, buttonholes are made on the left front side.

BUTTONHOLES

There are two types of buttonholes, *bound* and *worked*:

- *Bound Buttonholes.* These are finished with strips of fabric. They are made in the garment before the facing is attached. Bound buttonholes are often used when tailoring a jacket or coat. (Refer to BOUND BUTTONHOLES, page 455.)

- *Worked Buttonholes.* These are finished with thread and can be stitched by machine or by hand. They are made after the garment is completed.

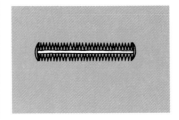

1. *Machine-worked buttonholes* can be easily stitched with a zigzag machine stitch. They can be used on almost all fabrics. However, they are not recommended for very lightweight fabrics that may pucker, or for heavy, loosely woven fabrics that may fray.

2. *Handworked buttonholes* are stitched with a buttonhole stitch (see page 413). They are used primarily on fabrics that are too lightweight or too loosely woven to machine stitch.

Before making any type of buttonhole on your garment, always make a sample buttonhole on a piece of scrap fabric.

Buttonhole Placement

The location of each buttonhole is indicated on your pattern pieces. If you have adjusted the length of your pattern, then changes may have to be made. Respace the buttonholes evenly between the top and the bottom buttonholes on the pattern. Sometimes a buttonhole may have to be added or subtracted.

Buttonholes should extend a little beyond the button placement marking to allow for the shank of the button. *Horizontal buttonholes* begin ⅛″ (3 mm) beyond the button marking toward the fabric edge. *Vertical buttonholes* begin ⅛″ (3 mm) above the button marking. Vertical buttonholes are often used on shirt bands or for a row of small buttons.

If you chose a larger size button than the pattern rec-

ommends, double check the buttonhole placement. Be sure the buttonholes are placed far enough from the edge of the garment so that the buttons will not extend beyond the edge when the garment is buttoned.

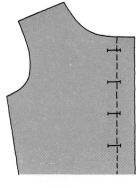

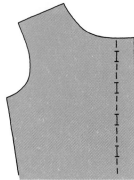

Buttonhole Length

The length of the buttonhole is determined by the size of the button. The length should equal the diameter of the button, plus its thickness. The pattern piece has buttonhole markings equal to the diameter of the recommended button size plus ⅛" (3 mm). If you choose a different size button, you will have to adjust the length of the buttonhole.

Buttonhole Markings

Machine-worked buttonholes are stitched from the right side of the fabric. It is important to choose a marking method that will not leave a permanent line on the outside of your garment. Hand basting is usually used for marking. Use contrasting thread and a long, uneven basting stitch, or machine baste. If you use tailor's chalk, always test to see that the marks can be removed easily from your fabric.

Several lines should be marked:

- *center lines* that must meet when closing is fastened,
- *short lines* that indicate the ends of each buttonhole,
- *long lines* that indicate the length of each buttonhole.

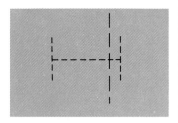

Machine-Worked Buttonholes

Some sewing machines have a built-in buttonhole attachment. Others are operated manually by changing the zig-zag-stitch width. Special buttonhole attachments can also be purchased. Always check to be sure there is plenty of thread on the bobbin. It is difficult to rethread in the middle of a buttonhole:

1. *Mark* location of the buttonhole on the right side of the garment.
2. *Stitch* the buttonhole, following the instructions in your sewing machine manual.
3. *Place* a pin across each end of the buttonhole to prevent cutting through end stitching.
4. *Cut* the buttonhole opening, using small, sharp scissors. Insert the scissor blade in the center of the buttonhole, and cut from the center in both directions.

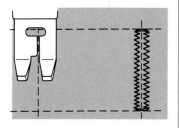

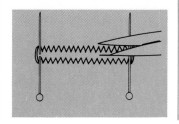

BUTTONS

Buttons are available in a wide variety of sizes, shapes, and designs. Your pattern envelope will list the size of button to be used, stated in fractions of an inch. The size of a button is the measurement of its diameter.

Button Placement

Mark the placement of the buttons through the buttonhole openings, rather than from the pattern. This will assure that each button will be in the correct position:

1. *Overlap* the fabric edges with the buttonhole on top. Match the center lines or overlap lines.
2. *Place* a pin through the buttonhole, ⅛″ (3 mm) from the end, along the center line.
3. *Slip* the buttonhole over the head of each pin and separate the garment sections. Be careful when doing this step.

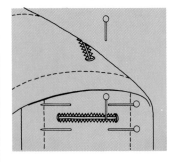

Attaching Buttons

Buttons should be sewn with a double strand of thread. Heavy-duty thread or but-

tonhole twist can be used for extra strength on heavier garments. Thread can also be pulled through special beeswax to make it stronger.

The two basic types of buttons are *sew-through buttons* and *shank buttons*. They are attached differently.

• *Sew-Through Buttons.* These have holes or "eyes" in the face of the button. Buttons used only for decoration can be sewn flat against the fabric. Buttons used with a buttonhole should be attached with a thread shank. The shank allows the buttonhole to fit smoothly between the button and the under fabric. The length of the thread shank is determined by the thickness of the fabric:

1. *Secure* the thread at the button marking with small backstitches.
2. *Place* a toothpick, heavy pin, or matchstick on the top of button.
3. *Bring* the needle up through one hole, over the toothpick or other object, and down through second hole. Continue to make several stitches through the button and fabric. If the button has four

holes, repeat stitching at the other pair of holes. End stitches with the needle and thread under the button.

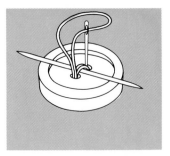

4. *Remove* the object and pull the button to the top of the thread loop.

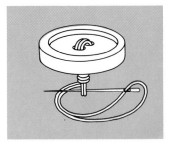

5. *Wind* the thread tightly around the stitches under the button to form a thread shank. Fasten the thread securely in the fabric under the button.

Sew-through buttons can also be attached with zigzag machine stitching. Follow instructions in your sewing manual.

• *Shank Buttons.* These have a metal or plastic loop on the back of the button. Thread is stitched through the shank to attach the button to the fabric.

1. *Secure* thread at the marking with backstitches.
2. *Stitch* through the shank and fabric with four or five small, even stitches.
3. *Fasten* the thread securely in the fabric under the button.

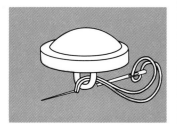

Sometimes buttons on heavy fabric or in areas of extra strain need reinforcement. Sew a small, flat button to the wrong side of the garment as you are stitching the sew-through or shank button in place.

ZIPPERS

Zippers are available in different types, weights, and lengths. The most common type of zipper is the *conventional zipper,* which has a stop at the bottom. Specialty zippers, such as separating, decorative, and heavy-duty zippers, are also available. Your pattern envelope will recommend the type and length of zipper to choose for your project.

Zippers can be stitched in a variety of ways. The meth-

ods are known as *applications.* Refer to your pattern guide sheet for which application to use. You will also find instructions for applications in the zipper packages.

The Conventional Zipper

The conventional zipper can be used for the three most common applications.

Zipper Guidelines

For a smooth zipper application, follow these general guidelines:
- Preshrink zipper.
- To shorten a zipper, machine zigzag or whipstitch across the teeth or coil in one place to form a new bottom stop. Cut away the zipper ½" (1.3 cm) below the stitching.
- Staystitch any curved or bias seamlines to prevent stretching.
- If seam allowances are less than ⅝" (1.6 cm), stitch seam tape to the edge for extra width.
- Check your pattern guide sheet to see if the zipper should be stitched before or after any facing is attached.
- Check the length of the zipper opening. Place the zipper teeth or coil ¾" (1.9 cm) from the top edge of the fabric. If some type of fastener will be sewn above the zipper, place the zipper 1" (2.5 cm) below the top edge. Mark the fabric where the teeth or coils end at the bottom of the zipper.
- Stitch the seam below the zipper marking, using a regular machine stitch. Backstitch ¼" (6 mm) to secure the seam.
- Machine baste the zipper opening. Clip the basting every inch (2.5 cm) to make it easier to remove after the application is finished. Press the seam open. Be sure to match plaids and stripes carefully.
- If sewing the zipper by machine, use a zipper foot attachment so you can stitch close to the zipper.
- If sewing the zipper by hand, use a pickstitch.
- Always stitch both sides of the zipper in the same direction to prevent any wrinkles or puckers in the zipper placket.

- *Centered Zipper Application.* It has the zipper in the center of the seam with two rows of stitching along each side. Equal amounts of fabric cover the zipper teeth or coil on either side. It can be used in center front and center back seams.

- *Lapped Zipper Application.* This has one placket, or lap of fabric, covering the zipper. Only one row of stitching shows on the outside. It can be used in side seams, as well as center front and center back seams.

- *Fly Front Application.* This is similar to the lapped zipper, but the lap is wider. It can be used as a front closing on pants or skirts.

Inserting the Zipper

Always follow the directions in your pattern guide sheet for inserting a zipper. Or use the following methods:

Centered Zipper Application

1. *Machine baste* the seam and press open.
2. *Place* the zipper face down on the open seam

Centered Zipper Application

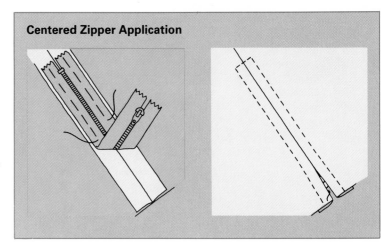

allowance. Center the zipper teeth or coils exactly on top of the basted seam. Hold the zipper in place with hand basting or sewing tape.
3. *Spread* the garment flat, right side up. Mark the bottom stop of the zipper with a pin. Attach the zipper foot.
4. *Begin stitching* at the lower end of the zipper on the right side of the fabric. Stitch across the end, pivot, and up along one side ¼″ (6 mm) from the basted seam.

5. *Begin* again at the lower end and stitch the other side in the same manner.
6. *Pull* the thread ends at the bottom to the wrong side of fabric and knot.
7. *Remove* the machine basting. Press.

Lapped Zipper Application

1. *Machine baste* the seam and press open.
2. *Open* the zipper. Place it face down on the back seam allowance with the teeth or coil at the seamline. Pin, baste, or tape in place.

Lapped Zipper Application

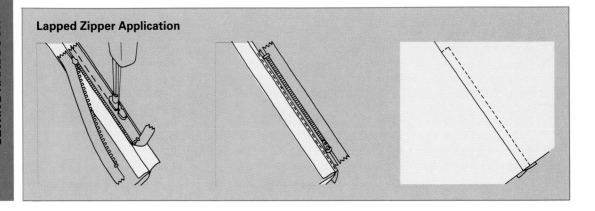

3. *Machine stitch* through the zipper tape and seam allowance only, from the bottom to top of zipper. Use the zipper foot to stitch close to the edge of the zipper.

4. *Close* the zipper and turn it face up. Smooth the fabric away from the zipper, forming a narrow fold between the zipper coil and basted seam.

5. *Machine stitch* close to the fold, beginning at the lower end of the zipper. Sew through the folded seam allowance and zipper tape only.

6. *Open* out the fabric and place the zipper face down on the front seam allowance. Turn the tab up. Pin in place.

7. *Machine baste* through the tape and seam allowance only, starting at the top of the zipper. This will hold the zipper in place for the final stitching.

8. *Stitch* from the right side of garment, beginning at the lower end of the zipper. Stitch across the bottom, pivot, and go up the side of the lap. Stitching should be ⅜" to ½" (9–13 cm) from the seam.

9. *Pull* the thread ends to the wrong side of the fabric and knot.

10. *Remove* the basting stitches and press.

Fly Front Application

Follow the same steps as for the lapped zipper application.

CHAPTER 13
Hems

A hem is used to finish the bottom edge of a shirt, jacket, sleeve, skirt, or pants leg. Hem lengths vary according to fashion trends. However, it is important to select a hem length that is flattering to your own body proportions.

A well-made hem should not be noticeable.

- The stitches should not show on the outside of the garment.
- The hem edge should be flat and smooth.
- The garment should hang evenly around your body.

However, hems can also be an important part of the garment design. A decorative binding or topstitching can add special interest to a hemline.

Hems can be made in a variety of ways, depending upon the type of fabric and the design of your garment. However, most hems are made by turning the raw edge of fabric to the inside of the garment. Then the edge of the hem is held in place by hand stitching, machine stitching, or fusing.

To *finish a hem,* follow these four basic steps:

1. *Mark* the hem length.
2. *Turn* up the hem.
3. *Finish* the hem edge.
4. *Attach* the hem to the garment.

Mark Hem Length

Your garment should hang on a hanger for at least 24 hours before the hem is marked. This allows any bias areas of the garment to stretch and prevents the hemline from sagging.

Put on the garment with the same clothes and shoes that you will wear with it. Fasten all openings and any belt. Stand in your normal posture with your weight on both feet. For complete accuracy, have someone else mark the hem for you. You should remain standing still, and the person doing the marking should move around you.

Choose a hem length that suits the style of the garment and your own body proportions.

- *Skirts and Dresses.* Use a yardstick, meterstick, or skirt marker. Be sure to keep the marker at right angles to the floor. Place pins every 3" or 4" (8–10 cm) around the hemline. Or mark with chalk. Turn the hem to the inside along the markings and pin to check length. Readjust if necessary.

- *Pants.* Fold under the edge of the fabric and pin. The front of the pants should just touch the top of the shoe; the back should be

Marking Hem Length

about ½" (1.3 cm) longer than the top of the shoe.

• *Jackets.* Fold under the fabric along the hemline marked on the pattern and pin. Adjust the length according to your own body proportions. Be sure that the hem is even around your entire body.

• *Sleeves.* Bend your arm so that your hand is in the center of your waistline. Fold under the edge of the sleeve until it just covers the wrist bone. Pin in place.

Turn Up Hem

After the hemline is marked, the hem must be trimmed to the proper width and any extra fullness eliminated.

Trim Width Your pattern will recommend the proper width of the finished hem. Most hems are 2" to 3" (5–8 cm) in depth. This gives added weight to the hemline and helps it to fall evenly. However, the width of the hem will depend on the flare of the garment and the weight of the fabric. A curved edge will have a narrower hem than a straight edge. Knitted or heavier weight fabrics may have a narrower hem. Sheer fabrics usually have a narrow rolled hem or a very deep hem. Follow these steps:

1. *Fold* the hem up along the marked line.
2. *Measure* an even distance from the folded edge with a sewing gauge or a small ruler.
3. *Mark* the desired hem width with chalk.
4. *Trim* away excess fabric.
5. *Remove* any pins and lightly press the fold of the hem.

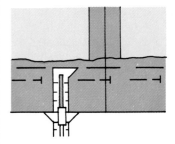

Eliminate Fullness If the garment is flared, the turned up hem will be wider at the upper edge than the garment.

This fullness must be eased in to fit flat against the garment:

1. *Machine baste,* 6 to 8 stitches per inch (3–4 mm in length), ¼″ (6 mm) from the upper edge of the hem.
2. *Turn* the hem up and pin at each seam and at the center.
3. *Use* a pin to pick up a stitch of the bobbin thread of the machine basting. Gently pull the thread toward a seam to ease in the extra fabric.
4. *Press* the hem allowance to shrink out fullness.

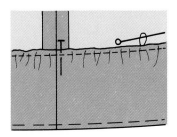

On fabrics that cannot be eased, remove the extra fullness by tapering the seamline below the hem. Take the same amount off each seam. Remove the original stitching and trim the seam allowances to remove the bulk. Press the seam open.

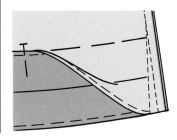

Finish the Hem Edge

The type of hem finish to use depends upon the fabric and the type of garment. The same finishes used for seams can also be used for hems. (Refer to CHAPTER 4, page 405.)

If the fabric ravels, some type of finish must be used to prevent fraying and raveling. Most knits do not need a finish. If you want to cover the edge of the hem, you can use seam tape, bias tape, lace, or other decorative trim.

• *Machine Zigzag Finish.* Use for all weights of fabrics. Zigzag close to edge of fabric.

• *Pinked Finish.* Use for more firmly woven fabrics. Pink edge, or stitch ¼″ (6 mm) from the edge and then pink.

• *Hemmed Finish.* Use for light to mediumweight fabrics. Turn under the raw edge ¼″ (6 mm) and stitch.

• *Seam Tape, Bias Tape, or Lace Finish.* These can be used on all fabrics. Place the tape or trim ¼″ (6 mm) over the raw edge and stitch, overlapping the ends.

Attach Hem to Garment

The hem can be attached to the garment by *hand stitching, machine stitching,* or *fusing.*

Hand Stitching   To hem by hand, use any of the following stitches: *blindstitch, catchstitch, slipstitch,* or *hemming stitch.* Use a single thread for hemming. Make sure that your stitches do not show on the outside of the garment. Keep stitches slightly loose

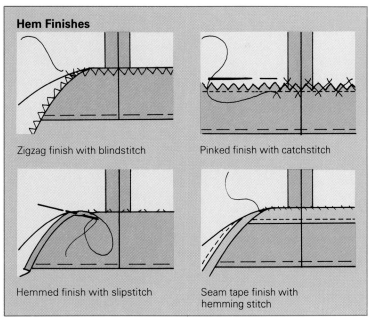

Hem Finishes

Zigzag finish with blindstitch

Pinked finish with catchstitch

Hemmed finish with slipstitch

Seam tape finish with hemming stitch

so that the fabric does not pull or ripple. (Refer to CHAPTER 6, page 392, for specific directions for making each of the stitches.)

- *Blindstitch.* This can be used with all types of fabrics and hem finishes. It shows less than any other type of stitch and allows for movement without pulling.

- *Catchstitch.* This is good for hemming knits and stretch fabrics. It can be done at the edge of the hem or as a blind catchstitch inside the hem.

- *Slipstitch.* It is used to join a folded edge, such as a hemmed finish, to the garment. Excellent for narrow, hand-rolled hems.

- *Hemming Stitch.* This can be used to stitch a hem with seam tape or lace finish.

Machine Stitching Machine stitching can be used for both decorative and invisible stitching. It is a fast, easy way to complete a garment or other type of sewing project.

Topstitching can be used to attach the hem and trim the garment at the same time. Fold the hem to the de-

sired width. For woven fabrics, turn under the raw edge ⅜″ (9 mm) and press. Stitch close to the upper edge. Knitted fabrics can be stitched single thickness and then trimmed close to the stitching. Use two or more rows of stitching for a more decorative finish. Be sure to keep the rows straight and parallel.

Some machines may have a built-in blindstitch. Fold back the garment ¼″ (6 mm) below the hem edge. Machine stitch so that the straight stitches fall on the hem allowance and the single zigzag stitch just catches the garment along the fold line.

Fusing Place fusible web between the garment and hem about ¼″ (6 mm) below the top of the hem. This helps to prevent the hem outline from showing on the right side of the garment. Also, it prevents any web from accidentally touching the iron and sticking to it. Press to fuse, following the manufacturer's directions accurately.

To alter a fused hem, press the area with steam until the two fabric layers can be gently pulled apart.

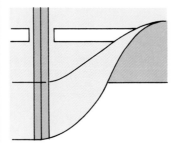

SPECIAL HEM TECHNIQUES

Some hems require special hemming techniques.

Hand-Rolled Hem

A narrow hand-rolled hem is used for sheer or lightweight scarves, blouses, and lingerie:

1. *Machine stitch* ¼″ (6 mm) from the raw edge and trim close to the stitching.
2. *Roll* the edge under between your thumb and forefinger until the stitching is concealed.
3. *Slipstitch* the hem in place, completing one small section at a time.

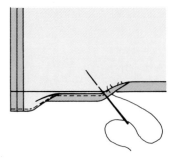

Faced Hem

A hem may be faced if there is not enough fabric for the hem allowance. Facings are also used if the hem edge is an unusual shape, such as scallops, or if the fabric is very heavy or bulky. Purchase bias hem facing or cut your own fabric facing.

1. *Pin* the facing to the garment, right sides together, overlapping the ends.
2. *Stitch* a ¼″ (6 mm) seam.

3. *Turn* the facing to the inside of the garment and slipstitch in place.

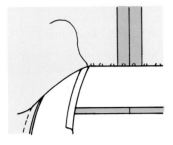

Hem with Pleat

1. *Clip* the seam allowance above the hem area.
2. *Press* the seam allowance open below the clip and trim to reduce the bulk.
3. *Complete* the hem.

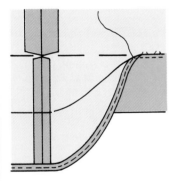

4. *Press* the pleat with the seam on the edge of the fold.
5. *Edgestitch* through all thicknesses.

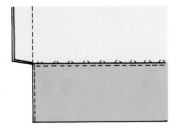

Pressing

Good pressing techniques are as important as good sewing skills. They work together to help you achieve professional results. Pressing starts with making sure that your pattern and fabric are wrinkle-free for accurate cutting. Pressing continues through every step of construction as it helps to smooth and shape your garment.

You should keep your pressing equipment near your sewing machine so that you will not be tempted to skip pressing as you sew. You will need an ironing board, a steam iron, and a press cloth. Either a tailor's ham or a press mitt should be used for pressing curved areas. Other types of pressing equipment can make the job easier but are not necessary. (See page 371.)

PRESSING BASICS

1. *Press; do not iron.* Pressing differs from ironing. When you iron, you slide the iron back and forth across the fabric. This may cause wrinkling and stretching of the fabric. In pressing, the iron is lowered to the place to be pressed, then raised off the fabric, and lowered again at the next spot. The heat and steam do most of the work so that heavy pres-

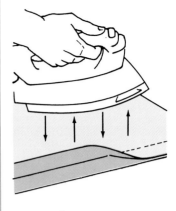

sure is not necessary. This helps to prevent stretching.

2. *Use the correct temperature setting for your fabric.* Set the temperature according to the fiber content of your fabric. However, do not use the cotton and linen settings for pressing as there is danger of scorching the fabric. If your fabric is a blend, use the setting for the most heat-sensitive fiber in the blend.

3. *Always test your fabric for any reaction to heat, steam, and pressure.* Use a scrap of fabric and check to be sure that it is not damaged or marked by the iron. If the fabric sticks, puckers, or melts, then the iron is too hot. Check to see if the fabric water spots. Too much pressure can crush napped fabrics or create press marks on the right side.

4. *Press on the wrong side of the fabric whenever possible.* Pressing on the inside prevents shine on the right side of the fab-

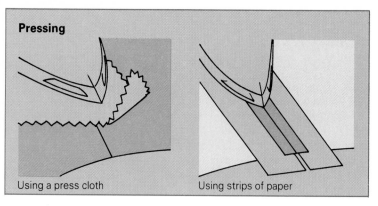

Pressing

Using a press cloth

Using strips of paper

ric. Also, seams can be seen clearly and pressed correctly.

5. *If pressing on the right side of the fabric, always use a press cloth.* Some areas, such as pleats and pockets, may have to be pressed on the outside of the garment. A press cloth will prevent a shiny mark being left on fabric.

6. *Never press over pins.* Pins will leave an impression on your fabric and may scratch your iron.

7. *Always press seams and darts before other seams are stitched across them.* This helps to reduce bulk and prevent any lumps in your finished garment.

8. *Press directionally with the grain of your fabric.* This will prevent stretching.

9. *Press seams flat before you press them open.* This allows the stitches to settle into the fabric. It also eliminates puckers and creates a smoother seam after it is pressed open.

10. *Press curved areas over a curved surface.* For example, use a tailor's ham or press mitt to maintain the curved shape of the fabric.

11. *Prevent press marks on the right side of the fabric.* Place strips of paper or an envelope under the edges of seam allowances, darts, and pleats to prevent impressions from appearing on the right side.

12. *Check the fit of the garment before you press any sharp creases, such as pleats.*

13. *Do not overpress.* Avoid heavy pressure and let the steam do the work. Use the tip of the iron in small places. Never press the fabric completely dry.

14. *When pressing an entire garment, start with the small areas.* First press the collar, cuffs, and other detail areas. Then press the small areas, such as sleeves and yokes. Finally, press the large flat areas of the garment.

15. *Follow safety procedures when using an iron and other pressing equipment.*

PRESSING TECHNIQUES

The pressing method to use depends upon whether the garment area is flat, curved, enclosed, gathered, or eased.

Flat Areas

Flat areas, such as straight seams, can be pressed flat on the ironing board.

1. *Place* the garment on the ironing board with both seam allowances to one side. Press the seamline to blend the stitches into the fabric.

2. *Open up* the fabric and place it over the ironing board. Press the seam allowances open, using your fingers and the tip of the iron to open the seam completely. Check on right side to be sure seam is perfectly smooth.

If a seam is to be pressed to one side, such as for a yoke or waistline, first press the seam flat. Then press the

seam allowances open. Finally, press the seam allowances toward one side.

Curved Areas

All darts or curved seams should be pressed over a curved tailor's ham or press mitt to maintain their shape:

1. *Press* dart or seam flat to blend stitches into fabric. Press darts only up to the point, and not beyond, to prevent pressing in a crease.
2. *Place* the fabric wrong side up over a tailor's ham or press mitt. Press the seam open. Press darts to one side. Vertical darts are pressed with the fold toward center front or center back. Horizontal darts are pressed with the fold down. Deep darts are pressed open after being slashed and trimmed to within 1″ of the point.

Enclosed Seams

Enclosed seams, such as those on the edge of a collar, facing, or cuff, should be pressed flat and then pressed open. This will give the seam a sharper edge when the piece is turned to the right side:

1. *Press* the seam flat to blend the stitches.
2. *Press* the seam open. Use a point presser to press all the way into the corner with the iron tip.
3. *Turn* right side out. Gently push out the corner or point.

4. *Press* the piece flat on the ironing board, slightly rolling the seam to the underside. This helps to prevent the seam from showing at the edge of the completed garment.

Gathered Areas

Gathers and ruffles should ripple softly below the seamline. They should not be pleated or crushed by the iron:

1. *Press* the seam allowances together to flatten the fabric above the seamline.
2. *Slip* the garment over the end of the ironing board. Turn the seam allowance away from the fullness.

3. *Press* directly up into the gathers with the point of the iron. Hold the seam allowance taut above the gathers with your other hand and lift it slightly up from the ironing board. This will help to prevent you from pressing folds into the gathers at the seamline.

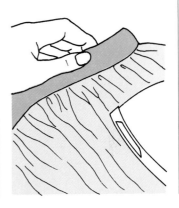

Shrinking in Fullness

Sometimes it is necessary to shrink in fullness. Press the curved seam of a sleeve cap over rounded end of ironing board or sleeve board. A hem can be pressed flat on the ironing board:

1. *Hold* the iron above the fabric to allow steam to penetrate before pressure is applied.

2. *Use* your fingers to pat out any folds and flatten the fabric.
3. *Press* the edge of the fabric to shrink in the fullness. Check to be sure that the sleeve or hem looks smooth on the right side of the garment.

FINAL PRESSING

If you have done a good job of pressing throughout the construction of your garment, then only a light pressing will be needed to remove any final wrinkles caused by handling. This final pressing should be merely a touch-up job. It should never be a cure-all for poor pressing during the construction.

Pressing Safety

- Don't touch a hot iron except on the handle.
- Keep hands and face away from steam.
- Do not overfill iron or the water can boil out. Use distilled water, if recommended by the iron manufacturer.
- Take care that the cord does not dangle off the ironing board. The iron could be accidentally pulled off onto you or the floor.
- Always rest the iron on the heel, not flat down on the soleplate.

- Turn off and unplug the iron after each use. Some irons should be drained of water each time.
- Keep the soleplate of the iron clean. Remove any substances that stick to the iron by rubbing back and forth over a clean piece of fabric. Or use a commercial iron cleaner.
- Store the iron in a protected place where it won't fall.
- Keep the cover of the ironing board clean. Check that the board is well padded.

CHAPTER 15

Fitting

Good fit is important to every garment. Clothes that fit well look attractive and are comfortable to wear. You will feel more confident when you know that your clothes are fitted just right for you.

Bodies are like fingerprints. No two are identical. So even though you started with a pattern in your correct size and figure type and made any necessary adjustments on the pattern, you still may need to do some fitting.

APPEARANCE

A well-fitting garment hangs smoothly on your body without obvious pulls and wrinkles. The center and side seams hang straight. The darts taper smoothly toward the fullest part of your body. The design details, such as collars and pockets, are flattering. The hemline is the right length for you.

The fit of a garment also depends on the style of the garment. Some designs are meant to be very full and loose, while others are snug and close-fitting. The amount of ease depends upon the fashion trend and the particular design.

Even your choice of fabric can affect the fit. For example, heavy or bulky fabrics require more ease in a garment than do lightweight fabrics. Knit fabrics and stretch fabrics require little ease because they stretch with your body.

Your own personal choice also influences the fit of your clothes. You may like your clothes to fit more loosely or snugly.

COMFORT

Good fit is necessary for ease of movement. You should be able to raise your arms, bend over, and sit down comfortably. You should be able to move about without having to constantly readjust your clothes.

There should be enough ease across the shoulders and sleeves to allow you to stretch out your arms. Buttonhole closings should not gap or pull as you move and bend. The waistline or waistband should fit comfortably at your natural waist and not ride up or down as you move. The waistline seam for men's pants should rest just above the hip bone.

Belts should stay in place. Pants and skirts should not wrinkle or pull across the hips or thighs. They should not have any baggy areas in either the front or the back. Jackets and coats should fit comfortably over other clothes.

FITTING AS YOU SEW

Don't wait until your garment is completed before you try it on. By then it may be too difficult or impossible to make necessary changes. Instead, take time to check the fit as you sew.

Try on the garment, right side out, as soon as the major seams are joined. A wrinkle here or there is easy to correct at this early stage. Be sure to do your fitting over the undergarments that you intend to wear with the garment. Stand in front of a full-length mirror and analyze the fit of your garment according to the guidelines on page 426. Begin at the top and work your way down. The fit at the top affects the fit of the lower part of the garment. A wrinkle or a break line in the fabric indicates a problem. A wrinkle usually points to the place which needs some adjustment.

Make any necessary fitting changes. Try on the garment again to be sure that the problem has been corrected before you go on to finish the neckline, closing, and hem. Taking time to check fit during construction will result in a more attractive and comfortable garment that you will enjoy wearing.

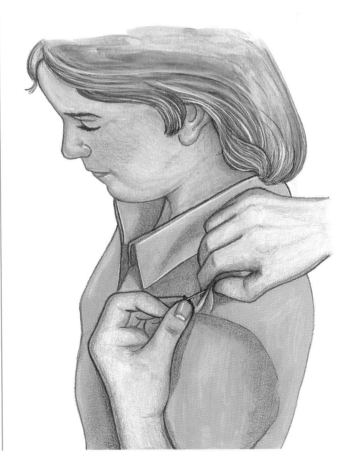

Fitting Guidelines

- Does the neckline lie smooth with no pulling or gapping?
- Does the collar roll evenly and are the points identical?
- Do the shoulder seams rest smoothly over the shoulders?
- Does the seamline of a set-in sleeve lie at the tip of the shoulder bone?
- Do the darts taper toward the fullest part of the body?
- Do the sleeves hang straight from the shoulders to the elbow?
- Does the sleeve or cuff end at the wristbone?
- Are the center front and center back seams in the center of the body and perpendicular to the floor?
- Do the side seams hang straight?
- Does the buttoned closing lie flat without any gapping?
- Is the waistline seam at the natural waistline or just above the hip bone and not too snug?
- Is the crotch length comfortable for sitting?
- Do the pants or skirt fit smoothly through the hips and thigh area with no wrinkles or extra fabric?
- Are hemlines even and parallel to the floor?
- Do pants cover the top of the shoe in back?
- Can you stand, sit, stretch, and bend comfortably?

UNIT 3

Someone once said, "Sewing is its own reward." It is a way to pass the time not only creatively, but profitably. It builds up a skill that can be used throughout life, and that gives people the chance to personalize their clothes.

The following chapters show you various special sewing techniques that need to be used when constructing a complete garment. Collars, sleeves, cuffs, pockets, waistlines, special buttonholes and loops, as well as bindings and bands, ruffles and trims, are discussed.

The last chapter in this unit deals with tailored garments. This chapter will give you many shortcut tips on constructing a garment that has a "tailored" look.

Good luck on your sewing adventures! With the skills that you are learning from your *Sewing Handbook,* countless sewing possibilities are open to you to please both yourself and your friends.

CHAPTER 16
Special Seams

Different types of seams can be used for a variety of purposes in sewing. **Self-finished seams** *enclose the seam allowances as the seam is stitched.* **Decorative seams** may *use topstitching or cording to create special effects.* Other situations require special techniques for stitching seams.

SELF-FINISHED SEAMS

Self-finished seams are used for a more attractive appearance or to strengthen the seam. They include the *French seam, mock French seam, flat-felled seam, double-stitched seam,* and *over-edge-stitch seam.*

French Seam

The French seam is used on sheer fabrics because no raw edges show through the fabric. It looks like a plain seam

on the outside of the garment and a narrow tuck on the wrong side. It can be used on straight seams, but is not flexible enough for eased or curved seams.

1. *Pin* wrong sides of fabrics together.
2. *Stitch* ⅜" (9 mm) from raw edges. Trim seam allowances to ⅛" (3 mm). Press seam allowances open.
3. *Fold* fabric along seamline with right sides together, and press.
4. *Stitch* ¼" (6 mm) from folded edge. The two seams, ⅜" (9 mm) and ¼" (3 mm), combine to make a ⅝" (1.6 cm) seam.

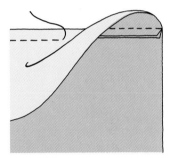

Mock French Seam

This seam looks like a French seam when finished, but it can be used on curved seams of a sheer garment.

1. *Stitch* ⅝″ (1.6 cm) standard seam, with right sides of fabric together. Trim seam allowances to ½″ (1.3 cm).
2. *Turn* in the edge of each seam allowance ¼″ (6 mm), and press. The folded edges should meet exactly.
3. *Stitch* folded edges together.

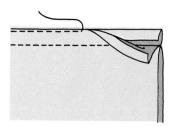

Flat-Felled Seam

This is a very sturdy and durable seam used for shirts, jeans, sportswear, pajamas, and other garments. Two rows of stitching show on the outside of the garment. Contrasting thread can be used as an accent.

1. *Pin* wrong sides of fabric together.
2. *Stitch* ⅝″ (1.6 cm) standard seam. Press open.
3. *Press* both seam allowances to one side.
4. *Trim* the under-seam allowance to ⅛″ (3 mm).
5. *Turn* under the edge of the upper seam allowance ¼″ (6 mm)

and place it over the trimmed seam allowance. Press.
6. *Stitch* close to the folded edge through all thicknesses.

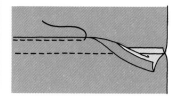

Double-Stitched Seam

This seam can be used for curved seams, such as armhole or crotch seams.

1. *Stitch* a ⅝″ (1.6 cm) standard seam, with right sides of fabric together.
2. *Stitch* again about ⅛″ (3 mm) from the seamline in the seam allowance. A narrow zigzag or patterned stitch can be used for this second row of stitching.
3. *Trim* seam allowances close to stitching.

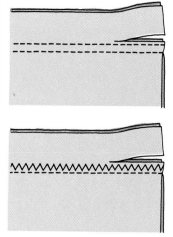

Overedge-Stitch Seam

If your machine has this special stitch, you can sew and finish the seam in one step.

1. *Trim* seam allowances to ¼″ (6 mm).
2. *Stitch* so that the straight stitches go along the seamline and the zigzag stitches cover the raw edges.

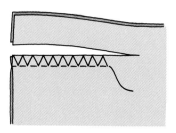

DECORATIVE SEAMS

Decorative seams can give a sporty, tailored, or contrasting finish to a garment. They include the *topstitched seam*, *welt seam*, *lapped seam*, and *piped* or *corded seam*.

Topstitched Seam

Topstitching can be used to hold bulky seam allowances flat and to emphasize the seams of a garment. Topstitching can be done on one side or on both sides of the seam:

1. *Stitch* a ⅝″ (1.6 cm) standard seam. Press seam allowances open.
2. *Topstitch* along each side of the seam, through both layers of fabric. Keep your stitching straight and equal distance from the seamline.

3. *Or press* both seam allowances to one side as indicated on your pattern. Topstitch through all three layers of fabric.

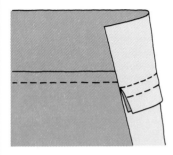

Welt Seam

This seam is used for a tailored finish on heavier fabrics and is less bulky than the flat-felled seam.

1. *Stitch* a standard seam, with right sides of fabric together. Press seam open.
2. *Press* both seam allowances toward one side.
3. *Trim* the seam allowance against the garment to ¼″ (6 mm).
4. *Stitch* from the outside through the garment and the wider seam allowance. Keep stitching an even distance from the seamline.

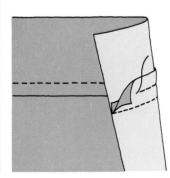

Lapped Seam

This seam is used when one piece is lapped over the other and topstitched in place. It is often used with natural or synthetic leather and suede:

1. *Turn* under the seam allowance on the section to be lapped, and press. For leather and suede, trim away the seam allowance.
2. *Lap* the folded or trimmed edge over the other piece at the seamline, wrong side to right side.
3. *Edgestitch* along the folded or trimmed edge.
4. *Topstitch* again ¼″ (6 mm) from edge.

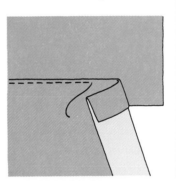

Piped or Corded Seam

Piping or cording covered with bias strips of fabric can be inserted into a seam while it is stitched.

1. *Pin* the piping or cording to the right side of one fabric section along the seamline. Be sure it is facing the garment with the seam allowance toward the edge of fabric.
2. *Stitch,* using a zipper foot, beside seamline in the seam allowance.
3. *Pin* second piece of fabric over the piping or cording, with right sides together.
4. *Stitch* along seamline through all thicknesses, using a zipper foot.

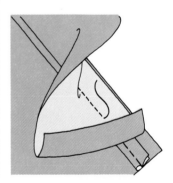

SPECIAL SEAM SITUATIONS

Special techniques are needed for stitching *bias, curved, gathered, eased, intersecting,* and *corner seams.*

Bias Seam

When stitching two bias edges, stretch the fabric slightly so that the seam will not pucker. When joining a bias edge to a straight edge, stitch with the bias side up to prevent puckers and to control stretching.

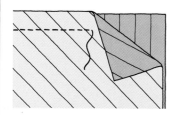

Curved Seam

If both fabric edges curve the same direction, clip or notch seam allowances so that the fabric will lie flat.

If one fabric edge curves inward and the other curves outward, staystitch both curved edges ½" (1.3 cm) from edge. Clip the inward curved edge up to the staystitching. Stitch seam with clipped side up. Press seam

open or to one side. Clip and notch until the seam allowances lie flat.

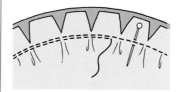

Gathered Seam

This seam is made by gathering a long piece of fabric into soft folds to fit a shorter edge. (See GATHERING, page 400.)

Eased Seam

This seam is used when one edge of fabric is only slightly longer than the other. The extra length is eased in without creating any folds or gathers. (See EASING, page 401.)

Intersecting Seams

Stitch one seam and press open. Then stitch the second seam and press open. With right sides together, place a pin through both seams to be sure they match exactly. Stitch intersecting seam. Trim corners diagonally to reduce bulk.

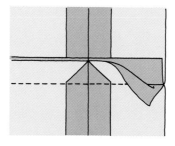

Corner Seam

Reinforcement stitches, 15 to 20 stitches per inch (1–1.5 mm in length) are used to strengthen a corner or point. If both pieces of fabric have the same angle, use reinforcement stitches for an inch (2.5 cm) on either side of the corner when you stitch the seam. Pivot at the corner or take 1 diagonal stitch across a sharp point. (See PLAIN SEAMS, page 402.)

If a corner is to be stitched to a straight edge or to a corner with an opposite angle, the inner corner or straight edge must be clipped. Stitch just inside the seamline with reinforcement stitches for about an inch (2.5 cm) on either side of the point. Clip up to but not through the stitches. Place a pin at the corner to prevent clipping too far. Stitch seam with clipped side up, pivoting at the corner.

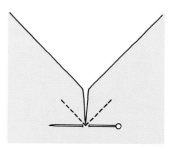

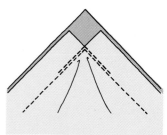

Tucks and Pleats

Tucks and pleats are folds of fabric used to control fullness or add design interest. **Tucks** are *narrow folds of fabric that are stitched partway or the entire length.* **Pleats** are *wider folds of fabric that are stitched or pressed in place.*

TUCKS

Tucks can be stitched so that the folds are on the outside or on the inside of the garment. The width of the tucks and the spacing between the tucks can vary depending upon the design. Follow your pattern guide for stitching directions. You can add your own tucks to a garment by tucking the fabric before cutting out the pattern pieces:

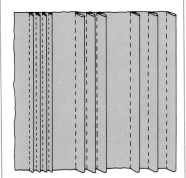

Tucks

1. *Mark* the stitching lines of each tuck on the side of fabric that will be stitched. If tucks will be stitched from the right side, use tailor's tacks or thread basting.

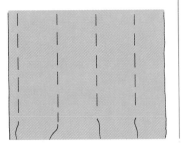

2. *Fold* tucks, matching stitching lines.

3. *Stitch* each tuck from the side of the tuck that will be seen after the tuck is pressed flat. Keep the stitching straight and even.

4. *Press* each tuck flat, as stitched. Then press each tuck to one side as it is shown on guide sheet.

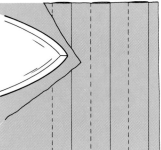

PLEATS

One single pleat or an entire series of pleats can be used in a garment. Pleats can be pressed sharp along the edges or fall in soft folds. They can also be stitched for a more tailored look.

Various effects can be created by the way pleats are turned. *Knife,* or *side, pleats* have the folds turned in one direction. *Box pleats* and *inverted pleats* are made by turning two pleats toward each other.

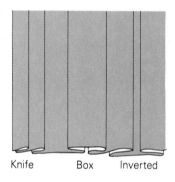

Knife   Box   Inverted

Follow your guide sheet for specific instructions for folding, pressing, and stitching pleats.

Folding Pleats

1. *Mark* both the fold line and the placement line for each pleat. If pleats are to be made from the right side, mark the lines with uneven basting stitches or tailor's tacks. Use one color of thread for the fold line and another color for the placement line.
2. *Fold* the fabric, matching fold and placement lines, and pin. An arrow on the pattern piece will show in which direction to fold.
3. *Baste* each pleat in place through all thicknesses.

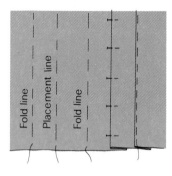

4. *Staystitch* pleats along upper seamline.

Pressing Pleats

1. *Press* pleats gently from inside of garment. If pleats leave an impression on the fabric, slip strips of paper under each fold before pressing.
2. *Turn* the garment to the right side.
3. *Press* pleats in place, using a press cloth. For soft pleats, press lightly. For sharp pleats, use lots of steam and a damp press cloth.
4. *Let* pleats dry on the ironing board.

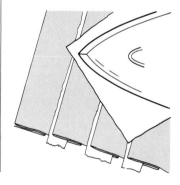

Stitching Pleats   Pleats may be topstitched or edgestitched for a smoother appearance and to hold the pleats in place. For pleats that are both edgestitched and topstitched, do the edgestitching first.

Edgestitching gives a sharper crease along the outer or inner fold of a pleat:

1. *Complete* the hem.
2. *Stitch* from bottom of pleat to top as close to fold as possible.
3. *Repeat* on other fold of pleat, if desired.

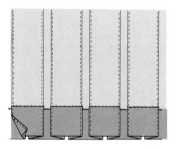

Topstitching is stitched only part way, usually between the waist and hip areas:

1. *Topstitch* from the right side through all thicknesses. Begin at the hip; do not backstitch. Stitch to top of pleat.
2. *Pull* threads to the under side and tie.

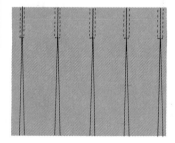

CHAPTER 18
Interfacing, Underlining, and Lining

Interfacing, underlining, and lining are inner construction fabrics. They do not show on the outside of a garment, but they help to shape and support the outer fabric.

• **Interfacing.** This is a layer of fabric placed between the facing and the outer fabric.

• **Underlining.** This is a layer of fabric stitched to the back of each piece of the outer fabric.

• **Lining.** This is constructed separately from the outer garment and then joined at one or more major seams.

Special inner construction fabrics are made in a variety of fibers, weights, and degrees of crispness. Some fabrics, such as taffeta and silk, can also be used as inner construction fabrics. With sheer fabrics, a piece of self-fabric can be used.

When choosing an inner construction fabric, always drape your garment fabric over the shaping fabric. Check to see how the two fabrics look and feel together.

• Is it too soft or too crisp for the shape that you want?
• Does the color of the shaping fabric show through or change the color of your outer fabric?
• Is the fiber content of the two fabrics compatible?
• Can they both be washed or dry cleaned in the same manner?
• Do they require pressing?

Read the labels carefully to avoid any disappointment in the future.

INTERFACING

Interfacing can be used to give shape to collars, cuffs, and waistbands. It can prevent edges, such as a neckline or front closing, from stretching. It can give added body to a belt, bag, or hat.

Sometimes a separate pattern piece will be provided for the interfacing. If not, the interfacing is cut from the facing, collar, cuff, or waistband pattern piece.

Special woven and nonwoven interfacing fabrics are available in many different types and weights. Sew-in interfacings can be stitched by hand or by machine to your garment. Fusible interfacings can be pressed and fused directly to the fabric with your iron.

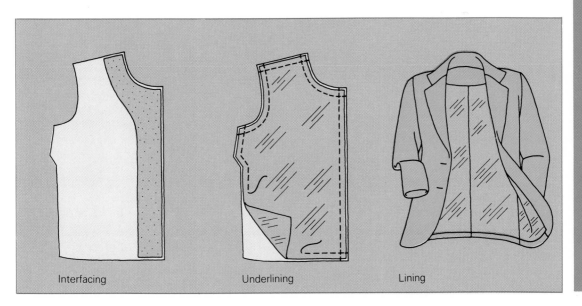

Interfacing   Underlining   Lining

Usually, the interfacing should be about the same weight or slightly lighter than your outer fabric. Some fusible interfacings are crisper after they are fused.

Sew-In Interfacing

Cut interfacing pieces following the directions on your guide sheet. Light to mediumweight interfacing can be stitched into the seam of a garment:

1. *Pin* interfacing to the wrong side of the garment or facing.
2. *Machine baste* ½" (1.3 cm) from fabric edge.
3. *Trim* interfacing close to the stitching.
4. *Catchstitch* interfacing by hand along a folded edge, such as an extended facing or cuff.

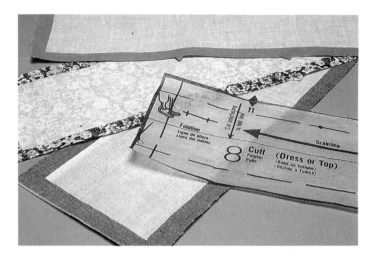

Heavier weight interfacings may be used in tailoring a jacket or coat. They are usually too bulky to be stitched into the seam. Instead, all seam allowances and darts are trimmed away. Then the interfacing is stitched by hand to the wrong side of the garment. (See TAILORING, page 465.)

Fusible Interfacing

Always pretest a fusible interfacing on a scrap of your fabric before applying it to your garment. If the interfacing leaves an outline or ridge along the edge, then fuse it to the facing rather than to the garment:

1. *Trim* away all seam allowances on interfacing.
2. *Place* adhesive side of the interfacing on the wrong side of the fabric, matching the cut edges of the interfacing to the seam lines.
3. *Fuse* in place, following the manufacturer's directions.

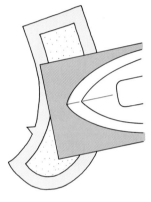

UNDERLINING

An underlining is used to give support to the outer fabric. It is cut from the same pattern pieces as the outer fabric. Then the two layers are stitched together and handled as one throughout construction. Facings, interfacings, and hems can be sewn to the underlining so that no stitches or ridges show on the right side of the garment. Use a lightweight, firmly woven fabric that is recommended for underlining or lining.

An underlining can be used with sheer fabrics to prevent see-through in certain areas of the garment. With loosely woven or stretchy fabrics, an underlining helps to prevent stretching. It gives more support than a separate lining:

1. *Make* all markings on the underlining fabric instead of the outer fabric.
2. *Pin* underlining to the wrong side of the outer fabric.
3. *Staystitch* ½" (1.3 cm) from the outer edge, stitching directionally.

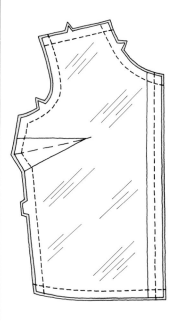

For darts, machine baste along fold line of each dart through both layers of fabric. Extend basting about 1" (2.5 cm) beyond point of dart. Fold and stitch dart, treating both fabrics as one. Remove basting.

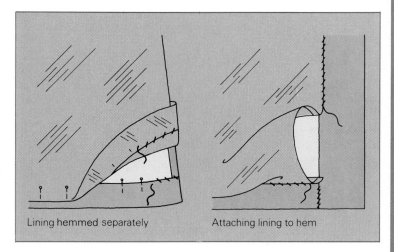

Lining hemmed separately

Attaching lining to hem

LINING

A lining is used to give an attractive appearance to the inside of a garment. It also helps to prevent stretching and wrinkling of the outer fabric. Use a firmly woven fabric with a smooth, slippery texture. Some coat linings are backed with a napped finish or insulation for added warmth.

A lining may be cut from the same pattern pieces as the outer fabric. Some coat or jacket patterns have separate pattern pieces for the lining.

Stitch the lining pieces together following your pattern guide sheet. A coat or jacket lining may have a center back pleat to allow for movement. Seam finishes are not necessary on either the outer fabric or on the lining unless the fabric ravels easily.

Use machine or hand stitching to attach the lining to the garment along the facing or the waistline seam.

Lining Hems

Some linings are hemmed separately; others are sewn to the garment. Coat, skirt, and dress linings are usually hemmed separately. Make the lining hem ½" to 1" (1.3–2.5 cm) shorter than the outer garment. (See HEMS, page 417.) Use French tacks to hold the hems together at the seam lines of a coat.

Jacket, sleeve, and pants linings are usually attached to the garment hem. The hem should be at least ½" (1.3 cm) above the edge of the garment. The lining should form a small tuck at the hemline to allow for movement:

1. *Match* the folded hem edges of the lining and garment.
2. *Pin* the folded edge of the lining at least ½" above garment edge, creating a tuck.
3. *Slipstitch* the edge of the lining to the garment hem.

CHAPTER 19
Collars

Collars come in many different sizes and shapes. However, there are four basic types of collars:

- *Flat Collar.* It lies flat against the garment. Both the upper and lower collar are cut from the same pattern piece.

- *Rolled Collar.* This stands up at the back of the neck and then turns down to create a rolled edge around the neck. It can be cut with a one-piece upper collar and a two-piece under collar that is slightly smaller. Or the entire collar can be cut as one piece and folded at outer edge.

- *Shirt Collar.* It has a separate stand, or band, that attaches the collar to the neckline.

- *Standing Collar.* It is a band that stands straight up or folds over to create a turtleneck.

Because a collar is close to your face, it attracts attention and should be well made. The collar should circle the neck smoothly without rippling. The front points or curves should be identical in shape. The under collar should not show along the edge. A rolled and a shirt collar should cover neck seam in back. The collar should be carefully pressed.

Interfacing is used in collars to give added shape and support. It is usually stitched or fused to the under collar.

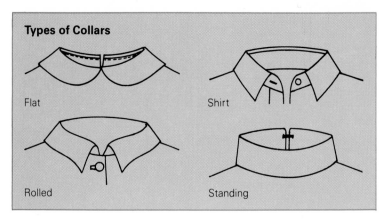

Types of Collars

Flat

Shirt

Rolled

Standing

However, if the outer fabric is lightweight, the interfacing can be stitched to the upper collar to prevent the seam allowances from showing.

There are two basic steps to making a collar:

1. *Construct* the collar.
2. *Attach* collar to garment.

CONSTRUCT THE COLLAR

Cut out the collar and any facings. The upper and under collar may be cut from the same pattern piece or from separate pieces. Or the collar may be cut from one piece of fabric and folded lengthwise:

1. *Stitch* or fuse interfacing to the wrong side of the under collar. (See INTERFACING, page 433.) For a one-piece collar, catchstitch the interfacing along the fold line. Stitch center back seam of the under collar, if necessary. Press the seam open and trim.

2. *Pin* the collar sections with right sides together.

Follow your pattern guide sheet for specific directions.

3. *Stitch* the outer seam of the collar. Reinforce corners or points with reinforcement stitches, 15–20 stitches per inch (1–1.5 mm in length).

4. *Trim* and grade seam allowances. Trim corners close to the stitching for crisp, sharp points. Clip or notch curved areas. Press seam open.

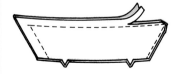

5. *Turn* the collar to the right side. Gently pull out the points. Don't push them out with the points of your scissors or you might poke a hole in the fabric.

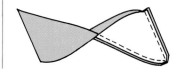

6. *Press* the outer seam, rolling it slightly to underside of collar.
7. *Understitch* the undercollar to the seam allowances. This will help to prevent the under collar from showing at the edge. Or topstitch around the edge of the collar.

For a shirt collar, stitch the collar band to the upper collar and the under collar at the inner edge. Trim, grade, clip, notch, and press the seams.

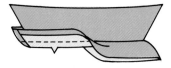

ATTACH THE COLLAR TO GARMENT

A collar may be stitched to a garment with a complete neckline facing, a partial facing, or no facing.

Collar with Facing

This method is used for flat collars and rolled collars.

1. *Stitch* facing sections together. Trim and press seams. Finish outer unnotched edge of facing.
2. *Staystitch* the garment neckline and clip.
3. *Machine baste* the neckline edge of upper and under collar together.
4. *Pin* the collar to the neckline, matching notches and markings. Stitch just inside the seamline in the seam allowance.

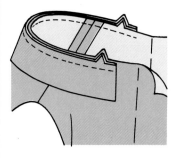

5. *Pin* facing to the neckline, with right sides together. Match all markings and seamlines. Stitch seam. Trim, grade, and clip seam allowances.

6. *Turn* facing to inside and press.
7. *Understitch* facing to the neckline seam allowances.
8. *Tack* the edge of the facing to the shoulder seam allowances.

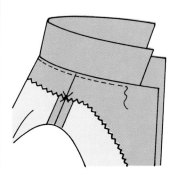

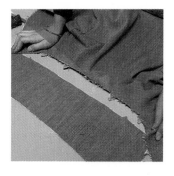

Collar without Facing

This method is used for shirt collars and standing collars.

1. *Staystitch* the garment neckline, and clip.
2. *Pin* under collar or band to the neckline, right sides together, matching all markings. Stitch seam, trim, and clip. Press seam toward collar.

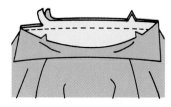

3. *Turn* in the seam allowance of the upper collar or band, and press. Trim the seam allowance to ¼" (6 mm).
4. *Pin* the folded edge over the neckline seam. Machine stitch close to the edge, or slipstitch by hand.

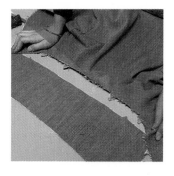

CHAPTER 20

Sleeves

Sleeves come in many different lengths and shapes. From a short cap sleeve to a long shirt sleeve with French cuffs, sleeves require a variety of sewing techniques.

There are three basic types of sleeves:

• *Set-In Sleeve.* This sleeve is joined to a garment by an armhole seam that circles the arm near the shoulder.

• *Raglan Sleeve.* This has a front and back diagonal seam that extends from the armhole up to the neckline.

• *Kimono Sleeve.* This is cut in one piece with the front and back of the garment.

Sleeves can be finished at the bottom edge with a hem, facing, casing, or cuff.

SET-IN SLEEVE

A set-in sleeve is the most common type of sleeve, but it is also the most difficult one to construct. A set-in sleeve always measures more than the armhole into which it must fit. The extra fullness in the sleeve is needed so that the sleeve will fit over the top curve of your arm and allow movement.

Some set-in sleeves will be very full across the *cap,* or *top,* of the sleeve. This fullness must be eased into the seam without any gathers or puckers. Other sleeves, such as a

Set-in

Raglan

Kimono

tailored shirt, will have a short sleeve cap and will be only slightly larger than the armhole.

There are two methods for sewing a set-in sleeve:

1. In the *closed-sleeve method* the underarm seam of the sleeve and the side seam of the garment are stitched before the sleeve is attached to the armhole.

2. In the *open-sleeve method* the sleeve is stitched to the armhole, and then the side seam and underarm seam are stitched in one continuous seam.

Closed-Sleeve Method

This method is also called the *unit method* of construction because the sleeve is completed before it is attached to the armhole. This method is used for sleeves that have extra fullness across the sleeve cap. Use two rows of ease stitching, about 8 stitches per inch (3 mm in length) to ease in the fullness of the sleeve:

1. *Machine baste* close to the ⅝″ (1.6 cm) seamline in the seam allowance, stitching around the top of the sleeve between the notches.

2. *Machine baste* a second row of ease stitching ⅜″ from the outer edge.

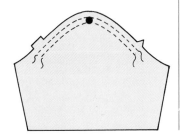

3. *Stitch* the underarm seam of the sleeve, and press open.
4. *Pull* up the bobbin thread ends of the ease stitching until the sleeve cap fits the armhole. Adjust the fullness evenly between the notches.
5. *Place* the sleeve cap over the rounded end of the ironing board or sleeve board. Gently steam and press the edge of the fabric to shrink in the fullness.
6. *Turn* the garment wrong side out. Turn the sleeve right side out and slip inside armhole.
7. *Pin* the sleeve to the garment, with the right sides together . Match the underarm seams, shoulder markings, and notches. Adjust fullness. Place pins at right angles to the seamline so they can be easily removed as you sew.

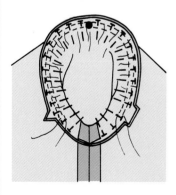

8. *Stitch* the sleeve to the armhole with the sleeve side up. This allows you to control the fullness and prevents tucks or puckers from forming.

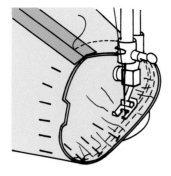

9. *Reinforce* the underarm section of armhole seam with a second row of stitches ⅜″ (9 mm) from the outer edge. Stitch from notch to notch. Trim seam allowances in the underarm section close to stitching. Or the entire armhole can be double-stitched and trimmed. This method is used for knitted fabrics.
10. *Press* the seam allowances together from the sleeve side, using the side of the iron. Do not press the seam from the right side of the garment. An armhole seam is supposed to be gently curved. Turn seam allowances toward the sleeve.

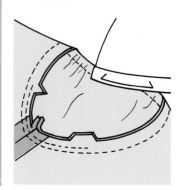

Open-Sleeve Method

This method is called the *flat construction* method because the sleeve is stitched to the armhole, while both the sleeve and garment seams remain open. This method is fast and easy. However, it can only be used for sleeves that require little easing, such as tailored shirts, sports shirts, and shirts with dropped shoulders. Usually the sleeve can be pinned to the armhole without any ease stitching:

1. *Match* sleeve to garment, right sides together, and pin. If the sleeve is ease stitched, adjust fullness evenly.
2. *Stitch* the seam with sleeve side up. Ease in any fullness with your fingers as you sew.

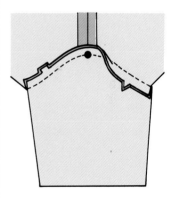

3. *Stitch* a second row of stitching ⅜″ (9 mm) from the outer edge. Trim close to stitching. Press seam allowances toward the garment. Or topstitch on the outside of the garment ¼″ to ⅜″ (6–9 mm) from the seam on the body side.

4. *Match* and pin the side seam and underarm sleeve seam.
5. *Stitch* the seam from the bottom of the garment to the end of the sleeve in one continuous line of stitching. Press seams open.

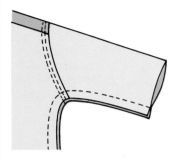

RAGLAN SLEEVE

A raglan sleeve is loose-fitted and comfortable to wear. It has a shoulder dart or seam to shape the sleeve over the shoulder area:

1. *Stitch* shoulder dart or seam. Slash and press open.

2. *Pin* diagonal seams of the sleeve to the garment, right sides together, matching notches, markings, and underarm seams.

3. *Stitch* seams.

4. *Stitch* again along underarm section, between notches, ⅜″ (9 mm) from outer edge.
5. *Clip* at the end of second row of stitching. Trim the underarm close to stitching. Press the seams open between notches and neckline.
6. *Stitch* underarm seam of sleeve and side seam.

KIMONO SLEEVE

This is the easiest sleeve for a beginner to make. It is simply an extension of the garment front and back.

1. *Stitch* the shoulder seam, right sides together. Press open.
2. *Stitch* the underarm seam.
3. *Reinforce* the underarm seam with a second row of stitching ⅜″ (9 mm) from outer edge.
4. *Or sew* a piece of seam tape over the curved underarm seam, stitching through all layers, to give the seam extra strength.
5. *Clip* the curve of the seam, but be careful not to clip the seam tape. Press the seam open.

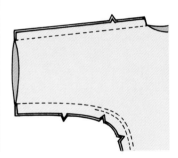

CHAPTER 21
Cuffs

Cuffs give a tailored finish to the end of a sleeve. There are three basic types.

- *Fold-Up Cuff.* This is actually a deep hem at the bottom of a sleeve or pants leg that is folded to the right side of the garment.

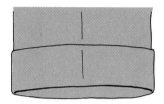

- *Band Cuff.* It has no opening and must be large enough for your hand to slip through easily.

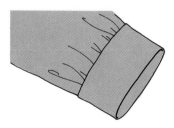

- *Buttoned Cuff.* It fits snugly around the wrist and fastens with a button or some other fastener. There must be some type of opening in the sleeve to allow the cuff to slide over your hand.

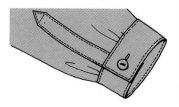

SEWING CUFFS

Fold-Up Cuff

1. *Finish* the lower edge of fabric with a machine zigzag, hemmed, or bound finish. (See SEAM FINISHES, page 405.)
2. *Turn* cuff to inside along fold line and pin.
3. *Hem* by hand or machine stitching.

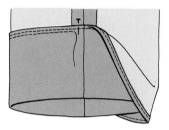

4. *Turn* the lower edge of garment to the right side along hemline to form cuff.
5. *Tack* cuff in place at each seam. Or stitch-in-the-ditch along the seam.

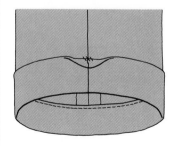

Band Cuff

1. *Interface* cuff following your pattern guide sheet and the information on INTERFACINGS, page 433.
2. *Fold* unnotched seam allowance of cuff to inside, and press. Trim seam allowance to ¼″ (6 mm).

3. *Pin* the notched edge of the cuff to the bottom edge of the sleeve, right sides together, matching markings. Adjust fullness. Stitch seam with the sleeve side up. Trim, grade, and press seam allowances toward cuff.

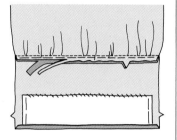

4. *Stitch* sleeve seam and cuff seam. Trim cuff and press seams open.

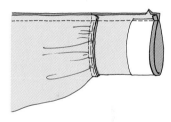

5. *Fold* the cuff in half along the foldline, wrong sides together.
6. *Pin* the folded edge of the cuff over the seamline. Slipstitch the edge in place. Or topstitch from the right side.

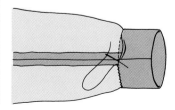

Buttoned Cuff The opening should be sewn before the sleeve seam is stitched. Your pattern guide sheet will give complete directions for making the opening (See SLEEVE OPENINGS, following.)

A buttoned cuff can be cut in one piece and folded lengthwise. Or it can be cut in two pieces and stitched along the outer edge:

1. *Complete* the sleeve opening.
2. *Interface* the cuff.
3. *Fold* the long unnotched edge of the cuff to the inside and press. Trim to ¼″ (6 mm).
4. *Stitch* the ends of the cuffs, right sides together. Or stitch the cuff sections together along the outer edge. Trim and grade the seams; press. Turn the cuff to the right side.

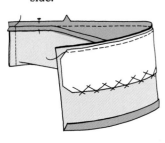

5. *Pin* the cuff to the gathered sleeve edge, right sides together, matching the notches and markings. For a shirt sleeve, the cuff edges will be even with the placket edges. For cuffs with a faced or bound opening, the cuff will extend beyond the back edge of the placket.

6. *Stitch* the seam. Trim, grade, and clip the seam allowances. Press seam allowances toward cuff.

7. *Place* the folded edge of the cuff over the seam and extension end. Slipstitch in place. Or topstitch from the right side through all thicknesses.
8. *Make* machine buttonholes and attach buttons.

SLEEVE OPENINGS

The three most common types of sleeve *plackets,* or *openings,* are a *banded* placket, a *faced* placket, and a *bound* placket. These openings can also be used for other parts of garments, such as a neckline or waistline placket.

Banded Placket

This placket gives a tailored or sporty finish to a sleeve or front of a shirt. The placket can be one or two pieces:

1. *Reinforce* the sleeve opening with stitching.
2. *Slash* and clip into corners.

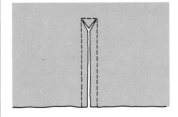

3. *Stitch* the underlap to back edge of opening, following instructions.

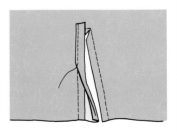

4. *Stitch* the overlap to the front edge of the opening.
5. *Overlap* placket and stitch at the upper edge. Stitch through all thickness across the point and around edges.

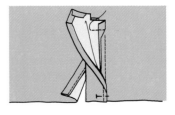

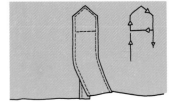

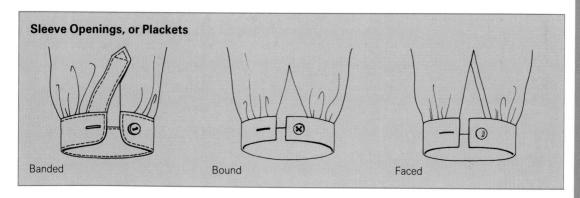

Sleeve Openings, or Plackets

Banded   Bound   Faced

Faced Placket

This forms a split opening, that can be used for a sleeve or neckline placket:

1. *Finish* the edge of the placket facing.
2. *Center* the placket over the sleeve opening, with right sides together.
3. *Reinforce stitch,* 16 to 20 stitches per inch (1–1.5 mm in length), along the stitching lines. Take one small stitch across the point.
4. *Slash* carefully up to the point.
5. *Turn* the facing to the inside and press.

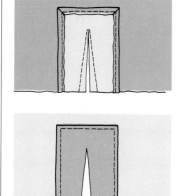

Bound Placket

This forms a narrow binding that overlaps at the opening. It can be used for a sleeve placket or a waistline placket on skirts, pants, or shorts. Cut fabric for binding 1½" wide (3.5 mm) and twice the length of the slash:

1. *Staystitch* the placket opening along the stitching lines, using reinforcement stitches. Take one small stitch across the point.
2. *Slash* carefully up to the point. Open the slash until the line of stitching is straight.

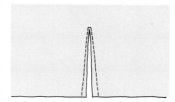

3. *Pin* the cut edge of the binding strip under the slash, right sides together, so that the stitching line is ¼" (6 mm) from the edge of the strip. Edges will not match.

4. *Stitch* along the first row of stitching, using reinforcement stitches. Press binding away from sleeve.

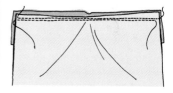

5. *Turn* in the raw edge of the binding ¼" (6 mm) and place over the seam.
6. *Slipstitch* or topstitch in place. Press. Fold under the binding on the front edge of placket before attaching cuff.

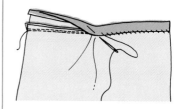

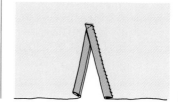

CHAPTER 22
Pockets

Pockets can be functional, decorative, or both. A pocket concealed in a side seam is purely functional, while a patch pocket is both functional and decorative.

Check the location of the pocket to be sure that the placement is correct for your height and body shape. You may have to raise or lower it for convenience or for better proportion.

There are many different types of pockets. Some are located inside the garment and open through a seam or a slash. Others are stitched on the outside of the garment. Some may have a flap covering the top of the pocket.

Three types of pockets that are easy to make are the *in-seam pocket,* the *patch pocket,* and the *front hip,* or *Western, pocket.*

IN-SEAM POCKET

This is the easiest type of pocket to make. The pocket is attached to the side seam of the garment. It can be cut as part of the garment front and back. Or it can be cut from a separate pattern piece and stitched to the seam. If the outer fabric is bulky or heavy, cut the pocket pieces from lining fabric. All of the construction is done on the inside of the garment:

1. *Stitch* a piece of seam tape or twill tape along the front and back fold line or seamline to prevent stretching.

2. *If* the pocket is cut separately, stitch pocket pieces to front and back opening, right sides together. Press seam allowances toward pocket pieces.

3. *Pin* the garment front to garment back, matching markings at seamline and pocket.

4. *Stitch* directionally along seam and around pocket in one step. Use reinforcement stitches, 15 to 20 stitches per inch (1–1.5 mm in length), at the corners. Press seam allowances flat.

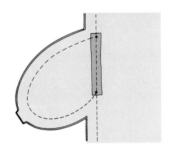

5. *Turn* the pocket toward the front of the garment. Clip back seam allowance above and below pocket so that the seam allowances of the garment can be pressed open.

6. *Finish* seam allowances, if necessary.

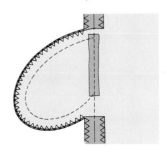

PATCH POCKET

These are made from the same fabric as the garment and stitched to the outside by hand or machine. If using a plaid, stripe, or printed fabric, match the pocket to the garment. Or cut the pocket on the bias for a special design effect. When making a pair of patch pockets, be sure that both pockets are the same size and shape. Attach the pockets to the garment evenly.

Patch pockets may be lined or unlined. A lining is needed for fabrics that stretch or sag. Fabrics that are firm enough to hold their shape can be used without a lining. Sometimes a flap is stitched above the pocket.

Unlined Patch Pocket

1. *Turn* under top edge of pocket hem ¼" (6 mm), press, and stitch.
2. *Turn* the hem to the right side of the pocket along fold line, and pin.

3. *Staystitch* around the pocket on the seamline, beginning at fold line of the hem. The staystitching will act as a guide for turning and pressing the edges and corners.
4. *Trim* and grade hem seam allowances. Clip upper corners. Turn hem right side out and press.

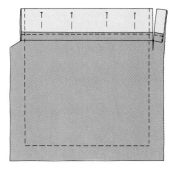

5. *Fold* in seam allowances along stitching and press. Square corners must be mitered; rounded corners must be notched.

6. *Stitch* the edge of the hem to the pocket by hand, or topstitch from right side.

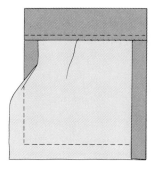

7. *Pin* the pocket to the garment. Slipstitch around the pocket by hand. Or topstitch edges in place. Reinforce corners by backstitching or by stitching a small triangle or square.

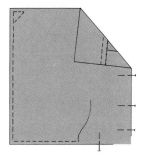

For a square or rectangular pocket: You will need to *miter* the corners to eliminate bulk to form flat, square corners:

1. *Open* out seam allowances.
2. *Trim* each corner diagonally to ¼" (6 mm) from fold.
3. *Fold* in corner diagonally and press.

4. *Refold* seam allowances on both sides of corner to form a square edge, and press again.

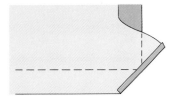

For a rounded pocket follow these steps:

1. *Machine baste,* 6 to 8 stitches per inch (3–4 mm in length), around the curved edges ½" (1.3 cm) from the outer edge.
2. *Pull* on the bobbin thread until the seam allowance curves in and lies flat.
3. *Trim* and *notch* seam allowance to eliminate bulk and puckers.
4. *Press.*

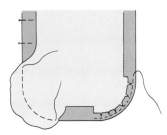

Lined Patch Pocket

1. *Pin* upper edge of lining to upper edge of pocket, right sides together. Stitch on seamline, leaving a 1" (2.5 cm) opening in center for turning.

Press seam toward lining.

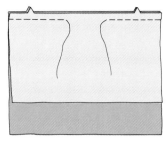

2. *Fold* the pocket, right sides together, along upper fold line.
3. *Pin* and *stitch* lining to pocket around all three sides. Trim and grade the seam allowances. Clip the corners and notch curved areas.

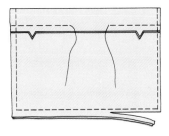

4. *Turn* the pocket right side out through the opening. Roll the seam slightly toward the lining and press.
5. *Slipstitch* the opening closed.

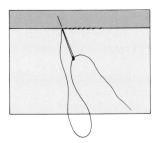

6. *Pin* the pocket to the garment, and slipstitch or topstitch in place.

Pocket Flap

1. *Interface* the outer half of the flap.
2. *Fold* the flap in half, right sides together, and stitch the end seams. Or pin two flap sections together and stitch around the outer edge.

Trim and grade seam allowances. Notch any curved areas. Turn the flap right side out and then press.

3. *Pin* the flap above the pocket, with the outer side of the flap against the outside of the garment. Match the seamline of the flap to the placement line on the garment.
4. *Stitch* through all thicknesses. Trim seam allowance next to garment close to stitching.

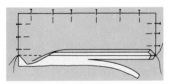

5. *Fold* under the long edge of the upper seam allowance, turning ends in diagonally. Pin over the trimmed edge, and edgestitch.
6. *Turn* the flap down and press.
7. *Slipstitch* the upper corners of the flap to the garment to hold in place.

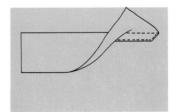

FRONT HIP, OR WESTERN, POCKET

This style of pocket is often used on pants and shorts. It is a diagonal or curved pocket that attaches to the waist and side seams. The back section of the pocket must be cut from the garment fabric because it is part of the main garment at the front of the hip. The inside front section of the pocket can be cut from the same fabric or lining fabric:

1. *Reinforce* the upper edge of the pocket with interfacing or seam tape to prevent stretching.
2. *Pin* the front edge of the garment to the front pocket section, right sides together. Stitch, trim, and grade seam.

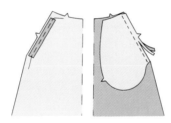

3. *Turn* the pocket to the inside of the garment and press. Understitch or topstitch a diagonal or curved seam to prevent the pocket from rolling to right side of garment.

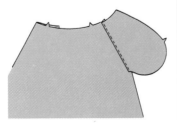

4. *Pin* the back section of pocket to the front section, right sides together. Stitch around the seamline being careful not to catch in the garment front. Press the seam flat and finish raw edges with zigzag stitching.

5. *Pin* and stitch the side seams, catching in the back section of the pocket as part of the garment front.
6. *Finish* the waistline according to the pattern directions.

CHAPTER 23

Waistlines and Belts

The waistline of a garment can be finished in several different ways. The waistline may have a seam that joins the top and bottom parts of a garment together. Or the waistline can be finished with a waistband, a facing, or a casing.

WAISTLINE SEAM

Most waistline seams fall at the natural waistline. However, some garments may have a raised or lowered waistline, depending upon the design. A *stay,* or *support,* can be stitched over the waistline seam to prevent stretching. The stay can be made from seam tape, twill tape, or grosgrain ribbon:

1. *Pin* the top and bottom sections of the garment together, following pattern directions. Match seams, notches, and markings. Pin seam allowances and darts so they will lie flat. Adjust any fullness evenly along seamline.

2. *Stitch* the waistline seam with the gathered or eased side up to control fullness and prevent puckers or pleats from forming. Press the seam flat.

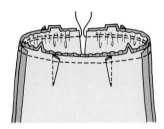

3. *To attach* a stay, cut tape or ribbon the same length as the waistline measurement of the garment. Pin stay to seam allowance on the bottom section of the garment, with one edge along the waistline seam. Machine stitch just above the waistline seam through stay and seam allowances. Trim seam allowances even with stay; grade if fabric is heavy. For fabrics that ravel, stitch upper edge of stay and seam allowances together.

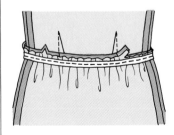

4. *Press* waistline seam toward top section of garment.

WAISTBANDS

A waistband is a strip of fabric attached to the waistline of pants, skirts, or shorts. It can be cut *straight* or *curved*. Both types of waistbands are attached to the garment in the same way. However, a straight waistband usually has a fold along the upper edge while a curved or shaped waistband has a seam.

The waistband should be about 1″ (2.5 cm) larger than your actual waistline to allow for movement and comfort. It should not fit too tight. The garment is eased or gathered onto the waistband to allow for the curve of your body below the waistline.

Usually the zipper is stitched before the waistband is applied. A side opening is always on the left side, and the waistband laps from front to back. If the opening is in the front or back, the waistband overlaps in the same directions as the lapped zipper application.

Interface waistband to prevent stretching or wrinkling. Usually the side that will be on the outside of the garment is interfaced. Follow your pattern directions.

There are two methods of applying a waistband:

• *Plain Waistband.* This is stitched to the right side of the garment, turned to the inside, and stitched by hand.

• *Topstitched Waistband.* It is stitched to the wrong side of the garment, turned to the outside, and topstitched in place.

Your pattern guide sheet will state which method is best for your garment.

Plain Waistband

1. *Interface* the waistband.
2. *Turn* in the seam allowance on the unnotched edge of the waistband and press. Trim seam allowance to ¼″ (6 mm).

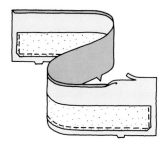

3. *Pin* waistband to garment, right sides together. Match notches and ease garment to waistband between markings. Check that the extension is on the correct side of the opening.
4. *Stitch* waistband to garment along seamline. Trim interfacing close to stitching. Trim and grade seam allowances. Clip if necessary. Press the seam flat and then up toward the waistband.
5. *Fold* ends of waistband, right sides together. Pin carefully, being sure that the folded and trimmed edge exactly meets the seamline.
6. *Stitch* both ends. Trim and grade seam allowances. Clip corners, and press.

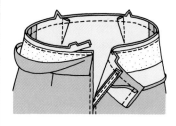

7. *Turn* waistband right side out. Pin folded edge over seam.
   Slipstitch in place, continuing across the extension.

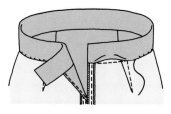

8. *Attach* fasteners.

Topstitched Waistband

1. *Interface* waistband.

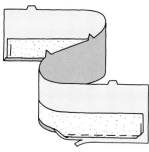

2. *Pin* the right side of the waistband to the wrong side of the garment, matching notches and markings. Check to be sure that the waistband will flip over so the right side will be on the outside of the garment.
3. *Stitch* the seam. Grade seam allowances so that the widest layer will be toward the outside of the garment. Clip if necessary. Press seam allowances up toward waistband.

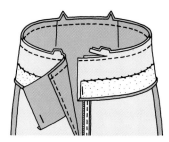

4. *Turn* in the long edge of the waistband along the stitching line and press. Trim to ¼″ (6 mm).
5. *Stitch* ends of waistband with right sides of fabric together. Trim, grade, clip corners, and press.

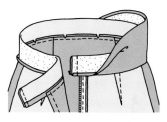

6. *Fold* the waistband over the seamline to the right side of the garment. Press and pin. Topstitch along the bottom edge of the waistband close to the fold.
7. *Attach* fasteners.

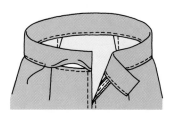

WAISTLINE FACING AND CASING

A facing can be used to finish a waistline edge. It allows the finished edge of a garment to rest right at the natural waistline.

Prevent stretching by either interfacing the waistline seam or by attaching a waistline stay. Attach interfacing according to pattern directions. Or stitch a piece of seam tape to inside of garment directly on top of the seam line.

Facing

1. *Prepare* facing and finish the outer edge.
2. *Stitch* the facing to the garment, right sides together. Match seams, notches, and markings. Trim, grade, and clip seam allowances. Press seam allowances toward the facing.

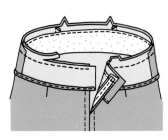

3. *Understitch* the facing to the seam allowances.

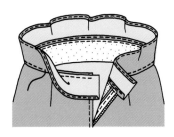

4. *Turn* the facing to the inside of the garment, and press. Tack at the seams with small cross stitches. Turn the under ends of the facing at garment opening. Slipstitch to zipper tape.

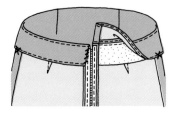

Casing

A casing can be made at the waistline edge of a garment or within a garment. It can be used with either elastic or a drawstring.

BELTS

Belts can be made of the same fabric as the garment or from contrasting fabric that accents the waistline. They can be wide or narrow, soft or stiff. They can fasten with a knot, bow, buckle, snap, or even lacing. Two basic types of belts are the *tie belt* and the *covered belt*.

Tie Belt

A tie belt, or sash, can be cut on the straight grain or on the bias, according to your pattern directions.

1. *Fold* the fabric in half lengthwise, right sides together.
2. *Stitch* across both ends and along the long edge, leaving a 3″ to 4″ (7.5–10 cm) opening in the center for turning. Trim seams and clip corners diagonally.

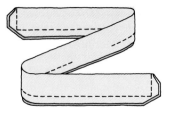

3. *Turn* to the right side through the opening. Press. Slipstitch the opening closed.

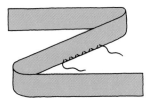

Belts that are narrow or made from heavy fabrics, such as corduroy, are difficult to turn:

1. *Press* all seam allowances toward the wrong side and trim.
2. *Fold* the belt in half lengthwise with the wrong sides together. Match the edges carefully.
3. *Edgestitch* through all thicknesses.

Covered Belt

A covered belt is made with belting or heavier weight interfacing to give body and stiffness to the belt. Or you can buy a commercial belting kit that contains all the materials.

1. *Cut* fabric on lengthwise grain twice the width of the finished belt, plus 1″ (2.5 cm) for seam allowances. The belt should be at least 6″ (15 cm) longer than your waist measurement.
2. *Trim* one end of the belting or interfacing into the desired shape, such as a point.
3. *Fold* fabric over the belting with the right side against the belting. Stitch a lengthwise seam close to belting, using a zipper foot. Be careful not to catch belting in the stitching. Trim seam allowances to ¼″ (6 mm).

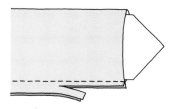

4. *Slide* the seam around to the center of belting. Press the seam open.
5. *Stitch* around the point of the belting and trim.

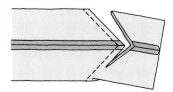

6. *Remove* belting from inside belt. Turn fabric right side out. Slip the belting back into the belt, pointed end first.
7. *Finish* the end of the belt after attaching buckle.

Belt Buckles

If the buckle does not have a prong, slip the belt through buckle and fold back the unfinished end of belt. Turn in the seam allowance and stitch to back of belt.

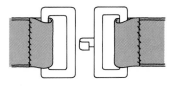

If the buckle has a prong, punch a hole with an awl on the unfinished end of the belt. If necessary, overcast raw edges of the hole. Slip the buckle prong through the hole. Fold back belt and stitch.

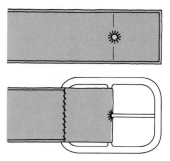

At the other end of belt, you can add one or more eyelets. Use a buttonhole stitch to make handsewn eyelets. Or purchase metal eyelets.

Belt Carriers

A belt carrier is a fabric or thread loop stitched to the garment to hold a belt in place. It can be made from a narrow strip of fabric used for the garment. Thread loops are made by hand stitching.

- *Fabric Carrier.* The length of each carrier should equal the width of the belt plus 1″ (2.5 cm) for seam allowances and ease.
  1. *Cut* the fabric strip from the selvage edge to reduce bulk. The width of the strip should be three times the desired width of the carrier. The length of the strip should be long enough to be cut apart to form as many belt carriers as necessary.
  2. *Make* two lengthwise folds, as shown, with the selvage edge on top. Press.
  3. *Stitch* the selvage in place by hand. Or topstitch along both edges of strip. Cut strip into individual carriers.

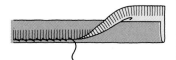

  4. *Fold* ends under about ¼″ (6 mm). Place on garment and stitch by hand or by machine.

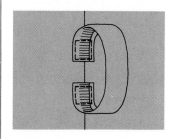

- *Thread Carriers.* Use a blanket stitch or a chain stitch to form thread loops. (Refer to HAND STITCHING, page 395.)

CHAPTER 24

Special Buttonholes and Loops

Buttons are used to fasten many different types of garments. Usually they are combined with machine-worked buttonholes that can be easily made with zigzag stitching. (Refer to FASTENERS, page 410.)

However, there are special times when some other type of button closing may be desired. A more detailed or decorative finish may be preferred. Or the design may call for a very inconspicuous closure.

Special buttonholes can be used on any edge that overlaps, such as the front of a shirt or jacket, a cuff, or a waistband.

Loops are buttonholes that extend beyond the edge of the garment opening. They can be used on edges that just meet, such as a slit opening or above a zipper. They can also be used on overlapping edges. Loops can be made from fabric or thread.

• *Fabric Loops.* These are made from bias strips of fabric. They can be used singly or in rows on blouses, dresses, and jackets.

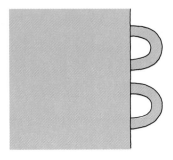

• *Thread Loops.* These are formed by blanket stitches or a chain stitch. A thread loop makes an almost invisible buttonhole at a neckline, on a collar, or above a back zipper.

• *Handworked Buttonholes.* These are made with tiny buttonhole stitches around the buttonhole edges. They are used for menswear jackets and coats and for delicate fabrics.

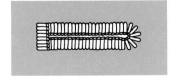

• *Bound Buttonholes.* These are finished with two narrow strips of fabric. They are used on tailored jackets, dresses, and coats.

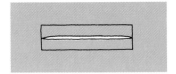

FABRIC LOOPS

The fabric is cut on the bias so that the loops will be flexible and can be shaped to fit around any size button. The fabric can be stitched and turned right side out to form *bias tubing.* Or the fabric can be stitched and turned with a cord inside to make *corded tubing.* (Refer to BIAS BINDINGS, page 456.)

Here are the steps in making fabric loops:

1. *Make* the bias tubing or corded tubing long enough to be cut apart

into as many loops as necessary. Each loop must be long enough to fit over the button plus seam allowances.

2. *Form* loops with seamed side up and the loops pointing away from the edge. Hold loops in place with tape. Stitch close to seamline in the seam allowance.

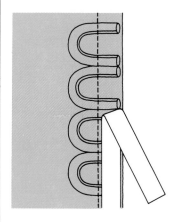

3. *Pin* facing over the loops. Stitch along the seamline, next to the first row of stitching, with garment side up. Trim ends of the loops to reduce thickness.

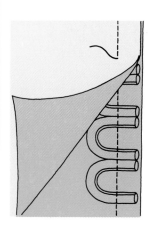

4. *Grade* seam, and turn facing to the inside. Press carefully to avoid making imprints on the outside of the garment.

THREAD LOOPS

Use a double thread or a single strand of buttonhole twist to form a chain stitch or to make blanket stitches. (Refer to HAND STITCHING, page 395.)

HANDWORKED BUTTONHOLE

Here are the steps to prepare a handworked buttonhole:

1. *Attach* facing and press.
2. *Mark* location and length of buttonhole.

3. *Stitch* a rectangle ⅛″ (3 mm) from the buttonhole marking, using reinforcement stitches 15 to 20 stitches per inch (1–1.5 mm in length). For a horizontal buttonhole, round end nearest garment edge.

4. *Cut* along the buttonhole marking through all thicknesses.

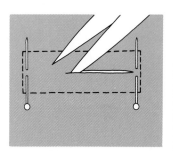

5. *Make* buttonhole stitches around the cut edge of the buttonhole, working from right to left. (Refer to HAND STITCHING, page 395.) Keep stitches evenly spaced and the same depth all around. For a horizontal buttonhole, fan the stitches out at the rounded end. Reinforce the other end with a bar tack. Make bar tacks at both ends of a vertical buttonhole.

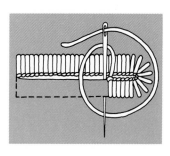

BOUND BUTTONHOLE

The size and location of each buttonhole will be marked on your pattern pieces. However the exact length depends upon the size and shape of your button. (See BUTTONHOLES, on page 412, for tips on buttonhole placement and length.)

Always make a test buttonhole in a scrap of fabric before making the buttonholes in your garment. Check that the buttonhole has square corners. The strips on each side of the opening should be even.

Make bound buttonholes before attaching the facing. The buttonholes are made through the outer fabric and the interfacing. If heavy or stiff interfacing is used, make the buttonholes before attaching the interfacing.

The Five-Line Method

There are several different ways to make bound buttonholes. One of the easiest and simplest methods to use is the *Five-Line Method*.

1. *Mark* the center line, and location and length of each buttonhole on the interfacing. Transfer all markings to the right side of the fabric, using hand or machine basting.

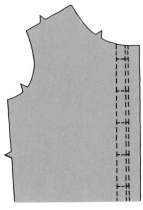

2. *Cut* a fabric patch 2½" (6 cm) wide and 2" (5 cm) longer than the finished button. Cut the patch on straight grain; sometimes plaid fabric is cut on the bias for contrast.

3. *Center* the fabric patch over the buttonhole marking on the outside of the garment, right sides together, and pin. Machine baste through the center of the patch exactly on top of the buttonhole marking.

4. *Baste* two more lines, ¼" (6 mm) above and below center basting. Measure to be sure that all three basting lines are parallel.

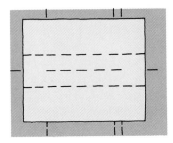

5. *Fold* the top edge of the patch down along outer basting line and press. Machine stitch, using 15 to 20 stitches per inch (1–1.5 mm in length) exactly ⅛" (3 mm) from the fold. Begin and end exactly at the marking lines for the buttonhole length. Backstitch at ends to secure stitches. Or tie thread ends securely on wrong side of garment.

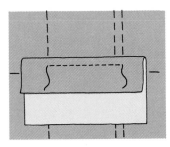

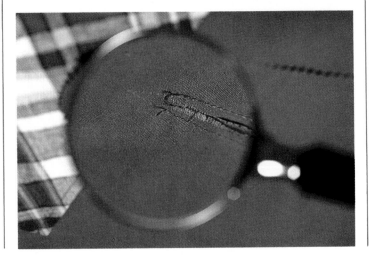

6. *Fold* the other edge of the patch up along the basting line to form a second fold. Press and stitch as above.

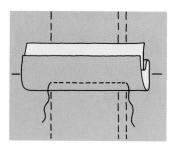

7. *Measure* on the wrong side of the garment to check that the five rows of stitching are of equal length and spaced ⅛" (3 mm) apart.

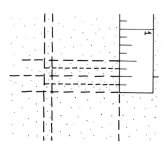

8. *Remove* the three rows of basting. Carefully cut through the center of the patch, without cutting into the garment fabric.

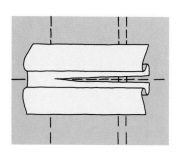

9. *Cut* the buttonhole open along the center line, using points of scissors, on the wrong side of the garment. Cut diagonally into corners. Be very careful not to cut through any stitches.

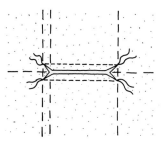

10. *Pull* the patch through the slash to the wrong side of the garment, and press. Baste buttonhole edges together.

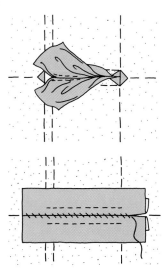

11. *On the outside,* fold the garment back over buttonhole to show the small triangle at end of the buttonhole. Stitch back and forth across

the base of the triangle several times to square corners and strengthen the end. Repeat at the other end of buttonhole.

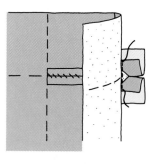

12. *Press* the buttonhole from the wrong side of the garment. Remove all marking stitches.

To complete a bound buttonhole, attach facing to garment edge. Pin facing around the buttonhole area. Stick a pin through each corner of the buttonhole opening from the outside. Be sure that the grain line of the facing is in line with the pins. Slash the facing between the pins, cutting diagonally into the corners. Fold under raw edges and stitch in place.

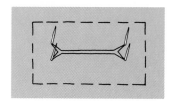

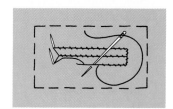

CHAPTER 25

Bindings and Bands

Bindings and bands are versatile, double-duty finishes. They are used to create a decorative trim around an edge, as well as to cover the raw edge of fabric. Bindings and bands can be used instead of a facing or hem at the neckline, armhole, or hemline of a garment. They are also used to finish the edge of placemats, pillows, backpacks, wallhangings, and many other items.

• *Bindings.* These are narrow trims made from a bias strip of fabric. Bias bindings are very flexible and can be used on curved as well as straight edges. You can cut your own bias strips or purchase single-fold or double-fold bias tape. Fold-over braid trim can also be used for binding. Ready-made bindings come in several widths and a variety of colors to match or contrast with your fabric.

• *Bands.* These are wider trims made from woven or knitted fabric. They can be cut in different shapes to add a decorative design to the garment. Bands extend beyond the edge of a garment or can go part way down the front of a garment to form a placket. Knit bands are often used for the neck or sleeve edge of a knitted shirt, sweater, sweatshirt, or parka. They can be cut from knitted fabric or purchased as ribbing.

BIAS BINDINGS

Bias bindings are made by cutting strips of fabric on the true bias and attaching to the edge of the garment or item. Your pattern guide sheet will give cutting and stitching directions for self-fabric bindings. The pattern envelope will list the type of bias tape or fold-over braid that can be used as binding.

Bias strips of fabric can also be used to make piping or tubing to use as trim, loops, ties, shoulder straps, and belts.

Cutting Bias Strips

There are two methods for cutting bias strips, depending on the amount you need. For a large amount, use the *continuous bias strip method.* For smaller lengths, you can cut and stitch individual strips together in the *cut and piece method.*

Continuous Bias Strip Method

1. *Cut* a square or rectangular piece of fabric. Fold one corner on the true bias by matching crosswise grain to lengthwise grain. Cut fabric along fold line.

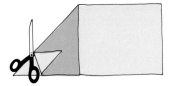

2. *Mark* parallel lines the desired width of bias strip on wrong side of fabric. For most purposes, use 1½″ (3.8 cm) unless your pattern states otherwise.

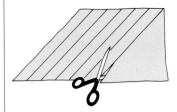

3. *Pin* fabric, right sides together, to form a tube, as shown. Be sure that one strip width extends beyond edge at each end of tube.
4. *Stitch* a ¼″ (6 mm) seam and press open.
5. *Cut* along marked line at one end to create a continuous bias strip of fabric.

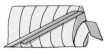

Cut and Piece Bias Strip Method

1. *Fold* the fabric diagonally, matching crosswise grain to lengthwise grain, to find true bias.
2. *Mark* bias strips on wrong side of fabric and cut apart.

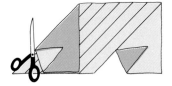

3. *Pin* ends of strips, right sides together, matching straight grain. The two strips will form a right angle.
4. *Stitch* a ¼″ (6 mm) seam along straight grain of fabric. Press seam open.

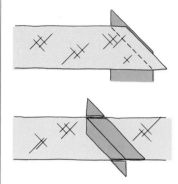

Attaching Binding

Bias strips can be attached using either a one-step or a two-step method. Always follow the directions in your pattern guide sheet for the best method to use for your particular design.

- *One-Step Method.* This method is usually used for attaching double-fold bias tape and fold-over braid, which have one edge folded slightly wider than the other. The binding is slipped over the edge of the fabric and stitched in place with one row of machine stitching:

1. *Trim* away seam allowance from edge to be bound.
2. *Slip* binding over raw edge with wider edge on wrong side of garment. Turn under ends, overlapping if necessary, and pin.

3. *Machine stitch* close to edge of binding through all layers.

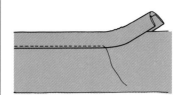

- *Two-Step Method.* This method is used for single-fold bias tape or for bias strips you cut yourself. One edge of the binding is stitched to the fabric. Then the binding is folded over the fabric edge and stitched again by hand or machine.

Your pattern will give directions for cutting self-fabric strips. Usually the bias strip is four times the finished binding width. This is sometimes called a "single binding." For sheer fabrics, the strip may be six times the finished width and folded in half lengthwise before applied. This may be called a "double binding":

1. *Trim* away seam allowances from fabric edge.
2. *Pin* the edge of the binding to the fabric, right sides together.
3. *Stitch* equal distance from edge, according to pattern directions. For single-fold bias tape, stitch along crease line of binding.

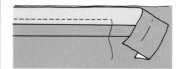

4. *Turn* bias over the seam allowance and pin. Slip-stitch in place.

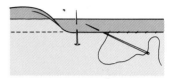

5. *Or* binding can be stitched to wrong side of garment. Flip binding to right side of garment and edgestitch in place.

Corners and Curves

Special techniques are needed to create smooth curves and sharp corners:

- *For Curves:* Preshape binding with a steam iron before stitching to fabric. Lay tape on top of pattern piece, shaping to fit curve. Press with steam to shrink out excess fullness and prevent puckers.

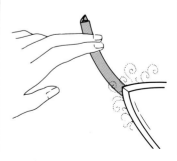

• *For Outward Corner:* Stitch binding to one edge, ending exactly where seamlines meet. Fold binding diagonally at corner and pin to other edge. Start at corner and continue stitching edge. Form a neat *miter,* or diagonal fold, on both sides of the binding at the corner. For the two-step method of application, finish by stitching inside edge of binding in place. For wider bindings, edgestitch or slipstitch along mitered fold to secure.

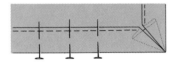

• *For Inward Corner:* Reinforce corner with small machine stitches, 15 to 20 stitches per inch (1–1.5 mm in length). Clip into corner.

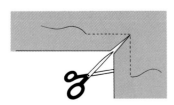

For the one-step method, slip binding over one edge and stitch to clip. Form neat miter at corner. Slip binding over other edge and continue stitching. Edgestitch along mitered fold if necessary.

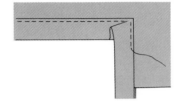

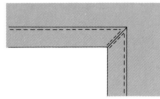

For the two-step method, stitch binding to edge up to the clip. Spread fabric at clipped corner to form a straight edge and continue stitching. Fold binding over edge, forming a miter on both sides at the corner. Finish by stitching inside edge by hand or machine.

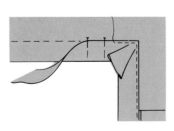

OTHER BIAS TECHNIQUES

Bias strips of fabric can be used for piping and tubing.

Piping is stitched into a seam to accent the seamline or outer edge of a garment. It is sometimes used around a neckline, edge of a collar or cuff, or along a yoke seam.

Tubing is stitched and turned right side out so that the seam allowances are inside the tube. It can be used for shoulder straps, button loops, and belts.

Both piping and tubing can be stitched over cable cord for a thicker trim.

Piping

1. *Cut* a bias strip of fabric twice as wide as finished piping, plus 1¼″ (3 cm) for seam allowances. Then press the strip lengthwise with the wrong sides together.
2. *Pin* piping to the right side of the garment, with the cut edges even.
3. *Machine baste,* 6 to 8 stitches per inch (3–4 mm in length), just inside seamline in seam allowance. Clip seam allowance of piping around curves.

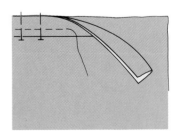

4. *Pin* and *stitch* seam to finish.

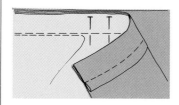

Corded Piping

1. *Fold* bias strip over cording with cording on inside of fabric. Using a zipper foot, stitch as close as possible to cording.

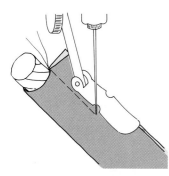

2. *Pin* corded piping to right side of garment so stitching rests on top of seamline.
3. *Machine baste* just inside the original stitching line in the seam allowance. Clip around curves.

4. *Pin* seam and stitch along seamline using zipper foot.

Bias Tubing

1. *Cut* a bias strip of fabric two times the finished width of tubing plus seam allowances.
2. *Fold* the fabric in half lengthwise, right sides together. Stitch, stretching the bias slightly as you sew. At the end, slant the stitches out toward the raw edge to make the tube easier to turn.

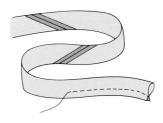

3. *Trim* the seam allowances of lighter-weight fabrics the same width as tubing. Use the seam allowances to fill the tubing. For heavier fabrics, trim the seam allowances closer to stitching.
4. *Turn* the tubing by attaching heavy thread to the wide end of the seam and pulling through the tube with a large needle or bodkin. Or use a loop turner.

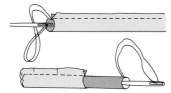

Corded Tubing

1. *Cut* cording twice the length of the bias strip plus 1″ (2.5 cm). Cut bias strip wide enough to fit around the cord plus seam allowances.
2. *Fold* bias over cord with right sides together and edges even. Stitch across cord and bias at the center of the cording.
3. *Stitch* long edge close to cord, stretching bias slightly, using a zipper foot. Trim seam allowances.

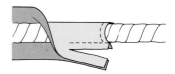

4. *Turn* right side out by gently pulling the fabric down over the cord and working the fabric along with your hands. Trim off excess cording.

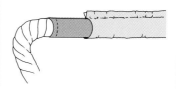

BANDS

Three types of bands are the *extended band, placket band,* and *knit band.* The method for attaching the band depends upon the design of your garment. Specific instructions will be given in your pattern guide sheet.

Extended Band

This type of band extends beyond the garment to form a shaped band around the neckline or armhole. Most bands have a separate facing cut the same shape as the outer band. Or the band may be designed with an extended facing that folds back to form the facing. The band may be interfaced, if it is necessary.

1. *Staystitch* garment edge and clip around curved edges.
2. *Pin* band to garment, right sides together, matching notches and seams. Stitch. Grade, clip, or notch seam allowances, and press toward band.

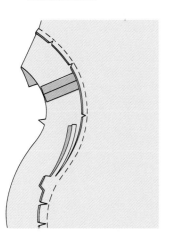

3. *Turn* under seam allowance at edge of facing and press.
4. *Stitch* facing to band. Trim, grade, and clip seam allowances. Press.
5. *Turn* facing to inside of garment and pin edge along seamline. Stitch in place by hand or machine.

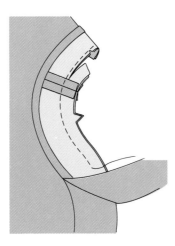

6. *For some bands,* the facing is stitched to the garment. Then the outer band is folded over to outside of garment and topstitched in place.

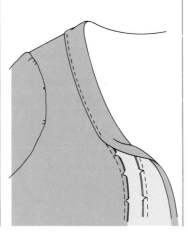

Placket Band

A placket band can be used for a neckline or sleeve opening. It may be cut in one piece or in two pieces. Transfer all markings to the wrong side of the band sections:

1. *Pin* right side of band to wrong side of garment, matching markings.
2. *Stitch* along stitching lines, pivoting at corners. Reinforce corners with small stitches, 15 to 20 stitches per inch (1–1.5 mm in length).
3. *Slash* between stitching lines and clip diagonally into corners. Grade seam.

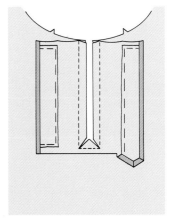

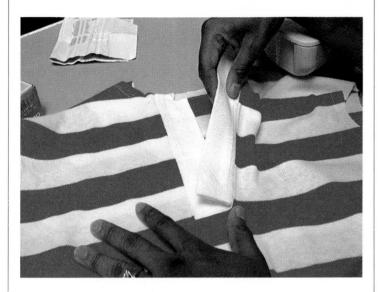

4. *Turn* placket to right side of garment. Press placket along fold lines and pin in place.
5. *Stitch* close to edge of each placket section, being careful not to catch other side of placket into stitching.

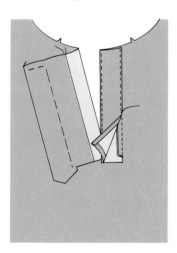

6. *Overlap* the two placket sections, one on top of the other. Topstitch bottom of placket to

secure the overlap to the underlap, as indicated on pattern piece.

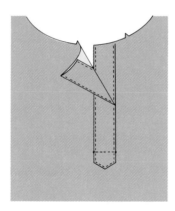

Knit Band

A knit band is cut a little shorter than the garment edge and then stretched slightly as it is stitched to the garment. A knit band can be cut from self-fabric or you can purchase ribbing:

1. *Form* band into a tube, right sides together. Stitch seam. Stitch again

⅛″ (3 mm) from seam in seam allowance and trim close to stitching.

2. *Fold* band in half lengthwise, wrong sides together. Pin band to right side of garment, stretching band to fit.
3. *Stitch* seam with band side up, being careful not to stretch garment edge.

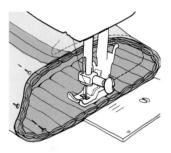

4. *Stitch* ⅛″ (3 mm) away from first row of stitching with a straight or zigzag stitch. Trim close to stitching. Press seam allowances toward garment.

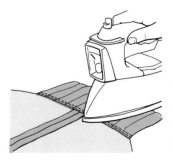

CHAPTER 26

Ruffles and Trims

Many different types of ruffles and trims can be used to decorate garments, accessories, and home decorating items. They can be bold and colorful or soft and subtle. It is important to coordinate the type of trim to your fabric and project design.

RUFFLES

Ruffles can be used around the edge of a neckline, collar, cuff, or hem. They can decorate curtains, dust ruffles, and pillows.

There are two basic types of ruffles:

• *Straight Ruffle.* This is made from a straight strip of fabric. It can be gathered along one edge and stitched in a seam or to the edge of the fabric. Or it can be gathered down the center or off-center and stitched to the outside of a garment or curtain.

• *Circular Ruffle.* It is created by stitching two or more circles of fabric together. The ruffle fits smoothly along the edge joined to the garment and ripples softly on the outer edge of the ruffle.

The amount of fullness in a ruffle depends on the width of the ruffle. Wide ruffles should have more fullness

than narrow ruffles to keep them from looking skimpy. Straight ruffles should be two to three times the length of edge or area to which they will be stitched.

Straight Ruffle

The outer edge of the ruffle can be finished with a narrow hem stitched by hand or machine. On lightweight and sheer fabrics, the ruffle may be cut twice the desired width and folded lengthwise to create a double thickness.

1. *Gather* the ruffle along upper edge. (Refer to GATHERS, page 400 for gathering details.)

2. *Pin* ruffle to edge of garment, adjusting fullness evenly. Stitch in place with ruffle on top to prevent stitching tucks into seam.

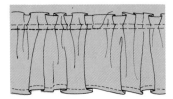

3. *Double-edged ruffle* can have trim, such as rickrack, stitched on top of the gathering stitches to cover them.

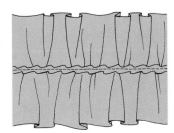

Circular Ruffle

1. *Cut* out circles, following pattern directions. Stitch circles together with a narrow seam to form ruffle. Finish outer edge of ruffle with a narrow hem. Sometimes the ruffle is cut as two layers and stitched together at the outer edge. Trim, clip and turn ruffle right side out.
2. *Staystitch* the inner edge of the ruffle ½″ (1.3 cm) from edge. Clip up to the row of staystitching.

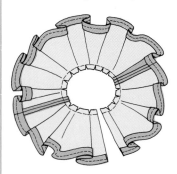

3. *Staystitch* garment edge to prevent stretching.
4. *Pin* the ruffle to the garment, right sides together, and stitch. Press seam allowances flat and trim.
5. *Finish* the inside edge with facing or a double row of stitching.

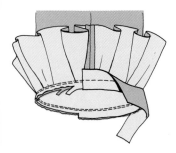

TRIMS

Trims are available in a wide variety of types, shapes, sizes, and colors. Rickrack, braid, ribbon, lace, eyelet, piping, and fringe are different types of trims. Fabric appliqués can also be used.

Be sure that the trim you select can be washed or dry-cleaned in the same manner as the outer fabric to which it will be stitched. Preshrink trims by placing them in hot water for 30 minutes. You can leave them wrapped around the cardboard, which should be bent slightly to allow for any shrinkage. Let trim dry.

Three basic methods are used to apply trim: *flat method, edging method,* and *inserted method.*

Flat Method

This method can be used for any trim that is finished on both edges, such as braid, ribbon, and rickrack. Use narrow trims for curved areas and press with a steam iron to shape before stitching in place:

1. *Pin* trim in place along placement line.
2. *Stitch* along one edge, both edges, or through the center. Rickrack should be stitched with a straight row of stitching down the center.

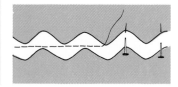

3. *Miter* corners of wider trims by stitching outside edge of trim up to corner.
4. *Lift* presser foot, pivot at corner, and continue stitching in new direction.
5. *Make* a neat diagonal fold in the trim at the corner and pin.

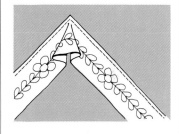

6. *Stitch* inside edge of trim. Stitch mitered fold, if necessary.

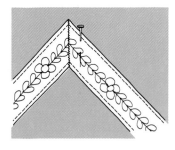

Edging Method

Use this application for trims that have only one finished edge, such as piping, gathered lace, gathered eyelet, and fringe. The trim can be stitched to the edge of a garment or inserted into a seam:

1. *Pin* trim to garment along edge or seamline with right sides together. Be sure trim is toward garment.
2. *Stitch* close to trim, using a zipper foot if necessary.

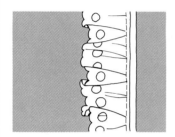

3. *Edge* may then be *finished* with facing or by turning seam allowance to inside and topstitching through all thicknesses.

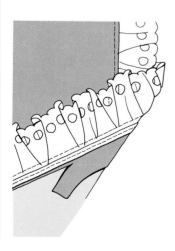

4. *For a seam,* place other section of fabric on top of trim with right sides together. Stitch seam and trim in one step.

Inserted Method

This application can be used on any straight section of a garment, such as down the front of a blouse or shirt, or around the bottom of a jacket or skirt. It cannot be used for curved areas. Choose flat trims such as lace or eyelet:

1. *Cut* fabric along placement line.
2. *Turn under* each fabric edge ½ the width of the exposed trim. Press edges.

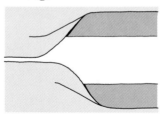

3. *Place* flat trim under folded edge of fabric.
4. *Edgestitch* through all thicknesses.

Finish Ends

There are several different ways to finish the ends of trims to create a neat appearance:

- Stitch trim to fabric before stitching seams so ends will be hidden in seam.

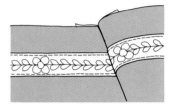

- Turn ends to wrong side and slipstitch.

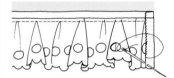

- Taper ends into a seam line.

- For overlapping ends, fold one end under ¼" (6 mm). Overlap folded end and stitch in place.

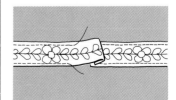

- For heavy trims, fold both ends under ¼" (6 mm), so that ends just meet and stitch.

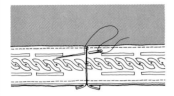

Fabric Appliqués

An appliqué is a cutout piece of fabric that is stitched to a larger background for decoration. You can purchase appliqués or make your own by cutting out a design from one or more fabrics. Do not use fabrics that ravel easily:

1. *Pin* or *baste* appliqué in place.
2. *Stitch* around edge with close zigzag machine stitching, covering edge completely. To stitch by hand, fold under edge and stitch with small blanket stitches or invisible slipstitches.

3. Or *fuse* in place with fusible web, following the manufacturer's directions.

Tailoring

A tailored garment is one that looks like it was custom-made by a good tailor. It has straight, simple lines and a trim fit. Suit jackets, blazers, coats, and even some dresses can be tailored.

What exactly is "tailoring"? **Tailoring** is *the shaping and molding of fabric by using special sewing and pressing techniques.* The shape is actually built into the garment with inner construction fabrics and special hand stitches. Tailoring takes extra time and skill. Yet, once the shape is built into a jacket or coat, it will remain throughout repeated wearings and dry cleanings.

Years ago, all suits and coats were hand-tailored. You can still buy hand-tailored clothes from a tailor or a specialty store. However, a hand-tailored garment will be very expensive because of all the labor involved in its construction.

Today, most tailored jackets and coats are made using shortcut tailoring methods. Machine stitching and fusible interfacings have replaced many of the traditional hand-sewing methods.

Many patterns are now designed with a tailored look, yet they are constructed using less complicated and time-consuming methods. Some blazers, casual jackets, and coats can be stitched almost entirely by machine. They may use only a few tailoring methods. Some jackets are left unlined for even easier construction.

After you have learned the basic sewing and pressing skills, you are able to tailor a simple jacket. Follow your pattern guide sheet carefully. You can also refer to special tailoring books for added information.

TAILORING TECHNIQUES

Traditionally, wool fabric was chosen for hand tailoring because it can be shaped and molded easily. A hair canvas was used for the jacket front and collar interfacing. Today, wool and wool-blended fabrics continue to be used.

However, many other fabrics, such as corduroy or velvet, can be used for tailored jackets. Several different types of sew-in and fusible interfacings are also available.

Basic tailoring techniques include *interfacing, rolled collar* and *lapels, pad stitching,* taping, shaped shoulders, bound or handworked buttonholes, interfaced hem, and lining.

Interfacing

The interfacing is usually a little heavier in weight such as a hair canvas, and is full cut to give extra support. Most patterns will provide separate interfacing pattern pieces that extend across the shoulder and around the armhole of both the front and back of the jacket.

Heavier-weight interfacings are not stitched into the seam except at the armhole. Instead, the seam allowances of the interfacing are trimmed away. Then the interfacing is catchstitched to the garment along the seamlines.

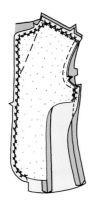

Shortcut methods include using fusible interfacings or lighter-weight interfacings that can be stitched into the seams by machine.

Rolled Collar and Lapels

Most tailored garments have a rolled collar attached to lapels. The under collar is interfaced and hand stitched for shaping. It is stitched to the garment neckline. A man's suit jacket may have the under collar made of a feltlike fabric.

The upper collar is stitched to the neckline facing. Then the outer seam of the collar, lapels, and garment front is stitched. Careful clipping, trimming, and pressing is essential to create sharp points and corners on the collar and lapels.

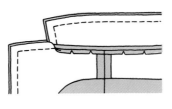

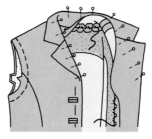

Shortcut methods include using fusible interfacing or machine stitching to shape the under collar.

Padstitching

Padstitching is a series of small diagonal stitches made by hand through the interfacing and outer fabric. It is done on the under collar and lapels to shape and mold the fabric.

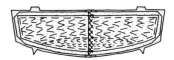

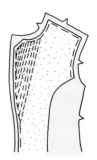

Shortcut methods include machine stitching the interfacing to the fabric or fusing the interfacing in place.

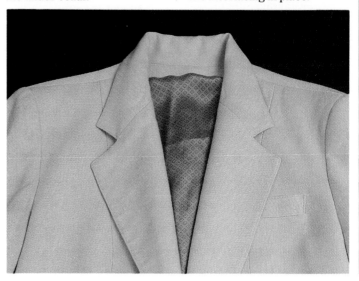

Taping

Some edges of a jacket or coat are taped to prevent stretching. Twill tape or seam tape is hand stitched along the seamline or fold line to stabilize bias or curved areas. Tape is usually used along the *roll line,* where the lapels fold back, and around the neck seam. The front edge, shoulder seams, armhole seams, and pocket or sleeve openings can also be taped.

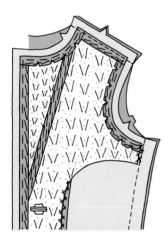

Shortcut methods include stitching the tape by machine instead of by hand.

Shaped Shoulders

The two-piece set-in sleeve is the classic tailored sleeve. Shoulder pads are often used to give shape and support to the shoulder line. Sometimes a sleeve heading, or padding, is inserted around the sleeve cap for added support.
Shortcut methods include using ready-made shoulder pads.

Buttonholes

Bound buttonholes are usually made on women's jackets and coats. Traditional men's wear has handworked buttonholes with a keyhole opening near the garment edge.
Shortcut methods include making machine-worked buttonholes.

Interfaced Hem

The sleeve hem and lower hem of a jacket or coat is usually interfaced with a bias strip of interfacing. The strip is cut about ½" (1.3 cm) wider than the hem to prevent a hem imprint from showing on the right side of the garment. The interfacing is stitched to the garment by hand, and then the hem is stitched only to the interfacing.

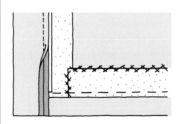

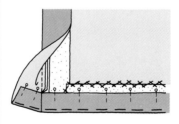

Shortcut methods include stitching the interfacing to the hem by machine or using fusible interfacing.

Lining

A jacket or coat lining is constructed separately and then stitched to the garment facing with tiny slipstitches. The center back pleat and shoulder tucks are held in place with cross stitches. A jacket lining has the hem attached to the garment, with a narrow tuck at the bottom for movement. A coat lining is usually hemmed separately and held in place with French tacks at the seams.

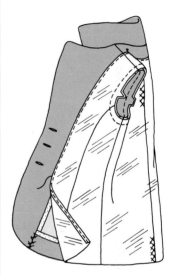

Shortcut methods include stitching the lining to the facing by machine.

Pressing

Careful pressing is essential in tailoring. Good pressing techniques help to shape and mold your tailored garment. (See Chapter 14, PRESSING, for guidelines.) Sometimes special pressing equipment is used to achieve smooth curves or sharp edges. (Refer to pages 371 and 421.)

Glossary

abba: cloak made from two rectangles sewn together at the shoulders and at the sides; worn by people from parts of Africa, Turkey, and Persia.

abrasion: a worn spot that develops when the fabric rubs against something.

absorbency: how well a fabric takes in moisture.

accented neutral color scheme: a color matched with white, black, or gray.

accessories: items that can add polish to an outfit; includes scarves, shoes, hats, belts, socks, jewelry, sunglasses, ties, and handbags.

acne: facial and body pimples.

acquired roles: roles that you take on a part-time or day-to-day basis.

adornment: decoration.

aerobic: a form of exercise which benefits the heart and lungs.

aesthetic: artistic.

agitation: stirring.

agrarian society: one that lives in one place and grows what it needs.

analogous color scheme: two or more colors that are next to each other on the color wheel.

annual percentage rate: percent of interest charged each year.

anorexia nervosa: a severe loss of appetite resulting in extreme loss of weight.

antiperspirant: a substance that prevents perspiration and odor from forming.

apparel designer: develops original ideas for clothing or translates other people's ideas into clothing for a particular market.

apparel industry: garment industry.

applied casing: made by sewing a separate strip of fabric or bias tape to the garment.

appliqué: sewing one or more pieces of fabric to the top of a larger piece of fabric.

apprenticeship: formal on-the-job training program.

appropriate: suitable

arbitration: the settlement of a dispute by a person or panel that listens to both sides and issues a decision.

assembly line: each worker specializes in a certain part of construction.

asymmetrical balance: space divided unequally within a garment.

balance: the way the internal spaces of a design work together.

barong tagalog: long-sleeved off-white embroidered shirt worn for formal events by Philippine men.

barter: trade one's goods and skills for someone else's goods and skills.

base salary: minimum salary.

batik: fabric that has been decorated by applying layers of wax and dye.

beadwork: the craft of stitching beads to fabric to form intricate and colorful designs.

blends: different fibers combined into one yarn.

block printing: the method of dyeing fabric by pressing it with an ink-covered block.

boll: the seed pod of the cotton plant.

bolt: fabric rolled or folded onto a cardboard or metal form.

bonded: fabric permanently joined to other fabric or material.

boutique: a type of specialty store featuring very fashionable or unique designs, usually higher priced.

braiding: the process of overlapping and wrapping several strips of yarn, fabric, or leather around each other.

brand label: a label identifying who is responsible for the product and giving other information on it.

breatheability: the ability for air or moisture to pass through fabric.

budget: a spending plan or schedule to adjust expenses to income during a certain period of time.

bulimia: an abnormal craving for large amounts of food, followed by vomiting or the use of laxatives.

bulk yarns: yarns that are permanently set into ripples, waves, zigzags, or various twists.

cable yarn: two or more ply yarns twisted together.

calorie: a unit of energy.

candlewicking: a series of knot stitches done in a coarse cotton thread.

care requirements: information on how to care for the product.

casing: a closed tunnel of fabric that holds a piece of elastic or a drawstring inside.

cellulose: a fibrous substance found in plants.

cellulosic fibers: produced primarily from wood pulp with a minimum of chemical steps.

certification: official approval or authorization.

chain: a large retail company with stores in many cities and towns.

charm: something worn or carried and believed to have magic powers.

chemisier: shirtmaker.

chicken scratch embroidery: a special form of crossstitch embroidery done on gingham fabric.

chiton: early Greek tunic which was made from two rectangles of fabric joined together at the shoulders.

choosing: making a decision about something.

circumference: the distance around.

classic: a traditional style that stays in fashion for a very long time.

client: customer.

clothing expectations: thoughts about how people in different roles should dress.

C.O.D.: cash on delivery; money for the purchase paid to the delivery person.

color scheme: the way that you use a color or combination of colors when planning an outfit or decorating a room.

colorfastness: the color in the fabric will not change.

commission: percentage of the purchase price on every sale.

comparison shopping: looking at quality, price, and design to compare value.

complementary color scheme: a combination of colors that are direct opposites.

complementary colors: colors that are opposite each other on the color wheel.

compromise: a settlement or give-and-take between two points.

conformity: expressing yourself as being similar to others.

conservation: the protection and preservation, or saving, of resources.

consideration: thoughtfulness or helpfulness.

consignment: giving a product to a store, but not receiving payment until the product is purchased by a customer.

consignment store: a store that pays you a percentage of the selling price after it sells your clothes.

cosmetics: anything used on the body to cleanse or change its appearance.

cost per wearing: purchase price plus cleaning costs, divided by a number of wearings.

costume jewelry: jewelry made from less expensive metals or other materials.

cotton gin: machine, invented in 1793 by Eli Whitney, which sepa-

rated cotton fibers from the seeds.

counted cross-stitch embroidery: a series of small "x's" carefully combined to form a picture or design.

courses: crosswise stitches in a knit fabric.

courteousness: the quality of being polite and considerate toward others.

cover letter: a letter sent with a résumé requesting an interview.

crewel embroidery: embroidery done with loosely twisted wool yarn.

crochet: the process of interlocking one strand of yarn or thread to form a fabric or garment.

culture: the collection of ideas, skills, values, and institutions of a society at a particular time in history.

curator: person in charge, such as for a museum.

curriculum: course of study.

curved lines: lines which are circular or gently waved.

cuticle: the little ridge of skin that grows at the base of the nails.

dandruff: flaking of the scalp.

decorative seams: seams that use topstitching or cording to create special effects.

dental hygiene: the care of your teeth and gums.

deodorant: substance that covers up or destroys body odor.

department store: stores that carry a wide selection of many different types of merchandise.

dermatologist: a skin specialist.

design ease: extra fullness built into clothes by the designer to create a particular style or silhouette.

designer: a person who is creative enough to have new ideas and practical enough to know how to turn those ideas into a product.

detergent: a cleaning agent made from chemicals or petroleum; works well in either hard or soft water.

diagonal lines: lines which move at an angle.

disability: a permanent or temporary condition that hampers a person in some way.

disposable income: money left over after fixed expenses are paid.

dowry: property given by the bride's family to the groom.

dry cleaning: the process that uses special liquids containing organic solvents to clean fabrics.

dry goods store: stores that sold fabric, thread, and ribbons, later selling mass-produced clothing.

durability: characteristics that affect how long a garment or item can be worn or used.

dyes: compounds that penetrate and color fibers.

easing: a method used to control fullness along a seamline; used when one edge of fabric is only slightly larger than the other.

economical: inexpensive and of good value.

economics: the way that a society produces, distributes, and spends its wealth.

elasticity: the ability to stretch and return to shape.

electrical engineer: responsible for the plant's general operating systems.

elements of design: the "building blocks" a designer uses: line, shape, space, texture, and color.

embroidery: many different types of decorative stitches used on fabric.

emphasis: the focal point, or center of interest, of a garment.

entrepreneur: a person who organizes and manages his or her own business.

ethnic: a term used to identify a particular race or nationality.

etiquette: acts that show consideration for events and people.

eyed needle: needle that allows thread to be pulled through a fabric in one step.

fabric: cloth of any kind.

fabric designer: helps to develop new weaves, patterns, prints, and colors or textile.

fabric stylist: spots trends and makes recommendations for color combinations and print designs.

factory: a place that houses many machines and many workers.

fad: a fashion that is very popular for a short time; a fashion cycle that happens quickly.

family structure: refers to the number, ages, and relationships of the family members.

fashion: anything that is currently "in."

fashion babies: small dolls used in the late 1700s that were dressed in the latest styles; used to spread fashion news.

fashion promotion: all the ways that manufacturers and retailers try to get your attention so that you will want to buy their product.

felting: when wool mats and shrinks due to heat, moisture, rubbing, or pressure.

fiber: the basic hairlike unit from which fabric is made.

figure type: size categories determined by height and body proportions.

filling yarns: crosswise yarns of a woven fabric.

finance charge: service charge, added to bill if the full amount is not paid.

fine jewelry: jewelry usually made from gold, silver, or platinum and may contain precious or semi-precious stones.

finishes: any special treatments that are applied to fabrics.

first impression: an initial image that is created in someone's mind by another person.

fixed expenses: items that must be paid on a regular basis and always cost the same amount of money over a period of time.

flammable: easily set on fire or which burns quickly.

flax: a tall, slender plant that is used to make linen fabric.

fleece: the hair of sheep used for wool.

flexibility: ability to change; ability to adapt to new opportunities and situations.

fluctuate: to go up or down.

free-lance: self-employed people who sell their work to different stores or companies.

gathers: soft folds of fabric formed by pulling up basting stitches to make the fabric fit into a smaller space.

generic name: the name that indicates a general classification of fibers or similar composition.

generic product: a product which has no brand name.

given roles: roles that occur automatically.

goal: something that you want to accomplish or hope to obtain.

good taste: high standards of art and beauty.

grading: converting a pattern into different sizes.

gray goods: fabric as it comes from the loom before it is finished.

grooming: caring for your body to make it look neat, clean, and attractive.

group: a number of people who share something in common.

hand: how a fabric handles and feels.

handicrafts: forms of art that are created by using your hands.

harmony: the pleasing arrangement of all parts of garment.

haute couture: high fashion.

heading: a width of fabric between the casing and the edge of the garment.

heritage: the body of culture and tradition that has been handed down from one's ancestors.

hidden costs: store expenses for customer carelessness, theft, and returns.

hierarchy: arranging needs according to their level of importance.

high fashion: style or trend when it is first introduced and becoming popular.

himation: an early Greek draped garment which was an oblong piece of fabric nearly five yards or meters long.

horizontal lines: lines which go across.

hue: name of a specific color.

illusion: something that deceives or misleads us when we look at it.

imitate: copy.

impression: an image that is transferred from one place to another.

impulse: buying suddenly, without any thought or planning.

individuality: the characteristics that make you unique or distinctive from others.

industrial engineer: makes sure all the operations in a plant are running smoothly and efficiently.

Industrial Revolution: a term that describes the changes in 19th-century society that resulted from the invention of power tools and machinery and the growth of factories.

insignias: badges or emblems that show membership in a group.

intensity: the brightness or dullness of a color.

interfacing: a layer of fabric placed between the facing and the outer fabric.

intermediate color: the combination of a primary color with a secondary color.

interview: a meeting between an employer and applicant for a job.

inventory: physical count of merchandise; comparison of written stock records to actual count of merchandise.

ironing: a method of smoothing away fabric wrinkles, done with a back and forward motion of the iron.

irregulars: garments with small imperfections.

job application: a company's record of every person who applies for a job.

kibr: a hooded robe with sleeves; an Arabian garment.

kilt: clan blankets with special plaid patterns wrapped around the body to form a short, belted-on, all-purpose garment: Scots in origin.

kinesics: the science that explores the meaning of messages expressed through body movement.

kleptomania: an abnormal and persistent impulse to steal.

knitting: a method of looping yarns together.

knock-off: a less expensive copy.

lacemaking: the process of making lace; the most complicated of the knotting and looping arts.

latex: milky liquid from rubber trees from which natural rubber is made.

laundering: washing fabric by hand or by machine with a soil removing product.

lay-away: purchase plan of an initial down payment, plus regular payments, until the total amount is paid.

leisure time: free or spare time.

line: a series of points connected together to form a narrow path; manufacturer's collection of clothes.

line of credit: maximum amount that can be owed on a credit card account.

lining: constructed separately from the outer garment and then joined at one or more major seams.

logical: practical and sensible.

logo: symbol.

long staple fibers: seed bolls with fibers as long as 2 inches (5 cm).

luster: a gloss or sheen.

macaronies: exaggerated versions of the pompadour-style hairdo, worn by men in the late 1700s.

macramé: the decorative art of tying knots.

mandatory: required by law.

manufactured fibers: fibers developed through scientific experimentation from substances such as wood pulp, petroleum, natural gas, and air.

market: location of designers' and manufacturers' showrooms.

marketing: ways to advertise, promote, and distribute a product for sale.

market research: the study of consumer needs and attitudes; investigating the potential market for a product or a service before you begin to produce it.

mass-produced: many garments made at the same time in a factory.

mechanical engineer: responsible for maintaining and developing the plant's equipment and machinery.

media: method used to communicate an advertising message.

mercerized: give cotton fiber added strength and luster.

merchandising: all the decisions that go into the selling of a product.

merino: breed of sheep, developed in Spain by the Romans.

modesty: what people feel is the proper way for clothing to cover the body.

money order: similar to a check, can be purchased from a post office or a bank.

monochromatic color scheme: the value and intensities of just one color.

monofilament: the simplest yarn, having only one strand of filament.

muumuu: a loosely flowing garment made from a bright cotton print, Hawaiian in origin.

natural fibers: fibers that come from natural sources, such as plants and animals; cotton, flax, wool, and silk.

neutral: colors with no true pigment; white, black, and gray.

noncellulosic fibers: made from molecules derived from petroleum, natural gas, air, and water.

nonverbal messages: your appearance and behavior.

nonwoven fabrics: made by interlocking the fibers with heat and moisture or with an adhesive agent.

notions: small items, such as buttons and thread, that go into a garment.

novelty yarn: made from two or more single yarns that are not alike.

nutrients: substances needed by your body, including proteins, carbohydrates, fats, vitamins, minerals, and water.

nutrition: the act of nourishing or feeding yourself.

nutritionally dense foods: foods that are low in calories and high in nutrients.

obsolete: no longer useful.

old-fashioned: any style that we have grown tired of looking at.

optical illusions: special effects that make you think that your eyes are playing tricks on you.

outlet: a store that sells merchandise produced by the manufacturer or factory that owns it.

overlock seam: special combination of stitches that joins the fabric and finishes the edges in one operation.

overrun: excess merchandise.

patchwork: the technique of sewing small shapes of fabric together to form larger shapes.

pattern: a project that contains all the instructions you will need for constructing your sewing project.

pattern grading: converting a pattern from one size into many sizes.

patternmaker: develops a master pattern in the manufacturer's standard size.

peer group: members who have equal standing within the group.

peer pressure: pressure by the peer group to conform.

permanent finishes: those that last throughout the life of the fabric.

personality: the combination of all your unique qualities.

piecework: paid so much per piece or garment instead of by the hour.

pile: the raised surface on a fabric.

pill: to form tiny balls of fiber on a fabric.

pills: balls of fiber forming on the surface of a fabric.

plaque: a thin layer of mucus on teeth that contains harmful bacteria.

pleats: wider folds of fabric that are stitched or pressed in place.

pliable: able to bend without breaking.

ply yarn: two or more single yarns twisted together.

portfolio: collection of work, in the form of sketches or photos.

pressing: a method of smoothing away fabric wrinkles accomplished by raising and lowering the iron from one area to the next.

primary colors: the basic colors of red, yellow, and blue.

principles of design: the artistic guidelines (balance, proportion, emphasis, rhythm, harmony) for using the various design elements in a garment.

printing: transferring color to the surface of a fabric.

priorities: preferences.

prioritize: rank.

promotion: a form of free advertising.

properties: characteristics of fibers.

proportion: the size relationship of each of the internal spaces within a garment to one another and to the total look.

quality: the condition of the garment's appearance and construction; refers to superior characteristics or features.

quality control expert: people trained to carefully examine the finished products for flaws.

quillwork: the craft of stitching quills onto clothing in patterns that form designs.

quilting: stitching together two layers of fabric with a soft material in between.

ready-to-wear: mass-produced garments.

recreational shopping: window shopping or shopping just for fun.

recycling: reclaiming items for another use.

redesigning: changing a garment to better meet your needs.

regulations: laws.

reliability: the quality of being dependable.

retailing: selling goods to customers.

resilient: able to spring or bounce back into shape.

resources: money, time, and skill.

résumé: a written summary of who you are and what you have done.

rhythm: the flow of the lines, shapes, space, and texture of a garment.

role: a particular function or purpose of a group member.

sales analysis: the study of what has sold in the past in order to predict what will sell in the future.

sales promotion: a subtle form of advertising.

sales representative: sells company's products to its customers.

samplemaker: works with the designer to develop sample garments.

sari: a piece of silk or cotton fabric worn by women in India.

sarong: a wrapped and draped skirt, Malaysian in origin.

scissors: a smaller cutting tool, which has handles of the same shape.

secondary color: equal amounts of two primary colors; green, orange, and violet.

secondary school: junior high school or high school.

seconds: goods with major flaws.

self casing: folding over the edge of the garment and stitching in place.

self-finished seams: to enclose the seam allowances as the seam is stitched.

self-image: how you perceive all of your characteristics; how you see yourself.

selvage: self-edge of a woven fabric.

seminar: workshop on a special topic.

serger: overlock machine.

sewing: the art of using stitches to join pieces of fabric together.

sewing plate: an early sewing tool made of a flat piece of bone, used to push the needle through hide or fabric.

sewing supplies: items that become part of your garment or project.

sewing tools: equipment used during the different stages of sewing.

shades: colors darkened by the addition of black.

shape: the outline, or silhouette, of an object.

shears: a cutting tool with long blades, which has two handles that are shaped differently.

shirtwaists: simple skirts and white linen blouses; Gibson Girl look, named after illustrations drawn by Charles Dana Gibson.

shuttle: an instrument used to weave crosswise threads on a loom; the flying shuttle, invented by John Kay in 1733.

silhouette: the outer shape of an object.

silk-screen printing: a method of dyeing fabric by allowing dye to seep through unsealed areas of a screen.

sinews: tendons of an animal.

soap: a cleaning agent made by mixing an alkali with a fat; works best in soft water.

society: a group of individuals who live together in a particular area.

software: information systems or programs for a computer.

solvent: a substance used to dissolve another substance.

space: the area inside the shape, or outline, of an object.

specialty store: a store that carries only a limited range of merchandise.

spectrophotometer: a computerized piece of equipment that analyzes the color of one item and tells what formulas to use to exactly reproduce that color in a variety of yarns and fabrics.

spectrum: the band of colors reflected by light.

spindle: rod or stick used for spinning yarn.

spinning jenny: an invention developed in 1767 by James Hargreaves, containing eight spindles so that eight yarns could be spun at the same time.

spinning mule: machine invented in 1779 by Samuel Crompton that could produce as much yarn as two hundred hand spinners.

split complementary color scheme: one color used with the two colors on either side of its direct complement.

standard of living: goods and services necessary to maintain a certain level of living.

standards: specific measurements or models to which similar products are compared.

statement: bill

status: position or rank within a group.

status symbols: clothes or other items that offer a sense of status for the ordinary person; an item of clothing that gives the wearer a special feeling of importance or wealth.

stereotype: an opinion based on ideas that you already have, whether they are accurate or not.

stretchability: the fabric's ability to "give" and stretch with the body.

style: the shape of a particular item of clothing that makes it easy to recognize.

stylist: a person who takes other people's ideas and puts them together in a way that looks fresh and original.

sumptuary laws: medieval laws made to regulate what each class could wear.

sunblock: lotion or cream that prevents tanning and burning.

sunscreen: lotion or cream that allows skin to tan, but which protects against burning.

sweatshop: a dark, airless, unhealthy factory.

symbol: something visible that represents something else.

symmetrical balance: space divided into equal parts within a garment.

synthetic: term used to refer to manufactured fibers produced from chemicals.

tacked: fastened.

tailoring: the shaping and molding of fabric by using special sewing and pressing techniques.

tanned: skins treated to stay soft.

target audience: a very specific audience.

tartar: plaque that has hardened on the teeth.

technology: the way a culture uses its scientific knowledge to produce things.

temporary finishes: those that may last through only one or two cleanings.

tensile strength: ability to withstand tension or pulling.

textile chemist: responsible for creating new fibers, new dyes, and new finishes.

texture: the surface characteristics, or feel, of an object.

thrift shops: stores that carry second-hand, or used, clothing and household items.

tie dyeing: the method of tying knots into fabrics before dyeing.

tints: colors combined with white.

toga: a crescent-shaped piece of fabric with one straight end wrapped and draped around the body, worn by the early Romans.

toxic: poisonous.

trademark: symbol, design, word, or letter to distinguish a manufacturer's product.

trade name: the name given to manufactured fibers and registered as trademarks and protected by law.

trade-off: an exchange of one thing for another.

traditions: customs used to emphasize various ceremonies or ways of doing things throughout a long period.

trend: a fashion cycle that happens quite slowly.

triadic color scheme: three colors that are of equal distance from one another on the color wheel.

tucks: narrow folds of fabric that are stitched part way or the entire length.

tuition refund plan: company payment of all or part of school costs.

turban: cloth wrapped about the head to absorb sweat during the day and insulate the head at night, Middle Eastern in origin.

underlining: a layer of fabric stitched to the back of each piece of the outer fabric.

understitching: a row of stitches used to prevent a shaped or extended facing from rolling to the outside of a garment.

unit construction: everything is completed on the smallest unit possible before you begin to sew the separate units together.

value: lightness or darkness of a color.

values: your ideas about what is important or good.

variety store: sells many different types of products.

verbal message: the tone of your voice and choice of words.

versatile: able to be worn or combined in a variety of ways.

vertical lines: lines which go up and down.

voluntary: given freely and not regulated by law.

wage: certain amount of money per hour or per day of work earned by a worker.

wales: lengthwise rows of stitches in a knot.

wardrobe plan: a clothing review.

warp yarns: yarns that run the length of the fabric.

warp knits: knits made with several yarns.

warranty: pledge or assurance that the product will meet certain standards.

water frame: a machine powered by water, invented by Sir Richard Arkwright in 1769.

waterproof: no water will penetrate.

water-repellent: resists water, but eventually will become wet.

wearing ease: the amount of fullness needed for movement and comfort.

weaving: interlacing two sets of yarns at right angles to each other.

weft knits: knits made with only one yarn; also known as filling knits.

wicking: a fabric's ability to draw moisture away from the body.

wool: fleece or hair of sheep.

yarn: bits of plants, reeds, horse hair, or bark spun into one continuous stand.

yarns: created from fibers twisted together or laid side by side.

Index